Inerrancy and the Church

Edited by

John D. Hannah

MOODY PRESS
CHICAGO

Library of Congress Cataloging in Publication Data
Main entry under title:

Inerrancy and the church.

Includes bibliographical references.
Contents: The doctrine of Scripture in the early
church / John D. Hannah — Augustine's doctrine of
biblical infallibility / Wayne R. Spear — Biblical
authority and scholastic theology / John F. Johnson —
Luther and biblical infallibility / Robert D. Preus —
[etc.]
1. Bible — Evidences, authority, etc.—History of
doctrines—Addresses, essays, lectures. I. Hannah,
John D.
BS480.I424 1984   220.1'3   84-6671
ISBN 0-8024-0327-1

1 2 3 4 5 6 7 Printing / GB / Year 89 88 87 86 85 84

Printed in the United States of America

Contents

Series Editor's Introduction

This book is part of a series of scholarly works sponsored by the International Council on Biblical Inerrancy (ICBI). They include the following areas:

GENERAL—*Inerrancy* (Zondervan, 1979), Norman L. Geisler, ed.

PHILOSOPHICAL—*Biblical Errancy: Its Philosophical Roots* (Zondervan, 1981), Norman L. Geisler, ed.

THEOLOGICAL—*Challenges to Inerrancy* (Moody, 1984), Gordon Lewis and Bruce Demarest, eds.

HISTORICAL—*Inerrancy and the Church* (Moody, 1984), John Hannah, ed.

HERMENEUTICAL—*Hermeneutics, Inerrancy, and the Bible* (Zondervan, 1984), Earl Radmacher and Robert Preus, eds.

The ICBI is a coalition of Christian scholars who believe that the reaffirmation and defense of biblical inerrancy is crucial to the life and vitality of the Christian church. In addition to these scholarly books, the Council has produced two landmark statements: "The Chicago Statement on Inerrancy" (1978) and "The Chicago Statement on Hermeneutics" (1982). These two documents represent a consensus of evangelical scholarship on these fundamental topics.

The ICBI does not endorse every point made by the authors of this book, although all the writers are in agreement with the ICBI stand on inerrancy. Freedom of expression of this commitment was exercised throughout the various books. All wrote with the hope that believers in Christ will become increasingly assured of the firm foundation for our faith in God's inerrant Word.

NORMAN L. GEISLER
General Editor, ICBI

Introduction

꒐

The publication of *Biblical Authority* (edited by Jack Rogers) in 1977 alerted many in evangelical churches, as well as in the religious community at large, that a new theological polarization was emerging. That book, however, was by no means the harbinger of the theological contest. The lines of demarcation among evangelicals became more distinct with the publication of another important work, *The Authority and Interpretation of the Bible: An Historical Approach* (1979), coauthored by Jack Rogers and Donald McKim, that expanded and buttressed the assumptions of the previous book. Generally speaking, it now appears that there are two parties within the evangelical movement that have become sensitive to the issue of the nature of the Bible's uniqueness. Both sides affirm the gospel message of the Scriptures; the contested point is the mode in which that unique message is expressed.

One of the responses to the point of view presented in *Biblical Authority* was the formation of the International Council on Biblical Inerrancy (ICBI) in 1978. That organization drew widespread ecclesiastical and denominational support at its initial gathering in Chicago. It has challenged the theological, philosophical, biblical, and historical assumptions of those evangelicals who seek to separate the Bible's saving message (its function) from the words (the form) in which that message has been communicated to us.

This volume, like others in the ICBI series, addresses the crucial issue of biblical inerrancy from a consensus of contemporary evangelical scholarship. In particular, it addresses the historical thesis proposed by Jack Rogers and Donald McKim in *The Authority and Interpretation of the Bible: An Historical Approach.* Those authors assert that the historic position, the "central church tradition," has been to regard the Bible's message as genuine and authoritative but its words as fallible. That view suggests that the Bible is authoritative in matters of religion and life, but not inerrant; it is true, but not wholly so.

The corollary to that view is the belief that the idea of inerrancy is novel, that it is a product of post-Reformation Protestant Scholasticism. Supposedly, the origins of inerrancy are to be found in the seventeenth century followers of the Reformers, who sought to recast their teaching in a rationalistic, Aristotelian mold. Theodore Beza, Francis Turretin, and others preferred the theological method of Aquinas so that "reason was given priority over faith, and Scripture came to be treated as a compendium of proposition from which logical deductions could be drawn" (p. 188). Therefore, the authors argue, from the earliest attempts to systematize the doctrine of Scripture by Origen, Jerome, and Augustine to Luther, Calvin, and the Westminster Assembly, the church has recognized that the doctrine of accommodation presupposes errancy; to believe otherwise is unwise, a misuse of Scripture, and a perversion of history. The accommodationist, errantist, or authoritarian position ought to be recovered from the catastrophically negative impact of the inerrantists who seek to establish faith on a frail, inadequate foundation of Thomistic methodology. Therefore, Rogers and McKim see spokesmen for the authority but not the inerrancy of the Scriptures—men like James Orr, Herman Bavinck, Karl Barth, and G. C. Berkouwer—as the true defenders of the historic position of the church; those spokesmen present the only viable structure for Christian truth in the twentieth century.

Are such assertions correct? Is there a "central church tradition" that asserts the authority but denies the inerrancy of the Bible? Are inerrantists a novel species on the stage of history? Does the testimony of the church support the position of Rogers and McKim?

The following essays seek to address that constellation of questions. The thesis of this book is that the position of the church, as it has been delineated by scholars, clerics, and teachers, is that of the absolute authority and inerrancy of the Scriptures. That was the view of Augustine, Luther, and Calvin, as well as of the entire church; inerrancy is the "central church tradition." The novel interpreters of the doctrine of Scripture were not Turretin, Hodge, and Warfield but Orr, Barth, Berkouwer, and Rogers. Those who argue that belief in an inerrant Bible is a novel historical position, that accommodation has been its "central tradition," grievously err in calling the great figures of the church to witness for them.

Part 1

The Tradition of the Infallibility of Scripture in European Christianity

1

The Doctrine of Scripture in the Early Church

John D. Hannah

In recent decades within the evangelical community the doctrine of Scripture has been warmly debated. Some have come to the studied conclusion that the teaching of the infallibility of the Bible is both a recent phenomenon—an aversion to the rise of Scientism ·after the Reformation—and a departure from the historic position of the church that emerged in an articulated form from the Alexandrian tradition in the third century, principally in the works of Origen. The historical argument for that position has been set forth in a recent volume, *The Authority and Interpretation of the Bible: An Historical Approach.* That book has received an array of reviews among evangelicals, from Clark Pinnock, who believes that it may forge "a non-fundamental evangelical consensus on the inspiration and authority of the Bible" that should "warn educated evangelicals prepared to look at the history not to join the ranks of the inerrancy militants,"[1] to the conclusions of W. Robert

1. Clark H. Pinnock, "The Real Battle for the Bible, A Review of *The Authority and Interpretation of the Bible*," *Sojourners* 9 (1980): 36.

JOHN D. HANNAH, B.S., Philadelphia College of Bible, M.A., Southern Methodist University, Th.M., Th.D., Dallas Theological Seminary, is department chairman and professor of historical theology at Dallas Theological Seminary. He has contributed articles to such periodicals as *Bibliotheca Sacra* and the *Grace Theological Journal* and is a member of the Society of Church History, Organization of American Historians, and the American Historical Association.

Godfrey that "the book fails to be a trustworthy analysis of either the theology or the history of the doctrine of the Bible's authority."[2]

The purpose of this chapter is to consider the doctrine of Scripture from Clement of Rome to the fourth century. Did the early church maintain the authority but not the inerrancy of the Bible? Did Origen articulate the "central church tradition" that affirmed authority but denied infallibility? Though the Fathers were often unspeculative in their writings and did not attempt to write systematic theology, and though they did not set forth a theology of the Scriptures per se, this chapter presents evidence that they did believe in the inerrancy of the Bible. Indeed there is evidence that even Origen, the supposed fountainhead of the "central church tradition," affirmed the infallibility of the Word of God.

In the previous century James Bannerman stated that though other doctrines were minutely scrutinized in the early church, the doctrine of the Scriptures was assumed. He said,

> The question of the authority and infallibility of Scripture did not, however, pass through this process until many centuries afterwards. There are no definitions and limitations of the doctrine on one side and another, elaborately drawn out and reduced to systematic form, as if armed on every side to repel assault, or fortified around to prevent controversy or misunderstanding. The belief of the early Church in an infallible Bible was too simple to require to be fenced about with the safeguard of explanations, and too unanimous to need support from argument. There was neither controversy nor theorizing demanded to satisfy the faith of Christians; nor did the one or the other appear in connection with inspiration for the first eight hundred years.[3]

Geoffrey W. Bromiley, who has articulated the essential thesis of this chapter, advances the same evaluation. He says,

> When we turn to the patristic period, we are struck at once by the

---

2. W. Robert Godfrey, "An Errant Guide: A Review of *The Authority and Interpretation of the Bible: An Historical Approach*," *Christianity Today* 25 (1981): 68.
3. James Bannerman, *Inspiration: The Infallible Truth and Divine Authority of Holy Scripture*, vol. 2 (Edinburgh: T. & T. Clark, 1865), p. 123.

way in which all writers accepted the inspiration and authority of Holy Scripture as self-evident. The actual writings of the Old and New Testaments are seen to derive from the Holy Spirit and therefore carry the divine message. Nor is this merely a general inspiration; it extends to the detailed phraseology of the Bible in accordance with the sayings of Christ in Matthew 5:18.[4]

It is our contention that the infallibility of Scripture was never disputed in the early church; only those outside the church viewed it otherwise. Though there was controversy about what the Bible taught, its essential nature was unquestioned.

THE INTEGRITY OF THE SCRIPTURES AND THE EARLY CHURCH —A GENERAL OVERVIEW

THE CHURCH AND THE BIBLE

⌐The equality of the testaments, though a moot point in the current inerrancy debate, does offer abundant proof that early Christians received the New Testament as equal in authority and inspiration to the Old Testament. Years before the famous fourth-century bishop of Alexandria, Athanasius, sought "to set before you the books included in the Canon," and handed down, and accredited as Divine,[5] church scholars equated the two testaments as coordinate in authority. Origen, the third-century Alexandrian scholar, is quite specific in his commentary: "And likewise he becomes a third peacemaker as he demonstrates that which appears to others to be a conflict in the Scriptures is no conflict, and exhibits their concord and peace, whether of the Old Scriptures with the New, or of the Law with the Prophets or of the Gospels with the Apostolic Scriptures, or of the Apostolic Scriptures with each other."[6] Origen believed in the harmony of the Scriptures, in their noncontradictory nature, and argued for a sin-

4. Geoffrey W. Bromiley, "The Church Doctrine of Inspiration," in *Revelation and the Bible*, ed. Carl F. H. Henry (Grand Rapids: Baker, 1958), p. 207.
5. *Letter*, 39. Unless otherwise indicated, all patristic citations are from Alexander Roberts and James Donaldson, eds., *The Anti-Nicene Fathers* (Grand Rapids: Eerdmans, 1977) or Philip Schaff and Henry Wace, eds., *The Nicene and Post-Nicene Fathers* (Grand Rapids: Eerdmans, 1975).
6. *Matthew*, 2.

gle authorship. "This just and good God, the father of our Lord Jesus Christ, Himself gave the Law, and the prophets, and the Gospels, being also the God of the apostles and of the Old and New Testaments."[7] Origen's understanding (as well as that of the church before and after him) of the nature and equality of the testaments is reflected in his statement,

> Since, in our investigation of matters of such importance, not satisfied with the common opinions, and with the evidence of visible things, we take in addition, for the proof of our statements, testimonies from what are believed by us to be divine writings, viz., from that which is called the Old Testament, and that which is styled the New, and endeavour by reason to conform our faith; and as we have not yet spoken of the Scriptures as divine, come and let us, as if by way of an epitome, treat of a few points respecting them, laying down those reasons which lead us to regard them as divine writings.[8]

The general manner of the Holy Spirit's influence in the conveyance of divine revelation strongly implies that the Scriptures are from God. Bannerman summarizes the point well by stating, "If the Holy Spirit is to be considered as the author of Sacred Scripture in such a sense that its qualities are directly referable to him alone, then the Scripture must be infallible."[9] Early Christian scholars referred to the Spirit's influence as inspiration. Clement of Rome, an early second-century writer (perhaps late first century), wrote, "Take up the epistle of the blessed Apostle Paul. What did he write to you at the time when the Gospel first began to be preached? Truly, under inspiration of the Spirit, he wrote to you concerning himself, and Cephas, and Apollos, because even then parties had been formed among you."[10] He wrote to the Corinthians, "Look carefully into the Scriptures, which are the true utterances of the Holy Spirit."[11] Justin Martyr, the second-century

7. *De Principiis*, Preface 4.
8. Ibid., IV.1.
9. Bannerman, 2:65. For similar statements from Origen consult *De Principiis*, Preface 4, IV.16 and I.1.
10. *First Epistle*, 47.
11. Ibid., 45.

apologist, wrote, "And the prophets are inspired by no other than the Divine Word, even you, as I fancy will grant;"[12] Justin accredited the Scriptures to Jesus Christ. Most usually, however, Martyr argued that the Spirit influenced the writers of the Bible: "Again the same prophet Isaiah, being inspired by the prophetic Spirit, said, 'I have spread out my hands to a disobedient and gainsaying people.' "[13] In speaking of the Psalmist's ability to foretell the things of Christ, he wrote, "And hear how it was foretold concerning those who published His doctrine and proclaimed His appearance, the above-mentioned prophet and king speaking thus by the Spirit of Prophecy."[14] He further described the influence of the Spirit as filling. He said,

> There existed, long before time, certain men more ancient than all those who are esteemed philosophers, both righteous and beloved by God, who spoke by the Divine Spirit and foretold events which would take place and are now taking place. They are called prophets. These alone saw and announced the truth to men, neither reverencing nor fearing any man, not influenced by a desire for glory, but speaking those things alone which they saw and which they heard, being filled with the Holy Spirit.[15]

A near contemporary of Justin Martyr was the Athenian philosopher Athenagoras, who had embraced Christianity. In his apology to the Emperor Marcus Aurelius, he wrote of the Scriptures, "We have for witnesses of the things we apprehend and believe, prophets, men who have pronounced concerning God and the things of God, guided by the Spirit of God."[16] In another place he wrote, "The Holy Spirit Himself also, which operates in the prophets, we assert to be an effluence of God, flowing from Him, and returning back to Him like a beam of the sun."[17]

In the western church three writers were particularly influential: Hippolytus, a deacon in Rome, Irenaeus, bishop in Gaul,

12. *The First Apology*, 33.
13. Ibid., 34.
14. Ibid., 40; cf. *Dialogue with Trypho*, 32.
15. *Dialogue with Trypho*, 7.
16. *Plea for the Christians*, 7.
17. Ibid., 9.

and Tertullian of Carthage. Hippolytus wrote, "This is the Spirit that at the beginning 'moved upon the face of the waters,' by whom the world moves, by whom creation consists and all things have life, who also wrought mightily in the prophets, and descended in flight upon Christ."[18] Tertullian's testimony is equally pungent, "Hence there is among us an assured faith in regard to coming events as things already proved to us, for they were predicted along with what we have day by day fulfilled. They are uttered by the same voices, they were written in the same books—the same Spirit inspires them."[19] Irenaeus simply stated, "We should leave things of that nature (unknowable things) to God who created us, being most assured that the Scriptures are indeed perfect, since they were spoken by the Word of God and His Spirit."[20] Irenaeus connected the influence of the Holy Spirit with an infallible product; the Scriptures, given by the Spirit of God, are true and errorless.

The testimony of the two great third-century Alexandrian scholars, Clement and Origen, provides a firm basis for understanding their views of the Spirit's influence in the writing of the Scriptures. Clement, for example, wrote, "Jeremiah the prophet, gifted in consummate wisdom, or rather the Holy Spirit in Jeremiah, exhibits God."[21] Of false teachers he declared, "So then, they are not pious, inasmuch as they are not pleased with the divine commands, that is, with the Holy Spirit."[22] In another passage Clement argued both the divine origin of Scripture and the equality of the two testaments. "For we have, as the source of teaching, the Lord, both by the prophets, the Gospels, and the blessed apostles. . . ."[23] Origen spoke for the churches of his day when he said, "This Spirit inspired each one of the saints, whether prophets or apostles; and that there was not one Spirit in the men of the old dispensation, and another in those who were inspired at the advent of Christ, is most clearly taught throughout the

18. *Discourse on the Holy Theophany*, 9.
19. *Apology*, 20.
20. *Against Heresies*, II.38.2.
21. *Exhortation to the Heathen*, 8.
22. *The Stromata*, VII.16.
23. Ibid.

churches."[24] In the same treatise he argued, "And that this testimony may produce a sure and unhesitating belief either with regard to what we have still to advance, or to what has been stated, it seems necessary to show, in the first place, that the Scriptures themselves are divine, i.e., were inspired by the Spirit of God."[25] Explicitly, he wrote in the same book, "The Scriptures were written by the Spirit of God."[26] Again, "We, however, in conformity with our belief in that doctrine, which we assuredly hold to be divinely inspired, believe that it is possible in no other way to explain and bring within the reach of human knowledge this higher and diviner reason as the Son of God, than by means of those Scriptures alone which were inspired by the Holy Spirit, i.e., the Gospels and Epistles, and the law and the prophets, according to the declaration of Christ Himself."[27]

The fourth-century Cappodocian theologian Gregory of Nyssa, who was a contemporary and sympathizer with Athanasius of Alexandria, wrote, "The Scripture, 'given by inspiration of God,' as the Apostle calls it, is the Scripture of the Holy Spirit and its intention is the profit of men."[28]

The specific manner of the Holy Spirit's influence in giving the words of the Scriptures (i.e., the quotation formula) provides strong evidence that the early church understood the words of the human authors to be the words of God. Though the church affirmed the Spirit's general providence over the content of His revelation, the Fathers believed that the Spirit superintended and chose the words the human writers employed. Clement of Rome, for example, quoted from Isaiah 53, but prefaced the passage with these words, "As the Holy Spirit had declared regarding Him. For He says."[29] In casting Jeremiah 9:23-24; 1 Corinthians 1:31, and 2 Corinthians 10:17 into a single quotation he wrote, "For the Holy Spirit saith."[30] In quoting Psalm

24. *De Principiis*, Preface 4.
25. Ibid., IV.1.
26. Ibid., Preface 8.
27. Ibid., I.3.1.
28. *Against Eunomius*, 7.1.
29. *First Epistle*, 16.
30. Ibid., 13.

34 he declared, "For He (Christ) Himself by the Holy Ghost thus addresses us."[31]

Hippolytus of Rome, in quoting Isaiah 53, stated, "For the Holy Spirit indeed, in the person of the apostles, has testified to this, saying, 'and who has believed our report? ' "[32] In explaining the meaning of Paul's statement in 1 Corinthians 4:9, "We have become a spectacle to the world, both to angels and to men," Tertullian wrote, "To prevent, however, your using such an argument as this, the Holy Ghost has providentially explained the meaning of the passage thusly."[33] Again he wrote elsewhere, " 'Covetousness,' the Spirit of the Lord has through the apostle pronounced 'a root of all evils,' " when quoting from 1 Timothy 4:11.[34] Cyprian, bishop of Carthage in the third century, has many similar notations. Before quoting Proverbs 16:16 he wrote, "The Holy Spirit speaks in the sacred Scriptures, and says,"[35] and in a reference to Psalm 68:6, "The Holy Spirit designates and points out in the Psalms saying."[36] Of Song of Songs 4:9 he said, "The Holy Spirit in the Song of Songs designated in the person of our Lord and says."[37]

Clement of Alexandria in the third century quoted Moses' words in Deuteronomy 32:10-12 and wrote, "Somewhere in song the Holy Spirit says with regard to Him."[38] Eusebius, the fourth-century historian, quoted Isaiah 53:8 and said, "Wherefore also the divine Spirit says in the prophecies."[39] Before quoting Psalm 98:1-2 he wrote, "Obeying the Divine Spirit which exhorts us in the following words."[40] A lengthy example from Gregory of Nyssa is most instructive.

All things the Divine Scripture says are utterances of the Holy Spirit. For "well did the Holy Spirit prophecy"—this he says to the

---

31. Ibid., 22.
32. *Against the Heresy of One Noetus*, 17.
33. *Against Marcion*, V.7.
34. *Of Patience*, 7.
35. *On Works and Alms*, 2; *Treatises*, 8.
36. *On Unity*, 8.
37. Ibid., 4.
38. *The Instructor*, I.7.
39. *Church History*, I.2.2.
40. Ibid., X.1.3.

Jews in Rome, introducing the words of Isaiah; and to the Hebrews, alleging the authority of the Holy Spirit in the words, "wherefore as saith the Holy Spirit," he adduces the words of the Psalm which are spoken at length in the person of God; and from the Lord Himself we learn the same thing—that David declared the heavenly mysteries not in himself (that is, not speaking according to human nature). For how could anyone, being but man, know the supercelestial converse of the Father with the Son? But being "in the Spirit" he said that the Lord spoke to the Lord those words which He has uttered.[41]

The synonyms and epithets applied to the Bible by the early church leaders indicate the high regard they had for the Scriptures. Descriptive phrases for the Scriptures abound in the early writings. Justin Martyr denominated the Scriptures as "the Divine Word,"[42] Theophilus, the second-century bishop of Antioch, as the "Sacred Scripture,"[43] and Hippolytus as "the Holy Scriptures."[44] Tertullian said of the Scriptures, "Do you look into God's revelations, examine our sacred books."[45] Elsewhere he referred to them as "our sacred writings"[46] and "the Divine Scripture."[47] In a remarkable statement Tertullian confided, "To make up for our delay in this we bring under your notice something of even greater importance; we point to the majesty of our Scriptures, if not to their antiquity. If you doubt that they are as ancient as we say, we offer proof that they are divine."[48] Irenaeus referred to the Bible as "Scriptures of truth"[49] and ventured to argue "that the Scriptures are indeed perfect."[50] Cyprian spoke of the Scripture as "Holy Scriptures"[51] and "Sacred Scripture."[52] Such epithets are numerous also in Origen's writings: "Holy

41. Against Eunomius, 7.1.
42. The First Apology, 33, 36.
43. To Autolycus, II.10.
44. Against the Heresy of One Noetus, 9.
45. Tertullian, Apology, 31.
46. Ibid., 49.
47. On Modesty, 5.
48. Apology, 20.
49. Against Heresies, III.20.1.
50. Ibid., II.38.2.
51. On Unity, 10; cf. Treatises, II.10; VII.9.
52. Epistles, 63; cf. Treatises, VII.2.

Scripture,"[53] "Holy Scriptures,"[54] "Sacred Scripture,"[55] "Divine oracles,"[56] "the oracles of God,"[57] "Sacred Scriptures,"[58] "the divinity of Scripture,"[59] and "Holy Writings."[60] He also wrote, "Do you then, my son, diligently apply yourself to the reading of the sacred Scriptures. . . . And apply yourself thus to the divine study, seek aright, and with unwavering trust in God, the meaning of the Holy Scriptures, which so many have missed."[61] Athanasius of Alexandria referred to the Bible as "the sacred and inspired Scriptures,"[62] "the Divine Scriptures,"[63] "the divinely inspired Scriptures,"[64] and "accredited as divine."[65]

THE CHURCH AND THE WRITERS OF THE BIBLE

The early church's understanding of the mode of inspiration appears to border on mechanical dictation. The early Apologists, as far as they attempt any rationalization of the inspiration of the Bible, reveal the influence of the Alexandrian Philo; they viewed the writers as passive, though not unconscious, as they recorded God's revelation. Of the passive figures of speech employed by the Apologists, Vawter writes, "Metaphors of this kind are so common, the reader of this patristic literature can hardly be blamed for taking away the idea, as many have, that Philo of Alexandria had prevailed over the early church however little he had succeeded in persuading his fellow Jews."[66] Though the early Fathers regarded the human authors of Scripture as passive instruments, it does not logically follow that those Fathers were strict mechanicalists. The early church simply did not develop a detailed or

53. *De Principiis*, Preface 10, 11.
54. Ibid., IV.1.
55. Ibid., Preface 4.
56. *Commentary on Matthew*, II.
57. *Against Celsus*, VII.10.
58. *De Principiis*, IV.8.
59. Ibid., IV.7.
60. Ibid., IV.8.
61. *Letter to Gregory*, 3.
62. *Against the Heathen*, 1.
63. *Letter*, 39.2.
64. Ibid., 39.3.
65. Ibid.
66. Bruce Vawter, *Biblical Inspiration* (Philadelphia: Westminster, 1972), p. 25.

coherent theory of inspiration. What does emerge is an attempt by the church to defend the integrity of the Scriptures as the Word of God. As Bromiley notes, "The apologists may not have meant to teach mechanical inspiration, but there can be no mistaking that they held to divine, inerrant inspiration."[67] Thus, as Klotsch echoes, "Only in this way, the Fathers thought, was the infallibility of the divine revelation secured."[68]

It should also be recognized that the early churchmen did not mean to imply that the human authors of Scripture were unconscious, not rational, and passive. In this regard the Montanists of the third century apparently helped the church to articulate more carefully the doctrine of inspiration. The Montanists believed that the state of inspiration was a circumstance in which sensation and self-consciousness were completely lost. The church's reaction to that Christian sect allowed the church to perceive more clearly what was involved in the divine-human event of communication. According to Kelly, "They understood, therefore, what they were saying; and although Scripture sometimes depicts them as falling victims to ecstasy, it would be erroneous to deduce from this that they had lost the use of the reason."[69] According to Eusebius, the fourth-century church historian, Miltiades pointed out that fact. He said,

> But the false prophet falls into an ecstasy, in which he is without shame or fear. Beginning with proposed ignorance, he passes on, as has been stated, to involuntary madness of soul. They cannot show that one of the old or one of the new prophets was thus carried away in spirit. Neither can they boast of Agabus, or Judas, or Silas, or the daughters of Philip, or Ammia in Philadelphia, or Quadratus, or any others not belonging to them.[70]

The early church did not deny the human element of inspiration (i.e., they did not assert that the writers were passive); they

---

67. Geoffrey W. Bromiley, *Historical Theology: An Introduction* (Grand Rapids: Eerdmans, 1978), p. 27.
68. E. H. Klotsch, *The History of Christian Doctrine* (Grand Rapids: Baker, 1979), p. 44.
69. J. N. D. Kelly, *Early Christian Doctrines* (New York: Harper & Row, 1978) p. 63.
70. *Church History*, V.17.2-3.

attempted to defend the uniqueness of the divine revelation. With these facts in mind, a description of the Fathers' doctrine of inspiration is in order.

Justin Martyr argued that God spoke the Scriptures. According to Justin, "When you hear the utterances of the prophets spoken as it were personally, you must not suppose that they were spoken by the inspired themselves, but by the Divine Word who moves them."[71] Martyr's doctrine of inspiration, which appears to be mechanical, should be understood within its apologetic context. He was attempting to argue the superiority of Christianity by emphasizing its superior origins, which result in a superior and harmonious disclosure of truth. According to Justin,

> For neither by nature nor by human conception is it possible for men to know things so great and divine, but by the gift which then descended from above upon the holy men, who had no need of rhetorical art, nor of uttering anything in a contentious or quarrelsome manner, but to present themselves pure to the energy of the Divine Spirit, in order that the divine plectrum itself, descending from heaven, and using righteous men as an instrument like a harp or lyre, might reveal to us the knowledge of things divine and heavenly. Wherefore, as if with one mouth and one tongue, they have in succession, and in harmony with one another, taught us both concerning God, and the creation of the world, and the formation of man, and concerning the immortality of the human soul, and the judgment which is to be after this life, and concerning all things which it is needful for us to know, and thus in divers times and places have afforded us the divine instruction.[72]

For the same apologetical reasons, Athenagoras explained the guidance of the Spirit in the disclosure of truth by saying, "It would be irrational for us to cease to believe in the Spirit from God, who moved the mouths of the prophets like musical instruments, and to give heed to mere human opinions."[73] He described the Old Testament prophets as "lifted in ecstasy above the natural operations of their minds by the impulses of the Divine Spirit,

---

71. *The First Apology*, 36.
72. *Hortatory Address to the Greeks*, 8.
73. *A Plea for Christians*, 7.

uttered the things with which they were inspired, the Spirit making use of them as a flute player."[74] Theophilus attempted to commend the Bible by comparing it to the Sibylline oracles; the Bible is authoritative simply because it is from God. The psychic state of the receptor of the divine oracle was not a point of issue; the quality and authority of the written disclosure was.

> But men of God carrying in them a holy spirit and becoming prophets, being inspired and made wise by God, became God-taught, and holy, and righteous. Wherefore they were also deemed worthy of receiving this reward, that they should become instruments of God, and contain the wisdom that is from Him, through which wisdom they uttered both what regarded the creation of the world and all other things. For they predicted also pestilences, and famines, and wars. And there was not one or two, but many, at various times and seasons among the Hebrews; and also among the Greeks there was the Sibyl; and they all have spoken things consistent and harmonious with each other, both what happened before them and what happened in their own time, and what things are now being fulfilled in our own day: wherefore we are persuaded also concerning the future things that they will fall out, as also the first have been accomplished.[75]

The obscure churchman Caius stated that "the impious adulterate the simple faith of the divine Scriptures" as they question them, "for either they do not believe that the divine Scriptures were dictated by the Holy Spirit, and are thus infidels; or they think themselves wiser than the Holy Spirit, and what are they then but demoniacs?"[76] It is noteworthy that Caius understood belief in verbal superintendence to be orthodox and its denial a characteristic of infidels. Hippolytus of Rome reflected Justin Martyr's terminology in the words "For these fathers were furnished with the Spirit, and largely honoured by the Word Himself; and just as it is with instruments of music, so had they the

74. Ibid., 8.
75. *To Autolycus*, 2.9.
76. *Fragments*, 3.

Word always, like the plectrum in union with them, and when moved by Him the prophets announced what God willed."[77]

Thus the early Fathers conceived of the writers of Scripture as musical instruments actuated by the Holy Spirit. That does not imply that the Fathers dismissed the human dimension; they were attempting to express in illustrative form the phrase "inspired by God" in 2 Timothy 3:16 and "men moved by the Holy Spirit spoke from God" in 2 Peter 1:21. But they may have created a false impression centuries later for those who accommodated their illustrations to the ecstatic, passive receptacles of the Sybilline oracles, who in affirming the divine origin of truth depreciated the human dimension of inspiration. One weakness of their terms for divine disclosure is their susceptibility to manipulation by a wrongly applied hermeneutic. As Lee states, "the tone and quality of the (musical) note depend(s) as much upon the instrument itself, as upon the hand which sweeps over the strings."[78] It should be emphasized that the Fathers were zealous to preserve the authority of Scripture. According to Vawter, "To return to the Fathers: if 'author' is not applied to God in the early Greek literature or generally in the Latin literature before Augustine, enough kindred terminology turns up to nourish the suspicion that the simplistic notion of God as writer of the Bible has venerable roots in christian antiquity."[79]

The human element of inspiration was not entirely neglected by the early churchmen, though when attempting to argue the supernatural origin and authority of Christianity such elements would reasonably receive less stress. Indeed, Lee asserts, "The language made use of plainly denotes that the human element was not thought to have been suppressed or suspended, but to have been reanimated and exalted by the divine illumination and to this notion belongs that entire system of illustration so familiar to the fathers from the earliest times."[80] The question may be posed as follows, Does the evidence of the Fathers suggest that their con-

---

77. *Treatise on Christ and Antichrist*, 2.
78. William Lee, *The Inspiration of Holy Scripture* (Dublin: Hodges, Smith and Co., 1864), pp. 81-82.
79. Vawter, p. 25.
80. Lee, p. 81.

cept of inspiration is the same as a prophecy by a follower of Montanism or the articulation of a Sybilline oracle? Were the writers of the Scripture lifted beyond their conscious state into a sphere of nonrational passivity?

Even Justin Martyr, who emphasized the apologetic value of ascribing revelation to God alone, recognized the human, rational processes in the communication of Scripture: "Before the period (the Greeks) existed only the history of the prophet Moses, which he wrote in the Hebrew character by the divine inspiration."[81] Hippolytus suggested that the writers retained their reasoning abilities; God operated "in union with them" and "convinced" them of the propriety of what they were recording. Further,

> For these fathers were furnished with the Spirit, and largely honoured by the Word Himself; and just as it is with instruments of music, so had they the Word always, like the plectrum, in union with them, and when moved by Him the prophets announced what God willed. For they spake not of their own power (let there be no mistake as to that), neither did they declare what pleased themselves. But first of all they were endowed with wisdom by the Word, and then again were rightly instructed in the future by means of visions. And then, when thus themselves fully convinced, they spake those things which were revealed by God to them alone, and concealed from all others.[82]

If the human writers were passive instruments in a state of ecstasy in which personal nuances of literary style were obliterated, the logical result would be uniformity of grammar and syntax throughout the entire Bible. Similarly, the recognition of literary style logically implies denial of absolute mechanicalism. Irenaeus, for example, built a biblical argument by stressing Paul's unique grammatical style and mental genius.[83] Tertullian, who in some ways was attracted to the Montanists, attributed the words of Scripture to the individual writers, as well as to God. He wrote, "The preachers of whom we have spoken are called prophets, from the office which belongs to them of predicting the future.

81. *Address to the Greeks*, 12.
82. *Treatise on Christ and Antichrist*, 2.
83. *Against Heresies*, III.2-2.

Their words, as well as the miracles which they performed, that men might have faith in their divine authority, we have still in the literary treasures they have left, and which are open to all [italics added]."[84] The Scriptures were understood by the Fathers to be the Word of God and the words of men; they assumed that the writers were active, rational agents, not men who were coerced so that they were nonpersonal vehicles of transcription. Cyprian stated, "Moreover, the blessed Apostle Paul, full of the grace of the Lord's inspiration, says."[85] The dual authorship of Scripture was captured by Clement of Alexandria thusly, "Jeremiah the prophet, gifted with consummate wisdom or rather the Holy Spirit in Jeremiah exhibits God. . . . And again by Isaiah."[86] And as Origen noted, "The prophets have therefore, as God commanded them, declared with all plainness those things which it was desirable that the hearers should understand at once for the regulation of their conduct; while in regard to deeper and more mysterious subjects, which lay beyond the reach of the common understanding, they set them forth in the form of enigmas and allegories, or of what are called dark sayings, parables, or similitudes."[87] Eusebius stated that Daniel wrote the prophecies in his book, thereby implying some degree of reason in the process of recording the data. If God made men passive, unthinking recorders of revelation, could it be said that they wrote the Bible? For instance, Daniel the prophet, under the influence of the divine Spirit, seeing God's end-time kingdom, was inspired to describe the divine vision in language fitted to human comprehension.[88]

Inspiration was understood to extend not only to the message of the Bible but also to the words that enshrined and conveyed that message. Kelly notes that "it goes without saying that the fathers envisaged the whole Bible as inspired. It was not a collection of desperate segments, some of divine origin and others of merely human fabrication."[89] Bannerman summarized the thought of the early churchman in much the same way.

84. *Apology*, 18.
85. *On Works and Alms*, 8, The Treatise 8.9.
86. *Exhortations to the Heathen*, 8.
87. *Against Celsus*, 7.10.
88. *Church History*, I.2.24.
89. Kelly, *Early Christian Doctrines*, p. 61.

The inspiration of Sacred Scripture was, with the Ancient Church, one of the most important assumptions of christian faith. This assumption of inspiration was applied both to the writers and also through them to the writings of the Bible: Such is the conclusion from the entire manner of speech employed by the Church Fathers."[90]

Clement of Rome seems to have argued both for the extensive and intensive inspiration of the Scriptures. In his words, "Look carefully into the Scriptures, which are the true utterances of the Holy Spirit. Observe that nothing of an unjust or counterfeit character is written in them."[91] Hippolytus of Rome, in the early third century, extended the inspiration of the Holy Spirit to the words of Scripture by writing, "For we do not attempt to make any change one way or another among ourselves in the words that were spoken of old by them, but we make the Scriptures in which these are written public, and read them to those who can believe rightly."[92] His belief that the Spirit inspired the actual words used to record the revelation helps us to understand the following passage.

> Whatever things, then, the Holy Scriptures declare, at these let us look; and whatsoever things they teach, these let us learn; and as the Father wills our belief to be, let us believe; and as He wills the Son to be glorified, let us glorify Him; and as He wills the Holy Spirit to be bestowed, let us receive Him. Not according to our own will, nor according to our own mind, nor yet as using violently those things which are given by God, but even as He has chosen to teach them by the Holy Scriptures, so let us discern them.[93]

In the same century Irenaeus extended the inspiration of the Spirit not only to all the Scriptures but also to its exact words. He wrote, "Since, therefore the entire Scriptures, the prophets, and the Gospels, can be clearly, unambiguously, and harmoniously understood by all, although all do not believe them . . . as I have

90. Bannerman, 2:69-70.
91. *The First Epistle*, 45.
92. *Treatise on Christ and Antichrist*, 2.
93. *Against the Heresy of One Noetus*, 9.

shown from the very words of Scripture."[94] Tertullian shared the same views but drove the point home more poignantly by arguing that the inspiration of the Scriptures extends to the very letters that compose the inspired words. He wrote, "The Divine Scripture has made us concorporate; the very letters are our glue."[95] When he argued the authority and applicability of the Enoch narrative, Tertullian stated, "But since Enoch in the same Scripture has preached likewise concerning the Lord, nothing at all must be rejected by us which pertains to us; and we read that all Scripture suitable for inspiration is divinely inspired."[96]

When arguing against the heretic Marcion, as well as the Gnostics, he stated that they had divested the words of Scripture of their natural and inspired meaning:

> One man perverts the Scriptures with his hand, another their meaning by his exposition. For although Valentinus seems to use the entire volume, he has none the less laid violent hands on the truth only with a more cunning mind and skill than Marcion. Marcion expressly and openly used the knife, not the pen, since he made such an excision of the Scriptures as suited his own subject matter. Valentinus, however, abstained from such excision, because he did not invent Scriptures to square with his own subject matter, but adapted his matter to the Scriptures; and yet he took away more, and added more, by removing the proper meaning of every particular word, and adding fantastic arrangements of things which have no real existence.[97]

In the western church, Novatus attempted to defend the deity of the second person of the Trinity by arguments predicated on the divine authority and superintendence of the words in Matthew 1:23. He argued,

> "The Holy Spirit shall come upon thee, and the power of the Highest shall overshadow thee; therefore also the Holy Thing which is born of thee shall be called the Son of God." If, then, say

94. *Against Heresy*, II.27.2.
95. *On Modesty*, 5.
96. *On the Apparel of Women*, I.3.
97. *On Perspective Against Heretics*, 38.

they, the angel of God says to Mary, "that Holy Thing which is born of thee," the substance of flesh and body is of Mary; but he has set forth that this substance, that is, that Holy Thing which is born of her, is the Son of God, Man, say they, himself, and that bodily flesh; that which is called holy, itself is the Son of God. That also when the Scripture says that "Holy Thing," we should understand thereby Christ the man, the Son of man; and when it places before us the Son of God, we ought to perceive, not man, but God. And yet the divine Scripture easily convicts and discloses the frauds and artifices of the heretics. For if it were thus only, "The Spirit shall come upon thee, and the power of the Highest shall overshadow thee; therefore that Holy Thing which is born of thee shall be called the Son of God," perchance we should have had to strive against them in another sort, and to have sought for other arguments, and to have taken up other weapons, with which to overcome both their snares and their wiles; but since the Scripture itself, abounding in heavenly fullness, divests itself of the calumnies of these heretics, we easily depend upon that what is written, and overcome those errors without any hesitation.[98]

Writers in the eastern segment of the church similarly extended the inspiration of the Spirit to the entirety of the Scriptures, implying that the words were given by God. Clement of Alexandria wrote,

For we have, as the source of teaching, the Lord, both by the prophets, the Gospels, and the blessed apostles, "in divers manners and at sundry times," leading from the beginning of knowledge to the end. But if one should suppose that another origin was required, then no longer truly could an origin be preserved. He, then, who of himself believes the Scripture and voice of the Lord, which by the Lord acts to the benefiting of men, is rightly [regarded] faithful. Certainly we use it as a criterion in the discovery of things.[99]

In that same passage Clement argued that the message of the inspired writers was intrinsically united to the inspired words that they wrote. Regarding errant teachers he said, "And those have a

98. *Treatise Concerning the Trinity*, 24.
99. *The Stromata*, 7.16.

craving for glory who voluntarily evade, by arguments of a diverse sort, the things delivered by the blessed apostles and teachers, which are wedded to inspired words; opposing the divine tradition by human teachings, in order to establish heresy."[100] Clement's successor in Alexandria, Origen, continued the same tradition of extending the inspiration and divine authority to all the Scriptures. In writing his principles of biblical interpretation he noted, "And therefore great pains and labor are to be employed, until every reader reverentially understands that he is dealing with divine and not human words inserted in the sacred books."[101] According to Origen the inspiration of the Scriptures is extensive.

> But as (the doctrine of) providence is not at all weakened (on account of those things which are not understood) in the eyes of those who once honestly accepted it, so neither is the divinity of Scripture, *which extends to the whole of it,* lost on account of the inability of our weakness to discover in every expression the hidden splendour of the doctrines veiled in common and unattractive phraseology [italics added].[102]

In the fourth century Gregory of Nyssa summarized his understanding of the extensive and intensive inspiration of the Scriptures by stating, "Thus it is by the power of the Spirit that Holy men who are under Divine influence are inspired, and every Scripture is for this reason said to be given by inspiration of God, because it is the teaching of Divine afflatus."[103]

THE CHURCH AND THE INFALLIBILITY OF THE BIBLE

Though it may readily be granted that the early churchmen believed in the divine authorship of the Scriptures and in God's superintendence of the very words of that revelation, we must still consider whether the Fathers understood such revelation to be

---

100. Ibid.
101. *De Principiis*, IV.19.
102. Ibid., IV.7.
103. *Against Eunomius*, 7.2.

inerrant. Bannerman argued that the Fathers, though unspeculative, understood that the Scriptures were infallible:

> The opinion of the early Christian Church as to inspired Scripture did not differ from that of its Jewish contemporaries. From the time of Christ downwards, and for centuries afterwards, there was hardly any difference of opinion as to the infallibility of the Bible, and little comparatively, for a time, of the perilous attempts to define or limit by human speculations the methods through which the result was accomplished.[104]

Clement of Rome claimed that the Scriptures were errorless. "Look carefully into the Scriptures, which are the true utterances of the Holy Spirit. Observe that nothing of an unjust or counterfeit character is written in them."[105] Justin Martyr expressly stated that the Scriptures contain no conflicting or contradictory information.

> And I answered, if you spoke these words, Trypho, and then kept silence in simplicity and with no ill intent, neither repeating what goes before nor adding what comes after, you must be forgiven; but if you have done so because you imagined that you could throw doubt on the passage, in order that I might say the Scriptures contradicted each other, you have erred. But I shall not venture to suppose or to say such a thing; and if a Scripture which appears to be of such a kind be brought forward, and if there be a pretext [for saying] that it is contrary [to some other], since I am entirely convinced that no Scripture contradicts another, I shall admit rather that I do not understand what is recorded, and shall strive to persuade those who imagine that the Scriptures are contradictory, to be rather of the same opinion as myself.[106]

Irenaeus employed the same argument of noncontradictability when he wrote, "Since, therefore the entire Scriptures, the prophets, and the Gospels, can be clearly, unambiguously, and harmoniously understood by all, although all do not believe

104. Bannerman, 2:122.
105. *First Epistle*, 45.
106. *Dialogue to Trypho*, 65.

them . . . as I have shown from the very words of Scripture."[107] Of
the writings of the apostles he said, "The apostles, likewise, being
disciples of the truth, are above all falsehood; for a lie has no fellowship with the truth, just as darkness has none with light, but
the presence of the one shuts out that of the other."[108] In another
instance Irenaeus perceived that divine inspiration presupposes
infallibility:

> If, however, we cannot discover explanations of all those things in
> Scripture which are made the subject of investigation, yet let us not
> on that account seek after any other God besides Him who really
> exists. For this is the very greatest impiety. We should leave things
> of that nature to God who created us, being most properly assured
> that the Scriptures are indeed perfect, since they were spoken by
> the Word of God and His Spirit; but we, inasmuch as we are
> inferior to, and later in existence than, the Word of God and His
> Spirit, are on that very account destitute of the knowledge of His
> mysteries.[109]

Tertullian was swift to argue before the church's detractors that
the Scriptures contained no contradictory material nor error. He
argued,

> Now, what is there in our Scriptures which is contrary to us? What
> of our own have we introduced, that we should have to take away
> again, or else add to it, or after it, in order to restore to its natural
> soundness anything which is contrary to it, and contained in the
> Scriptures? What we are ourselves, that also the Scriptures are,
> (and have been) from the beginning. Of them we have our being,
> before there was any other way, before they were interpolated by
> you. Now, inasmuch as all interpolation must be believed to be a
> later process, for the express reason that it proceeds from rivalry
> which is never in any case previous to nor home-born with that
> which it emulates, it is as incredible to every man of sense that we
> should seem to have introduced any corrupt text into the Scrip-
> tures, existing, as we have been, from the very first and being the

107. *Against Heresies*, 11.27.2.
108. Ibid., III.5.1.
109. Ibid., II.38.2.

first, as it is that they have not in fact introduced it, who are born later in date and opposed to the Scriptures.[110]

In the east as well the churchmen appear to have understood Scripture as the inerrant Word of God. The surety of the Scriptures is put forth by Clement of Alexandria who wrote, "I could adduce ten thousand Scriptures of which not 'one tittle shall pass away' without being fulfilled; for the mouth of the Lord the Holy Spirit hath spoken these things."[111] He added in another place, "But if it is not enough merely to state the opinion, but if what is stated must be confirmed, we do not wait for testimony of men, but we establish the matter that is in question by the voice of the Lord, which is the surest of all demonstrations, or rather is the only demonstration."[112] Clement ventured to describe the Scriptures, not only as the voice of God, but as the "infallible criterion of faith."[113] He even argued that the truth is in the normal meaning of the words of Scripture:

> But, selecting ambiguous expressions, they wrest them to their own opinions, gathering a few expressions here and there; not looking to the sense, but making use of the mere words. For in almost all the quotations they make, you will find that they attend to the names alone, while they alter the meanings; neither knowing, as they affirm, nor using the quotations they adduce, according to their true nature. But the truth is not found by changing the meanings (for so people subvert all true teaching), but in the consideration of what perfectly belongs to and becomes the Sovereign God, and in establishing each one of the points demonstrated in the Scriptures again from similar Scriptures.[114]

Within the Alexandrian tradition, Origen has no peers. It is clear that he perceived the Scriptures as perfect and noncontradictory, with no irrelevant material. In his commentary on Matthew he wrote,

110. *On Perspective Against Heretics*, 38.
111. *Exhortation to the Heathen*, 9.
112. *Stromata*, 7.16.
113. Ibid., 2.4.
114. Ibid., 7.16.

And likewise he becomes a third peacemaker as he demonstrates that which appears to others to be a conflict in the Scriptures is no conflict, and exhibits their concord and peace, whether of the Old Scriptures with the New, or of the Law with the Prophets or of the Gospels with the Apostolic Scriptures, or of the Apostolic Scriptures with each other. For, also, according to the Preacher, all the Scriptures are "words of the wise like goads, and as nails firmly fixed which were given by agreement from one shepherd"; and there is nothing superfluous in them. But the Word is the one Shepherd of things rational which may have an appearance of discord to those who have not ears to hear, but are truly at perfect concord. For as the different chords of the psalter or the lyre, each of which gives forth a certain sound of its own which seems unlike the sound of another chord, are thought by a man who is not musical and ignorant of the principle of musical harmony, to be inharmonious, because of the dissimilarity of the sounds, so those who are not skilled in hearing the harmony of God in the sacred Scriptures think that the Old is not in harmony with the New, or the Prophets with the Law, or the Gospels with one another, or the Apostle with the Gospel, or with himself, or with the other Apostles.[115]

In the same context he continued,

For he knows that all the Scripture is the one perfect and harmonised instrument of God, which from different sounds gives forth one saving voice to those willing to learn, which stops and restrains every working of an evil spirit, just as the music of David said to rest the evil spirit in Saul, which also was choking him.[116]

The testimony of the Fathers in the fourth and fifth centuries reflects the same high regard for the inspiration of the Bible. Athanasius clearly affirmed the infallibility of the Scriptures when he wrote, "We, however, who extend the accuracy of the Spirit to the merest stroke and tittle, will never admit the impious assertion that even the smallest matters were dealt with haphazard by those who have recorded them, and have thus been borne in mind down

115. *Commentary on Matthew*, 2.
116. Ibid.

to the present day."[117] Basil of Caesarea wrote to his disciple, Chilo, that "all bread is nutritious, but it may be injurious to the sick. Just so all Scripture is God inspired and profitable, and there is nothing in it unclean: only to him who thinks it is unclean, to him it is unclean."[118] Jerome, defending his work of translation, stated, "I am not, I repeat, so ignorant as to suppose that any of the Lord's words is either in need of correction or is not divinely inspired; but the Latin manuscripts of the Scriptures are proved to be faulty by the variations which all of them exhibit, and my object has been to restore them to the form of the Greek original, from which my detractors do not deny that they have been translated."[119] After examining the evidence of the Fathers, Lee concludes, "The Church inferred the sufficiency, the infallible certainty, and the perfection of Scripture."[120] That appears to be a logical inference from the early writings of the churchmen.

THE INTEGRITY OF THE SCRIPTURES AND THE ALEXANDRIAN TRADITION—A SHARPENED FOCUS

The scholarly debate over the nature of the Scriptures is being waged between those who affirm inerrancy and those who defend the Bible's authority, believing that God safeguarded its message but not its words.[121] The basic thesis of those who support the second position is that truth is found in the function (use), not the form (words) of language.[122] The historical basis for such a claim is the thesis that the doctrine of inerrancy is a recent historical development, a product of post-Reformation scholasticism, and is therefore a departure from "central church tradition." In brief, "certain features of the central church tradition regarding the authority and interpretation of Scripture, which had been retained from the early church down through the Reformation, were lost in the post-Reformation reaction to the rise of scientific

117. *Orations*, 11.105.
118. *Letters*, 42.3.
119. *Epistles*, 27.1.
120. Lee, pp. 76-77.
121. Jack B. Rogers and Donald K. McKim, *The Authority and Interpretation of the Bible: An Historical Approach* (San Francisco: Harper & Row, 1979), pp. 3-22.
122. Ibid., p. 11.

criticism of the Bible."[123] By arguing that the early church believed that accommodation allowed for error on the one hand and the preservation of truth in errant words on the other, some recent scholars argue that that "central church tradition" was first articulated in the Alexandrian tradition in general and in Origen (185-254) in particular. "It began with the Alexandrian school and became the common property of the central tradition from Origen through Augustine and on to Luther and Calvin.[124] But by emphasizing the Alexandrian tradition, the writings of Clement of Rome, Justin Martyr, Irenaeus, Tertullian, and many others outside the Alexandrian orbit are ignored.[125] The evidence used to support the position that Origen's views differed appreciably from his contemporaries is suspect, as is the assertion that he systematized a "central church tradition" that came under attack only in the post-Reformation era. Since Origen is believed to have articulated early church orthodoxy, it is vital to understand the assertions made about his views and to investigate his writings.

The main thesis of those scholars who believe that Origen founded the "central church tradition" is that "the basic purpose of Scripture was to bring persons to salvation, and that to accomplish that purpose God had accommodated himself to human forms of thought and speech. It was the saving message, not the form of the words, that was wholly from God."[126] Thus the Bible's message of salvation is authoritative, though its historical and geographical data may be spurious. On the basis of such reasoning Rogers and McKim are able to write that "revelation, for Origen, did not consist in the human words used, but in the divine meaning expressed."[127] They assume that the concept of truth is not to be understood as that which corresponds to reality but functionally; they bifurcate the message from the commentary of the scriptural authors. The crucial concept in understanding Origen from that perspective is the theory of accommodation, which is defined as encompassing human culpability. They argue that Origen

123. Ibid., p. XVII.
124. Ibid., p. 12.
125. John D. Woodbridge, "Biblical Authority: Towards an Evaluation of the Rogers and McKim Proposal," *Trinity Journal* 1 (1980): 1713.
126. Rogers and McKim, p. 11.
127. Ibid., p. 12.

"acknowledged that the New Testament evangelists and Paul expressed their own opinions, and that they could have erred when speaking on their own authority."[128]

Sources for Origen's supposed understanding of accommodation (i.e., errancy) are drawn in part from Bruce Vawter's *Biblical Inspiration*, in which he argues that Origen rejected mechanical dictation as absurd, rejected the ecstatic idea of the Montanist heresy, and advocated the humanness of Scripture.[129] Since accommodation is presuppositionally inclusive of error by definition, on the basis of the evidence we must argue that Origen did not define accommodation as co-extensive with human error in the Scriptures. Vawter writes,

> It seems to be clear enough that, in company with most of the other christian commentators of the age, he most often acted on the unexpressed assumption that the Scripture is a divine composition through and through, and for this reason *infallibly true in all its parts*. He could say, in fact, that the Biblical texts were not the works of men but of the Holy Spirit [*De princ.* 4.9, *PG*11:360], and that from this is followed that they were filled with the wisdom and truth of God down to the very least letter. He could therefore entertain a notion of verbal inspiration or of the literary authorship of God that could appear quite crass indeed, and it was this notion that he frequently carried with him when he examined the Scriptures [italics added].[130]

Another scholarly evaluation of Origen's theory of the Scriptures is that of R. P. C. Hanson, Senior Lecturer in Christian Theology in the University of Nottingham. Though he personally has little regard for the inerrantist position, he maintains that Origen was an inerrantist and that that has been the common position of the church. He says, "Origen's frank recognition that the textual tradition of the Scriptures was open to deviation and error did not in the least affect his conviction that the Scriptures were not only inspired but verbally inspired. . . . That every word of the Scriptures was carefully designed by God was in Origen's day no new

128. Ibid., p. 8.
129. Vawter, pp. 26-27.
130. Ibid., p. 27.

doctrine."[131] Origen, argues Hanson, advocated a rigid theory of inerrancy because of his belief that the Holy Spirit was the author of Scripture and the clear parallel between the incarnate Word, Christ, and the written Word, the Holy Scriptures. He says, "Nothing could assure us more eloquently of Origen's conviction of the divine status and authorship of the Bible than this startling doctrine of the Bible as the extension of the Incarnation."[132] Hanson's conclusion is itself startling in the light of Rogers and McKim's definition of accommodation in Origen's doctrine. According to Hanson, "One of the consequences of the Scriptures being inspired in this way is that they must be inerrant."[133] It appears that Origen did not formulate a new theory of Scripture but gave expression to one that the church already held. The traditional theory that Origen shared, however unstructured, was predicated on the trustworthiness of the words of the Bible, not on a belief that accommodationism implied error. And so Origen was not the organizer of a "central church tradition" as such. It is important to note that Origen used allegory as an interpretative tool to decipher the obscure meaning of biblical texts. The important question to answer, however, is whether he employed such a hermeneutic because he believed a literal interpretation would reveal the presence of errors or because he felt that a nonliteral interpretation better preserved his doctrine of inerrant inspiration. Does a non-literal interpretation of a text presuppose that the words that comprise it are not individually inspired of God and therefore inerrant? Origen wrote,

> The prophets have, therefore, as God commanded them, declared with all plainness those things which it was desirable that the hearers should understand at once for the regulation of their conduct; while in regard to deeper and more mysterious subjects, which lay beyond the reach of the common understanding, they set them forth in the form of enigma and allegories, or of what are called dark sayings, parables, or similitudes.[134]

131. R. P. C. Hanson, *Allegory and Event: A Study of the Sources and Interpretation of Origen's Interpretation of Scripture* (Richmond: John Knox, 1959), p. 187.
132. Ibid., p. 194.
133. Ibid., p. 191.
134. *Against Celsus*, 7.10.

Though much is to be understood literally in the gospels, he similarly confided, "In those narratives which appear to be literally recorded, there are inserted and interwoven things which cannot be admitted historically, but which may be accepted in a spiritual signification."[135] Origen, though freely imposing more allegory than literalists may desire to accept, did not pass easily into a nonliteral hermeneutic (remember his literal rendering of Matt. 6:30). He wrote,

> But that no one may suppose that we assert respecting the whole that no history is real because a certain one is not; and that no law is to be literally observed, because a certain one, (understood) according to the letter, is absurd or impossible; or that the statements regarding the Saviour are not true in a manner perceptible to the senses; or that no commandment and precept of His ought to be obeyed; we have to answer that, with regard to certain things, it is perfectly clear to us that the historical account is true. For the passages that are true in their historical meaning are much more numerous than those which are interspersed with a purely spiritual signification. And again, who would not say that the command which enjoins to "honour thy father and thy mother that it may be well with thee" is useful, apart from all allegorical meaning, and ought to be observed, the Apostle Paul also having employed these very same words? And in the writings of the apostle the literal sense is to be retained. . . . The careful (reader), however, will be in doubt as to certain points, being unable to show without long investigation whether this history so deemed literally occurred or not, and whether the literal meaning of this law is to be observed or not. And therefore the exact reader must, in obedience to the Saviour's injunction to "search the Scriptures," carefully ascertain in how far the literal meaning is true, and in how far impossible; and so far as he can, trace out, by means of similar statements, the meaning everywhere scattered through Scripture of that which cannot be understood in a literal signification.[136]

It appears that Origen did not resort to a nonliteral hermeneutic because of textual corruption but for two other reasons: he

135. *De Principiis*, IV.16.
136. Ibid., IV.19.

could not understand the text in its normal literary function and he wanted to preserve what he believed to be senseless as the inspired Word of God. The question with Origen is not how much of the Bible is supernatural, divine, inspired truth; it is how much of this divine truth is to be understood literally. Origen appears to have resorted to allegory to preserve his high view of inerrancy. His view of inspiration is orthodox, though some of his interpretations are not. Hanson explained Origen's motive for allegorizing by saying,

> Origen's handling of Scripture was often uncongenial to our minds and even positively perverse; he is to be forgiven all because he held so firmly to the theory that there is a hidden sense in all the Scriptures. As a matter of fact Origen's theory of inspiration very often drives him into exasperatingly atomistic exegesis, just because he is determined to believe that every verse, and sometimes every word, is an oracle in itself, independently of its context; this is indeed a result which the embarrassing theory of a hidden sense latent in all Scripture is eminently calculated to promote.[137]

Justo Gonzalez states in his discussion of Origen's rationalistic hermeneutics, "Although Origen is very far from being literalistic in his interpretation of the sacred text he does firmly believe in the literal inspiration of every word in Scripture."[138] As Kelly says,

> Origen indeed, and Gregory of Nazianzus after him, thought they could perceive the activity of the divine wisdom in the most trifling verbal minutiae, even in the solecisms, of the sacred books. This attitude was fairly widespread, and although some of the fathers elaborated it more than others, their general view was that Scripture was not only exempt from error but contained nothing that was superfluous. "There is not one jot or tittle," declared Origen, "written in the Bible which does not accomplish its special work for those capable of using it." In similar vein Jerome stated that "in the divine Scriptures every word, syllable, accent and point is packed with meaning"; those who slighted the commonplace con-

---

137. Hanson, *Allegory and Event*, p. 188.
138. Justo L. Gonzalez, *A History of Christian Thought*, vol. 1 (Nashville: Abington, 1970), p. 217.

tents of Philemon were simply failing, through ignorance, to appreciate the power and wisdom they concealed. According to Chrysostom, even the chronological figures and the catalogues of names included in Scripture have their profound value; and he devoted two homilies to the salutations in Romans 16 in the hope of convincing his auditors that treasures of wisdom lie hid in every word spoken by the Spirit.[139]

CONCLUSION

The early churchmen evidence both in theory and in practice a conviction that the Scriptures were written by the Holy Spirit and are therefore the inerrant Word of God. Though admittedly the Fathers show little concern to systematize their understanding of the doctrine of Scripture, the integrity of the Bible was an inviolate principle. There appears to be little evidence that the Fathers bifurcated form and fact, words and message, that they perceived an infallible, redemptive message in a fallible revelation. The summary of Klotsch captures the thrust of this chapter.

> The Fathers of the ancient church were all agreed that the Scriptures were inspired but differed in their views as to the "how." Some maintained that the state of inspiration is the state of ecstasy, or at least a state from which all human agency is to be excluded. Others recognized the human element in the biblical writings though they never questioned the divine origin nor the inerrancy of the Scriptures.[140]

It must be granted that the early church recognized the orthodoxy of God's enormous condescension to mankind both in the incarnate Savior and in the Holy Scriptures. As the accommodation of the living Word did not involve sinful pollution in any innate sense, so the Spirit's accommodation in the written Word must be similarly conceived, as Origen suggested. Certainly, the early church believed in accommodation but not condescension to error in either the written or the living Word. The act of conde-

139. Kelly, *Early Christian Doctrine*, pp. 61-62.
140. Klotsch, pp. 44-45.

scension was that providence of stooping to be understood by errant humanity, not an incorporation of the errant nature of humanity. As Christ did not take on the sin of humanity in the incarnation, neither did the Spirit succumb to such lowliness in conveying the Scriptures. Or as Christ was born through the womb of sinful flesh and yet was impeccable, so the Holy Spirit bore the written word through fallible authors and yet it is infallible.

Furthermore, the church Fathers do not appear to differ from Origen in the doctrine of Scripture. It does not seem valid to argue that the Alexandrian tradition had a view that was distinct from the rest of the church. Nor did Clement of Alexandria and Origen establish as the "central church tradition" that Scripture was authoritative but errant. As has been suggested, Origen is rather silent on textual contradictions and overt error, though he frequently rejected a literal hermeneutic. His propensity for allegory was the result of his rational quest to preserve the unity and purity of the Scriptures; it was not the result of a belief that there were errors in the text. Indeed, it has been said of Clement of Alexandria, a cofounder of the supposed errantist "central church tradition," that he "never doubts the Scriptures are inspired of God. His assurance on this point is such that he never develops a theory of inspiration. God speaks in the Scriptures, and the manner in which this fact is related to the men who actually wrote the sacred text is not a problem of primary importance."[141] Belief in the verbal inspiration of Scripture was articulated prior to the Alexandrians by such apologists as Justin Martyr and was adopted by churchmen after him. Willis Shotwell says of Martyr, "It may be seen that the individual might say the words, but it was God who was doing the speaking. Justin held to a completely verbal doctrine of inspiration. Because it was God, not man, who was speaking, each word of Scripture was of inestimable value.[142] In the conclusion of his analysis of Martyr's view of inspiration he writes,

---

141. Gonzalez, 1:99.
142. Willis A. Shotwell, *The Biblical Exegesis of Justin Martyr* (London: S.P.C.K., 1965), p. 4.

This, then, is Justin's concept of the inspiration of the Scriptures. God had spoken to the Old Testament writers through the divine Logos or the Holy Spirit. These prophets had written down the messages given to them. Because the words were inspired and from God, they were of inestimable value and could not contradict one another. The inspiration of these words was beyond all proof and must be accepted by faith. Through this faith the grace to understand these words was given by God to men who were Christians.[143]

It is also interesting that Jerome, a devout follower of Origen, though impressed with the deeper spiritual signification of the text, did not neglect its historical sense.[144] Jerome, for example, believed in the historicity of the book of Jonah.[145] Augustine, that important figure in early church history, does not appear to have entertained any notions of the errancy of the Bible.

It seems valid to argue that Origen did not appreciably differ in his view of the Scriptures from the Fathers who preceded him, except in his extensive use of allegory, and that he did not perpetuate any new view of the Bible that was subsequently understood to be the definition of orthodoxy on that topic. Justin Martyr, Irenaeus, Clement of Alexandria, and Origen agreed together on the verbal, plenary inspiration of the Holy Scriptures.

143. Ibid., pp. 7-8.
144. J. N. D. Kelly, *Jerome* (London: Gerald Duckworth and Company, Ltd., 1975), p. 151.
145. Ibid., pp. 220-21.

2

Augustine's Doctrine of Biblical Infallibility

Wayne R. Spear

In the present debate among evangelicals concerning the inerrancy of the Bible, the ultimate ground of argument must be biblical and theological, not historical. Historical considerations are not, however, without importance. If it is argued that belief in errancy is a relatively recent development in Christian doctrine, the effect may be that people will be led to regard the doctrine as an unfortunate aberration that leads away from the mainstream of Christian thought and life. On the other hand, if it can be shown that inerrancy has been the main position of the church and her leading theologians down through the centuries, then there may be a greater openness to giving serious consideration to the biblical and theological evidence on which a case for inerrancy must ultimately rest.

The purpose of this article is to examine the writings of the great North African bishop of the fourth and fifth centuries, Augustine of Hippo. He was a church leader of enormous influ-

WAYNE R. SPEAR, B.A., Beaver College, diploma, Reformed Presbyterian Theological Seminary, Th.M., Westminster Theological Seminary, Ph.D., University of Pittsburgh, is professor of systematic theology at Reformed Presbyterian Seminary in Pittsburgh, Pennsylvania. His published works include *The Theology of Prayer* (1979).

ence, prolific in writing, the "only church father," according to Hans von Campenhausen, "who even today remains an intellectual power."[1] He has been described by many scholars, both Catholic and Protestant, as a defender of the inerrancy of Scripture. On the Roman Catholic side, the French Jesuit Eugene Portalie has written, "The teaching on inspiration also owes to Augustine its exact formulation in the sense of a 'strict biblicism,' that is, of the divine origin and consequently absolute inerrancy of the Sacred Books. . . ."[2] Von Campenhausen describes his view in these words,

> The Bible is God's book, inspired and dictated by His Spirit and deserves unlimited confidence. While bishops may err, one must "in no manner doubt or dispute whether anything is true or false, once it is established that it is written there" (*Bapt.* 2; 3, 4). This verdict is valid in principle even with regard to the accessory data and statements contained in the Bible; it is not limited to the assertions "significant for salvation."[3]

By way of contrast, in their recent important work on the inerrancy debate, Jack B. Rogers and Donald K. McKim have advanced the thesis that the "Augustinian" tradition in theology rejects the claim that the Scripture's authority lies in a "form of scientifically inerrant words." They regard such a claim as the product of Aristotelian scholasticism introduced into the Protestant churches by Melanchthon and Beza and elaborated by Turretin and the "Old Princeton" theology.[4] In the study of Augustine that follows, that thesis will be examined with the intention of showing that Augustine did hold to the inerrancy of the Bible,

1. Hans von Campenhausen, *The Fathers of the Latin Church*, trans. Manfred Hoffman (Stanford: Stanford U. Press, 1969), p. 183.
2. Eugene Portalie, *A Guide to the Thought of Saint Augustine*, trans. Ralph J. Bastian (Westport: Greenwood Press, 1975), p. 122.
3. Ibid., p. 271. See also David W. Kerr, "Augustine of Hippo," in *Inspiration and Interpretation*, ed. John F. Walvoord (Grand Rapids: Eerdmans, 1957), pp. 67-86.
4. Jack B. Rogers and Donald K. McKim, *The Authority and Interpretation of the Bible: An Historical Approach* (San Francisco: Harper & Row, 1979), pp. 457-59 (hereafter cited as *Authority and Interpretation*).

even with regard to "scientific" matters and the seemingly insignificant details of the text.

The amount of Augustine's writing that has survived is enormous, and some selection had to be made in this study. Primary attention has been given to *The Harmony of the Gospels* because that work constitutes Augustine's most detailed response to the charge that the Bible contains contradictions or erroneous statements.[5] Only works that have been translated into English have been consulted.

THE PLACE OF SCRIPTURE IN AUGUSTINE'S LIFE AND WORK

Augustine's view of Scripture was not an abstract, merely intellectual concept. In his developing spiritual experience, which he described so vividly in the *Confessions*, it is obvious that the Scripture—read, preached, and remembered—had a central role.[6] Aurelius Augustinus was born to a pagan father and a Christian mother, Monica, in A.D. 354, in what is now Algeria.[7] In his childhood and early youth he apparently had little knowledge of the Bible, though he had, as he said, taken in the name of the Savior with his mother's milk. In a time of illness he had begged for baptism, desiring to confess Christ for the remission of sins, but his wish was not granted.[8] When as a teenager he began to study Cicero, he was disappointed only by the absence of the name of Christ in the pagan philosophy. He decided to begin the study of Scripture but found it puzzling and inelegant in style.[9] His disappointment in that early contact with the Bible led Augustine on a long detour through sensuality and then into Manichaeanism, where he sought vainly for the power to live a pure life. He remained in that dualistic, pseudo-Christian sect for some nine years. During that time he studied astronomy (perhaps, more

5. Augustine, *The Harmony of the Gospels*, trans. S. D. F. Salmond, in *The Nicene and Post-Nicene Fathers*, ed. Philip Schaff (New York, 1888), 6:65-236 (hereafter cited as *Harmony*).
6. *Confessions*, trans. Vernon J. Bourke, in *The Fathers of the Church*, (New York: Fathers of the Church, Inc., 1953), vol. 21 (hereafter cited as *Confessions*).
7. Biographical information is taken from Warren Thomas Smith, *Augustine: His Life and Thought* (Atlanta: John Knox, 1980).
8. *Confessions*, 3.4.8; 1.11.17.
9. Ibid., 3.5.9.

accurately, astrology). He found many things in the Manichaean writings about the heavens that were contradictory, and he looked forward eagerly to hearing Faustus, a prominent Manichaean teacher who, he hoped, would resolve his doubts. When he found that Faustus was only eloquent, largely ignorant, and unable to resolve his scientific questions, Augustine began to look elsewhere in his search for truth.[10] The presence of contradictions and views that could not explain the seen world undermined his confidence in what he had heretofore regarded as sacred writings. Still, he did not know how to answer the criticism that the Manichaeans brought against the Scriptures of the catholic church.[11]

In A.D. 384 Augustine went to Milan, Italy, as a teacher of rhetoric, and there he went to hear the great Ambrose preach. At first Augustine was impressed with the preacher's oratory, but then his heart began to open to the message of the gospel. He began to regard the Christian faith as capable of defense. "This was especially so when I heard, rather often, one after another of the obscure passages from the Old Testament being explained . . . I now came to reprove my despair, which had led me to believe that the haters and mockers of the Law and the Prophets were altogether incapable of being resisted."[12] Augustine now decided to become a catechumen. He began to be persuaded of the necessity and authority of the Scripture. In his words,

> Thus, since we were too weak to discover the truth by clear reasoning, and because, as a result, we had need of the authority of holy Scripture, I had already started to believe that Thou wouldst never have granted such high authority throughout every land to that Scripture, unless Thou hadst willed that we believe in Thee through it and that we seek Thee through it.[13]

In Milan, Augustine came under the influence of Platonism as it was interpreted by Plotinus. Afterwards, he came to regret his enthusiasm for Platonic thought and his failure to defend Chris-

10. Ibid., 5.7.12.
11. Ibid., 5.11.21.
12. Ibid., 5.14.24 (Ambrose's method of interpretation was "spiritual," or allegorical).
13. Ibid., 6.5.8.

tian teaching against its errors.[14] At the time, however, it served to deepen his appreciation of the Scripture. He wrote,

And so, with great eagerness, I seized the venerable writings of Thy Spirit and above all, of Thy Apostle, Paul. Those difficult problems, on which at one time the text of his discourse seems to contradict himself and not to be in keeping with the evidence of the Law and Prophets, disappeared. The unified form of these chaste spokesmen became clear to me, and I learned to rejoice with trembling.[15]

The existence of seeming contradictions in the Bible, then, was a problem for Augustine when he was coming to faith in Christ, and the resolution of those problems was a step toward his conversion.

Augustine's conversion, the experience that he regarded as the decisive turning point in his life, involved the Scripture in a memorable way. He was inwardly torn as he considered turning his back on his old way of life and making a definite commitment to the service of God. In the famous garden scene he expressed his anguish in words from the Psalms. The resolution came when in response to a mysterious voice, he opened a copy of Paul's writings at random and found the words "put on the Lord Jesus Christ, and as for the flesh, take no thought for its lusts."[16] In the early days of his new peace and joy Augustine found words to express his experience in the Bible, especially in the Psalms.[17]

Following Monica's death, Augustine returned to Africa in A.D. 388, where he engaged in writing and tried to establish a monastic community. While in the city of Hippo, he was called to the priesthood by public acclamation and ordained in A.D. 391. Feeling keenly the responsibility of being one who administered the Word of God to the people, he received permission from his bishop for some months of free time in which to study the Scripture,

14. *The Retractions*, trans. Mary Inez Bogan, in *The Fathers of the Church* (Washington: Catholic U. of America Press, 1968), 60:10 (hereafter cited as *Retractions*).
15. *Confessions*, 7.21.27.
16. Ibid., 8.12.29.
17. Ibid., 9.4.8,10,11.

pray, and weep.[18] He became a preaching priest, and after A.D. 395, a preaching bishop. His ministry was a model of the advice he later gave to those who aspired to be teachers:

> Furthermore, a man speaks more or less wisely in proportion as he has made more or less progress in the Holy Scriptures. I do not mean in the extensive reading and memorizing of them, but in a thorough understanding and careful searching into their meanings . . . it is particularly essential for the man who should say with wisdom even what he cannot say eloquently to remember the words of Scripture . . . so that he may prove from them what he says in his own words and, although inferior in his own words, he may rise in distinction, as it were, by the testimony of the great.[19]

As well as preaching, Augustine devoted much of his energy to writing expositions of various portions of Scripture. In all, it has been calculated that he cited Scripture more than 40,000 times in his works.[20]

According to an early biographer, Augustine had the words of the Penitential Psalms pinned on the wall before him while he was dying, so that his thoughts might be directed by them. As in his search for truth, his conversion, and his ministry, so in his death, Augustine gave the Scriptures a central place.

This rapid sketch of his life, though providing some indications of his doctrine of Scripture, has not made clear precisely what Augustine believed about the origin, authority, and accuracy of the Bible. To those matters we now turn our attention.

AUGUSTINE'S VIEW OF INSPIRATION

Augustine had experienced the dynamic, saving efficacy of the Scripture in his own life and ministry. In his teaching he made clear that that power of the Scripture was in keeping with the

18. Letter 21, To Bishop Valerius, *Letters*, vol. 1, trans. Wilfrid Parsons, in *The Fathers of the Church* (Washington: Catholic U. of America Press, 1951), 12:47-51.
19. *Christian Instruction*, trans. John J. Gavigan, in *The Fathers of the Church* (New York: Fathers of the Church, Inc. 1947), 2:173-74 (hereafter cited as *Instruction*).
20. Smith, *Augustine*, p. 89.

divine origin of the words of the Bible, that is, their *inspiration*.[21]

Without departing from the devotional tone of the *Confessions*, Augustine wrote of the way in which Moses became the author of Genesis.

> Let all be far from me who think that Moses said false things. But as for those who are fed upon Thy truth . . . let me be joined together with them in Thee, O Lord, and may I be made joyful with them in Thee. Let us approach together the words of Thy Books and let us seek out in them Thy intention through the intention of Thy servant, by whose pen Thou didst dispense it.[22]

Whatever difficulties he might have had in understanding Genesis (and Augustine found it very perplexing), he was confident that the words written there were not false but expressed what God intended because they were written by Moses as the Lord's penman. What Moses wrote, God had commanded him to write.[23] The Scriptures may therefore appropriately be called the writings of God's Spirit.[24]

Augustine was so convinced of the Holy Spirit's authorship of the Bible that he appealed to the Spirit's intention when he attempted to solve the problem of an apparent mistake in Matthew 27:9, where a quotation from Zechariah is attributed to Jeremiah. After dismissing Origen's suggestion of a copyist's error, Augustine made the following proposal.

> How then, is the matter to be explained, but by supposing that this has been done in accordance with the more secret counsel of that providence of God by which the minds of the evangelists were governed? For it may have been the case, that when Matthew was engaged in composing his Gospel, the word Jeremiah occurred to his mind, in accordance with a familiar experience, instead of Zechariah. Such an inaccuracy, however, he would most undoubtedly have corrected (having his attention called to it, as surely

21. For a full and accurate treatment of the subject, see A. D. R. Polman, *The Word of God According to St. Augustine*, trans. A. J. Pomerans (Grand Rapids: Eerdmans, 1961).
22. *Confessions*, 12.23.32.
23. Ibid., 12.3.3.
24. Ibid., 7.21.27.

would have been the case, by some who might have read it while he was still alive in the flesh), had he not reflected that [perhaps] it was not without a purpose that the name of the one prophet had been suggested instead of the other in the process of recalling the circumstances (which process of recollection was also directed by the Holy Spirit), and that this might not have occurred to him had it not been the Lord's purpose to have it so written.[25]

The Spirit's purpose, as Augustine understood it, was to point to the essential unity of the words of the prophets. Because the same Spirit gave expression through the various prophets, "words spoken by Zechariah are really as much Jeremiah's as they are Zechariah's." Therefore Matthew, in leaving "Jeremiah" in his text, was bowing to the authority of the Holy Spirit "under whose guidance he felt his mind to be placed in a more decided sense than is the case with us. . . ."[26] If Augustine's explanation seems forced, it is nevertheless clear that he here presents a view that amounted to verbal inspiration—in the case of a word that seems at first to be incorrect!

One of the most vivid and theologically significant passages in which Augustine spoke of the inspiration of Scripture is his rebuttal of those who criticized Christianity for failing to possess writings from the hand of Jesus himself. Though that is true, Christ did leave His own message for later generations. Augustine said,

Accordingly, He who sent the prophets before His own descent also despatched the apostles after His ascension. . . . He stands to all his disciples in the relation of the head to the members of His body. Therefore, when those disciples have written matters which He declared and spoke to them it ought not by any means be said that He has written nothing Himself; since the truth is, that His members have accomplished only what they became acquainted with by the repeated statements of the Head. For all that He was minded to give for our perusal on the subject of His own doings and

25. *Harmony*, 3.7.30.
26. G. W. Bromiley, "The Church Doctrine of Inspiration," in *Revelation and the Bible*, ed. Carl F. H. Henry (Grand Rapids: Eerdmans, 1958), p. 208; cited in *Authority and Interpretation*, p. 64, n. 132.

sayings, He commanded to be written by those disciples, whom He thus used as if they were His own hands.[27]

That clear statement cannot be dismissed, as Bromiley does, by saying that "this does not mean more than that the members of Christ's body act in behalf of Christ himself as Head."[28] In the context Augustine was speaking specifically of the apostles. Furthermore, it is clear that the reliability of the New Testament writings, in his view, is due to Christ's appointment of only certain persons to communicate the gospel in writing, and to the Holy Spirit's special guidance of them. The writings of the apostles Matthew and John, and those of "followers of the apostles," Mark and Luke, are thus the only written records of Jesus' life "admitted to the canonical authority of the Holy Books."[29] It is on the basis of the gospel writers being the instruments of Christ that Augustine proceeded in the *Harmony* to answer the charge that they have given contradictory accounts of the Lord. He intended to show that those "members in that body have preserved a befitting harmony in the unity of the body itself, not only by identity of sentiment, but also by constructing records consonant with that identity."[30]

Augustine's view of inspiration has been called a "dictation theory," but he made it clear that the work of the Holy Spirit in producing the Scripture did not eliminate the active participation of the human authors. Moses' intention, as well as that of the Holy Spirit, is of great importance in understanding Genesis.[31] The evangelists remembered Jesus' words and actions. They had made inquiries about Jesus, His parents, and others concerning those events in Jesus' life that had occurred before they had become followers[32]; each one made his own judgment about what to include and how he would write. Augustine said,

For it is evident that the evangelists have set forth these matters

27. *Harmony*, 1.35.54.
28. Ibid., 1.1.2.
29. Ibid., 1.1.2.
30. Ibid., 1.35.54.
31. *Confessions*, 12 23.32.
32. *Harmony*, 1.1.1.

just in accordance with the recollection each retained of them, and just according as their several predilections prompted them to employ greater brevity or richer detail on certain points, while giving, nevertheless, the same account of the subjects themselves.[33]

For Augustine, the nature of memory is a key element in the process by which men wrote the Scriptures out of their own knowledge of things yet were fully guided by the Holy Spirit in doing so. In Book X of the *Confessions* he explored the amazing labyrinth of human memory, finding it analogous in its complexity to the incomprehensibility of God. Memory is a storehouse in which all sorts of things lie hidden and from which a person summons them into consciousness. But one does not have full control over his own memory; "Some things come forth immediately; others are hunted after for a longer time. . .; still others rush out in a mob, when something else is sought and looked for, jumping forth in the middle as if to say, 'Would we do, perhaps?' "[34] In the *Harmony of the Gospels* Augustine used his understanding of the nature of memory to explain why two evangelists record events in a different order.

For as it is not in one's power, however admirable and trustworthy may be the knowledge he has once obtained of the facts, to determine the order in which he will recall them to memory (for the way in which one thing comes into a person's mind before or after another is something which proceeds not as we will, but simply as it is given to us), it is reasonable enough to suppose that each of the evangelists believed it to have been his duty to relate what he had to relate in that order in which it had pleased God to suggest to his recollection the matters he was engaged in recording.[35]

Thus the divine and human elements operate together. There is human recollection of events and teachings, and there is the governing activity of the Spirit who brings these things to remembrance in a certain order, different in one evangelist than in

33. Ibid., 2.12.27.
34. *Confessions*, 10.8.12.
35. *Harmony*, 2.21.51.

another. Yet this is done in such a way that nothing is detracted from the truth.

After a much more detailed examination of the evidence than has been undertaken here, A. D. R. Polman has correctly summarized Augustine's view of the inspiration of Scripture in these words, *"The Bible was both the exclusive work of the Holy Spirit alone and at the same time the exclusive work of the Biblical writers.* . . . Thus the difference between the Gospels must be attributed to what it pleased the Holy Ghost to put in them and also to the spiritual tendencies of the Evangelists."[36]

It should be acknowledged that the words used by Augustine to express the Spirit's work in the inspiration of the Bible are also used in a more general way. He regarded the work of the translators of the Septuagint as being the result of supernatural guidance that preserved them from error.[37] Indeed, Augustine could speak of any assistance or direction of the Spirit in the lives of Christians by using the same words. However, the important point to be established is that Augustine believed that there was a body of literature that was unique because it was produced by specially appointed men who wrote under the special direction of the Holy Spirit. The evidence cited shows that he believed that the church possessed just such a body of literature in the Bible. It is a secondary, though still important, question, to ask where the line of demarcation between Holy Scripture and other literature is to be drawn. Disputes about the extent of the canon and about the accuracy of various translations could not take away Augustine's confidence that in the writings of the prophets and apostles, the church possessed the Word of God.[38]

The question to which we now turn has to do with the nature of the Scripture produced by the divine-human activity described by Augustine. Does the human element in some way limit divine guidance, so that the product is a combination of divine, saving, infallible truth, and human, fallible, mundane opinions? Or did

36. Polman, *The Word of God*, p. 51.
37. *Instruction*, 2.15.22.
38. See Polman, *The Word of God*, pp. 44-46, for a discussion of the terms used by Augustine. Polman also treats Augustine's view of the Septuagint at length, pp. 182-95.

the Spirit's direction keep the human authors from error in what they wrote?

AUGUSTINE'S DEFENSE OF BIBLICAL INERRANCY

It is not difficult to find numerous passages in the writings of Augustine in which he asserts in so many words that the Scriptures are without error. He wrote to Jerome, the translator of the Vulgate, "I think it extremely dangerous to admit that anything in the Sacred Books should be a lie; that is, that the men who have composed and written the Scriptures for us should have lied in their books."[39] In another letter to Jerome he said,

> . . . it is from those books alone of the Scriptures, which are now called canonical, that I have learned to pay them such honor and respect as to believe most firmly that not one of their authors has erred in writing anything at all. . . . And I think that you, my brother, feel the same way; moreover, I say, I do not believe that you want your books to be read as if they were those of Prophets or Apostles, about whose writings, free from all error, it is unlawful to doubt.[40]

The same distinction between Scripture and other writings with reference to inerrancy is expressed with great fullness and clarity in Augustine's *Reply to Faustus the Manichaean*. The passage is so important for an understanding of Augustine's view that it is quoted at length.

> As regards our writings, which are not a rule of faith or practice, but only a help to edification, we may suppose that they contain some things falling short of the truth in obscure and recondite matters, and that these mistakes may or may not be corrected in subsequent treatises. . . . Such writings are read with the right of judgment, and without any obligation to believe. In order to leave room for such profitable discussions of difficult questions there is a distinct boundary line separating all productions subsequent to apostolic times from the authoritative canonical books of the Old

39. Letter 28, *Letters*, 1:95-96.
40. Ibid., Letter 82.

and New Testaments. The authority of these books has come down to us from the apostles through the successions of bishops and the extension of the Church, and, from a position of lofty supremacy, claims the submission of every faithful and pious mind. If we are perplexed by an apparent contradiction in Scripture, it is not allowable to say, The author of this book is mistaken; but either the manuscript is faulty, or the translation is wrong, or you have not understood. In the innumerable books that have been written latterly we may sometimes find the same truth as in Scripture, but there is not the same authority. Scripture has a sacredness peculiar to itself . . . in consequence of the distinctive peculiarity of the sacred writings, we are bound to receive as true whatever the canon shows to have been said by even one prophet, or apostle, or evangelist. Otherwise, not a single page will be left for the guidance of human fallibility, if contempt for the wholesome authority of the canonical books either puts an end to that authority altogether, or involves it in hopeless confusion.[41]

For Augustine, it was an article of faith that there is no real discrepancy or contradiction in all of Scripture. That must be believed even when one is unable to find a satisfactory solution to a particular problem in the biblical text.[42] The *Harmony of the Gospels* is an extended attempt on Augustine's part to demonstrate that there is no falsehood at all in the accounts given by the evangelists.

How do those who claim Augustine's prestige and authority against the inerrancy position interpret such statements? Rogers and McKim, for example, contend that Augustine's view was radically different from that of reformed scholasticism, though they made use of some of these same quotes. They interpret them as something other than a defense of biblical inerrancy, however, by making four assertions that if true would limit or qualify Augustine's denial that the Bible contains any errors. Those four assertions must now be examined.

41. Augustine, *Reply to Faustus the Manichaean*, trans. Richard Stothert, in *The Nicene and Post-Nicene Fathers*, vol. 4 (Buffalo: Christian Literature Co., 1887), 11. 5., p. 180.
42. Augustine, *Lectures . . . on the Gospel According to St. John*, trans. John Gible, in *The Nicene and Post-Nicene Fathers*, ed. Philip Schaff, vol. 7 (New York, 1888), 112. 18. 1.

THE EXTENT OF THE SPIRIT'S GUIDANCE

According to Rogers and McKim, Augustine believed that the divine activity of the Holy Spirit was limited in the production of the Scripture, so that in some aspects of their writing the human authors were left to themselves and so were fallible. God's *permission* accounted for the variations in expression. "One must not suppose that . . . the evangelists must have been instructed by the Holy Spirit in their choice of words."[43] The Spirit is said to have "permitted this pluriformity of perspectives," to have "allowed" each of the gospel writers to arrange things as that writer chose.[44] That view of the permissive activity of the Spirit makes room, then, for fallible human work in which it was possible for less than accurate accounts to be given of the words and actions of Jesus.

In one important passage, Augustine did make use of the concept of permission in reference to the Spirit's activity. The Spirit ". . . has left one historian at liberty to construct his narrative in one way, and another in a different fashion. . . ."[45] In the context, however, that is not *mere* permission. Augustine said that the *reason* the Spirit acted in that way may be discovered by pious investigation; that is, the end result was according to the Spirit's design. Also, in the same sentence he spoke of the Spirit as the one who ". . . governs and rules the minds of the holy men themselves in the matter of suggesting the things they were to commit to writing. . . ." The Holy Spirit, Augustine believed, had His own purpose that is fulfilled in the varying orders in which the evangelists wrote their narratives.

Augustine's treatment of Matthew 27:9 must again be referred to in that connection. The substitution of the name of Jeremiah for Zechariah, at first regarded as the result of a lapse of memory on Matthew's part, is seen on further reflection to be due to the infallible guidance of the Spirit. He governed the mind of the evangelist in order, Augustine thought, to lead the reader to a deeper truth because of the apparent mistake.[46]

43. *Authority and Interpretation*, p. 29.
44. Ibid.
45. *Harmony*, 2.21.52, cited in *Authority and Interpretation*, p. 28.
46. Ibid., 3.7.30.

Augustine discussed at length a seemingly insignificant difference between Mark 15:25 and John 19:14 concerning the hour of Jesus' crucifixion. He did not account for it by appealing to the humanity of the writers but attributed it to the sovereign purpose of God. The one who finds a contradiction in the two accounts is exhorted to

> be content to reckon his own notion inferior to that of Mark the evangelist, who has judged it right to insert the statement just at the point at which it was suggested to him by divine inspiration. For the recollections of those historians have been ruled by the hand of Him who rules the waters, as it is written, according to his good pleasure. For the human memory moves through a variety of thoughts, and it is not in any man's power to regulate either the subject which comes into his mind or the time of its suggestion. Seeing, then, that those holy and truthful men, in this matter of the order of their narrations, committed the casualties of their recollections (if such a phrase may be used) to the direction of the hidden power of God, to whom nothing is casual, it does not become any mere man, in his low estate, removed far from the vision of God, and sojourning distantly from Him, to say, "This ought to have been introduced here"; for he is utterly ignorant of the reason which led God to will its being inserted in the place it occupies.[47]

Both the number of the hour and the place where it stands in Mark's account are due to the direction and will of God, and therefore there can be no mistake or error involved.

In Augustine's doctrine of inspiration the real participation of the human writers does not place a limit on the divine guidance that guarantees the trustworthiness of the Bible. Even the seemingly insignificant details of the narratives fulfill the purpose of the Holy Spirit. He does not act upon the writers of Scripture only in the mode of permission.

THE DEFINITION OF ERROR

It has been claimed that Augustine's notion of inerrancy differs from the more recent position because he had a limited definition

47. Ibid., 3.13.39.

of what constitutes an error. According to Rogers and McKim, "Error, for Augustine, had to do with deliberate and deceitful telling of that which the author knew to be untrue. It was in that context of ethical seriousness that he declared that the biblical 'authors were completely free of error.' "[48] Though no evidence is cited for that particular definition of error, it may be that Augustine's treatise *On Lying* is in view. There, he does make the intention to deceive to be the essence of lying. "For, a person is to be judged as lying or not lying according to the intention of his own mind, not according to the truth or falsity of the matter itself. . . . In reality, the fault of the person who tells a lie consists in his desire to deceive in expressing his thought."[49]

Augustine excluded any possibility that any of the biblical writers had lied in that way, even by using a so-called polite or serviceable lie. Good intentions would not justify any attempt to deceive, since the ultimate effect would be to destroy the credibility of the speaker. That holds also for the Bible: "If we once admit in that supreme authority any polite lie, there will be nothing left of those books, because, whenever anyone finds something difficult to practice or hard to believe, he will follow this most dangerous precedent and explain it as the idea or practice of a lying author."[50] It needs to be remembered that Augustine regarded the Holy Spirit as the ultimate author of the biblical text, and of course the intention to deceive cannot be attributed to the Spirit. The concept of accommodation needs to be used with great care in that respect, because whatever may be said of God's condescension to human weakness in giving his Word, Augustine's view will not permit the practice of well-meant deception to be a part of that gracious accommodation.[51] A definition of lying, however, considered as part of a discussion of ethical behavior, is not the same thing as a definition of error. An inadvertent mistake is not morally culpable, but it can still mislead, and it can undermine confidence in a person's testimony.

48. *Authority and Interpretation*, p. 31.
49. Augustine, *On Lying*, trans. Mary Sarah Muldowney, in *Fathers of the Church*, vol. 16 (Washington: Catholic U. of America Press, 1952; reprinted, 1965), 4. 4., pp. 55, 56.
50. Letter 28, *Letters*, 1:96.
51. See *Authority and Interpretation*, pp. 27-30.

When Augustine declared the Bible to be free from error, he explicitly rejected the presence of inadvertent mistakes as well as conscious deception. "It is only seemly, however, that no charge of absolute unveracity should be laid against the evangelists, and that, too, not only with regard to that kind of unveracity which comes by the positive telling of what is false, but also with regard to that which arises through forgetfulness."[52] In the *Harmony* in particular Augustine's concern was not so much with the evangelists' conscious aim as it was with the accuracy of the accounts that they wrote. He not only excluded erroneous motives on their part but also errors of fact. And that holds good for the rest of Scripture as well.

THE RELATIONSHIP BETWEEN WORDS AND MESSAGE

Rogers and McKim make the point repeatedly that Augustine found the truthfulness of the Bible in the meaning intended by the writers, rather than in their very words. They say, "Yet the unity of Scripture was in the consistency of its message, not in a formal harmony of all its verbal forms, in which God's message was expressed. . . . Augustine therefore focused on the meaning expressed, not the mechanics of expression. . . . Augustine knew that the truth of Scripture resided finally in the thought of the biblical writers and not in the form of their words."[53]

It is certainly true that Augustine was primarily concerned with the meaning of the words of Scripture. In harmonizing the gospel accounts, he referred frequently to that principle. He said,

> We ought not to suppose that any one of the writers is giving an unreliable account if, when several persons are recalling some matter either heard or seen by them, they fail to follow the very same plan, or to use the very same words, while describing, nevertheless, the selfsame fact . . . we should also understand that it is not so

52. *Harmony*, 2.12.29. In the preceding sentence where Augustine spoke of a "slip of memory," he was speaking of what appears to be the case, not what actually took place.
53. *Authority and Interpretation*, pp. 28-30.

much in mere words, as rather truth in the facts themselves that is
to be sought and embraced. . . .[54]

Because of the variations in the gospel records, it may be impossible in some cases to know what were the precise words spoken by Jesus on a particular occasion. However, inquiry about that is unnecessary since "the speaker's meaning . . . admits of being understood with the utmost plainness even under the diverse terms employed by the evangelists."[55]

Augustine was simply making a point about the nature of language. It contains such flexibility that the same thing may be said in more than one way without any loss of truth. Furthermore, diversity of expression has a positive advantage. When the same thing is expressed in two different ways, it becomes clearer since the second mode of expression removes any ambiguity that may have been present in the first. Commenting on a passage common to the three synoptic gospels Augustine wrote, "One and the same sense, therefore, is conveyed; and it is expressed all the better in consequence of these variations employed in some of the terms, while the matter of fact itself is left intact." Words found only in Luke "bring out the sense more clearly."[56]

Augustine dealt with the divergencies between the Hebrew codices and the Septuagint by appealing to the possibility of saying the same thing accurately in more than one way. Just as "harmonious diversity" characterizes the four evangelists, so the translators of the Septuagint ". . . while not departing from the real mind of God . . . gave a different form to some matters in their reproduction of the text." That was accomplished, he believed, ". . . without any failure from strict truth."[57]

Augustine did not conclude, however, that since meaning is the important thing, there may be error in the form of the words used

54. *Harmony*, 2.12.28.
55. Ibid., 3.2.8.
56. Ibid., 2.27.61; cf. 2.38.85.
57. Ibid., 2.66.128. See *Authority and Interpretation*, p. 65, n. 137. The sentence quoted seems to say that God has not given any words but only the truth, the "thing itself," in the Bible. In the context of a discussion of translation, however, it is clear that Augustine was denying that truth was so inseparably tied to Hebrew *sounds* (a preferable meaning for *sonis*) that it was incapable of being expressed in Greek or in some other language.

to express that meaning in the Bible. In the Scripture, there can be two or more true ways of saying the same thing. There are not false words that somehow are the vehicle of a true meaning. Augustine's approval of diversity of expression is limited by the accuracy of the alternative versions. "For as to writers who do not employ precisely the same modes of statement, if they only do not present discrepancies with respect to the facts and the sentiments themselves, we accept them as holding the same position in veracity."[58]

The most persuasive evidence of Augustine's belief that infallible words and infallible thoughts are inseparable is simply his *Harmony of the Gospels* taken as a whole.[59] Having examined almost every conceivable allegation of contradiction or discrepancy in the words of the gospel writers, he affirmed the entire truthfulness of what they have written. Never does he explain a problem by resorting simply to the occurrence of human error in the choice of words. Never did he say, "This is a mistake, but it does not matter because it is only in the words." Always he attempted to show that the form of expression was chosen by the author as the best way to express the truth in keeping with his particular purpose and that that choice was made under the clear guidance and direction of the Holy Spirit.

SCIENCE, HISTORY, AND THE BIBLE

One important aspect of the present debate about biblical inerrancy concerns the relationship between the truthfulness of the Bible and modern views in science and history. Rogers and McKim describe the "post-Reformation scholastic" view as holding that "the Bible was a repository of information about all manner of things, including science and history, which had to be proven accurate by then current standards." The Hodge-Warfield position, they argue, was that "the Bible is inerrant by modern standards in all matters that it mentions," including statements

58. *Harmony*, 2.12.28. See *Authority and Interpretation*, p. 29, where the significant qualification at the end of the sentence is omitted.
59. The expression is suggested by a quotation from A. A. Hodge and B. B. Warfield, cited in *Authority and Interpretation*, p. 377, n. 188.

having to do with the realm of science. Such a view is foreign to the thought of Augustine, they maintain, because for him ". . . the purpose of Scripture was not to bring people information in general, but to bring the Good News of salvation and guidance in the Christian way of life. The Bible was not a textbook of science or an academic tract."[60]

The description of the Hodge-Warfield position given by Rogers and McKim is problematical because it involves an instance of begging the question. When the position is said to require inerrancy "by modern standards," it is already assumed that such standards of inerrancy are quite different from those prevailing in other times, particularly from those used by Augustine. The view actually held by Augustine was simply that the Bible was without error in all matters that it mentions, including matters having to do with the external world and world history. It goes without saying that Augustine's "science" was not modern science, and that his knowledge of general history was that shared by his contemporaries. The point that must be established is whether or not Augustine felt it important to demonstrate that when the Bible touches on matters open to investigation by observation or examination of extrabiblical evidence, it was truthful.

Augustine was far from being uninterested in the question of the Bible's accuracy regarding scientific and historical information. He devoted a significant portion of *The City of God* to such questions, defending the truthfulness of the Scripture against various attacks as he traced the history of God's redemptive work. He discussed the question of the antiquity of the human race and vindicated the biblical chronology, as he understood it, which places the time of Adam's creation at not more than 6,000 years before Augustine's own day. In that connection he discussed and rejected the Egyptian chronologies with which he was familiar and also a purported letter of Alexander the Great that he thought was in conflict with the ". . . established authority of our inspired writings."[61] He responded to skepticism about the reference to giants in Genesis 6:4 by citing reports of the discovery of fossil bones of

60. Ibid., pp. xvii, xx, 26.
61. *The City of God*, Books VIII-XVI, in *The Fathers of the Church*, vol. 14 (Washington: Catholic U. of America Press, 1952), 12. 11 (hereafter cited as *City*).

immense size and telling of his own observation of a "human molar," one hundred times the size of an ordinary tooth, as he was walking on the beach at Utica.[62] He defended the biblical account of the longevity of the patriarchs before the Flood. In doing so he explained the differences between the numbers of the Septuagint and Hebrew texts as due to a copyist's error, regarding the "original text" as containing the account that conforms to the facts.[63] Long before the rise of modern historical geology, Augustine anticipated scientific objections to the Genesis story of the Deluge. Using the concepts of the "science" of his day, he argued for the physical possibility of the Flood, the ability of Noah and his sons to construct a vessel as enormous as the ark, and even considered the question of the food supply for the carnivorous animals who were on board! At the end of his treatment of the Flood, he made it clear that the "saving significance" of the story—which he drew out by his familiar allegorical method—cannot be separated from the factual details of the event. He said "a man is bound to believe that there was a purpose in committing these facts to writing and in handing them down to future generations; that the events really took place; that what took place had a symbolic meaning; that the meaning is a foreshadowing of the Church."[64]

Rogers and McKim assert that Augustine cautioned Christians not to take their science from the Bible, implying that the reason for that warning was that he did not regard the scientific information in the Bible to be accurate. They quote a passage from *Genesis According to the Literal Sense* that contains the following warning.

It is therefore deplorable that Christians, even though they ostensibly base their dicta on the Bible, should utter so much nonsense that they expose themselves to ridicule. While ridicule is all they deserve, they also give the impression that the Biblical authors are responsible for their mutterings, thus discrediting Christianity

62. *City*, 15.9 (it is thought the tooth may have been from an elephant).
63. *City*, 15.8-14. In chapter 14, however, he seems to say that there may be a divinely intended discrepancy between the Hebrew and the Septuagint, which "may conform to and even emphasize the truth." He leaves an explanation of that puzzling statement to "some more appropriate occasion."
64. *City*, 15.27.

before the world, which is led to assume that the authors of the Scriptures were ignorant fools also.[65]

The quotation does not make the point that Rogers and McKim believe it does. Augustine was speaking of those who only *ostensibly* take their scientific notions from the Bible. In fact, they are ignorant persons who parade their own foolish ideas as though they learned them from the writers of Scripture. Augustine's point was that the writers of the Bible were *not* the ignorant fools that that procedure made them out to be. It should be remembered that Augustine's disillusionment with Manichaeanism began when he observed the ignorance of Faustus, who was unable to reconcile the Manichaean writings with what Augustine understood to be the nature of the heavenly bodies. He was concerned lest a similar ignorance on the part of Christians turn away those who were seeking the truth. As for the biblical authors, Augustine said, "our authors knew the truth about the shape of the heavens," even though giving such information was not the primary purpose for which they wrote.[66]

It is not really a disputable matter that Augustine believed that the Bible was a book with a special purpose. Its historical accounts do not intend to record everything that happened because there is a selectivity on the part of the inspired historians that is related to the saving purpose of the Scriptures. Commenting on omissions in Old Testament history, he wrote,

> All that the writer had in mind, under the inspiration of the Holy Spirit, was to trace the succession in definite lines from Adam to Abraham and then from the children of Abraham to the people of God. The directing idea was that this people, as distinct from others, prefigured and preannounced what in the light of the divine Spirit the writer foresaw would be fulfilled in that City which is to continue eternally.[67]

65. Cited from Polman, *The Word of God*, p. 61. Rogers and McKim give what is virtually a paraphrase of Polman's remarks but omit his comments that show Augustine's confidence in the scientific accuracy of the Bible.
66. See above. Polman, *The Word of God*, p. 60.
67. *City*, 15.8.

The special purpose of biblical history does not eliminate the need for accuracy in the historical information that is given. Augustine devoted Book XVIII of *The City of God* to an explanation of how the events of the history of salvation, recorded in the Bible, can be correlated with the course of general history. It was his conviction that "in actual history the two currents of development [i.e., the City (kingdom) of God and the city of the world] flowed in a single stream . . . the two cities continued to progress concurrently and to give their respective colors to human history."[68] Moreover, Augustine was so confident of the historical accuracy of the Bible that he used it as the criterion to decide which secular historians could be believed. He argued,

> The very disagreement of historians among themselves affords us an opportunity to choose for credence those whose contentions are not at variance with the divinely inspired history to which we adhere. . . . We . . . have the support of divine authority in the history of our religion. Accordingly, whatever in secular histories runs counter to it we do not hesitate to brand as wholly false, while with respect to non-parallel matters we remain indifferent. For, whether they be true or untrue, they make no important contribution to our living righteous and happy lives.[69]

Rather than regarding the historical accuracy of the gospels to be irrelevant in view of their saving purpose, Augustine devoted painstaking labor in the *Harmony of the Gospels* to demonstrating that the evangelists were "veracious historians," who at no point could be charged with giving false information.[70]

Modern advocates of the doctrine of biblical inerrancy would not wish to be identified as holding the same understanding of scientific and historical facts as Augustine. The issue to be determined here is not whether his particular interpretations of certain biblical passages or his understanding of the world were correct. The question is whether he thought that the Bible was authoritative and reliable when it mentions matters that are within the

68. Ibid., 18.1.
69. Ibid.
70. *Harmony*, 1.7.10.

realm of scientific and historical investigation. The evidence that has been given shows that he did believe in a Bible that speaks with unerring authority when it addresses such matters. The centrality of the saving purpose of the Bible was an important hermeneutical principle for Augustine, but it does not eliminate the importance of bowing to the authority of the Scripture with regard to factual details.

INERRANCY AND FAITH

Faith is of monumental importance in the thought of Augustine—not merely as a theological concept but as the saving response to God and the gospel. To the present day, the relationship between faith and reason that he advocated is debated. "I believe that I may understand" is perhaps his best known statement. Defining what he meant by it has proved to be no easy task. Within the context of the inerrancy debate, the statement has been taken to mean that faith is the mode of response to the central meaning or the saving content of the Scriptures, and knowledge or understanding has to do with details or words or facts in the Bible. The priority of faith to understanding is then taken to mean that "The problems in the biblical text were problems for human understanding. They were not problems for Christian faith."[71] That interpretation does not correctly set forth Augustine's own view of the relationship between faith and the text of Scripture. Instead, that relationship is to be understood in terms of three propositions.

TO ACKNOWLEDGE THE EXISTENCE OF ERROR IN THE BIBLE IS TO BETRAY A LACK OF FAITH

At the beginning of his *Harmony of the Gospels*, Augustine indicated that the work is directed against "certain persons who, in impious vanity or in ignorant temerity, think to rob of their credit as veracious historians" the authors of the gospels.[72] Augustine used hard language about such persons. They exhibit "blindness,"

71. *Authority and Interpretation*, p. 30.
72. *Harmony*, 1.7.10.

"sacrilegious vanity," "hardness of impiety."[73] When they charge that Mark's account of Peter's denial is not in harmony with the other evangelists', it is "because they approach the question under the cloud of a prejudiced mind, in consequence of their being possessed by a hostile disposition towards the gospel."[74] If one objects to the order in which Mark has inserted the remark that Jesus was crucified the third hour of the day, "such a reasoner is simply imposing upon the historians of truth in his own overweening pride. . . ."[75] Augustine believed that such details in the text were questions for faith. It was unbelief that made a man willing to find mistakes in the Scripture.

THE PRESENCE OF ERRORS IN THE BIBLE WOULD BE A
BARRIER TO FAITH

The enemies of Christianity who were being addressed in the *Harmony* alleged the presence of contradictions and discrepancies in the gospels to prevent inquirers from becoming believers and also to upset the faith of those who had already become Christians.[76] Augustine's response was not to explain to those who were thus troubled that discrepancies in the Scripture did not matter. Instead, he dealt painstakingly with hundreds of possible problems in the details of the gospel accounts with the aim of showing that a plausible explanation for each difficulty could be given.

If doubt were permitted to remain about any part of the Scripture, there would be a kind of "domino effect." He wrote,

> Moreover, your spirit of devotion will force you to this conclusion, and make you recognize, that the authority of Divine Scripture is undermined—leaving anyone to believe what he likes and to refuse to believe what he does not like—once the opinion has gained ground that the men through whose ministry the Scriptures have come down to us should be guilty of falsehood.[77]

73. Ibid., 2.7.20; 2.30.77; 3.13.49.
74. Ibid., 3.2.7.
75. Ibid., 3.13.48.
76. Ibid., 1.7.10.
77. Letter 28 to Jerome, *Letters*, 1:97.

Though he condemned open hostility to the accuracy of the Bible, Augustine recognized that the presence of apparent errors could create a stumbling block to faith for those who lacked a proper understanding. Such persons should not be regarded with contempt but should be enlightened by the offering of explanations.[78] Those with unresolved questions were still regarded as having faith, but further instruction would be helpful in strengthening that faith.

TRUE FAITH INCLUDES CONFIDENCE IN THE INERRANCY
OF THE SCRIPTURE

In a dispute with Jerome about something the great biblical scholar had written, Augustine wrote, "I do not believe you want your books to be read as if they were those of the Prophets or Apostles, about whose writings, free from all error, it is unlawful to doubt."[79] It would be repetitious to include here the numerous statements of Augustine that have already been quoted, which make the same point. Believers like Augustine and Jerome agreed that full confidence could be placed in the truthfulness of Scripture. But that confidence was not a blind faith. A proper attitude toward the Bible does not make the task of harmonization irrelevant. Rather, faith provides the motivation that is necessary to seek solutions to problems and to harmonize apparent contradictions that are found in the text. "A man of piety," said Augustine, will "seek some worthier explanation than that of simply crediting the evangelist with stating what is false."[80] A "faithful son of the Gospel" will accept a plausible explanation of a problem, even if it seems somewhat unlikely, rather than conclude that the gospel is untrue.[81] Faith involves an attitude of submission to the authority of the Bible so that its statements are taken as the criteria by which all else is to be judged.

Augustine's faith in the accuracy and noncontradictory quality of the Scriptures led him to seek for means by which to under-

78. *Harmony*, 2.56.113.
79. Letter 82 to Jerome, *Letters*, 1:392.
80. *Harmony*, 2.3.7.
81. Ibid., 2.65.126.

stand the problems in the text. In doing so, he made full use of the intellectual resources available to him. He drew especially on his knowledge that he had obtained in his years as a teacher of rhetoric of what was involved in the communication of ideas. That meant that he recognized that the language of the Bible, as the instrument of God's communication to man, exhibited all the flexibility and richness of human speech. The effort at harmonization that faith requires is carried out by giving full weight to factors that make for variability, without harming the full accuracy of expression. Augustine affirmed that the authors of the four gospels give absolutely authoritative and reliable accounts, even though "they fail to follow the very same plan, or to use the very same words, while describing, nevertheless, the self-same fact."[82] In one very long sentence Augustine mentions a number of the factors that cause variation (given here, for clarity, in the form of an enumeration): (1) The order of words may be varied, (2) some words may be substituted in place of others, which nevertheless have the same meaning, (3) something may be left unsaid, either because it has not occurred to the mind of the recorder or because it becomes readily intelligible from other statements that are given, (4) one of them may introduce something that he does not feel called upon to expound as a whole at length but only to touch upon in part, (5) with the view of illustrating his meaning and making it thoroughly clear, the person to whom authority is given to compose the narrative makes some additions of his own, not indeed in the subject matter itself, but in the words by which it is expressed, and (6) though retaining a perfectly reliable comprehension of the fact itself, he may not be entirely successful, however he may make that his aim, in calling to mind and reciting anew with the most literal accuracy the very words that he heard on the occasion.[83]

Thus the writers of the Bible, when giving parallel accounts, do not exhibit a mechanical identity of expression. Nevertheless, because the Holy Spirit governs even their weaknesses to accom-

82. Ibid., 2.12.28.
83. Ibid.

plish His purpose, those variations do not affect the veracity of the Scriptures.

Augustine also took account of the fact that the writers of the Bible made use of well-known literary conventions, such as the use of round numbers and using the part for the whole. In setting forth guidelines for biblical interpretation he advised that "learned men should know that our authors have used all the modes of expression which grammarians call by their Greek name, 'tropes' . . . the knowledge of them is a considerable aid in understanding the Scriptures."[84] They are a part of the speech of the common people and therefore are an aid to effective communication. Recourse to them is useful when the literal sense is contrary to reason.[85]

Faith and reason are not in conflict, nor do they operate in separate spheres, according to Augustine. If anything is a problem for reason (reason understood in a Christian sense), then it is also a problem for faith. Faith in the God-given character of the Scripture will not allow the believer to rest easy when he is confronted with seeming contradictions or errors there. Faith gives him the motivation to find a solution that will be in keeping with right reason. If some problems do not immediately yield a satisfactory solution, the believer will keep seeking for one as he maintains his confidence that ultimately the Scripture will be found not to be in error.

Our brief investigation of some of the writings of Augustine has sought to establish the thesis that he was a defender of biblical inerrancy. I do not claim that his views were identical in every respect with those held by present-day advocates of inerrancy. His Platonic philosophy, his use of the allegorical method of interpretation, his views of the divine inspiration of the Septuagint and the extent of the canon, his understanding of science and history, are not generally shared by conservative evangelicals today. But the evidence presented here, it is believed, has shown that Augustine had a profound interest in demonstrating that the Bible was free from any real error—indeed, that it was "scientifically inerrant," if

84. *Instruction*, 29.40.
85. Ibid., 23.41.

that expression is used to refer to the scientific views of his own day rather than those of the present. Few, if any, books originating in the circles of "post-Reformation scholasticism" can begin to compare with his *Harmony of the Gospels* for meticulous attention to the details of the biblical records and for elaborateness of effort at harmonization. Augustine may be rightly claimed as one who taught the full, divine inspiration of the Bible and who defended inerrancy as the necessary result of that inspiration.

3

Biblical Authority and Scholastic Theology

John F. Johnson

Dr. Stanley Gundry has recently noted that North American evangelical Christians, by and large, are but minimally conscious of their relation to the Christian past as they deal with crucial theological and ecclesiological issues of the day.[1] Though Gundry does not explicitly identify that expanse of the tradition most often dismissed, it would not be far off the mark to suggest the medieval era as the most likely candidate—especially in terms of dealing with questions of biblical authority, infallibility, and interpretation.

Indeed, when many evangelicals think of medieval theology, the initial images that come to mind are titles of tomes like the *Sententiae* of Peter Lombard or the *Quaestiones Quodlibetales* of John Duns Scotus. Moreover, we often describe medieval theology as a

---

1. Stanley Gundry, "Evangelical Theology: Where Should We Be Going?" *Journal of the Evangelical Theological Society* 22 (1979): 8.

JOHN F. JOHNSON, B.A., Arkansas State University, M.Div., Vanderbilt University, M.A., Texas Christian University, Th.D., Concordia Theological Seminary, Ph.D., St. Louis University, is associate professor and chairman of the department of systematic theology at Concordia Theological Seminary, St. Louis, Missouri. He is the author of a number of articles in professional theological and philosophical journals, including *Faith and Reason, Kinesis*, and the *Concordia Journal*.

"scholastic" manner of thinking and presentation characterized by sophisticated divisions, stereotyped literary forms, definitions, syllogisms, and constant subtle delineations—all accompanied by an arrogant confidence in the inerrancy of human reason. In short, the expression "medieval Scholasticism" is still somewhat under the dark spell of Renaissance humanism and the Enlightenment. For the evangelical especially, the phrase conjures up the image of an arid intellectualism that seems to have neglected the vivid originality of the Holy Scriptures. There are few who would take issue with Luther's opposition to the use of Aristotle by that "chatter-box" (as Luther called him), Thomas Aquinas—an opposition that is evident from the fact that though Aquinas consistently referred to Aristotle as "the Philosopher," Luther just as consistently referred to him as "that . . . pagan" (in addition to other choice epithets that form a long and impressive catalog).[2] Nor is it to be doubted if most would dissent from Luther's estimate of Peter Lombard or hesitate to apply it even more generally to other medieval theologians. "Peter Lombard," Luther said, "was adequate as a theologian; none has been his equal. He read Augustine, Ambrose, Gregory, and also all the councils. He was a great man. If he had by chance come upon the Bible he would no doubt have been the greatest."[3] In other words, there is the suspicion among contemporary evangelicals that the Scriptures were so ignored or allegorized in the Middle Ages that the theology of the period is but bare rationalization or fanciful imagination.

However, what is less known but equally decisive for an accurate understanding of medieval theology and its literary expression is that Scholasticism was developed on the basis of and in the framework of what might be termed today an "evangelical movement." The period of the last third of the twelfth and the beginning of the thirteenth century was characterized by the breakthrough of a desire for biblical knowledge that could not be satisfied by means of glosses between the lines or on the margin of the text or by means of a meditation presented by an abbot to his

2. Quoted in Friedrich Nietzsche, *Luther und Aristoteles* (Kiel: Universitäts-Buchhandlung, 1883), p. 3.
3. Martin Luther, *Table Talk* (Philadelphia: Fortress, 1967), p. 26.

monks that was intended only for religious edification.[4] Obviously, that thirst for knowledge had a sociological dimension; from a more exact hearing of the biblical word arose an impulse toward a renewal of the church, and soon that evangelical movement expressed itself in new institutional forms such as, for instance, the Orders of the Franciscans and the Dominicans.[5] Yet that thirst for scriptural knowledge soon developed as an academic tendency in its own right. New methods were invented to diffuse the text of the Bible in greater quantity; corrected copies of the text were attempted in both Latin and the vernacular; the text was divided into pericopes; the first concordances appeared; and above all, the theological educational system was rearranged in harmony with those tendencies. The consistent presentation of systematic theology was the concern of the assistant professor, the *baccalureus*, who explained the *Sentences* of Lombard. The ordinary professor, *magister*, was alone concerned with continuous commentary on the Holy Scriptures. Only in public debate, *quaestiones disputatae*, did the magister teach as a systematician. And those *quaestiones disputatae* had also been developed from the commentary on the Scriptures, both as an academic exercise and as a literary form. For in the text of the biblical commentary, it had long been customary to deal with questions that arose in the context in the form of a systematic excursus. Thus the "magister in sacra theologia" has been produced by the "magister in sacra pagina" and not vice versa. At one time historians commonly assumed that masters in theology lectured on the *Sentences* as well, but in 1894 Heinrich Denifle demonstrated conclusively that the official textbook of masters in theology in the medieval university was the Bible.[6] Once a young man became a master, he was not allowed to lecture on Lombard; his task was to comment on the Bible. Even Thomas Aquinas wrote his chief work, the *Summa Theologiae*, without direct relation to his systematic academic work. He wrote the

---

4. See Beryl Smalley, *The Study of the Bible in the Middle Ages* (Oxford: Clarendon, 1952).
5. Ibid., pp. 264-305.
6. Heinrich Denifle, "Quel livre servait de base al'enseignement des Maitres en Theologie dans d'Universite de Paris," *Revue Thomiste* 2 (1894): 99.129-61.

Summa to help students in their work outside the classroom.[7] Except for the debates, his daily courses were concerned with the interpretation of the Scriptures.

In retrospect, then, that understanding of the Middle Ages that sees it as isolated from a concern for the Bible and its centrality for life is a caricature without historical basis. Great strides were being made in the study and accessibility of biblical truth. But was there a correlative commitment to the authority and infallibility of the Scriptures? That is the question the present essay seeks to address.

REASON AND REVELATION IN THE MIDDLE AGES

From the very beginnings of Christian theological reflection, the problem of the relationship between reason and revelation was one of vital importance. For medieval theology the nature of scriptural authority was inextricably bound up with that issue. In the early church positions varied on the question; they ranged from the stance of Tertullian, whose famous *credo quia ineptum* expressed what he held to be an irreconcilable antagonism between the Word of God and human reason, to the prophilosophical view of Clement of Alexandria.[8] However, many such preceding tendencies were synthesized by Augustine, and it was his conception of faith and reason that dominated the thought of the earlier Middle Ages.

Shortly after his conversion to Christianity, Augustine outlined his program for achieving wisdom:

> Whatever may be the nature of human wisdom, I see that I have not yet understood it. Nevertheless, although I am now in the thirty-third year of my life, I do not think that I ought to despair of understanding it some day, for I have resolved to disregard all the other things which mortals consider good, and to devote myself to

7. J. Van Der Ploeg, "The Place of Holy Scripture in the Theology of St. Thomas," *The Thomist* 10 (1947): 402.
8. For an extensive account of the problem of reason and revelation in the early church see Richard Kroner, *Speculation and Revelation in the Age of Christian Philosophy* (Philadelphia: Westminster, 1969), pp. 50-72, and Bernhard Geyer, *Die partistische und scholastische Philosophie* (Berlin: n.p., 1928).

an investigation of it. And, whereas the reasonings of the Academics used to deter me greatly from such an undertaking, I believe that through this disputation I am now sufficiently protected against those reasonings. Certainly, no one doubts that we are impelled toward knowledge by a twofold force: the force of authority and the force of reason. And I am resolved never to deviate in the least from the authority of Christ, for I find none more powerful. But, as to what is attainable by acute and accurate reasoning, such is my state of mind that I am impatient to grasp what truth is—to grasp it not only by belief, but also by comprehension. Meanwhile, I am confident that I shall find among the Platonists what is not in opposition to our Sacred Scriptures.[9]

In that program there are two guides to wisdom: the authority of Christ and His Word, and human reason. Augustine was convinced that human reason, left to itself, is not enough. In fact, from the moment of his conversion the Bishop of Hippo was never to forget that the safest way to reach truth is not the one that starts from reason and then goes on from rational certitude to faith, but the one that starts from faith and then goes on from divine revelation to reason. By reaching that unexpected conclusion Augustine was, as Etienne Gilson observes, "opening a new era in the history of western thought. No Greek philosopher could have ever dreamt of making religious faith in some revealed truth the obligatory starting point of rational knowledge."[10] Thus with Augustine a new age was beginning in which the highest type of speculative thinking would be that of the theologians.

To be sure, even the stance of an Augustinian presupposes a certain exercise of natural reason. One cannot believe something, even God's own Word, unless one finds some sense in the formulas that one believes. And it can hardly be expected that one will believe in God's revelation unless one has a reason to think that such a revelation has indeed taken place. As modern theologians would say, there are motives of credibility. Yet when all is said, perhaps the most forceful reasons to believe that God has spoken

9. *The Essential Augustine*, ed. Vernon J. Bourke (New York: New American Library, 1964), pp. 25-26.
10. Etienne Gilson, *Reason and Revelation in the Middle Ages* (New York: Scribners, 1966), p. 17.

truly cannot take one further than that belief itself. To believe that God has spoken and that what God has said is absolutely true is something essentially different from a rational comprehension of the truth that one holds by faith. For Augustine, that is to say, one *believes* that it is true; but no Christian can hope to know, at least in this life, the truth that he believes. Yet among those truths that he believes, the Christian finds the divine promise that he will later contemplate the God of his faith and in that contemplation find eternal beatitude. Thus already in this life he attempts to investigate the mysteries of revelation by the natural light of reason. The result of such an effort is precisely what Augustine called *intellectus*—some rational insight into the contents of revelation. Such is the ultimate meaning of Augustine's famous formula "Understanding is the reward of faith. Therefore seek not to understand that you may believe, but believe that you may understand."[11]

It would seem, then, that for Augustine one is invited by revelation itself to believe, that unless one believes one shall not understand, and that far from inviting one to do away with reason, the gospel itself has promised to all those who seek truth in the revealed Word the reward of understanding. But the point is that one accepts the truths of faith as true because they are rooted in the deposit of faith—the Bible. Only after the acceptance of such divine truth does reason intervene to aid in the understanding of what one believes. That, by and large, was the concept of Christian wisdom Augustine contributed to the Middle Ages. For him there was a critical difference between science that occupied itself with the things of the world and the wisdom of theology that nourished itself on eternal truth. The content of faith is higher than that of the sciences and distinct from it. Nevertheless, all of the resources of the human mind are brought into the service of theology. All of the truths discovered by man—the treasures of philosophy, science, history, and grammar—are considered to

11. *On the Gospel of Saint John*, XXIX, 6, in *Homilies on the Gospel of St. John*, trans. H. Browne and J. H. Parker (Oxford: Oxford U. Press, 1848), 1:440.

belong by right to Christians and to be for their use.[12] The integrity of biblical truth is not compromised per se by such resources.

The rise of rival schools of thought—the realists and the nominalists—in the tenth and eleventh centuries led to a dialectical treatment of fundamental dogmas of the church and reopened the question of the relationship between reason and revelation, over which Augustine's stance had held sway.[13] Many theologians of the period were suspicious of the employment of dialectic and attempted to discourage their pupils from applying it to matters of faith. Peter Damian, for instance, saw philosophy as a compromising influence in the Christian life. For him, Christ had spoken, and His Word should not be adulterated by dialectic and speculation.[14] Hildebert, Bishop of Tours, took a similar position. He stressed faith as opposed to reason, which he, like his contemporaries, identified with dialectic. God willed, Hildebert asserted, that He might be only partly comprehended in order that some merit might be attached to faith. Thus he defined faith as *voluntaria certitudo absentium, supra opinionem et infra scientiam constituta.*[15]

The realist school of thought, with its belief in universals, did not challenge the authority of the church. Realists treated logic and dialectic as useful but clearly subordinate tools. The nominalists, on the other hand, were inclined to give a very important place to human reason. An example of that tendency was Berengar of Tours. "Unless a man is stupidly blind," he wrote, "he will not contest that in the search for truth reason is undoubtedly the best guide. It is characteristic of a great mind always to have recourse to dialectics."[16] When Berengar himself employed dialectics to explain the Lord's Supper, he denied the doctrine of tran-

12. Etienne Gilson, *The Christian Philosophy of St. Augustine* (New York: Random House, 1960), pp. 115-26; cf., Odilo Lechner, *Idee und Zeit in der Metaphysik Augustins* (Munich: A. Pustet, 1964), pp. 28-30, 71-74.
13. For a history of the realist-nominalist conflict see M. H. Carre, *Realists and Nominalists* (Oxford: Oxford U. Press, 1946).
14. Peter Damian, *Opusula* (Rome, 1606-1640), XXXVI, 5, "Quae tamen artis humanae peritia si quando tractandis sacris eloquiis adhibetur, non debet jus magisterii sibimet aroganter arripere, sed valut ancilla dominae quodam famulatus obsequio subservire, ne si pracedit, oberret."
15. Hildebert of Tours, *Opera* (Paris, 1708), p. 1010.
16. Quoted in Armand H. Maurer, *Medieval Philosophy* (New York: Random House, 1962), p. 48.

substantiation. That led him to a controversy with Lanfranc, the teacher of Anselm, who accused Berengar of abandoning "sacred authority" and turning to dialectics.[17] However, Berengar and the dialecticians never seemed to think of giving faith in divine revelation and fallible reason an equal potency.

Thus the Augustinian conception that subordinated reason to God's Word dominated medieval theology until the end of the twelfth century. Anselm, for example, even surpassed Augustine and taught that all knowledge must ultimately be based on faith. Though scholars such as F. S. Schmitt have held that Anselm's method of thought is ineluctably rationalistic and unconcerned with the biblical witness,[18] it is clear that when one recalls Anselm's teaching on the primacy of faith as a lived totality of thought and action, that is not the case. Rather Anselm believed that an understanding of God and of man's relation to Him must always begin with faith, i.e., with the firm and complete assent to the truth that is based on the *divina auctoritas* of God revealing. In the hearing of the infallible Word of proclamation faith proceeds, through God's grace, from an upright will and a sincere heart. According to Anselm, the content of belief so surpasses human comprehension that the believer's assent is in no way forced by evidence. It is therefore a free decision to submit to God's self-disclosure. After that initial assent, however, faith can be expanded to include an *intellectus fidei* through the exercise of reason within the context of belief. In fact, as his interlocutor in the *Cur Deus Homo* remarks, those believers who are capable of such a rational quest would seem to lay themselves open to the charge of negligence if they fail to undertake it.[19] For their initial faith, if it is truly living faith, is a vital movement, through works of love,

---

17. Berengar argued that accidents cannot exist without substance, and since the accidents of bread remain after consecration, the substance of bread also remains. There is simply the addition of another form—that of the Body of Christ. See R. W. Southern, "Lanfranc of Bec and Berengar of Tours," *Studies in Medieval History* (Oxford: Clarendon, 1948), pp. 27-48.
18. F. S. Schmitt, "Die wissenschaftliche Methode in 'Cur Deus Homo,' " *Spicilegium Beccense* (Paris, 1959), 1:370.
19. Anselm, *Cur Deus Homo*, book 1, chap. 1, "Sicut rectus ordo exigit ut profunda Christianae fidei prius credamus, quam ea praesumaus ratione discutere, ita negligentia mihi videtur, si, postquam confirmati sumus in fide, non studemus quod credimus intelligere."

toward union with God (a movement Anselm designated by the Augustinian expression *credere in Deum*), and the *intellectus fidei* that they seek through the exercise of reason is an intermediary stage along the way to their goal of full union with God within the beatific vision.[20] Apart from faith, Anselm argued, the quest for such an understanding is doomed to failure. In his *Epistola de incarnatione verbi* he wrote that those who would dispute about truths revealed in the Scriptures without having first accepted them in faith simply lack the spiritual wings, given by the solidity of faith in the Word of God, that are required for rising to such lofty questions and thus, as blind bats presuming to argue with the clearsighted eagle, they inevitably fall into error.[21] The root of faith is *credere in Deum*, and for Anselm God was the God who revealed Himself to man in the Bible. The content of what was to be "proved," then, was given by faith, and in Anselm's mind "no one can deny the truth of what is contained in the Old and New Testaments."[22] Though he was confident in the power of the mind to formulate necessary reasons for such dogmas of faith as the Holy Trinity and the incarnation, the Bible was still the foundation; reason or dialectic was employed only to interpret the truths that faith revealed. The charge that Anselm discarded the notion of biblical authority and infallibility is based on a misinterpretation of his thought.

There were, however, indications that reason was beginning to tire of its subordination to faith. The first of those indications can be detected in the work of Peter Abelard. Though it would be a mistake to regard Abelard as a rationalist, he did aim to use dialectic as a dominant method of explaining to his students the meaning of the Christian message.

Abelard dealt with the problem of reason and revelation in three of his works: *De Trinitate*, the *Theologia Christiana*, and the *Introductio ad Theologiam*. The views that he set forth in the first two

20. Anselm, *Commendatio operis ad Urbanum Papam II*, in *Opera Omnia*, 2:40, 10-12, "Denique quoniam inter fidem et speciem intellectum quem in hac vita capimus esse medium intelligo: quanto aliquis ad illum proficit, tanto eum propinquare speciei ad quam omnes anhelamus existimo."
21. Anselm, *Epistola de incarnatione verbi*, chap. 1.
22. Victor W. Roberts, O.S.B., "The Relation of Faith and Reason in St. Anselm of Canterbury," *American Benedictine Review* 25 (1974): 504.

volumes were pre-eminently orthodox. He reflected a traditional acceptance of the inspiration and authority of the Scriptures and emphasized the inability of the human reason to fully comprehend Christian truth. However, in the *Introductio ad Theologiam*, Abelard's treatment of the relationship between reason and revelation is less conciliatory. He criticized, for instance, Bernard for his reliance on authority and authority alone. But Abelard knew well enough that the limited human mind cannot hope to exhaust the mysteries of faith; yet words, for him, were meant to convey a meaning, and he sought the human meaning of Scripture. That largely accounts for his concern with words and his contribution to medieval logic.

Abelard notwithstanding, the medieval position on reason and revelation remained Augustinian right up to the time of the discovery of Aristotle's writings. John of Salisbury, for example, compared and contrasted the Eternal Reason, which is infallible, with the human reason, which has been weakened by man's fall from grace. Similarly, Hugh of St. Victor held that the uncorrupted truth of things cannot be discovered by corrupted reasoning. He believed that profane knowledge must necessarily subserve revealed knowledge. Faith in God's revelation is a form of certitude relating to beliefs or things not present, which is more than opinion. Though cognitively speaking it may be less satisfactory than reasoned knowledge, it conveys greater merit. Hugh of St. Victor is especially noted for constantly stressing the importance of the historical and literal senses of the Bible—he condemned the neglect of those senses in his *De Scripturis* and the *Didascalicon*. In fact, he poked quiet fun at those who hurry over the literal sense in their haste to reach the allegorical.

> The mystical sense is only gathered from what the letter says, in the first place. I wonder how people have the face to boast themselves teachers of allegory, when they do not know the primary meaning of the letter. "We read the Scriptures," they say, "but we don't read the letter. The letter does not interest us. We teach allegory." How do you read Scripture then, if you don't read the letter? Subtract the letter and what is left?[23]

23. Hugh of St. Victor, *De Scripturis V*, 5:13-15.

The medieval understanding of the relationship between reason and revelation sketched above was, however, dramatically challenged by a new development that helped to shape biblical study in the "High Middle Ages" and led to a renewed effort to deal with the entire problem—the introduction of Aristotelianism into the theology of the church.

THE REDISCOVERY OF ARISTOTLE

For more than a century after the beginnings of dialectical activity in the schools of Italy and France, the masters of logic and philosophy had at their disposal only that fragment of ancient thought represented by the so-called old logic of Aristotle and the group of commentaries and treatises connected with it, composed for the most part by Boethius. Otherwise, for those who aimed at "higher knowledge," Plato was "the Philosopher." Toward the middle of the twelfth century, however, a great change began, and an epoch opened that was to last for more than a hundred years. It was the epoch in which ancient Greek and more recent Arabic thought and science became available to the West in larger and larger doses. That flood of new knowledge transformed European thought and life in many respects, but in the realms of philosophy and theology the principal transforming agent was the system of Aristotle, which was revealed piece by piece until he became, in place of Plato, "the Philosopher" to all the schools. That revelation, which began soon after 1100 and was not completed until 1270, was the result of a process of translation from Greek and Arabic on the part of a series of scholars who worked almost solely from a disinterested desire for knowledge.[24]

The significance of that phenomenon for the understanding and interpretation of the Bible in the Middle Ages is not to be seen in the use of new methods so much as in the close integration of language and thought it produced. That was significant for the medieval perspective on the Scripture's authority and infallibility, though it is often overlooked by commentators who persistently

24. A brief account of the importance of the rediscovery of Aristotle for Scholasticism is offered by David Knowles in *The Evolution of Medieval Thought* (New York: Random House, 1962), pp. 185-93.

argue that such a view of the Bible was eclipsed by speculative philosophy. It was realized, for instance, that interpretation cannot be isolated from the rules of thought that govern all areas of knowledge; it should be conducted scientifically, with adequate reasons given for the significations adduced. It would be well, incidentally, for contemporary evangelicals to explore that Aristotelian motif in view of the threat to modern biblical theology by a new nominalism that appears to question very radically the relation of language to thought.[25]

According to T. F. Torrance the impact of the rediscovery of Aristotle on medieval biblical study was basically felt in two interrelated ways. First, he writes, "it challenged the sharp distinction between sense and thought. According to the Platonic philosophical orientation, there is a world of ordered forms above and apart from the world of sense experience; they are reflected in it, but knowledge of them is reached only by transcending sense experience. That belief made it possible for the late patristic and early medieval ages to develop an entire world of elaborate allegory and spiritual meaning in detachment from history and event. Many think that such a perspective dominated the entire medieval view of the Scriptures. According to the Aristotelian view, however, the universal ideas exist only as expressed in the individual objects of the sensible world, and one has knowledge of them not apart from but only through sense experience. That belief had a sobering effect on exegesis. It disparaged the development of a world of meaning that could be correlated on its own without scientific reference to the historical sense of Scripture and careful examination of its words and concepts."[26] This means that Aristotelian philosophy refused to separate matter and form; they are two aspects of one and the same thing. Thus, a given object is matter as it is determined according to an organic pattern or form, and the form is the determinate structure according to which the object is organized. In terms of hermeneutics one cannot understand the Bible by radically distinguishing letter from

---

25. An example of such nominalist skepticism is James Barr, *The Semantics of Biblical Language* (Oxford: Oxford U. Press, 1961).
26. Thomas F. Torrance, "Scientific Hermeneutics According to St. Thomas Aquinas," *Journal of Theological Studies* 13 (1962): p. 259.

spirit and making a separate study of each—a tendency still in evidence today in biblical interpretation. As Beryl Smalley writes in her study of the Bible in the Middle Ages,

> Transferring his view of body and soul to "letter and spirit," the Aristotelian would perceive the "spirit" of Scripture as something not hidden behind or added on to, but expressed by the text. We cannot disembody a man in order to investigate his soul; neither can we understand the Bible by distinguishing letter from spirit and making a separate study of each.[27]

In the second place, says Torrance, one has to note the impact on biblical studies of the Aristotelian notion of science as that which establishes rational connections and gathers them around a center. Scientific knowledge is thus "the orderly arranging and demonstration of sequences of truths in a particular science according to the particular principles relevant to it (e.g., biological sequences within biology and geometrical sequences within geometry). Knowledge arises through a development from sense-experience by drawing out and disentangling what is implicit in it and so proceeds by abstraction to the formulation of general notions and to explanation by testing the relation of their causes to particular effects. To be sure, that does not mean that particular principles can be demonstrated any more than first principles; but if the critical work of reasoning is done properly, they will be pointed out, and one will discern the truth of them in their own nature."[28] The application of this to scriptural interpretation in the medieval era does not mean that the infallible truths of the Bible have to be demonstrated to the satisfaction of human reason but that the interpretation of the Scripture cannot be totally separated from careful analysis of propositions, for the interpretation of language is the interpretation of thought. Revelation is, after all, propositional. This, in turn, has a double effect on scholastic exegesis. Torrance continues: "on the one hand, it detached the interpretation of Scripture from a realm of mystical meaning that could not be rationally related to the text; thus it brought theolo-

27. Quoted in Torrance, p. 260.
28. Torrance, p. 260.

gy and exegesis into closer relation to one another. On the other hand, it introduced a powerful element of inferential reasoning into interpretation, whether of the linguistic signs used in the Bible (its words and sentences) or of the things they signified. As a result, there arose a natural theology side by side with revealed theology; and because the former could only be regarded as *praeambula fidei*, it tended to provide the general framework within which biblical interpretation was carried on," consequently, "everything depended upon the degree in which the metaphysical framework of natural theology was allowed not only to provide the thought-forms in which revealed theology was to be expressed, but to impose an alien form of thinking upon it and so to triumph over it."[29]

Taken as a whole, the translations of Aristotle gave western theologians (for the first time) matter on which to construct a full and mature theological system. However, the rediscovery of Aristotle also provided an important matrix for the interpretation of the Scriptures in the Scholasticism of the "High Middle Ages."

THOMAS AQUINAS AS BIBLICAL SCHOLAR

"St. Thomas Aquinas," David Knowles comments, "has been hailed by common consent in the modern world as the prince of scholastics."[30] It is legitimate, then, to look to Aquinas as a concrete example of how the two developments discussed thus far—the perennial medieval question of the relationship between reason and revelation, and the ramifications of Aristotelianism for hermeneutics—coalesced in the context of the scholastic notion of biblical authority.

At first sight, it might appear that the Bible has a small place in the theology of Thomas Aquinas, especially if one makes a superficial examination of the *Summa Theologiae*, the only basis for judg-

29. Ibid., p. 261.
30. Knowles, p. 255. For a general historical introduction to Thomas Aquinas see M. D. Chenu, *Toward Understanding St. Thomas* (New York: H. Regnery Co., 1964); Etienne Gilson, *The Christian Philosophy of St. Thomas Aquinas* (New York: Random House, 1956); H. P. Dondaine-D. Schluter O. H. Pesch, "Thomas von Aquin," in *Lexicon für Theologie und Kirche*, 10:119-34. The most recent scholarly study is by James A. Weisheipl, *Friar Thomas D'Aquino* (New York: Oxford U. Press, 1974).

ing his use of the Scriptures. There it has seemed to some that the use of the Bible is relegated to mere citations, often not clearly related to the subject. However, such an impression is not warranted, for St. Thomas, as Charles Callan has said, was "not a mere philosopher building on the sands of human reasoning, but a massive theologian erecting his structure on the rock of the divine Word."[31] In fact, according to Pope Leo XIII, Thomas was the leading exegete of Holy Scripture among the theologians of the scholastic age.[32]

Aquinas was, of course, a Dominican friar and very much committed to the medieval "evangelical" movement, a commitment sharpened in the midst of the antimendicant controversy that was at its zenith when he incepted at the University of Paris in 1256. In that year, and until his death in 1273, Thomas lectured on the Bible as a Master of Theology. He wrote commentaries on a number of biblical books: Isaiah, the Canticles, Lamentations, Jeremiah, Job, the Psalms, the gospel of Matthew, the epistles of St. Paul, and the gospel of John. To those commentaries must also be added the *Catena Aurea*, called by Aquinas himself *Glossae in Quatuor Evangelica* (it is not a commentary written by Thomas himself, but one continuous concatenation of texts of the Fathers, which explain the gospels). The material extent of all those commentaries is as large as that of the *Summa*, and from that point of view they occupy an important place among his theological works.

Aside from his full-length commentaries, he dealt with the Bible extensively in other theological works. He cited a great many biblical texts and interpreted separately a substantial number of them, for example, the first chapter of Genesis as discussed in the *Summa*.[33] He also dealt with questions of introduction, and though he did not write a treatise on inspiration, his opinions on the issue—an orthodox affirmation of the divine authorship of the Scriptures—may be gathered especially from his treatises on

31. Charles J. Callan, "The Bible in the Summa Theologica of St. Thomas Aquinas," *The Catholic Biblical Quarterly* 9 (1947): 37.
32. Pope Leo XIII, "Thomas Aquinas inter eos habuit palmam," in the Encyclical, *Providentissimus Deus* (*Enchiridion Biblicum*, No. 81).
33. *Summa Theologiae*, I-I, qq. 45-48. Hereafter cited as *ST*.

prophecy and from dispersed texts.[34] The question of the sense of Scripture was addressed by him several times.[35] In the beginning of his career as a teacher, he treated the question of the canon, which was not controverted in the Middle Ages,[36] though some Fathers and doctors followed the dissentient view of Jerome. In his first public lecture, or *principium* as it was termed in the Middle Ages, Thomas offered a short survey of the books of both Old and New Testaments. It was also in that inaugural address, which in many manuscripts bears the title of *Commendatio Sacral Scripturae*, that Thomas discussed the work of the theologian.

> The doctors of Holy Scripture must excel by their excellent conduct in life, to be apt to preach with good success; they must be illuminated, to be able to instruct well; they must be well instructed to be able to refute errors in their disputations, in accordance with the words of the Apostle, who says that the ecclesiastical authority must be able to admonish with sane doctrine and to refute adversaries.[37]

In other words it is clear that the newly created master was considered a doctor of Holy Scripture. He was first of all to preach sacred Scripture to the faithful because the revelation it contained had been given by God for the spiritual welfare of man; then he was to explain it to those who could study its deeper sense, i.e., to the clergy; and finally he was to defend it against those who attacked it or drew false conclusions from it.

Thomas, it seems, took his own characterization of a scriptural theologian quite seriously! During his stay in the Pontifical States of central Italy (1259-1269), Aquinas averaged teaching four lessons on the Scriptures each week. At Naples he conducted no scholastic disputations so that he could lecture on the Bible five times a week. He also fulfilled the first, and too often neglected, task of the *magistri*—preaching. During the whole of Lent, 1273, he preached daily to the students of Naples and the people of the

34. Ibid., II-II, qq. 171-74.
35. Ibid., I-I, q. 1, a. 10; *Quaestiones Quodlibetales*, 7, a. 14-16; *In Epist. ad Galatas*, 4, lect. 7.
36. *Opuscula*, 39.
37. Ibid., 40.

town. And, it is said, his very last work was to explain on his deathbed the Canticle of Canticles to the monks of Fossanuova.[38]

In his lectures it seems that Thomas first treated a book of the Old Testament and then one of the New. However, his selection of the biblical books did not proceed arbitrarily. After his graduation he chose as lecture matter the books of Isaiah and Matthew, which were often treated together in the Middle Ages. Of the four gospels, Matthew was the most in favor; and the prophet Isaiah was considered a precursor of the evangelists, or almost as one of them, because of his many predictions of Jesus and His work.

During his second stay at Paris ten years later, Aquinas chose the gospel of John, to his mind the most profound of the four gospels. Among the books of the Old Testament he chose Job, in which the problem of providence comes to the fore. The influence of Averroism, which Aquinas opposed as being contrary to scriptural teaching because it denied the existence of divine providence, undoubtedly determined his selection. At Anagni, the place where the papal court was residing and the central administration of the Roman Church was established, Thomas explained the Canticles. The bride in the Song of Songs was commonly taken to be a personification of the church, and that may have dictated his choice. Why Aquinas wrote a commentary on Jeremiah is not clear; it may be because Jeremiah was the second of the great prophets. But it seems to be clear why he dealt with the Psalms and the epistles of St. Paul, the latter twice. Both books were the two most used biblical texts, and since the time of the early Fathers a great many commentaries had been written on them.

The form of his commentaries was prescribed by custom. To modern readers it may seem somewhat artificial, with its many divisions and subdivisions, but those were deemed necessary in the medieval era since the good teacher was he who made good distinctions (*qui bene distinguit, bene docet*). However, Thomas demonstrated a significant degree of freedom from earlier exegetical methods as, for instance, in his admirable commentary on Job, called by a medieval scholar a *mirabile opus*.[39] His freedom from

38. Callan, p. 38.
39. John of Colonna quoted in P. Mandonnet, "Chronologie des écrites scripturaires de S. Thomas d'Aquin," *Revue Thomiste* (1928): 149.

tradition is indicated methodologically by the fact that his first exegetical rule was to explain the Bible by the Bible (reminiscent of the Reformation principle that "Scripture interprets Scripture"). Thus many passages of his exegetical works consist more of biblical texts than of the text of the author. It is also noteworthy that in comparison with citations from Scripture, the church Fathers are not cited as often by Aquinas as in earlier *biblical* commentaries. Furthermore, with regard to the sense of Scripture, Thomas gave first the literal and then the spiritual sense. Even in the latter case, he was much more judicious and faithful to the text than some of his contemporaries. In terms of Aquinas's respect for the text, Van der Ploeg wrote:

> In his commentaries he tries to be exact and accurate and to omit nothing, rightly judging that everything in the sacred text deserves the full attention of the exegete. It should not be thought that the great thinker, as a speculative theologian, gave attention only to that which, in his eyes, was of "theological" importance, that is, of importance for his theological system. His reverence for the true word of God was too great to do this. As a true exegete, he took notice of the smallest details of the text, of the names of persons and places, of the headings of the Psalms. He would leave nothing obscure or undiscussed. Thus he was fully what an exegete of those days and, *mutatis mutandis*, also of our days should be.[40]

Contrary to modern preconceptions regarding the Scholasticism he pre-eminently represented, Thomas Aquinas emerges as a biblical theologian who studied and commented on the Scriptures incessantly. They were central to his thought and writings. That is confirmed, however, by more than his lectures and commentaries; the authoritative place of Holy Scripture for him is also indicated by its role in his theological *system* and his approach to the problem of interpretation.

AQUINAS: THE BIBLE IN THEOLOGY

As noted earlier, the issue of the relationship between faith and

40. Van der Ploeg, p. 410.

reason was largely determinative for scholastic theology's view of biblical authority. That question similarly undergirds the Thomistic position on the place of the Scriptures in systematic theology. According to Thomas, there existed a unity between reason and revelation—what Etienne Gilson alludes to as the twofold certitude of philosophy and revelation.[41] In the light of that unity, far from seeing in revelation the downfall of true philosophy, Thomas viewed philosophical reasoning as a kind of *praeparatio evangelica* by which the minds of men were prepared to receive divine truth.

That idea is perhaps most explicitly elaborated in the initial book of the *Summa Contra Gentiles*. The object of wisdom for first philosophy, Aquinas argued, is the end of the universe. A wise man, therefore, is one who can arrange things as they ought to be arranged, to dispose of a thing with a view to its end.

> They are to be called wise who order things rightly and govern them well. Hence, among other things that men have conceived about the wise man, the Philosopher includes the notion that "it belongs to the wise man to order." Now, the rule of government and order for all things directed to an end must be taken from the end. For, since the end of each thing is its good, a thing is then best disposed when it is fittingly ordered to its end. And so we see among the arts that one functions as the governor and the ruler of another because it controls its end. Thus, the art of medicine rules and orders the art of the chemist because health, with which medicine is concerned, is the end of all the medications prepared by the art of the chemist. . . . They are therefore said to be wise with respect to this or that thing; in which sense it is said that "as a wise architect, I have laid the foundation." (1 Cor. 3.10)[42]

Moreover, since the end of an object is the same as its principle or cause, rational knowledge has for its object the study of first causes; "It belongs to the wise man to consider the highest causes."[43] Thomas, then, took under consideration that which is

41. Etienne Gilson, *The Spirit of Thomism* (New York: P. J. Kennedy and Sons, 1964), pp. 14-18. Also, see my "Philosophy and Christian Theology: A Thomistic Perspective," *Faith and Reason* 6 (1980): 147-59.
42. *Summa Contra Gentiles*, I, 1.
43. Ibid., I, 1.

the first cause or the final end of the universe. The final cause, he maintained, is that which its author, in making it, had in view. Since it can be demonstrated that the first author of the universe is an intelligible being, the end that He had in view in creating it must be the end of intelligence, which is truth.

> Now, the end of each thing is that which is intended by its first author or mover. But the first author and mover of the universe is an intellect, as will be shown later, the ultimate end of the universe must, therefore, be the good of an intellect. This good is truth.[44]

Thus truth is the final end of the universe. And since the object of first philosophy is the ultimate end of the universe, it follows that its proper object is truth. But the disposition of things in the order of truth is the same as that in the order of being—being and truth are equivalent. A truth, Thomas reasoned, that is to be the source of all truth can be found only in a being who must be the first source of all being. In a word, the true object of metaphysics or first philosophy is God. Philosophical inquiry is almost totally ordained to the cognition of God as its end.

In chapter 3 of book 1 of the *Summa Contra Gentiles*, Aquinas moved to the way in which divine truth is to be made known. Man has at his disposal two means. The first means, of course, is human reason. The natural reason is capable of grasping such truths as the existence of God, that He is one, and the like. In fact, Thomas observed, such truths about God have been proved demonstratively by the philosophers. The issue, rather, is whether the reason of man is an instrument sufficient to reach the goal of metaphysical inquiry, namely, the divine essence. Thomas concluded that it is not. It is evident that certain forms of knowledge concerning the nature of God exceed the power of human understanding. According to Thomas:

> That there are certain truths about God that totally surpass man's ability appears with the greatest evidence. Since, indeed, the principle of all knowledge that the reason perceives about some thing is the understanding of the very substance of that being . . . it is nec-

44. Ibid.

essary that the way in which we understand the substance of a thing determines the way in which we know what belongs to it. Hence, if the human intellect comprehends the substance of some thing, for example, that of a stone or of a triangle, no intelligible characteristic belonging to that thing surpasses the grasp of the human reason. But this does not happen to us in the case of God. For the human intellect is not able to reach a comprehension of the divine substance through its natural power. For, according to its manner of knowing in the present life, the intellect depends on the sense for the origin of knowledge; and so those things that do not fall under the senses cannot be grasped by the human intellect except in so far as the knowledge of them is gathered from sensible things.[45]

Perfect knowledge, therefore, consists in deducing the properties of an object by using its essence as the principle of the demonstration. Accordingly, the mode in which the substance of each thing is known to man determines the mode of the knowledge that he can have of the thing. God is a purely spiritual substance; man's knowledge, on the contrary, is only such as a being composed of a soul and a body can reach. It originates necessarily in sensation. The knowledge man has of God is only such as a person starting from sense data can acquire of a being who is purely intelligible. Thus the understanding of man, resting upon the testimony of his senses, can indeed infer that God exists, but it is evident that a mere examination of sensory objects, which are the effects of God and therefore inferior to him, cannot bring man to a knowledge of His essence.

That fundamental limitation on human reason led Thomas to discuss a second means man has in attaining the object of first philosophy—divine revelation. The necessity of scriptural revelation is emphasized in the first part of the *Summa Theologiae*, where Thomas contended that if the end of man is none other than God, and man must possess knowledge of his end to be able to order his intentions in relation to it, then revelation was necessary in order

45. Ibid., I, 4.

to bring to his knowledge a certain number of infallible truths that are incomprehensible to the light of reason.[46]

Man has, then, a twofold certitude; Aquinas thought that the ultimate object of both rational inquiry and theological inquiry is one and the same. There was, to be sure, an explicit and formal distinction between philosophy and revelation for Thomas, but there was some essential agreement. The knowledge of the first principles evident to the mind has been implanted in man by God, who is the author of his nature. The principles of human knowledge are part of divine wisdom, and thus one should trust implicitly the natural light of reason within the boundaries appropriate to it.

The foregoing discussion of the general relationship between reason and revelation is the frame of reference for his explicit treatment of the nature of theology. Actually, Aquinas very seldom used the word "theology." Indeed, he employed it only twice in the entire introduction to the *Summa Theologiae*. The first time the reference is precisely *not* to what one commonly understands by theology but to the fact that Aristotle had called his "first philosophy" by the name of theology.[47] But that, as Thomas subsequently remarked, is different in kind (*secundum genus*) from the theology that pertains to *sacram doctrinam*.[48] The second mention of the term is connected with a simple reference to the etymology of the word that is said to indicate *sermo de Deo*—talk about God.[49]

Always and invariably, then, the discussion in the introductory question of the *Summa* turns not on the nature and meaning of theology but on the nature and meaning of *sacra doctrina*. In other words, the kind of theology he was talking about has little in common with rational knowledge of God except its object. The latter is roughly equivalent to what one calls natural theology; the other

46. *ST*, I-I, q. 1, a. 1: "Primo quidem quia homo ordinatur ad Deum sicut ad quendam finem qui comprehensionem rationis excedit, secundum illud Isiae 44, (4): 'oculus non vidit Deum absque te, quae praeparasti diligentibus te.' Finem autem oportet esse praecognitum hominibus, qui suas intentiones et actiones debent ordinare in finem. Unde necessarium fuit homini ad salutem, quod ei nota fierent quaedam per revelationem divinam, quae rationem humanam excedunt."
47. *ST*, I-I, q. 1, a. 1.
48. Ibid., I-I, q. 1, a. 1, ad. 2.
49. Ibid., I-I, q. 1, a. 7.

is appropriately called "revealed theology," or sacred teaching. Sacred teaching proceeds from God—it is revealed by Him. It is quite significant that when he spoke in the *Summa* of the nature of theology, Thomas used the terms *sacra doctrina, sacra Scriptura, scientia divinitus inspirrata,* and *divina revelatio*—apparently indiscriminately. The Bible and *sacra doctrina* are even equalized by the word *seu* (*sacra scriptura seu doctrina*). Elsewhere Thomas was still more explicit, as he said in the preface of his commentary on St. Paul, when speaking of the Psalms and the epistles of the great apostle, "These writings contain the whole doctrine of theology." And in the same preface, written in Naples at the end of his life, he said, "In the New Testament one reads, after the Gospels, the doctrine of the apostles."[50]

Several important implications of that equivalence of sacred doctrine and the Bible are elucidated by Thomas in articles *iv-vii* of the first question in the *Summa*. There Aquinas developed the theme of the "transcendence" of sacred doctrine. Article *iv*, for example, asks whether scriptural teaching is a practical science. Thomas responded that *sacra doctrina* is not chiefly concerned with what man can do, as is the case with moral science, but rather with God, who is man's maker. However, scriptural teaching is the supreme science (*scientia* in the sense of certain knowledge). It is supreme because unlike knowledge based on human experience, it is based on the science that God has from Himself, and that is also the ultimate reason that Christians believe in the truth of the Bible, inspired by God, who is Himself nothing but truth. So sacred teaching cannot suffer the same circumscriptions as other kinds of knowledge. In terms of the original question, it is both speculative and practical.[51]

In article *v* Aquinas again affirmed the certainty of Scripture. It is more certain than all other knowledge because the certitude of *sacra doctrina* is derived from divine knowledge rather than through

---

50. Quoted in Van Der Ploeg, p. 411.
51. However, I would venture that for Thomas, as opposed to Bonaventure, for example, sacred doctrine was more formally speculative because divine revelation tells man more of divine things than of human actions.

the fallible light of human reason.[52] That led Aquinas to further underscore the superiority of sacred doctrine in article *vi* by asserting that it is the wisdom above all human wisdoms, an authority that adheres to it because it is given by God. In article *vii* Thomas affirmed, "All which is spoken of in Holy Scripture is spoken of God."[53] God is the subject of Scripture; everything treated in the Bible is treated *sub ratione Dei*; the principles of sacred doctrine are about God and from God. Since God Himself is truth, His revelation is truth. For Thomas, the point of biblical authority was rather simple; God was the author of Scripture; consequently, everything in Scripture was inspired by Him.[54]

Such conclusions are critical to any consideration of the theme of the place of the Holy Scriptures in the thought not only of Aquinas but of the vast majority of scholastic theologians. Reason can prove some of the truths that are proposed by the Christian faith; it can elucidate truth that cannot be proved, and it can defend the principles of the faith against detractors. But scholastic theology is not rationalistic in the absolute sense. For the salvation of men, Thomas observed, it was necessary that they be instructed by the author of all truth through His own revelation.

AQUINAS: BIBLICAL HERMENEUTICS

Aside from the importance of the scholastic concern over reason and revelation, it was noted earlier in this chapter that the rediscovery of Aristotle also had immense implications for the role of the Scriptures in their theology. Again, Thomas Aquinas represents clearly that development. But what brand of biblical hermeneutic emerges from a theologian whose understanding of the Word of God evolved in the matrix of Aristotelian influence? Is it a hermeneutic hopelessly mired in the bogs of scholastic subtle-

52. *ST*, I-I, q. 1, a. 5. Any doubts about the principles of faith arise, according to Thomas, from the weakness of man's intellect, not any deficiency in revelation. It might be observed that the confusion that seems to obtain today on the relationship of faith to reason has no other cause than that often neglected fact.

53. G. F. Van Ackeren, *Sacra Doctrina: The Subject of the First question of the Summa Theologiae* (Rome: Catholic Book Agency, 1952), offers a fine discussion of the implications of that comment by Thomas; see pp. 107ff.

54. Van Der Ploeg, pp. 411-12.

ties? Or is it a hermeneutic, deficient to be sure, but suggestive of some important motifs to which evangelicals can all resonate? The answers to such questions are at least intimated in the identification of those concepts that ground the scholastic hermeneutic of Thomas and their implications also for his view of the Bible.

In interpretation Thomas held that one has to determine the intention of the author and discern the significant form of what he has to say, through turning one's attention to the things signified and through noting the use of his words by examining their relation to the whole of his discourse.[55] In all of that, interpretation is fundamentally an act of the intellect or understanding (*intellectus*) in which the mind pierces through to see the *quid* of a thing, that is to say, to read the truth in the very essence of it (*interius in ipsa rei essentia rei veritatem quodammodo legere*).[56]

The etymology of *intelligere* as used by Thomas was from *intus legere*, to read within. That provides an important clue to the Thomistic notion of interpretation as an act of understanding or intimate knowledge (*intellectus*). In the *Summa* he wrote:

Sensitive cognition is concerned with external sensible qualities but intellective cognition penetrates into the very essence of a thing, because the object of the understanding that which is (*quod quid est*). But there are many kinds of things which lie hidden within, to which man's cognition ought to penetrate from the inside, as it were. For under the accidents lies hidden the substantial nature of the thing; under words lie hidden the things signified by the words; under similitudes and figures lie hidden effects, and conversely. But since man's cognition begins with sense as from without, it is manifest that the stronger the light of the intellect is, the farther it can penetrate into the inmost depths. However, the natural light of our intellect is of finite strength and hence can but reach to what is limited. Therefore man needs supernatural light, that he may penetrate farther in order to learn what he cannot learn through his natural light, and that supernatural light given to man is called the gift of understanding (*donum intellectus*).[57]

55. See Aristotle's *Perihermenias*, book 1, 1-7.
56. See Hans Meyer, *The Philosophy of St. Thomas Aquinas* (St. Louis: Herder, 1944), pp. 109ff.
57. Quoted in Torrance, p. 261.

By the supernatural light Thomas did not have in view some extraordinary grace but rather the gift of simple intuitive apprehension. Although he was critical of Augustinian Platonism, "Aquinas yet held that the power of the intellect, penetrating into the essence of a thing, into its ultimate structure or spiritual content, would not be possible were it not that man has been given to share in the divine light." To be sure, in the passage just cited Thomas was not discussing hermeneutics per se. But as he indicated, the same procedure applies to the interpretation of words, for one has to discern not only their sense but break through to their real meaning. To understand is to read the hidden meaning. That does not refer to some esoteric art but to the same sort of activity one employs when one seeks to know the quiddity or essence of anything.[58]

But how is one to think of that intuitive apprehension of essences when it is applied to the interpretation of the inspired writings of Scripture?

The Bible has two authors, Thomas argued; the principal author is God, but man is the instrumental author or secondary author. Thus, in interpreting Scripture the intellect "must penetrate through the sense of the words to the meaning of the human author and to the meaning of the divine author." That does not mean that the Bible is equivocal, for God reveals Himself through the literal sense intended by the human author. It does mean that one has to recognize the divine intention in the literal sense.[59]

On the one hand, then, one has to interpret the Scriptures as divinely inspired. In them, Thomas wrote, "The Word of the eternal Father, comprehending everything by His own immensity, has willed to become little through the assumption of our littleness, yet without resigning His majesty, in order that He may recall man who had been laid low through sin, to the height of His divine glory." Because it is the nature of man to learn intelligible truths through the sensible species the mind apprehends, God has provided revelation of Himself according to the capacity of human nature and has put forward in the Bible divine and spiri-

58. Borrowed from Torrance, p. 261.
59. Ibid., pp. 262-63.

tual truths through comparisons with material things. Thus, according to Aquinas, it is apparent that

> the divinely inspired scripture does not come within the philosophical disciplines that have been discovered according to human reason. Accordingly, there is needed another science divinely inspired beyond philosophical disciplines ... because man is ordained to God, to an end that surpasses the grasp of reason.[60]

The science of interpreting the Scriptures needs special illumination that the intellect may penetrate into the inner depth of the divine revelation, into the very heart of the truth. It will not, however, leave the literal sense behind nor deprecate it. It is only in and through the literal sense, Thomas was convinced, that the illuminated intellect can reach the spiritual content and the reality that lies behind it for him. The literal meaning is critical to biblical interpretation.[61]

• On the other hand, the Bible must be considered from the point of its human authorship. The fact that Aquinas distinguished the human author as the instrumental author means that he thought of the Bible's human authorship in terms of secondary causality. Thus, though God was the principal cause, the human author was given a relative freedom under Him as the secondary cause, so that what the human author produced must be investigated in its relative independence as a human composition. Thomas had no place for a type of mechanical dictation theory of interpretation. As Torrance suggests, "when the act of *intelligere* is directed to the human words of Holy Scripture, according to Aquinas, it penetrates beneath them to read them from their inner aspect, and so through the *sensus* it reaches what the author intended the words to signify, the *intellectus litteralis*. In determining that one has to consider the end to which they conduce and therefore the reason for them. Therefore, interpretation is concerned not only with the literal sense of the words but with the literal causes and reasons that lie behind them. If language and thought, words and reasons, belong so closely together, then a faithful interpretation of the text

60. Ibid., pp. 264-65.
61. Ibid., p. 265.

will be inseparable from an interpretation of the thought." Thus, in the Scriptures, one is concerned with rational communication, so that allied disciplines have to be used in their interpretation (e.g., science, philosophy, language, etc.).[62]

It is to be observed that when one penetrates into the literal reasons that lie behind the literal sense of the Bible, one is interpreting what is intended by the primary as well as the secondary author. For example, when one considers the reasons for the ceremonial laws in the Old Testament, one discovers that they involve a twofold end that should guide one's interpretation; they were ordained for divine worship to commemorate certain divine benefits, and they were also ordained to foreshadow Jesus Christ, the coming messiah. They may therefore be taken in two ways, but never in such a way that they go beyond the order of literal causes. Thus, even though one gives some of those ceremonies a distinctively Christological interpretation, one can only do that if it is congruent with the literal signification and rooted in it.[63]

In terms of biblical interpretation, Aquinas stressed that the primary necessity was to study the text. The interpreter of the Bible has to see the parts of scripture in relation to the whole message and the whole message in relation to the several parts that make it up. No part separated from the rest has the form of the whole any more than a hand separated from man has human form.

From start to finish Thomas Aquinas was a rigorous scientific thinker. It is not surprising, therefore, that he should act in the same way with regard to the Bible. A science, according to him, is the way of reasoning from things already known to a knowledge of things previously unknown. That reasoning process leads to certain knowledge (*scientia*) but no science can establish its own first principles, but it is in the light of them that it knows what is less knowable. In ordering its matter in the light of the first principles, it does succeed in connecting the contents rationally together and so directs attention back again to first principles. When this method is applied to theology, Thomas said, the Bible occupies

62. Ibid., p. 267.
63. *ST*, I-II, q. 102, a. 2, ad 1; cf. Torrance, pp. 267-69, on Thomas's use of the Old Testament Laws.

the place of first principles, and it is in the light of the infallible truths they reveal that the whole ratiocinative process of theological activity is undertaken.[64] But Thomas wrote that "sciences are of two kinds: some work from premises recognized in the innate light of intelligence, for instance, arithmetic, geometry, and sciences of the same sort; while others work from premises recognized in the light of a higher science, for instance optics start from principles marked out by geometry. In this second manner is Christian theology a science."[65] It is in that way that Thomistic Scholasticism unequivocally based the doctrines of theology on the Word of God. Theological science receives its principles immediately from God through the divine revelation given to the prophets and the apostles. The authoritative pronouncements of the canonical books have supreme place—sacred doctrine can only make use of other authorities or teachers as extrinsic and probable arguments.

In part, the reason for that is that Aquinas stressed the difference between human words and God's word. He made that point in the argument of the *De differentia divini verbi et humani*.

> The ... difference between our word and God's is that ours is imperfect, but God's word is most perfect, for we cannot express all the things that are in our soul by one word, and so there must be many imperfect words through which we express separately all the things that are in our knowledge. But in God it is not so. For since he understands and understands himself and whatever he understands, by his own essence, by one act, one unique word of God is expressive of all that is in God ... otherwise it would be imperfect.[66]

Thus it is by one word that God not only reveals Himself but relates all creatures to Himself, and the content of that word is the fullness of His divine knowledge. With human beings, words con-

64. Adapted from Torrance, p. 285.
65. *ST*, I-I, q. 1, a. 2, a. 3. Cf. also, Torrance, p. 287; and Herman Reith, *The Metaphysics of St. Thomas Aquinas* (Milwaukee: Bruce Publishing Co., 1958), pp. 141-44.
66. Ibid., I-I, q. 34, a. 3; see also Thomas's *The Division and Methods of the Sciences*, ed. Armand Maurer (Toronto: Pontifical Institute of Medieval Studies, 1963).

vey less than men know and are defective instruments, but that is not the case with God's word, for the whole of His wisdom is contained in it. The words of the Holy Scriptures are the visible, material representations of that Word of God impressed on the human authors of Scripture by divine inspiration. Consequently, "we must keep to that which has been written in Scripture," wrote Aquinas, "as to an excellent rule of faith so that we must add nothing to it, detract nothing, and change nothing by interpreting it badly."[67] That is quite a clarion call to biblical authority from one whom many are prone to dismiss as a scholastic theologian for whom the Scriptures were incidental.

CONCLUSION

Certainly, from the perspective of the evangelical theologian, there are many deficiencies in other aspects of scholastic biblical theology in general and of Thomistic hermeneutics in particular. There can be no doubt that in spite of his sincere intention to give the Scriptures their supreme place in his theological system, philosophy is more conspicuous and receives more extended consideration in Thomas than in the Reformation tradition. It is also the case that in refusing to allow the propositions of the Roman Church to come under the criticism of the Scriptures, Aquinas contributed to making the ecclesiastical authority dominant over the *prima veritas*. And finally, it is true that after Aquinas there emerged medieval theologians for whom the scholastic system was the principal matter and the interpretation of the Bible a secondary one.

However, it would seem that the stereotypical portrayal of scholastic theology as mere rationalism is not warranted, especially when such an analysis is utilized to demonstrate the relative "novelty" of a view of the Bible as the infallible Word of God. As Charles J. Callan notes, the scholastic theologians shared the traditional orthodox view of the Bible as the written Word of a God "who inspires human writers, illuminating their minds to conceive clearly and correctly what He wishes them to write,

67. *De Divinus Nominibus*, II, lect. 1.

moving their wills faithfully to write down the divine message which He gives them. . . . "[68] That is a significant point to remember if contemporary biblical Christianity is to capitalize on its wider connection with past Christian tradition and to mine that connection for all of its gold in defending the primacy and infallibility of the Word of God today.

68. Callan, p. 34.

4

Luther and Biblical Infallibility

Robert D. Preus

A FRAMEWORK AND CONTEXT FOR THE STUDY

If Luther were alive today would he believe in the inerrancy of Scripture? That, the subject of our present chapter, seems like a very unsound question, unworthy of a good scholar or historian or even a good theologian. After all, how could anyone know how Luther would have reacted to arguments pro and con on the subject of biblical inerrancy and to the mass of data available to us today as they impinge on that doctrine? The question, however, has been asked by just about every Luther scholar, historian or theologian, who has addressed Luther's use of the Scriptures and his attitude toward them. It has been phrased differently at times:

ROBERT D. PREUS, B.A., Luther College, B.D., Bethany Lutheran Theological Seminary, Ph.D., Edinburgh University, D.Theol., Strasbourg University, is president of Concordia Seminary in Ft. Wayne, Indiana. He previously served in the pastoral ministry and as a professor at Concordia Seminary in St. Louis, Missouri. His works include *The Inspiration of Scriptures* (1955), *The Theology of Post-Reformation Lutheranism* (2 vols. 1970, 1972), and *Getting into the Theology of Concord* (1977). He is a member of the Society for Reformation Research, Concordia Historical Institute, Medieval Society of America, Archaeological Society, and the Council of the ICBI.

e.g., Did Luther believe there were errors in the Bible? Did he believe that the Bible was wholly and in every respect true? My phrasing of the question, however, has a couple of advantages over the more scholarly and conservative posing of it. First, it reminds us of the great span of time separating Luther from us and of the very different motives and reasons and context for his reverent (I presume every Luther scholar would grant that) posture toward Scripture from that of modern theologians—whether liberal or conservative—and scholars. And it alerts us to the possible danger or inappropriateness of addressing a twentieth-century question to a sixteenth-century man. Second, the very unsoundness and unscholarly tone of the question is calculated to draw attention to the fact that we have no right as theologians or historians to speculate concerning how he would fit in with our present discussions concerning inerrancy; our duty is to determine what he actually believed and to rule out what he could not have believed in 1520 or 1546.

What I am getting at is not meant to imply that we cannot conclude that Luther (like Erasmus or Socinians later in the century) may well have been in advance of his day as he interpreted the Scriptures, or that Luther could have anticipated an understanding of the Scriptures' form that became explicit and accepted only after his day. But I would argue that such conclusions are unlikely (Luther, like every other historical figure we study, except Christ, was a child of his time); the burden of proof—irrefutable proof—lies squarely on the back of the scholar who proposes that Luther was in advance of his day, especially three or four hundred years in advance.

I realize that what I am saying may appear to reveal a strong bias on my part even before I examine the evidence and the secondary sources relevant to Luther's position on biblical authority and interpretation, and I readily admit that. However, that is not a theological prejudice on my part but a basic principle that ought to inform the method of any scholar who studies the history of Christian thought and to caution him against coming to facile, anachronistic conclusions.

I believe that my apprehension concerning that point of method is fully justified as one gives attention to Luther's doctrine of biblical authority and to all that has been written on the subject in recent years. It is distressing and aggravating, for instance, to hear modern theologians claiming that Luther was a father of the so-called historical-critical method[1] and thus had to believe that the Bible was less than inerrant. One might dismiss that false assertion as just another attempt to adduce the authority of Luther and the Reformers to support a modern theory; it is indeed just that. But such a claim is also the result of a deep methodological aberration, namely, the inability (or refusal) to see and study Luther in his own context, his own age, his own world of thought. And it is on that point that I would like to make a few comments.

It is entirely possible that the humanism of the Renaissance paved the way for the historical-critical method with its frank rejection of biblical inerrancy and everything supernatural in the biblical account—a method that was consciously put into play only about the time of Semler, almost three hundred years later. But if that is so, it is not the emphasis *ad fontes*, or the interest in textual criticism, or the rejection of the allegorical method of exegesis, or even the critical questioning of the authenticity of historical documents such as the Donation of Constantine—all common to humanism—that prefigured the historical-critical method, but humanism itself, that is, its basic philosophy, theology, and anthropology. And that humanistic frame of thought and approach to Scripture that we see so clearly in Erasmus,[2] an approach that resembles the theology of Semler and the classical

1. A recent statement by Warren Quanbeck is quite typical of that position. See "The Confessions and Their Influence upon Biblical Interpretation," in *Studies in Lutheran Hermeneutics*, ed. John Reumann (Philadelphia: Fortress, 1949), p. 182: "The historical-critical study of the Bible, set in motion by the Renaissance and the Reformation, has made great contributions to the understanding of the biblical message. It has underscored and reenforced the teaching of the reformers at many points, even corrected the reformers' interpretations." Interestingly, an article by Kurt Marquart, "The Incompatibility between Historical-Critical Theology and the Lutheran Confessions" (p. 113ff.), denies the very assumption of Quanbeck that the historical-critical method has its origins in the approach of the Reformers to Scripture. See also Robert Preus, "How Is the Lutheran Church to Interpret and Use the Old and New Testaments?" in *1973 Reformation Lectures* (Mankato, Minn.: Bethany Lutheran College, 1973).
2. *Ratio seu methodus compendio perueniendi ad veram theologiam* (Basel, 1520). Erasmus's theology is summarized in that short work. He preferred the simple theology of the gospels to the rest of Scripture and drew his teachings mainly from them. Jesus was represented as a great teacher and example. Erasmus showed no interest in the high priestly office of Christ. His emphasis was almost entirely on the ethics of Jesus.

liberalism of Harnack, is precisely what Luther and all the Reformers, including Melanchthon, rejected *in toto*. Luther's *De servo arbitrio* and Melanchthon's first *Loci communes* prove that point emphatically. Thus, the fact that Luther and all the Reformers (as well as Flacius and the strictest of the later Lutherans and Calvinists, such as Calov and the Buxdorfs) eagerly made use of the many adventitious contributions of the humanists does not even faintly suggest that they deviated intentionally or unintentionally from that view of Scripture and its divine authority that was the common possession of all western Christianity.[3]

But perhaps Luther unintentionally and inadvertently approached and said things about Scripture that might have given rise to the historical-critical method and the accompanying denial of inerrancy. In principle such a possibility exists and is not in opposition to my caveat that we study Luther strictly in his context. After all, someone in the course of history has to sow the seed of every new thought, and someone too has to advocate the thought explicitly. Why not Luther in this case? Again however, all evidence and careful thought militate against such a surmise.

First, the time between Luther and Semler is too great; why would no one in the intervening period draw attention to Luther's more liberal and innovative thoughts, if he had them, on the matter of biblical authority and truthfulness? And why would all his truly loyal followers adopt in time of controversy a position of strict biblical inerrancy? Second, and more significantly, by 1535 (and certainly by 1545) Luther had formed a very final position in all matters of doctrine, including the authority of Scripture and what that implied for hermeneutics and the whole theological enterprise. Furthermore, his position in his later career was definitely not *in transitu* but clearly self-conscious. We have every reason to believe that the mature Luther understood his own position and the implications of what he said on theological issues. Thus we cannot say with any confidence, "If Luther were alive today he would have said things differently," or, "Those are the implications of Luther's theology that, if he were alive today, he would

---

3. See John F. Johnson's chapter (in this volume) on the position of the early church Fathers.

embrace." One statement from Luther's great confession (1528) is perhaps significant to establish the point.

> I see that schisms and errors are increasing proportionately with the passage of time, and that there is no end to the rage and fury of Satan. Hence lest any persons during my lifetime or after my death appeal to me to misuse my writings and confirm their error as the Sacramentarians and Baptists are beginning to do, I desire with this treatise to confess my faith before God and all the world, point by point. I am determined to abide it until my death and (so help me God!) in this faith to depart from this world and to appear before the judgment seat of our Lord Jesus Christ. Hence if one shall say after my death, "If Dr. Luther were living now, he would teach and hold this or that article differently, for he did not consider it sufficiently," etc., let me say now as then, and then as now, that by the grace of God I have most diligently traced all these articles through the Scriptures, have examined them again and again in the light thereof, and have wanted to defend all of them as certainly as I have now defended the Sacrament of the Altar. I am not drunk or irresponsible. I know what I am saying, and I well realize what this will mean for me before the Last Judgment at the coming of the Lord Jesus Christ. Let no one make this out to be a joke or idol talk; I am in dead earnest, since by the grace of God I have learned to know a great deal about Satan. If he can twist and pervert the Word of God, what will he be able to do with my or someone else's words?[4]

If those prolegomonous remarks about the method of studying the thought of a sixteenth-century theologian are cogent, then one substantial conclusion becomes apparent and basic for any study

---

4. Cited in *FC, SD*, VII, 29-31. See *WA*, 26:499-500. See also *LW*, 37:360-61. In no work of his did Luther more emphatically teach biblical authority and affirm his adherence to the *sensus literalis* of Scripture than in that great work. See ibid., p. 308 passim.

Note the following keys to abbreviations used in this and following notes: *Er. Lat.* = Martin Luther, *Opera latina* (Frankfurt und Erlangen: Heyder und Simmer, 1865-73); *WA* = D. Martin Luther's *Werke, Kritische Gesamtausgabe* (Weimar: Bohlau, 1883–); *W1* = D. Martin Luther's *Sämtliche Schriften*, herausgegeben von Johann Georg Walch, 1. Auflage (Halle: Johann Justinus Gebauer, 1740-53); *W2* = Martin Luther's Sämliche Schriften, herausgegeben von Johann Georg Walch, 2. Auflage (St. Louis: Concordia, 1818-1930). *LW Luther's Works*, ed. Jaroslav Pelikan, Robert Fischer et al. (Philadelphia: Fortress, St. Louis: Concordia, 1955-).

of Luther's doctrine of Scripture; one should not impute any view regarding Scripture or its interpretation to Luther without solid, assertive evidence from his writings. And one ought to eschew innuendos, hyperbolic statements, outbursts, and snippets from Luther as evidence that he held a position toward Scripture in advance of his time, especially if there is no positive evidence to support such a contention. Luther, in his thousands of deliberate and definite remarks about Scripture and its interpretation, said many things that were clearly against the Romanists, *Schwaermer*, Zwingli, and many others of his day, and he said some things that were indeed novel. If he had held a view concerning the truthfulness or divine authority of Scripture different from the papists, or *Schwaermer*, or any adversary, or from tradition, we would expect him to have expressed himself plainly, as he did at Leipzig in 1519, at Marburg in 1529, against the heavenly prophets in 1525, and repeatedly throughout his career. But as far as I have been able to discern, his view (as we shall see), expressed so accurately in controversy, was invariably the highest view of Scripture and revealed a greater devotion to the written Word than that of his adversaries. And if occasionally an *obiter dictum*, ejaculation, or subjective opinion—so common to Luther—seems to make him appear radical or liberal at times in comparison with many of his contemporaries, we can only (without discounting them or psychologizing them away) balance such statements with the overwhelmingly massive evidence of Luther's mature and conservative view of Scripture.

LUTHER STUDIES: A HELP AND A HINDRANCE

To trace the discussions of Luther's doctrine of Scripture is in itself to write a history; that we cannot do. But we must mention how such studies have affected our understanding and appreciation of Luther's doctrine of biblical authority. With the exception of the apostle Paul, no theologian's ideas have been discussed so often and so heatedly as Luther's. Historians and theologians have had a kind of fascination for the man and his theology. That is so, perhaps, because he wrote so much, because he wrote so passionately and often changed his opinions until he became an older man; or perhaps it is because of the intensely important themes he addressed himself to: salvation, law, authority, human rights, war, etc. At any rate, one cannot handle all the vast bibliography of Luther, just as one can hardly get through all of his works in a lifetime. Not only is Luther one of the most debated figures in the history of Christian thought, he is one of the most popular, at least today. Almost everyone wants to claim Luther as an ally, it seems, at least in some respect: Roman Catholics, Lutherans, Reformed, Existentialists, Neo-Orthodoxists, conservatives, liberals, even East German Communists.

Because of the great interest in Luther's doctrine of biblical authority and the sharp disagreement and controversy among scholars as they have sought to portray his thoughts on the matter, there has been a tremendous amount of literature on the subject in recent times. The literature of the past one hundred and fifty years has repeatedly explored all the data, though radically different conclusions have been drawn.

Why should that be, when the same data are used by all the Luther researchers? Luther spoke prolifically about Scripture and its authority. Was he perhaps unclear on the matter, equivocal, unsure of his position? Hardly. Perhaps his extemporaneous manner of addressing questions, his dogmatism, his penchant for hyperbole give rise to different interpretations. At most, that can only be a partial explanation for the diversity of opinion regarding his true views on biblical authority. The better explanation lies in the scholars and theologians themselves who study Luther—in their respective ideologies that color their interpretation of him on many issues and their desire to have Luther as an ally for their own ideas. That is an undeniable fact, whether conservative or liberal scholars offer us their findings. Now it may appear that I am engaging at this point in a dubious practice, what the logicians call "poisoning the wells," as I suggest that the prejudices or beliefs of Luther scholars have determined their conclusions. And I am as well undermining whatever conclusions I might bring forth in this study of Luther's doctrine of biblical authority. But please notice that I am directing my charge against virtually all historians and theologians who have studied Luther, whether it be the dispassionate and objective Leopold von Ranke, who did not bother to discuss Luther's doctrine of biblical authority because he did not consider doctrine the stuff of history, the conservative Ewald Plass, who represents Luther's position in the form of Lutheran Church-Missouri Synod doctrine, existentialist Martin Heinecken, who portrays Luther's doctrine with a Kierkegaardian existentialist brush, or liberal Joseph Sittler, who denies that Luther even believed in the normative authority of Scripture (a "static" doctrine, according to Sittler), that is, that Scripture was divinely authoritative by virtue of its divine origin and form. And we could go on and on giving examples of that very thing. Isaac Dorner, the nineteenth-century Prussian Union historian and theologian, represented Luther as teaching that some portions of Scripture are more inspired than others and some not the Word of God at all.[5] In more recent times dialectical theologian Emil Brunner commended Luther for teaching a merely material theory of biblical authority, the authority of its evangelical content not its words,[6] a position shared by not a few Lutherans. In all those cases the theologian or historian quotes Luther and insists that he understands Luther's true position concerning Scripture.

How do we react to all that and explain the apparently conflicting data in Luther: on the one hand his derogatory statements about James, Hebrews, Esther, etc., his seeming impatience and criticism with certain statements in the Scriptures, his pitting one Scripture passage or pericope against another (let us call that negative data) and on the other hand his continuous affirmations concerning the divine authority, origin, and truthfulness of Scripture (let us call that the positive data)? Several solutions have been

---

5. Isaac A. Dorner, *History of Protestant Theology*, trans. George Robson and Sophia Taylor, 2 vols. (Edinburgh: T. & T. Clark, 1871), 1:243-45. Two historians of dogma who have transcended the tendency to interpret Luther in the light of their own ideologies are Adolf von Harnack and Otto Ritschl. Adolf Harnack, *History of Dogma*, trans. Neil Buchanan (London: Williams & Norgate, 1896). Otto Ritschl, *Dogmengeschichte des Protestantismus* (Leipzig: J. C. Hinrichs'sche Buchhandlung and Göttingen: Vandenhoeck & Ruprecht, 1908-27). Ritschl (1:70ff.) actually drew attention to the point mentioned above when he spoke of the "self-evident presuppositions" of the "modern theologians" of the day. He and Harnack both saw certain apparent conflicts in Luther, which they do not seek to harmonize, e.g., Luther's statements on canonicity as opposed to his very pious attitude toward Scripture as a whole.

6. *The Christian Doctrine of God, Dogmatics*, vol. 1., trans. Olive Wion (Philadelphia: Westminster, 1950), pp. 109-11.

tried. One can give the negative data priority over the positive data by interpreting the positive data as mere medieval nominalistic incrustations on the more progressive and advanced theology of Luther—incrustations that he could rid himself of no more than his belief in devils or the sin of usury. That solution is not compelling because of the massive amount of positive data and especially because Luther emphatically asserted and believed the statements that constitute the positive data, just as he also in fact believed in devils and that usury was sinful.

Another solution would discount the negative data on the strength of the magnitude of the positive data. There is some force in that solution that, however, probably makes Luther more inconsistent than he really was but fails to explain away the negative data. After all, if one makes assertions utterly at variance with one's own mature thought, the historian or researcher owes it to his research to offer some plausible explanation for such inconsistency.

Still another solution would be to accept the force of the vast positive data at its face value as representing Luther's firm and mature convictions regarding biblical authority and then meticulously to find or at least propose explanations one by one for the conflicting statements of Luther's found in the negative data. The trouble with that solution is that though many of Luther's statements that appear to conflict with his ordinarily high view toward Scripture can be explained away as hyperbole, unthinking and uncritical outbursts, or in some cases as inauthentic, his statements on matters of canonicity, though subsiding in intensity, continued throughout his life and cannot be explained away by any of the aforementioned felicitous expediencies.

Still another possible solution would be simply to let Luther's seeming contradictions concerning the Bible stand in all their contrariety. That solution (Adolf von Harnack?) is, I believe, methodologically unsound. One can in principle piously refrain from attempting to solve apparently conflicting statements only in the case of writings that one believes to be of divine origin and thus transcending critical human analysis (e.g., the doctrine of the Trinity or of any mystery of faith contained in the Bible). In the case of Luther such a procedure would be utterly self-defeating.

For if the scholar, in attempting to discover Luther's opinion, finds him to be simply and categorically in disagreement with himself, then *eo ipso* the scholar cannot know Luther's opinion on the subject under consideration. And of course, such a solution that merely collects data and makes no attempt to evaluate, assess, and harmonize when that is called for is no solution at all.

Now except for the last, all the aforementioned solutions to the seeming conflicts between Luther's statements concerning Scripture have been attempted and with varying degrees of success. Kahnis, Tholuck, Luthardt, Craemer, and in more recent times Emil Brunner, Joseph Sittler, Edgar Carlson, and many, many others have opted for the first solution, ignoring the copious positive data, and thus making Luther an anachronistic forerunner of positive theology, crisis theology, existentialism, neo-orthodoxy, or the historical-critical method.[7]

A smaller number of conservative scholars have opted for the second solution, tended to ignore the negative data, and simply concluded that Luther shared pretty much the nominalistic thinking of his day on inspiration, authority, and inerrancy—with the addition of a keen insight into the power of the Word.

The third approach to solving the problem of conflicting data in Luther has been the most fruitful and has been carried on by theologians and historians with both conservative and liberal bent. Among liberals two great historians of dogma stand out: Adolf von Harnack and, even more, Otto Ritschl. They concluded that there are basic conflicts in Luther that he was never fully able to resolve himself, and so he held to a high view of biblical authority and inerrancy and at the same time made highly questionable statements about Scripture and radically doubted and altered generally accepted ideas about canonicity. Among more conservative theologians we have Wilhelm Rohnert, Wilhelm Koelling, and Wilhelm Walther in Germany and in America C. F. W. Walther, Adolf Hoehnecke, Francis Pieper, and Michael Reu, the last Luther scholar to make a definitive study of Luther's doctrine of Scripture on the basis of primary sources. The conclu-

7. See Francis Pieper, *Christian Dogmatics*, trans. H. W. Romoser et al (St. Louis: Concordia, 1950), 1:276ff.; Joseph Sittler, *The Doctrine of the Word* (Philadelphia: Muhlenberg Press, 1948).

sions of those scholars are that many of the negative data are simply taken out of context and irrelevant to the subject of biblical authority; other negative data are careless or passing statements of Luther's that simply cannot be used to mitigate his clearly articulated position. And in the matter of canonicity they contend that Luther's position, which they usually reject, is again irrelevant to the subject of the inspiration of Scripture or its inerrancy and authority since the antilogomena were not considered to be Scripture by Luther.[8]

LUTHER'S EVANGELICAL HERMENEUTICS

The purpose of this study is to present Luther's doctrine of biblical infallibility. What do we mean by infallibility? What are we looking for as we study the writings of Luther in respect to that issue? We will not construct in advance a notion of biblical infallibility and then show how Luther taught it. Rather, we will examine his writings and his basic approach to Scripture and see what he said about Scripture and how he treated the Scriptures in order to learn just what his notion of biblical infallibility was. To do that I will examine Luther's views on three issues that are related to the idea of infallibility: the divine origin of Scripture, the authority of Scripture, and the truthfulness of Scripture. But

8. For bibliographical data on Luther's studies and the conclusions of Luther scholars on Luther's doctrine of Scripture, see Michael Reu, *Luther and the Scriptures* (Columbus, Ohio: The Wartburg Press, 1944). For bibliographical information after the mid-forties, see E. Thestrup Pedersen, *Luther som skriftfortolker, en studie i Luthers skriftsyn hermeneutik og eksegese* (Kobenhavn: Nyt Nordisk Forlag Arnold Busck, 1959). Reu's conclusions are based in part upon the data and conclusions of Wilhelm Walther, *Das Erbe der Reformation* (Leipzig: A. Duchert, 1918). It is interesting that Walther's monumental work in German and Reu's definitive study in English have been totally ignored by Rogers and McKim in their historical approach to the authority and interpretation of the Bible. See Jack B. Rogers and Donald K. McKim, *The Authority and Interpretation of the Bible* (San Francisco: Harper & Row, 1979). The only reference to Reu's work is the citation from Otto W. Heick, *A History of Christian Thought*, 2 vols. (Philadelphia: Fortress, 1976), in which Heick accuses Reu (for altogether wrong reasons) of being unreliable and giving a "distorted view of Luther." That, I think, is the most shameful put down and the most outrageous piece of bad scholarship I have ever encountered in anyone, except perhaps for Sittler, who has aspired to write on the history of Christian thought. Rogers and McKim do not even include Reu (or Heick, for that matter) in their selected bibliography.

first we must say a few words about Luther's exegetical approach to Scripture.

Luther's notion of biblical infallibility arose from his firm belief that the Bible is the Word of God and that God spoke to him there powerfully and authoritatively. That belief of Luther's was more assumed than articulated, though one can find scores of statements of Luther's in which he expressly asserts that Scripture is God's Word that saves poor sinners. As a theologian and teacher, Luther saw himself first and foremost as an exegete, an interpreter of Scripture, a *bonus textualis*, as he put it.[9] That in itself was a break with scholastic tradition that extolled scholastic theology and those who wrote commentaries on Thomas Aquinas and Peter Lombard. There can be no doubt that Luther's love for exegesis and lecturing on books of the Bible was due to what he discovered therein, namely the gospel of justification by faith that comforted his tired conscience and informed his exegetical lectures, whether on Romans, Galatians, Genesis, or Isaiah. The exciting activities of the humanists, as they studied the biblical languages and dug into the Scriptures, no doubt only confirmed Luther in his first theological love.

Luther's background in the Occamistic tradition of *sola scriptura* reinforced him in his devotion to the exegesis of the sacred Scriptures. So we would expect Luther in his multitudinous writings to extol the Scriptures and to urge every aspiring theologian to read and reread them, struggle with them, depend upon them, and embrace their content with avidity. And so he did.[10] To Luther, the theologian was simply to accept what Scripture says according to the clear meaning of the words.[11] Against the medieval scholastics he insisted that the sense of Scripture was single and was clear.[12] The simple purpose of the exegete was to determine and draw out the meaning of the biblical text and to apply it.

From his many exegetical works, but also from his other writings, we are able to learn a great deal about Luther's approach to the Bible (hermeneutics) and his attitude toward it (which affect-

9. *W2*, 5:456.
10. *W2*, 6:96; 13:1898; 15:1271; 18:332, 732.
11. *WA*, 10:I:1:447; cf. *W2*, 3:21; 22:577.
12. *W2*, 1:950-52; 11:313; 18:1447.

ed his hermeneutics). In our present study we cannot, unfortunately, offer any kind of summary of Luther's hermeneutics, an acquaintance with which would be helpful—though not indispensable—for a full appreciation of his idea of biblical authority and infallibility.[13] Neither can we precede our discussion of Luther's doctrine of biblical infallibility with a full summary of his entire doctrine of the Word of God in the broader sense, helpful as that might be to give us perspective. But we must say a few things relative to Luther's approach to Scripture, lest his views on biblical authority be distorted.[14]

First, as we have already mentioned, Luther believed fervently that the Holy Spirit made a person a theologian through the study of Scripture and in no other way. In his well-known statement on the theme *Oratio, meditatio et tentatio faciunt theologum* (prayer, study [of Scripture], and affliction make one a theologian), Luther, placing by far the greatest emphasis on the second point, *meditatio* (the assiduous study of Scripture), wrote:

> You should meditate, that is, not in the heart alone, but also externally, work on and ply the oral speech and the lettered words in the book, read them and reread them again and again, noting carefully and reflecting upon what the Holy Spirit means by these words. And have a care that you do not tire of it or think it enough if you have read, heard, said it once or twice, and now profoundly

---

13. We can only mention some of the studies on Lutheran hermeneutics: E. Thestrup Pedersen, ibid.; Jaroslav Pelikan, *Luther the Expositor* (St. Louis: Concordia, 1959); W. M. Oesch, "Die Lehre von der Inspiration und ihre Anwendung auf die Urgeschichte," in *Fuldaer hefte* (Berlin: Lutherisrhes Verlagashaus, 1960); John Warwick Montgomery, *Crisis in Lutheran Theology*, 2 vols. (Grand Rapids: Baker, 1967); John Reumann, ed., *Studies in Lutheran Hermeneutics* (Philadelphia: Fortress, 1979); Arnold J. Koelpin, ed., *No Other Gospel* (Milwaukee, Wis.: Northwestern Publishing House, 1980); Peter Meinhold, *Luthers Sprachphilosophie* (Berlin: Lutherisches Verlagshaus, 1958); Hans-Joachim Kraus, *Geschichte der historisch-kritischen Erforschung des Alten Testaments* (Neukirchener: Neukirchener Verlag, 1969); Werner Georg Kümmel, *The New Testament: The History of the Investigation of Its Problems*, trans. S. McLean Gilmour and Howard C. Kee (Nashville: Abingdon, 1970).

14. I briefly touched upon those before in "The Early Church Through Luther," in Norman Geisler, ed., *Inerrancy* (Grand Rapids: Zondervan, 1979), pp. 372-77.

understand it all; for in that manner a person will never become much of a theologian.[15]

Again in the same vein he remarked:

> He [the theologian] should adhere to this primary principle: in sacred matters there is no arguing or philosophizing; for if one were to operate with the rational and probable arguments in this area, it would be possible for me to twist all the articles of faith just as easily as Arius, the Sacramentarians, and the Anabaptists did. But in theology we must only hear and believe and be convinced in our heart that God is truthful, however absurd that which God says in His Word may appear to be to reason.[16]

There is no doubt that for Luther the Holy Spirit made a person a theologian by leading him into an understanding of the intended sense of Scripture and in no other way.

> This is our foundation: where the Holy Scripture establishes something that must be believed, there we must not deviate from the words as they sound, neither from the order as it stands, unless an express article of faith (based on clear Scripture passages) compels us to interpret the words otherwise, or arrange them differently. Else, what would become of the Bible?[17]

It is significant that Luther had assumed the divine authority and infallibility of Scripture, which is the Spirit's own Word, as he emphasized how the Holy Spirit makes a person a theologian.

Second, as we consider Luther's doctrine of biblical authority and infallibility, we must keep in mind what he believed about the main message of Scripture—the gospel, or the Christocentricity of Scripture. To Luther, all the Scriptures, both Old and New Testaments, point to Christ. "The entire Scripture points only to Christ," he wrote.[18] "All the words of the Scripture have the purpose that Christ might be known."[19] "Take Christ out of the

15. *W2*, 14:435.
16. *W2*, 5:456.
17. *WA*, 18:147.
18. *WA*, 2:73; cf. *WA*, 3:620; 17:2:334; 52:509.
19. *WA*, 14:97:2.

Scriptures and what else will you find in them?"[20] "The cross of Christ appears everywhere in Scripture."[21] "All Scripture teaches nothing else but the cross."[22] What Luther said about the Christocentricity of Scripture, namely that Christ and His atonement is the main message of the entire book, is no mere theoretical statement. Neither is it a mere hermeneutical principle, though it is certainly that. Commenting on Luther's principle of Christocentricity, Thestrup Pedersen rightly says, "If we misunderstood Scripture's main content, then ever so correct a philological, grammatical analysis of the individual words and sentences will not help us a bit."[23] The principle of biblical Christocentricity not only informed Luther's exegesis of Scripture and his approach to Scripture but also his attitude toward and love for Scripture. That is extremely important as we study Luther's attitude toward the Bible. Luther valued Scripture more because of its content than because of its form as God's Word. But that does not imply that he valued the form less; the very opposite is the case. If at times he seems to despise the Scripture as the mere crib that holds the Christ child, it is only because the crib cannot be compared to what it holds.[24]

According to Luther, Scripture was written for the sake of its message, the gospel. That must be borne in mind when at times

20. *WA*, 18:606:29.
21. *WA*, 3:63:1.
22. *WA*, 9:560:1; cf. *WA*, 4:153:27; 40:III:652:15; 54:29:3, 414:13; 56:5:9.
23. Ibid., p. 251.
24. Luther's beautiful statement, in which he likens Scripture to the crib that holds the Christ child, has often been used by scholars to show that he took a condescending attitude toward Scripture. The exact opposite is the case. The well-known statement reads as follows, "I beg and faithfully warn every pious Christian not to stumble at the simplicity of language and the stories that will often meet him there [in Scripture]. He should not doubt that however simple they may seem, these are the very words, deeds, judgments, and history of the high majesty and wisdom of God; for this is the Scripture which makes fools out of all the wise and prudent and is open only to babes and fools, as Christ says, Matthew 11:25. Away with your overweening conceit! Think of Scripture as the loftiest and noblest of holy things, as the richest lode, which will never be mined out, so that you may find the divine wisdom which God places before you in such foolish and ordinary form. He does this in order to quench all pride. Here you will find the swaddling clothes and the manger in which Christ lies, to which the angels directed the shepherds, Luke 2:12. Swaddling clothes are plain and ordinary, but precious is the treasure, Christ, lying in them." (*W2*, 14:3)

he seems to oppose Christ to the Scriptures. He said, for instance, "If our adversaries urge Scripture, we urge Christ against the Scripture." And again he wrote, "One must not understand Scripture contrary to Christ, but in favor of him; therefore Scripture must be brought into relation to Christ or must not be regarded as Scripture."[25] What he was saying in those two statements is that his opponents should not oppose Scripture to its own chief message. He was applying his own principle of biblical Christocentricity. His opponents were misusing Scripture by citing law against the biblical gospel. To cite a Scripture passage in order to militate against the force of the biblical gospel was an awful confusion of law and gospel to Luther and an abuse of Scripture. In such a context Luther was enhancing Scripture in its "servant role" of proclaiming Christ; what a noble, precious role the Scriptures have! It is in that role, and because of their content, not usually because of their form, that Luther extolled the Scriptures.[26]

Third, Luther believed in the power of the Word and of Scripture, an important reason for his valuing the Scriptures so highly and a factor important for us to understand as we seek to study Luther's doctrine of biblical infallibility in its proper context. Again, Luther's doctrine of the efficacy or power of Scripture was no mere theoretical consideration. Scripture not only comforts and strengthens the Christian throughout his faith-life,[27] it not only instructs us in worship and theology,[28] but it is the Holy Spirit's own vehicle—an intrinsically powerful vehicle—to quicken, regenerate, and work faith in the lost sinner. "All the works which

25. *W2*, 19:144.
26. Almost invariably it is in its soteriological purpose that Scripture became so precious and valuable to Luther. *W2*, 9:1819: "God gave us Holy Scripture that we should not only read it, but also search, meditate, and ponder on it. In this way one will find eternal life in it" (cf. *W2*, 9:111, 655, 885, 1788, 1792, 1802). *WA*, 48:122: "The matter of greatest importance is that the readers of Scripture are not only diligent but also believing. This is what the Lord means when He says, 'How readest thou?' What are you learning? He says in effect, see to it that you believe when you read Scripture and that you rightly divide the Word of Truth, that you look for nothing in it except Me, without Whom no one comes to the Father and that from Scripture you teach this to others."
27. *W2*, 1:1344; 2:1200ff., 1385; 3:18; 4:2098; 5:274; 6:439.
28. *W2*, 4:1424; 13:573, 2215-16; 14:435.

Christ performed are recorded in the Word, and in the Word and through the Word He will give us everything, and without the Word He will give us nothing."[29] The Word brings us to faith, and the Holy Spirit comes through it.[30] It brings us to eternal life and gives life.[31] To be sure, the preached Word has all the power to convert and save that the written Word of Scripture possessed; Luther never ceased to exalt the power of the preached Word.[32] At times, he even gave prominence to the preached Word, not because it is intrinsically different or more powerful than the written Word of Scripture, but because the usual mode of proclaiming the gospel and carrying out Christ's Great Commission is by preaching, oral proclamation.[33] There is no question, however, that Luther saw no intrinsic difference between the power of the written and the preached gospel. And of course, as we shall see, the preached Word must be based squarely on the written Word of Scripture.[34]

SCRIPTURE IS THE WORD OF GOD

Nothing is more evident as one reads the works of Martin Luther than that he believed Scripture to be the very Word of God. There is nothing strange about that. Practically everybody in those days, except perhaps for a few renegade humanists, would have affirmed the divine origin of Scripture. What is remarkable about Luther in that regard, however, is the profoundness of his belief and how it affected his exegesis, his theology, and his career as a Reformer. Very definitely, it affected his notions concerning biblical infallibility. And so in the present study, we must first see how Luther spoke and what he meant when he described Scripture as divine and as God's Word.

29. *W2*, 13:1556; cf. *WA*, 8:491; 10:I:1:168; 52:2.
30. *W2*, 3:760; 5:271, 415; *WA*, 11:33.
31. *W2*, 9:1819; cf. p. 1788.
32. *WA*, 37:437; *WA*, 47:120.
33. *WA*, 10:I:625-27. E.g., p. 627: "Gospel means nothing else than preaching, and a crying out of the grace and mercy of God through our Lord Jesus Christ. . . . In essence it is not what stands in books or is written with letters, but much more a preaching by mouth and living Word, a voice which sounds forth into the whole world and is publicly cried so that everybody hears it. . . ."
34. *WA*, 2:446ff.; 7:96ff.; cf. *WA*, 12:278.

For Luther, Scripture was a divine Word. He made that point in a great variety of ways. "God declares His Word" in the Bible, Luther said, speaking on 1 Corinthians 15:39-44.[35] We should read the Bible, he wrote, "because therein God has written His own wisdom."[36] What we in the Bible read and hear God Himself "speaks to us,"[37] for the Bible is "the holy Word of God."[38] Very often Luther employed the terms "Scripture" (which he uses much more often than the term "Bible") and "Word of God" epexegetically, or in apposition to each other, as virtual synonyms. For instance, he spoke of *"verbum Dei et sacra scriptura"* or *"Gottes Wort und die heilige Schrift"* in many contexts, referring to the same thing by both phrases.[39] In that way he identified Scripture as the Word of God. On other occasions Luther used the terms "Scripture" and "Word of God" within a single sentence or context, so that the reader knows that he is referring to the same thing by both terms and thus using the terms interchangeably. For instance he wrote, "When the Lord Christ says in John 5:39, 'Search the Scriptures,' He wills that we diligently search and reflect upon God's Word."[40] In that way once again Luther identified Scripture and the Word of God. On other occasions Luther put the little word "or" (*oder, sive*) between the two terms, as when he said that the Enthusiasts would not submit to "God's Word or the Holy Scripture."[41] In many contexts Luther simply said that Scripture "is" God's Word, as when he said that "the bad conscience of the pope always reminds him that the Holy Scriptures are the Word of God."[42]

Very often Luther spoke of the "divine Scripture" (*göttliche Schrift, scriptura divina*), thus referring either to its divine origin, or,

---

35. *WI*, 8:1303.
36. *WI*, 22:1069.
37. *WI*, 9:1800.
38. *WI*, 22:3.
39. *WI*, 3:717, 1536; 4:1697; 8:26:1111, and especially 8:1316 where the phrase *"Gottes Wort und die heilige Schrift"* occurs several times. Cf. also *WI*, 1:57, 152; 5:805, 1067; 8:301, 600, 1107, 1226, etc.
40. *WI*, 3:1817; cf. 6:438; 7:178, 1984; 10:473, 1645, etc.
41. *WI*, 14:413; cf. 8:1111, 1129.
42. *WI*, 4:2118; 7:1541, 1549; 9:86, 1818: "We ourselves hold that the Holy Scriptures are God's saving Word which makes us forever blessed"; *WI*, 12:637: "Now we Christians have Scripture, and we are sure that it is the Word of God."

more likely, to its divine form as God's Word, or perhaps to its divine origin and saving message.[43] Or Luther simply referred to God's speaking to us in the Scriptures as the author of the Scriptures. For instance, he wrote, "God does not deal with us according to His majesty, but takes a human form and speaks with us throughout the entire Scripture, as a man speaks with another man."[44] In that connection it is interesting that Luther translated *legei* in Galatians 3:16 as its cites the Old Testament as "Er (God) spricht," not "Es (Scripture) spricht." And Luther, the exegete, said, "You are so to deal with it [the text of Scripture] that you believe that God Himself is saying this."[45]

Another common practice for Luther was to call Scripture God's book, or God's letter to us, in contrast to all human books. That too was his way of stressing the divine authorship of Scripture. Within the words of Scripture "are not the words of men" but "God speaks to us and does it Himself."[46] According to Luther, God has given the Scriptures to us.[47] The Scriptures are "God's letter" to us,[48] "our letter from God."[49] And so the Scriptures are a book that "no man ever wrote."[50] The very serious and even polemical context in which we find Luther using that kind of phraseology prevents us from concluding that he was speaking metaphorically as he stressed the divine authorship of Scripture and called it "God's Book," or "God's Epistle," or that he was

43. *W1*, 1:924; 4:867; 7:1086; 10:927, 1570.
44. *W1*, 1:1422; cf. 2:901: "God Himself" speaks in Scripture; cf. also 3:273; 9:1800, 1845, 1853 (on 2 Timothy 3:16). *W1*, 10:1018: "So then Scripture is God's own testimony concerning Himself"; *W1*, 14:491: "God has spoken the whole Scripture" ("*Die ganze Schrift had Gott geredet*").
45. *W1*, 3:21; 14:4. There is no reason to suppose that Luther was speaking metaphorically or hyperbolically when he said that God speaks the Scriptures or speaks in the Scriptures and is therefore the author of the book. He was speaking about what is actually the case. Otherwise, there is no accounting for outbursts such as the following, "It is cursed unbelief and odious flesh which will not permit us to see and know that God speaks to us in the Scriptures and that it is God's Word, but tells us that it is the word merely of Isaiah, or Paul, or some other mere man who has not created heaven and earth" (*W2*, 1:1800).
46. *W1*, 3:68; cf. 3:753.
47. *W1*, 9:1819.
48. *W1*, 9:1808.
49. *W1*, 1:1069.
50. *W1*, 4:211; cf. 1:1278. The language of Scripture is not human but divine (*W1*, 8:1230).

uncritically following the language of his day. Listen to one of his outbursts that touches on the matter. Commenting on 1 Peter 3:15 he wrote, "Therefore if the people will not believe you, you are to keep silent. For you are under no obligation to force them to hold that Scripture is God's Book, or Word."[51] Luther often called Scripture "God's Book."[52] When he called Scripture God's book, he was not thinking of God as the content of Scripture but as the author of Scripture. He was, of course, not ruling out the human authors of Scripture as willing, thinking, feeling instruments of God, but he was affirming that God is the author of Scripture in the primary sense and that Scripture represents His thoughts, His message to mankind.

Luther very often also called Scripture "God's wisdom" or "divine wisdom."[53] He wrote, ". . . the Holy Scriptures are not human, but divine wisdom." In such a phrase *wisdom* refers to the content of Scripture, the gospel and mysteries of faith, and the term *God's* refers to the origin and nature of that wisdom.

Having observed Luther's common terminology as he spoke of Scripture in reference to its origin and nature, we now turn our attention briefly to some of his more outstanding statements concerning its divine origin. Luther's common terminology in itself has clearly demonstrated what his doctrine concerning the divine origin of Scripture is; the few statements now to be cited will serve only to clarify and heighten his position.

Specifically, Luther attributed the entire Scripture to the Holy Spirit as its author.[54] The Spirit of God is directly the author of Scripture; He stands behind the Psalms of David.[55]

> And so the entire Holy Scriptures are attributed to the Holy Ghost, together with the outward Word and Sacrament, which touch and move our outward ears and senses; just as our Lord Jesus Himself ascribes His words to the Holy Ghost when He in Luke 4:18 cites Isaiah 61:1, "The Spirit of the Lord is upon Me." . . . What a glo-

51. *W1*, 9:1071; cf. *W1*, 9:1238.
52. *W1*, 9:1830; *W1*, 22:5: "Die heilige schrift ist das höchste und best Buch Gottes."
53. *W1*, 1:2:149, 152; 2:2; 5:610; 8:700; 9:1789.
54. *WA*, 2:556; *W2*, 15:1481.
55. *WA*, 31:I:393.

rious, proud pride this is: He who can boast that the Spirit of the Lord is speaking through Him and that His tongue is speaking the Word of the Holy Spirit must truly be very sure of His position. This will not be David, the son of Jesse, born in sins, but He who has been aroused to be prophet by God's promise. Should not he compose lovely psalms who has such a Master to teach him and speak through him? . . . David will not countenance the words to be ascribed to him. They are "pleasant, agreeable psalms of Israel," he says, but I did not make them up; rather, "the Spirit of the Lord has spoken through me." . . . The Holy Scriptures are spoken through the Holy Ghost according to the statement of David.[56]

Of course, human authors wrote the Scriptures as God's spokesmen and instruments, but their word was the Spirit's Word and revelation. Concerning creation Luther wrote, "Hence when Moses writes that God made heaven and earth and all that is in them in six days, you are to accept that it was six days and not to develop an explanation that six days were only one day."[57] But then he went on to say, "If you cannot understand how it could have been six days, then accord the *Holy Spirit* the honor that He is more learned than you. For you are to deal with the Scriptures in such a way that you think that God Himself is speaking to you there." Luther understood the Holy Spirit as the direct author of Genesis and of all Scripture. Yes, Moses, Isaiah, Paul, and other men wrote the Scriptures. But "there is a great difference between the Word which was sent from heaven and that which I devise by my own choice and devotion. The Holy Scriptures did not grow on earth."[58]

Now what does all that strong language of Luther's tell us about his doctrine of Scripture? Two things: (1) God is the author of Scripture (*Deus locutus est*), and (2) Scripture is formally God's Word right now (*Deus loquens*) and thus carries with it the power, the majesty, the authority, and infallibility of God Himself. We shall speak later of the implications of those two conclusions.

Does the fact that he considered God to be the author of Scrip-

56. *W2*, 3:1889.
57. *W2*, 3:21.
58. *W2*, 7:2095.

ture mean that for Luther Scripture was verbally inspired? Definitely. The evidence already presented should settle that matter. But since certain liberal theologians and scholars have questioned that conclusion, we might offer a few statements from Luther that indicate that, if he was unaware of the later formulation, he clearly anticipated the doctrine of verbal inspiration on several occasions.

Luther, by his very identification of Scripture as God's Word, had in mind the very words of Scripture. He said, "The Holy Scriptures are the Word of God, written and (as I might say) lettered and formed in letters."[59] To Luther, all the words of Scripture were weighted, counted, measured divine words (*omnia verba Dei sunt in pondere, numero, mensura*).[60] The very words and phrases in Scripture are divine, according to Luther.[61] Luther did not seem to be advanced or sophisticated enough to distinguish between the *res* and the *verba* of Scripture, as Calixt and certain seventeenth-century Lutherans did in their denial of verbal inspiration. When Luther attributed Scripture to the Holy Spirit or to God,[62] he was speaking very probably of Scripture distributively. Certainly, he did so in cases where he specifically attributed certain texts to the Holy Spirit.[63] In his commentaries he again and again cited the Holy Spirit as the author of a given verse or even word, and he pored over each word as given by the Holy Spirit.

Luther did not teach a "mechanical inspiration" or "dictation theory" of inspiration. Neither did any follower of his teach or suggest such a thing, for that matter.[64] But he did speak of the Holy Spirit's placing His Word in the mouth of the prophets,[65] and spoke of the holy writers as penmen of the Holy Spirit.[66] Again and again, as we have seen, he attributed the authorship of all Scripture to the Holy Spirit. "The Holy Scriptures were writ-

59. *W2*, 9:1770.
60. *WA*, 3:64.
61. *WA*, 40:III:254: Non solom enim vocabula, sed et phrasis est divina, qua Spiritus Sanctus et scriptura utitur.
62. *WA*, 40:I:83; 40:II:457; 5:491.
63. *WA*, 5:536, 543, 547; 54:39.
64. See Robert Preus, *The Theology of Post-Reformation Lutheranism* (St. Louis: Concordia, 1970), 1:287-91.
65. *W1*, 3:785.
66. *W1*, 3:1889; cf. *W1*, 9:356, 1774-75; 14:349.

ten by the Holy Ghost," he wrote.[67] It is true, as Bodamer has pointed out, that "in Luther we never find a dogmatic presentation of the teaching of verbal inspiration, as we find it in the later Lutheran Dogmaticians."[68] Pedersen puts the matter differently, and perhaps not at all misleadingly, when he says that Luther had no definite "doctrine" or "theory" of inspiration at all but rather a belief in inspiration.[69] By that he means that Luther never explained how Scripture is God's Word but merely believed it. But that Luther believed and affirmed what at a much later date came to be called verbal inspiration—that he believed, confessed, and taught that everything in Scripture and every single word of Scripture is God's Word—is subject to no doubt. And if he did not have a "doctrine" of inspiration, as Pedersen says, that means only that he did not try to explain philosophically, psychologically, or in any other way *how* (*pōs*) Scripture was the Word of God, though he affirmed at the same time *that* (*hoti*) it was so.

Since the Holy Spirit is the author of Scripture, since He spoke through the prophets and the apostles, since Scripture is "His Book," through the Scriptures He preaches and speaks to the world.[70] Scripture is the clearest and most lucid book in all the world.[71] "The Holy Spirit is the most simple writer and speaker in heaven and earth; therefore His words have only one sense, the most simple one which we call the literal sense."[72] To Luther, the intrinsic clarity of Scripture, which is a corollary of its divine origin and the result of it, was a fundamental principle for both exegesis and the entire theological enterprise. Luther was talking here about the intrinsic clarity of Scripture, that Scripture "in itself is

---

67. *WI*, 9:770.
68. W. Bodamer, "Luther's Stellung zur Lehre von der Verbalinspiration," *Theologische Quartalschrift* 34 (1936): 244. See Althaus, *The Theology of Martin Luther* (Philadelphia: Fortress, 1966), p. 50 passim; Eugene Klug, *From Luther to Chemnitz* (Amsterdam: J. H. Kok N. V. Kampen, 1971), pp. 17-38. Bodamer's presentation of Luther's doctrine is the most extensive in terms of documentation, especially from Luther's exegetical works, ever written. He has unearthed over a thousand citations from Luther clearly asserting that the Bible is the Word of God; over one hundred of those are found in this article. I have drawn extensively from his data, which is according to *WI*.
69. Ibid., p. 202.
70. *WI*, 2:1664; 3:358, 1907; 9:349, 356; 14:349.
71. *WI*, 22:577.
72. *WA*, 7:650; cf. 7:638.

the most certain, easy to understand, clear and consistent of all books; thus all other books are proved by it, judged by it, and illumined by it."[73]

In that and many other contexts Luther clearly was speaking of the clarity of Scripture *as it is written*, not its capacity to convince us of the truthfulness of its message (which Luther of course also believed).[74] *Per sese*, Scripture is a light, like the sun, objectively and cognitively clear, so that all may understand it. That was what Luther called the "external clarity" that exists in the Scriptural message itself as opposed to the internal clarity of Scripture that occurs in the believer when the Spirit of God convinces him of its message.[75] That external clarity of Scripture is really a very simple concept for Luther; he referred simply to the fact that the words of the Bible, as they stand and in their context, are not equivocal, solecistic, or obscure but understandable and lucid to the reader. That does not imply that there are not grammatical, contextual, and historical problems related to the text that will engage scholars at times in debate.[76] Nor was he contradicting himself when he said that Christ was the center of Scripture and understanding the gospel was essential for the exegete to understand the Scriptures at all.[77] The fact that we do not know the meaning of a *hapax legomenon* or cannot identify a geographical location does not impugn the intrinsic clarity of the book. That an understanding of the gospel and of the distinction between law and gospel are essential to a correct hermeneutical approach to the Scriptures is simply a datum that is drawn from the clear

73. *WA*, 797: per sese certissima, facillima, apertissima, sui ipsius interpres, omnium omnia probans, judicans et illuminans.
74. H. Ostergard-Nielsen, *Scriptura sacra et viva vox* (Munich: C. Kaiser, 1957), p. 24, says that Luther's notion of biblical clarity meant that the Scriptures had the ability to make their message clear and to convince one of their assertions. Pedersen (p. 52) calls that theory "metaphysical theology" and accuses Ostergard-Nielsen of confusing the objective authority of Scripture with its inner persuasive power.
75. *WA*, 12:439; 18:609.
76. *WA*, 18:606:22: Hoc sane fateor, esse multa loca in scripturis obscura et abstrusa, non ob maiestatem rerum sed ob ignorantiam vocabulorum et grammaticae, sed quae nihil impediant scientiam omnium rerum in scripturis; cf. 18:653:30.
77. *WA*, 18:606:24.

Scriptures themselves; it is not an imposition of a foreign hermeneutical principle employed to clarify their message.

The practice of pious exegesis, which was Luther's greatest love, was predicated on the fact that Scripture was God's own cognitive and clear language about God. That he yielded always and without qualification to the conclusions and findings of his exegesis was predicated on his conviction that Scripture was God's Word and carried with it God's authority and truthfulness as it conveyed God's saving message of the gospel.[78] As we now proceed to examine what Luther believed about the authority and truthfulness of Scripture, we shall easily perceive how essential his notion of the external clarity of Scripture was to his thoughts on biblical authority.

THE DIVINE AUTHORITY OF SCRIPTURE

In the hundreds of contexts where Luther spoke of the divinity and majesty of the Scriptures, where he affirmed that Scripture was God's Word and book and that God speaks (present tense) in and through it so that when Scripture speaks God speaks to us, Luther was *eo ipso* referring to the authority and infallibility of Scripture. He was, in fact, expressing himself in just such a fashion about Scripture for the very purpose of affirming its divine authority and infallibility and applying that to the reader. For the affirmation of the divine authority and nature of Scripture was never an end in itself to Luther, but was always for the sake of the gospel (as we have seen) and to assure the reader that the cognitive gospel presented in Scripture comes with divine power and infallible authority. The statements of Luther's we have studied thus far do not tell us the exact nature and function of biblical authority and infallibility. We shall now examine some of Luther's statements where he directly addresses that topic.

Luther inherited his basic notion of biblical authority from the

78. I must add at this point that not only the "external clarity" that we have been talking about but also the "internal clarity," namely, that the believer is enlightened and convinced by the Word of Scripture, is predicated on the fact that Scripture is in fact the Word of the Holy Spirit. *WA*, 18:609:5ff.

Fathers, Occamists,[79] and Nominalists,[80] but he did not inherit their hermeneutics. Already in Leipzig in 1519 (and before) he adhered, like the Nominalists, to a principle of *sola scriptura*, according to which neither the church nor pope possessed authority that could militate against the authority of the Bible.[81] However, the papists of his day also believed in the divine authority of Scripture to prove doctrine, as did the scholastics before them,[82] that is, in principle. In practice they insisted that only an authoritative interpretation of the divine Word could be accepted. Thus they made Scripture a "waxen nose" that could be turned any way the authoritative interpreter pleased.[83] That was the way the pope became lord over Scripture—by his refusal to bow to the clear and plain *sensus literalis* whenever it did not suit him and by his willful and bad interpretative propensities.[84] Such was the situation when Luther entered church history. In a highly significant statement Luther described that deplorable situation.

> All admit that Jesus says, John 10:35; "The Scripture cannot be broken," and that its authority is absolutely inviolable, so that no man may contradict or deny it. That premise, or *major*, that the perfect knowledge of God, theology, must be derived from Scripture all and everyone admits. But where the *minor* is concerned, the soldiers at once make a farce out of Scripture through their arbitrary glosses and distinctions, so that the power and authority of all Scripture goes by the board. For today, too, you cannot prove anything to the pope or any Thomist by Scripture, even though they acknowledge the authority of Scripture. "Let us not rend the coat," they say, "but cast lots for it," (John 19:24). For is that not playing a game of chance with Scripture, if one deals with it arbitrarily and twists it according to his whim? Do not our teachers of the universities take unto themselves the right to interpret Scripture? And it has reached such a pass that they laugh at him who

79. Reu, pp. 133-36; Fr. Kropatschek, *Das Schriftprinzip der lutherischen Kirche*, I, Die Vorgeschichte das Erbe des Mittelalters (Leipzig: A. Deichertsche, 1904), pp. 438ff.
80. Reinhold Seeberg, *Lehrbuch der Dogmengeschichte* (Leipzig: A. Deichert, 1930), 4:724.
81. *WA*, 5:643, 645.
82. *WA*, 10:I:633.
83. *WA*, 5:208; 6:305; 46:464. See Pedersen, p. 48.
84. *WA*, 5:646; 7:98, 100.

simply quotes Scripture, while they, as they say, operate with irrefutable arguments from reason. This is the game they play. They do not teach what Scripture demands, but each one tries his luck as to how he may square Scripture with his own ideas, how much of Scripture he can win. And in this game the pope is—and he deserves it—the chief of the soldiers, for he has passed a law, binding upon all, that it is his prerogative and his alone to interpret Scripture definitively. Others may interpret the Scripture, but only magisterially, by way of disputation and investigation, but not in such a way that the interpretation is final. Well, he plays with his partners in such a way that the die must fall in his favor, in that he alone has the right to interpret Scripture.[85]

That statement indicates that to Luther the issue in his day with the papists was centered in the *sola scriptura*, not in the mere question of authority. And the *sola scriptura* principle is violated by any intrusion on the plain authoritative meaning of the Scripture. To Luther, it was simply axiomatic that if Scripture is not alone the source and norm of Christian doctrine, it is not the source and norm at all; any violation of the *sola scriptura* principle is a violation of biblical authority per se.[86]

It was not long before another equally dangerous adversary to the *sola scriptura* raised his ugly head, the Enthusiast, who too imposed his own arbitrary interpretations on the Scriptures when the spirit moved him. The authority crisis that Luther faced so steadfastly was centered in those two parallel antitheses to the *sola scriptura*.[87] And so from very early in his career, we find Luther defending the Word of God and its authority above pope, church, and councils.[88] Commenting on Galatians 1:9, he stated: "It is damnable to think that the pope is lord and arbiter over Scripture or that the church has any power over Scripture. The pope and the church are to approve and commend and preach the Scrip-

---

85. *W2*, 4:307ff; cf. *W2*, 18:425ff.
86. Luther was followed in that understanding of the *sola scriptura* by all Lutherans, cf. John Andrew Quenstedt, *Theologia didactico-polemica, sive systema theologiae* (Leipzig, 1715), P. 1, C. 3, S. 2, q. 1 (1:49).
87. See Smalcald Articles, III, VIII; cf. Robert Preus, "Biblical Authority in the Lutheran Confessions," *Concordia Journal* 4 (1978): 16-24.
88. *WA*, 6:505-6; 9:561; 17:I:99.

tures, but that does not mean that they are over Scripture."[89] The church of God has divine authority only when it follows the Word of God, according to Luther.[90]

All that corresponds with Luther's larger doctrine of the Word that we have already touched upon. To him, the church lives by the Word of God and is thus bound by that Word.[91] The authority of God does not somehow come upon the Word in an event, situation, or ecclesiastical interpretation but is intrinsic to the Word as Word of God. And so the church is completely under that Word and can in no way manipulate it. "The church does not create the Word, but is created by the Word."[92] Thus nothing should be presented in the church unless it is proved by the authority of both Testaments and agrees with Scripture.[93] Luther did not view biblical authority as some legalistic club that coerced the church into obedience but as God's own voice in her midst to lead and bless her. God's Word accomplishes everything good in the church, Luther insisted, even though we sleep and are having a good time.[94] God keeps and protects His church through the Word.[95] And so the Word is the most valuable possession the church or Christians can have, worth more than angels, saints, and all creatures.[96]

Luther's principle of *sola scriptura* outlaws not only the authority of pope, church, and council as sources and norms of doctrine but also human reason and experience. Whatever our senses or experience may say to the contrary, we must always yield to Scripture, he maintained.[97] "God's Word is not for jesting. If you cannot understand it, take off your hat before it."[98]

> In matters of Faith that pertain to the divine essence and will and to our salvation we must close our eyes and our ears and all our

89. *WA*, 41:I:119; cf. 40:III:435.
90. *WA*, 40:431.
91. *WA*, 6:561; cf. *WA*, 7:131.
92. *WA*, 8:597; cf. Reu, p. 36.
93. *WA*, 4:180.
94. *W2*, 20:21.
95. *W2*, 15:2506.
96. *W2*, 18:1322.
97. *WA*, 4:517.
98. *WA*, 20:571.

senses and just hear and observe diligently what and how Scripture speaks. We must wrap ourselves completely in the Word and follow it without assessing our reason.[99]

And so Luther again and again called the Word of Scripture our "touchstone," our "rule."[100] What destroyed all progress at the colloquy with Zwingli at Marburg was, according to Luther, Zwingli's refusal to face up to the clear affirmations of Scripture, though professing, like the papists, adherence to the infallible authority of the Bible.[101]

But did not Luther himself employ reason as he interpreted Scripture? Of course he did. He recognized reason, even in a fallen sinner, as a gift of God, as he said in his little catechism. And he did not despise logic for one moment. Neither did he eschew a ministerial use of reason in the exegetical and theological task.[102] But reason cannot sit in judgment of Scripture.[103] It has been said that Luther's great confession at Wurms placed reason alongside Scripture as a source of doctrine. He wrote, "Unless I shall be convinced by testimonies of the Scriptures and by clear reason . . . I am conquered by the writings [in Scripture] cited by me, and my conscience is captive to the Word of God."[104] Here, however, Luther was referring to a regenerate reason that simply attempts to understand and submit to the Word, not reason in any independent sense.

Luther derived his doctrine of biblical authority from the divine origin of Scripture as God's Word. He argued, "Whoever concedes that the evangelists wrote the word of God, with him we will

99. *WA*, 23:699.
100. *WA*, 33:304; 36:501; 37:44; 46:780.
101. Reu, pp. 54-55. See also Hermann Sasse, *This Is My Body* (Minneapolis: Augsburg, 1959), pp. 215-300; cf. *WA*, 11:434; 23:119.
102. *WA*, 50:654ff. For Luther's ideas on the use of reason see Bengt Hagglund, *Theologie und Philosophie bei Luther und in der Occamistischen Tradition* (Lund: CWK Gleerups Forlag, 1955), pp. 115ff. See also Brian Albert Gerrish, *Grace and Reason* (Oxford: Oxford U. Press, 1962), pp. 28ff.
103. *WA*, 51:123, 192; cf. 51:194.
104. *WA*, 7:838: Nisi convictus fuero testimoniis scripturarum aut ratione evident . . . victus sum scripturis a me adductis et capta conscientia in verbis dei. . . . See Reu, pp. 28-35; Hans Preuss, *Die Entwicklung des Schriftprinzips bei Luther bis zur Leipziger Disputation* (Leipzig: R. Voigtlanders Verlag, 1901), p. 62.

meet. Whoever denies this, with him I will not even speak. For in such a case he has no part in Christian discussion. We must not even discuss things with one who denies the foundations (*principia*) of the faith."[105] And so against the sentences of the Fathers, against the authority of men, against angels and devils, Luther placed the Word alone. There he took his stand as a theologian. In that Word he boasted and defied Thomists, Sophists, Henry VIII, and all the gates of hell. And why? Because "God's Word is above all; divine majesty is on my side."[106]

The authority of Scripture, which springs from its divine origin, was infallible to Luther. Commenting on 1 Peter 3:15 he wrote:

> When the unbelievers and adversaries argue and say, You preach that the teaching of men should not be held, even though Peter and Paul, yes, and Christ Himself, were men—when you hear such people who are so completely blind and hardened that they deny that what Christ and apostles spoke and wrote is the Word of God and who have doubts concerning it, then just keep silent, do not speak one word to them, let them go their way. Just say this: I will give You ample evidence from Scripture. If you believe this, fine. If not, be on your way.[107]

And so Scripture, because it is God's wisdom and Word, is the final, divine, and infallible authority in matters of theology and Christian doctrine. "We must maintain this, that everything that we praise as an article of faith is confirmed clearly and purely and with evident testimony from Scripture."[108] "Paul takes them all together," Luther wrote, "himself, an angel from heaven, teachers on earth and masters of all kinds, and he subjects them to the Holy Scripture. Scripture must reign as queen, all must obey her and be subject to her, not teachers, judges and arbiters over her."[109]

For Luther, the authority of Scripture meant that when Paul or Isaiah spoke, God spoke. Deriving its authority from its divine

105. *WA, Tr.* 3:2884a.
106. *W2,* 19:337.
107. *W2,* 9:1238.
108. *WA* 6:560; cf. 6:321ff.
109. *WA,* 40:I:102.

authorship, Scripture always has a divine authority. In practice that means that Scripture is the *principium cognoscendi* of theology, as the later Lutherans were wont to say,[110] the source of everything we can know or say about God. All doctrine must be proved by Scripture, the divinely authoritative Word. The later, explicitly articulated doctrine that Scripture was the *principium cognoscendi* was clearly adumbrated by Luther; he insisted that Scripture was authoritative specifically as a cognitive source of theology.

> Therefore nothing but the divine words are to be the first principles (*prima principia*) for Christiano. All human words, however, are conclusions which are deduced from them and must again be subjected to them and approved by them. . . . If this were not true, why should Augustine and the holy fathers, whenever they contradict each other, go back to the Holy Scriptures as the first principles of truth (*ad sacras literas seu prima principia veritatis*) and illumine and approve by their light and trustworthiness their own dark and uncertain views? By doing this they teach that the divine words are more understandable and certain than the words of all men, even their own. . . . I do not want to be honored as one who is more learned than all; but this I desire, that Scripture alone rule as queen, and that it not be explained through my spirit or other men's spirit but be understood by itself and in its own spirit.[111]

Again Luther said that the first principles of all Christians are based upon the divine Word and that all theological conclusions are to be drawn from that Word.[112] And so Scripture was authoritative as a *principium*, as the cognitive source of all theology in the church.

At this point I must mention two gross misunderstandings of Luther's doctrine of biblical authority and comment on them. First is the caricature that Luther did not adhere—or did so only inconsistently and at times—to the so-called proof-text method of

110. See Preus, 1:256-62.
111. *WA*, 6:506.
112. *WA*, 7:98.

theologizing.[113] How do we respond to that bizarre allegation? Certainly, one can show that Luther on thousands and thousands of occasions proved his doctrine from Scripture, that is, from pericopes and specific passages of Scripture. And on thousands of occasions he showed that one clear Bible verse is enough to establish an article of faith. And Luther insisted that each article of faith must have its own proof, that is, its own biblical basis. That was one of the chief issues with Zwingli at the colloquy in Marburg. Zwingli had used passages from Scripture that did not deal with the Lord's Supper to mitigate the force of passages that did, according to Luther. Luther's principle against such reductionistic exegesis was the following: "Every article of faith is in itself its own principle and receives no corroboration [proof] by means of another [article of faith]."[114] If one will not accept every article of faith because of itself, that is, because God has revealed it clearly in Holy Writ, he despises God, so far as Luther was concerned, and in the end is in danger of rejecting everything God has said in His Word. "He who makes God into a liar in one of His words and blasphemes, saying that it is unimportant if He is despised and made out to be a liar, blasphemes God in His entirety and considers all blasphemy a trifling thing."[115]

Luther clearly inveighed against anyone who would only at times and inconsistently use the proof-text method in his theological work. To Luther everything was to be believed and followed in Scripture or nothing, "For whoever despises a single word of God does not regard any as important."[116] And again he wrote:

113. For instance, Joseph Sittler (p. 25) seems to think that only in certain extraordinary situations, such as in his controversy over the meaning of the words of institution of the Lord's Supper, did Luther insist "upon a literal acceptance of the biblical words." Sittler accuses anyone who attempts to argue from such extraordinary situations that Luther was committed to the proof-text method of using an "apologetic which triumphantly seizes upon a detached [sic] word of Luther, brushes aside all historical and theological context by which such a word is to be understood—and then flails about with a chance epigram as if it were a sufficient club to silence all enquiry." I rather suspect that those last bombastic words are meant to describe those of us who affirm that Luther, like every other theologian of his day, believed in *dicta probantia*.
114. Walter Koehler, *Das Marburger Religionsgespräch 1529* (Leipzig: M. Heinsius Nachfolger Eger & Sievers, 1929), p. 34.
115. *WA*, 23:85.
116. *WA*, 26:449.

And whoever is so bold that he ventures to accuse God of fraud and deception in a single word and does so willfully and again and again after he has been warned and instructed once or twice will likewise certainly venture to accuse God of fraud and deception in all of His words. Therefore it is true, absolutely and without exception that everything is believed or nothing is believed [*omnia vel nihil redari*]. The Holy Spirit does not allow Himself to be separated or divided so that He should teach and cause to be believed one doctrine rightly and another falsely.[117]

According to Luther, the Christian theologian simply repeats and teaches what the prophets and apostles have said.[118] That means that every article of faith must have a *sedes*. As far as Luther was concerned, if one "pooh poohs" a *sedes* for one article of faith, he despises the whole of Scripture. Against the Sacramentarians he wrote,

> They are revealing what kind of spirit is in them and how much they think of God's Word, ridiculing these precious words [the words of institution] as five poor, miserable words; they do not believe that these are God's words. Or if they believe that they are God's words, they would not call them miserable, poor words, but would prize one little word and letter more highly than the whole world.[119]

In the same vein Luther said again in one of his better known statements concerning the authority of Scripture, "It will not do to make articles of faith out of the holy fathers' words or works. Otherwise what they ate, how they dressed, and what kind of houses they lived in would have to become articles of faith—as happened in the case of relics. This means that the Word of God shall establish articles of faith and no one else, not even an angel."[120] But how else can the written Word establish articles of faith except as individual statements, pericopes, *sedes* are interpreted to yield the articles of faith? How else would Luther have

117. *WA*, 54:158; cf. 32:59; 50:269.
118. *W2*, 3:1890.
119. *W2*, 20:1040.
120. *SA*, II:II:15.

affirmed the article of justification by faith, for instance, except on the basis of *dicta probantia* such as Romans 1:16; 3:28; Galatians 2:20; and others? Certainly such an article of faith cannot be proved by the whole of Scripture or by passages not dealing with justification. To assert that Luther did not use the proof-text method is nonsense and renders his doctrine of biblical authority meaningless and inapplicable.

A second misrepresentation of Luther's principle of biblical authority portrays him as teaching that the authority of Scripture resides in its content, or message (the gospel), rather than in the very words, or divine form, of Scripture.[121] That notion has been taught by Lutherans and attributed to Luther in many different forms until our very day, when it is considered "Lutheran" to derive the authority of Scripture, or its infallibility, from its gospel-content rather than from its origin.[122] Like the first misrepresentation, this portrayal of Luther's position describes him as placing biblical authority in something other than the biblical words themselves. Thus the Bible itself is not the normative authority for all doctrine, but the biblical gospel is. Of course, to Luther the biblical gospel (also as it was preached from the pulpit and taught in the church) was the power of God unto salvation, and he extolled the power of that gospel in his writings.[123] But again and again Luther made clear that to him the normative authority of Scripture resided not in its subject matter, the gospel, but in its words. Thus he based all his theology on the text of Scripture as such. The very sentences and assertions and words of Scripture, in their proper context, were authoritative to him.[124] "A single letter,

---

121. See I. A. Dorner, *History of the Development of the Doctrine of the Person of Christ*, trans. W. L. Alexander and D. W. Simon (Edinburgh: T. & T. Clark, 1878), 1:231.
122. Kent S. Knutson, "The Authority of Scripture," *Concordia Theological Monthly* 40 (1969): 160, 163 passim; Edmund Schlink, *Theology of the Lutheran Confessions*, trans. Paul F. Koehneke and Herbert J. A. Bouman (Philadelphia: Muhlenberg Press, 1961), p. 29. For the opposite view, which shows the reductionistic tendency in such a misrepresentation of Luther's authority principle, see Holsten Fagerberg, *A New Look at the Lutheran Confessions*, trans. Gene Lund (St. Louis: Concordia, 1972), pp. 30ff.; Gerhard Maier, *The End of the Historical-Critical Method*, trans. Edwin W. Leverenz and Rudolph F. Norden (St. Louis: Concordia, 1977), pp. 27ff.
123. *WA*, 47:120; cf. 37:437.
124. *W2*, 14:435.

yea, a single tittle, of Scripture counts for more than heaven and earth."[125]

The view attributed to Luther that Scripture is authoritative by virtue of its evangelical content, rather than its divine origin, suggests that some of Scripture may be less authoritative than the rest or that certain teachings of Scripture are not divinely authoritative at all. That is surely not Luther's view, as we have seen. It is true, of course, and of very great significance that Luther saw certain books of Scripture to be of more value than others and the article concerning Christ and His atonement to be the central teaching of Scripture.[126] But at the same time he insisted that nothing in the Scriptures was vain or contemptuous. Commenting on Psalm 16:10, he said that there are no insignificant matters (*levicula*) in Scripture.[127] He wrote on another occasion, "It is impossible that there is a single letter in Paul which the entire church should not follow and observe."[128] And though much in the Mosaic law applies only to the Jews of the Old Testament,[129] nevertheless everything in Moses is in some way edifying to the Christian community.[130] And so the authority of Scripture to Luther was the authority of the words of Scripture as such; it was a plenary authority, and it was absolute. Every assertion of Scripture, however near or far from its gospel center, was an authority for Christian belief; every command of Scripture, if it applies to the New Testament Christian, was an authority for action in life.

THE INFALLIBILITY OF SCRIPTURE

As we address ourselves to Luther's notion of biblical infallibility (that Scripture cannot err), we must make two observations by way of introduction. First, as we have seen, Luther understood the God of grace and salvation as a speaking God. He spoke to mankind through the prophetic and apostolic Scriptures that are His Word. The human writers of the Scriptures were His instruments

125. *W2*, 9:650.
126. *Er.*, 40:324ff.; 48:18; 50:26-29; *Er. Lat.*, 10:137.
127. *WA*, 5:463; *Tr.* 1:736.
128. *W2*, 19:20.
129. *W2*, 3:9; 12:1037; 20:146.
130. *W2*, 20:153.

(*organum spiritus sancti*).[131] To hear and read the Scriptures, therefore, is nothing else than to hear God.[132] No wonder, therefore, that the Word of God was so precious to Luther; it came from "the mouth of God" and was "written for us" in order to serve and save us.[133] Thus the inerrancy of the Bible, or its truthfulness, was a corollary of its authority for Luther. "In theology one thing only is necessary, that we hear and believe and conclude in our heart: God is truthful, however absurd what He says in His Word may seem to our reason."[134] That truthfulness of God in His Word, of the biblical message, was of crucial importance to Luther because the message itself was so important to him. "I let you in your hostility cry that the Scripture contradicts itself, ascribing righteousness now to faith, and at other times to works. But it is impossible that Scripture contradict itself; it only seems so to foolish, coarse, and hardened hypocrites."[135] It is clear that to Luther the notion of an authoritative Word of God that nevertheless contains errors or contradictions would be a cruel piece of nonsense.

Second, Luther's insistence that the *bonus textualis* not merely determine the *sensus literalis* of the text of Scripture but accept it in spite of all other considerations and difficulties can only be explained by his total adherence to biblical inerrancy, and that as a basic principle of biblical interpretation. Why else would he insist on the real presence of Christ's body and blood in the sacrament of the altar? Why else would he insist that the right hand of God is everywhere and thus Christ is omnipresent in His state of exaltation also according to His human nature?[136] To Luther, the exegete is constantly engaged in taking his reason captive to the written Word against the sensible dictates of reason, experience,

131. *WA*, 3:262.
132. *WA*, 3:14, 41, 451; 4:318.
133. *WA*, 4:535.
134. *WA*, 40:II:593.
135. *WA*, 40:I:420.
136. *W2*, 47:213; *TR*, 4:4812; 26:244, 346, 437.

and all evidence.[137] We shall have occasion to come back to that subject a bit later.

Luther's view of the truthfulness, or inerrancy (to use a later term), of Scripture is a very clear and straightforward one. He simply believed in the truthfulness of the assertions of the biblical text.[138] He wrote, "You must follow straight after Scripture and accept it and speak not one syllable against it, for it is God's mouth."[139] And what will be the result when you follow such a procedure? You will find that "the Scriptures have never erred,"[140] that "the Scriptures cannot err,"[141] that "it is certain that the Scripture cannot disagree with itself,"[142] that "it is impossible that Scripture should contradict itself; it only appears so to senseless and obstinate hypocrites"[143] "for it is established by God's Word that God does not lie, nor does his Word lie."[144] No, "it is cursed unbelief and the odious flesh which would not permit us to see and know that God speaks to us in Scripture and that it is God's Word, but tells us that it is the word merely of Isaiah, Paul, or some other mere man, who has not created heaven and earth."[145] We are not all apostles, Luther insisted; they were infallible teachers sent by God, but not we; they were unable "to err or be mistaken in the faith."[146]

From the quotations above, which could be greatly multi-

---

137. *WA*, 56:329:27: Sapientia carnis aduersaria est verbo Dei, verbum autem Dei est immutabile et insuperabile. Ideo necesse est sapientiam carnis mutari et suam formam reliquere ac formam verbi suscipere. Quod fit, dum per fidem seipsam captiuat et destruit, conformat se verbo, credens verbum esse verum, se vero falsam. Cf. *WA*, 16:594:36.

138. His view of inerrancy or truthfulness has nothing to do with the transmission of the text. Luther not only recognized errors and the possibility of errors of transmission (like any humanistic lower critic of his day) but even suggested—sometimes too facilely—copyists' errors to solve vexing problems that could not be solved any other way. For instance, in reference to the seeming contradiction between Acts 13:20 and 1 Kings 6:1, Luther suggested (*W2*, 4:600) that the copyist might well have written *tetrakosiois* for *triakosiois*; cf, *W2*, 14:491. Such a practice only confirms his commitment to the inerrancy of the original text of Scripture.

139. *W2*, 19:337.

140. *W2*, 15:481.

141. *W2*, 19:1073.

142. *W2*, 20:798; cf. 14:491; 15:1481; 19:1073.

143. *W2*, 9:356.

144. *W2*, 20:789.

145. *W2*, 9:1800.

146. *WA*, 39:I:48.

plied,[147] we can draw three conclusions. First, Luther believed all the assertions of Scripture to be truthful, not merely those that were central or seemed to be of prime importance. Second, he believed in absolute, a priori inerrancy, that is, the infallibility of all biblical assertions. Notice how often he said that Scripture cannot err, cannot disagree with itself. Third, his notion of the nature of biblical truthfulness is the simple, unsophisticated notion that (1) Scripture does not affirm anything that is contrary to fact, and (2) Scripture does not contradict itself. Such a notion of the nature of inerrancy is utterly essential for the theologian—and Luther made that plain—if, on the basis of Scripture, he is ever to arrive at a knowledge of the truth and thus proclaim the true doctrine.

But what about the seeming discrepancies and contradictions of the Scripture? Did Luther, like an obscurantist, deny or ignore them? By no means. He recognized those difficulties and tried to cope with them. Commenting on Peter's denial in John, Luther wrote,[148] "John creates a confusion here. . . ."[149] Again he said in his comments on Matthew 27:9,[150] "Matthew does not hit the right place in his Scripture quotation. . . ."[151] But in none of those cases did Luther solve the problem by crying "error" and thus attribute to Scripture what he had consistently denied. Rather, he let the difficulty rest, if he could not solve it. That is the role of good scholarship, he believed, and pious respect for the Scriptures and their Author, the Holy Spirit. Concerning John 2:13-16 Luther commented:

> Here the question arises how the statements of Matthew and John harmonize with each other. . . . These are questions and remain questions which I will not solve. But nothing much depends upon it. What do I care that there are many sharp and very clever people who raise all kinds of questions and demand an answer on every single point.[152]

147. See Pieper, p. 281, passim. Reu, pp. 65-102.
148. *WA*, 28:269.
149. Cf. *WA*, 46:726.
150. *WA*, 23:6:42.
151. Cf. *W2*, 1:721: "Here in the case of Abraham 60 years are lost. . . ."
152. *W2*, 7:1780.

Such Bible difficulties simply did not threaten the authority and integrity of Scripture, as far as Luther was concerned. In some cases what appears to be a difficulty or error in Scripture represents in fact only poor exegesis or hermeneutics on the part of the interpreter. For instance, if we should demand that the evangelists observe strict chronological order as they record things, there will indeed appear to be discrepancies in Scripture. But the evangelists do not observe order in their chronology.[153] "Let it be as it will, whether it be before or after, one or two occurrences; our faith does not suffer thereby." In his Genesis commentary Luther noticed that according to Genesis 11·11, it appears as though the chronology of Arpachshad was confused. He commented as follows, "One offers one solution, another offers another. But in the first place we will not be hurt at all if we cannot find a perfect solution. . . . ." A bit later Luther added the words "For it is certain that Scripture does not lie."[154]

If Luther's solution, or reaction, to the apparent discrepancies within the Bible seems to be somewhat cavalier, it is not simply because he was a careless exegete; it is because he was so utterly convinced that the Scriptures are reliable and do not contradict themselves. Because of that, he did not really feel bound to defend the Scriptures on every issue. Furthermore, Luther knew how difficult it was for a sixteenth-century exegete to get at the immediate context and intention of texts written long ago. But perhaps most important, Luther realized how prone to error he himself was, how prone his flesh was to draw wrong inferences from Scripture, how prone he was to solve problems in the wrong way—especially when the Scriptures speak of the great mysteries of faith that are so hard for even the sanctified Christian to comprehend and apply. On one occasion he wrote:

> I am much displeased with myself and I despise myself because I know that all that the Scriptures say about Christ is true and nothing can be greater or more important or sweeter or the source of greater joy than this; it should intoxicate me with the greatest joy because I see that Scripture is consonant with itself in all and

153. *W2*, 7:1781.
154. *W2*, 1:714.

through all and agrees with itself in such a way that it is impossible to doubt the truth and certainty of such a weighty matter in any detail. And yet I am hindered by the malice of my flesh and I am "bound by the law of sin" that I cannot let this gift permeate into my limbs and bones and even into my marrow as I should like.[155]

The inerrancy of Scripture was of immense importance to Luther because the gospel of Scripture was of such immense importance, and that gospel permeates all of Scripture. When he dealt with Scripture, Luther felt that he was dealing with God's Word and salvation. And so in standing before that Word he could only say, "I am bound. . . . The text stands there too mightily."[156] On the face of it Scripture seems to be a poor, miserable, unholy, contemptible book, unworthy of the Holy Spirit. And so every carnal person is offended by the Scriptures' simplicity. But Scripture mortifies the flesh and speaks contrary to our way of thinking. That is the struggle that every Christian exegete finds himself involved in as he reads and interprets the divine Word of Scripture.[157]

Luther's intense belief in the utter truthfulness of Scripture was in total harmony with his idea of revelation and his *theologia crucis*. The center of the Scriptures and of God's revelation to us, according to Luther, is Christ—not in His majesty[158] but in His humanity and humiliation, His cross and death.[159] But in just that revelation of Christ and His cross is the gospel, the only possible good news for fallen man.[160] For in His humiliation and death Christ atoned for our sins, and therefore we are justified by His grace through faith in Him. And where does that faith in God as He really is and as He has graciously revealed Himself have its source? In the Word of revelation, Scripture.[161] And so faith is directed toward the Word whose central message is the crucified Christ, a message that is foolishness to the natural man, which the natural man can-

155. *WA*, 40:III:652.
156. *W2*, 15:2050.
157. *WA*, 16:82:5; *WA, DB*, 8:10:24.
158. *WA*, 40:I:75:9; 43:403:20.
159. *WA*, 4:153:27; 14:97:2; 40:I:76:9; 56:5:9, 414:13.
160. See Pedersen, p. 99.
161. *WA*, 3:279:30; 29:199:3; 56:240:15. See Pedersen, pp. 17, 140 for more references.

not believe by his own reason and strength. But by the grace of the Holy Spirit we believe just that Word, that offensive Word that seems so wrong, so absurd, so error-ridden. Commenting on Galatians 3:6 Luther wrote, "This is the way faith speaks, God, I believe you when you speak to me. But what does God say? Impossible things, lies, stupid things, unsound, abominable, heretical, devilish things—if you consult your reason."[162]

The fact that the very central message of God's revelation to man, the gospel of justification, goes against the grain gives the Christian a context and posture for reading Scripture in the light of its utter truthfulness. For as we have seen, neither pope, nor church, nor Fathers, nor reason, nor experience judges Scripture; but Scripture is the judge, judge even—and especially—when it speaks of the article on which the church stands or falls, the sinner's justification before God for Christ's sake. And so the good theologian not only seeks the intended sense of Scripture and none other but also sticks with that intended sense, all evidence to the contrary notwithstanding. And the centrality of the work of Christ in Scripture, far from becoming an interpretative cipher that makes inerrancy an unnecessary *theologoumenon* and hermeneutically unworkable, lends support to the inerrancy of Scripture and is a basic hermeneutical principle for serious exegesis. For Luther, the divine form of Scripture and its evangelical center and content, the infallibility (truthfulness) of Scripture and its power, the normative authority of Scripture and its causative authority, the formal principle of theology and its material principle, all entail

---

162. (*Nam fides ita dicit: ego credo tibi Deo loquenti. Quid loquitur Deus? Impossibilia, mendatia, stulta, infirma, absurda, abominanda, haeretica et diabolica, si rationem consultas.*) Cf. *WA*, 10:III:23; 14:330:4; 40:I:360:2; 43:671:32ff. It is not our province to understand the hows and whys of Scripture, but we are simply to accept what it says. *WA*, 3:516:39; 4:511:11ff. For instance, Luther said that if you cannot understand how God could create the world in six days, let it stand and "accord the Holy Spirit the honor that He is more learned than you" *W2*, 3:21. And in another context when he was unable to harmonize some of the chronology connected with Abraham, Luther wrote, "I conclude the matter with the humble confession of my own ignorance, for it is only the Holy Spirit Who knows and understands everything" *W2*, 1:721.

each other, belong together, and work together.[163] What I have just said is the only conclusion that fits the data we have just surveyed.

CONCLUSION

We have now concluded our brief study of Luther's doctrine of biblical infallibility in the context of his notion concerning the divine origin, authority, and truthfulness of Scripture. It is my hope that on the basis of this study, which merely reviewed well-known data and traversed well-known paths of Luther research, the reader will understand and appreciate not only that Luther believed in biblical infallibility but what his teaching really was. My conclusions on the basis of the data are the same as those of Wilhelm Walther and Michael Reu and, among dogmaticians, Adolph Hoehnecke and Francis Pieper. I make no apology for leaning heavily on the findings of those earlier scholars, especially Reu. No one since him has offered any substantive study of Luther's doctrine of biblical authority on the basis of primary sources. I only regret that the results of his research, which presents all the data pertinent to Luther's position, have not been consulted by so many modern theological dilettantes who, ignoring the caveat mentioned in the introduction to this chapter, have helter skelter consulted often tendential, secondary, and tertiary sources that have found in Luther every whim and theological trend that comes along today from higher criticism to process theology.[164] There is really nothing one can do about that except to

163. The finest discussion of the intimate and necessary relationships of the concepts mentioned above is by Harry Huth, *Gospel and Scripture, The Interrelationship of the Material and Formal Principles in Lutheran Theology* (St. Louis: Concordia, 1972).

164. The best example of such faulty and unscholarly method in recent times is the book by Rogers and McKim, mentioned above. The authors avoid any direct reading of Luther as he addressed himself in thousands of places to the subject of Scripture's authority, power, and intelligibility. They could at least have availed themselves of the *Registerband* of *W2* or the relatively good indexes of the monumental American edition of Luther's works, with their hundreds and hundreds of references to "God's Word" and "Scripture." Equally reprehensible is the fact that the secondary sources used by those authors are the wrong ones, in many cases not those of Luther scholars at all, but systematic theologians or historians whose *tendenz* Rogers and McKim apparently share.

voice the prayer that the present modest contribution to the subject of Luther and the infallibility of Scripture may to some degree counteract the aprioristic subjectivism that marks so much theological scholarship today and renders scholars incapable of analyzing or even describing the data that are—or ought to be—the basis of all their research.

Is Luther's doctrine of biblical authority evangelical? That question, which I think is quite legitimate, is answered affirmatively by most commentators who bother to answer it at all (but for different reasons, not all of which are valid). For instance, the modern proponent of the historical-critical method views Luther through his colored glasses and concludes mistakenly that his view of biblical authority was evangelical because he anticipated a more liberal view of Scripture. But that is to confuse obscurantism with legalism and so-called scholarship with evangelicalism. More subtly, however, such a conclusion is based on the assumption that one's (Luther's) doctrine of biblical authority is evangelical if it is based on the right understanding of Scripture's *form*. That assumption is fallacious. Non-Christian religions have holy books that are deemed to be God-given and inerrant, but such religions know nothing of the Christian gospel. Cults in America, such as the Jehovah Witnesses, have a very high view of Scripture in terms of its authority and inerrancy but reject the biblical gospel. It is not one's doctrine of the *form* of Scripture that marks his position as evangelical but his understanding concerning the *contents* and *goal* of Scripture. If that is true then Luther's bibliology and his doctrine of the Word were indeed evangelical. For as we have shown, he not only believed that the central teaching of Scripture was the evangelical doctrine of justification by grace for Christ's sake through faith, but that Scripture was written for the sake of that gospel. And he believed that that biblical gospel, whether read or preached, was a mighty power not only to offer but also to impart and confer forgiveness, life, and salvation. That is the sense and context in which Luther's approach to Scripture, his doctrine of biblical authority, and his doctrine of the power of the Word are truly evangelical.

Luther affirmed both the *auctoritas normativa* (to which we have been addressing ourselves primarily in this chapter) and the *auctoritas causativa* of Scripture—the causative as well as the normative authority of Scripture. The normative authority of Scripture may be defined as the infallible authority of the Scriptures as a source and norm of all doctrine and teachers in the church. The causative authority of Scripture is the inherent power of the biblical gospel to create faith in the hearts of sinners and to confer forgiveness and eternal life. Those two "authorities," so consistently emphasized by Luther, do not conflict with each other but agree perfectly and work together.[165] Without the former one has no sure word of prophecy, no certain basis for his teaching; without the latter one preaches a gospel that is subject to error or change and has no power to convert. As I read Luther those two strong emphases come through loudly and clearly, almost uniquely among the Reformers (certainly with greater force than in the others), and mark his doctrine of Scripture and its divine authority as truly and eminently evangelical.

165. For the best discussion of that double aspect of Luther's doctrine of biblical authority, see Huth and Maier.

5

John Calvin and the Inerrancy of Holy Scripture

J. I. Packer

This chapter has a threefold aim. First, it seeks to determine what Calvin's view of Scripture actually was, with special reference to points on which scholars have disagreed. Second, it tries to show how Calvin's view relates to the questions that are currently debated among English-speaking evangelicals about biblical inerrancy. Third, it attempts a critique of the account of Calvin's bibliology and the suggestions as to its relevance that Jack Rogers and Donald McKim offered in 1979 in their widely, rather than deeply, learned essay *The Authority and Interpretation of the Bible.*[1]

1. Jack B. Rogers and Donald K. McKim, *The Authority and Interpretation of the Bible: An Historical Approach* (San Francisco: Harper & Row, 1979). A major critical review by John D. Woodbridge ("Biblical Authority: Towards an Evaluation of the Rogers and McKim Proposal") appeared in the *Trinity Journal* 1 (1980): 165-236. McKim replied in *TSF Bulletin*, April 1981. An expanded critique by Woodbridge, *Biblical Authority: A Critique of the Rogers and McKim Proposal*, has been released by Zondervan (1982).

JAMES I. PACKER (D.Phil., Oxford University) is professor of systematic and historical theology at Regent College, Vancouver, British Columbia. He was previously Senior Tutor at Tyndale Hall, Warden of Latimer House, and Assistant Principal of Trinity College in Oxford. His major writings include: *Fundamentalism and the Word of God* (1958), *Evangelism and the Sovereignty of God* (1961), *Knowing God* (1973), *God Has Spoken* (1979), *Knowing Man* (1979), *Beyond the Battle for the Bible* (1980), and *God's Words* (1981). He also served as editor for the *New Bible Dictionary* (1962) and *The Bible Almanac* (1980).

Some preliminary discussion is called for if that threefold aim is to be achieved.

THE MODERN INERRANCY DEBATE

The arguments about inerrancy now in progress among evangelicals are the product of a century's interaction between confessional theology and critical biblical scholarship. The word *inerrancy* (Latin, *inerrantia*) has a long history in Roman Catholic theological vocabulary but became a significant term in American Protestant usage only about a hundred years ago. Previously, the preferred term for expressing the conviction that Scripture never misinforms or misleads was infallibility,[2] but when Presbyterians began to construct reduced accounts of infallibility, those who still wished to confess the Bible's unqualified trustworthiness began to use the language of inerrancy for their purpose.[3] That shift of vocabulary does not seem to reflect any hardening of response to the questions that biblical criticism raised (conservative response to critical skepticism about the factual truth of Scripture had in fact been firmly negative from the start). What it reflected, rather, was recognition that the word *infallibility* was no longer clear enough to express what conservative Protestants still wanted to say to the world about the reliability of biblical affirmations.

However, there was a point about halfway through the nineteenth century when discussion of the truth of Scripture began to be dominated by the agenda, preconceptions, and claims of the historical-biblical criticism that had emerged in Germany, and at that point a watershed really was passed. Formerly, any queries

---

2. The fact that the Westminster Confession speaks of the "infallible truth" of Holy Scripture is no doubt a main reason for that. Presbyterians, who affirmed infallibility without inerrancy at the end of the nineteenth century, included W. Robertson Smith, T. M. Lindsay, and James Denney in Scotland and C. A. Briggs in the USA. Cf. Rogers and McKim, pp. 380-85 on Lindsay, 348-61 on Briggs.

3. It is noteworthy that the famous essay by A. A. Hodge and B. B. Warfield "Inspiration," first published in the *Presbyterian Review* 2 (1881): 225-60, now reprinted with introduction and appendixes by Roger R. Nicole (Grand Rapids: Baker, 1979), which is often treated as the classic statement of inerrancy, does not use the word, but speaks of infallibility only. It looks as if the free use of the term by critics of the older position, e.g., Briggs in *Whither?* (New York: Charles Scribner's Sons, 1889), was an incentive to the orthodox to embrace and defend it.

about the truth of biblical statements had been
attacks on the Bible's theology, made in the interests
tic unbelief. But biblical criticism professed to be conc
with the history and historicity of the records, not with
and its exponents insisted (some perhaps naively, some p
disingenuously) that it was theologically neutral. Calvin, th
himself as sensitive to the historical dimensions of Bible study
any scholar of his day, stands on the farther side of that water
shed. Heresy founded on misreading of Scripture he met in plenty,
but nothing existed in his time like the modern biblical criticism
that finds Scripture rich in errors of fact yet claims to aid faith.
We should not, therefore, ever suppose him to be speaking to anything like the self-styled sheep in wolf's clothing we meet today.

The direct antecedents of the current evangelical debate[4] were:
(1) Dewey M. Beegle's book *The Inspiration of Scripture* (1963,
enlarged and reissued as *Scripture, Tradition and Infallibility*, 1973),
an attack by a professed evangelical on the idea of inerrancy, (2)
the view of Scripture taught (and the use of it modeled) in some
professedly evangelical seminaries during the sixties and seventies,
and (3) Harold Lindsell's strident *Battle for the Bible* (1976), the
first blast of his trumpet against what he saw as the monstrous
regiment of biblical errantists in the modern evangelical world.
Representative reassertions of the mainstream Protestant and,
indeed, historic Christian view of Scripture in relation to current
historical, scientific, and philosophical questions can be found on
a grand scale in Carl F. H. Henry's magnum opus, *God, Revelation
and Authority* (six volumes, 1976-) and more briefly in the Chicago
Statement and other literature produced by the International
Council on Biblical Inerrancy.[5] Lindsell understands inerrancy as

---

4. Cf. J. I. Packer, *Beyond the Battle for the Bible* (Westchester: Cornerstone, 1980),
   pp. 47-50 for a review of the debate.
5. The Chicago Statement can be found in J. I. Packer, *God Has Spoken* (Down-
   ers Grove, Ill.: Inter-Varsity, 1979), pp. 139-53 and in Carl F. H. Henry, *God,
   Revelation and Authority, IV: God Who Speaks and Shows* (Waco: Word, 1979), pp.
   211-19. Other relevant ICBI publications are: James M. Boice, ed., *The Foundation of Biblical Authority* (Grand Rapids: Zondervan, 1978); Norman L. Geisler, ed., *Inerrancy* (Grand Rapids: Zondervan, 1979); Norman L. Geisler, ed.,
   Biblical Errancy: An Analysis of Its Philosophical Roots (Grand Rapids:
   Zondervan, 1981). See also John W. Montgomery, ed., *God's Inerrant Word*
   (Minneapolis: Bethany, 1974).

'calism's last stand in our time. Simi-
lled it "the watershed of the evan-
\at inerrancy is crucial, they echo
ities as John Wesley, who wrote:
ny error in Scripture, shake the
there be one falsehood in that
. of truth."[6] Some today dismiss
...al, but it is arguable, to say the least,
.. Lindsell, Schaeffer, and Wesley has reason
..i sense on its side.

. that debate, and in Protestantism generally, four types of
positions regarding inerrancy can be distinguished. Each is best
approached as belonging to a view about biblical authority, for
that has always been the heart of Protestantism's theological and
religious concern vis-a-vis the Bible, and historically it is in relation to authority that each view has been worked out. First, some
say that Scripture has divine authority because it is God's own
testimony and teaching given in the form of human testimony and
teaching, and they see its inerrancy as entailed by its divine origin. Twentieth-century exponents of that, the historic mainstream
view, include B. B. Warfield, A. H. Strong, Herman Bavinck,
Louis Berkhof, Geoffrey Bromiley, Cornelius Van Til, and Carl
Henry. Second, some, having affirmed biblical authority on the
basis of the divine origin of what is written, go on to say that the
God-given text may yet contain technical errors in history and
science. They explain such errors as God's accommodation to the
mental and cultural limitations of either His human messengers,
His human audience, or both. That view is inherently dialectical,
for it requires one to affirm that biblical affirmations are God's
truth from one standpoint but not God's truth from another.
(Whether such a dialectic does not induce unreality rather than
understanding is a question waiting to be asked, but this is not the
place to ask it.) Rogers and McKim apparently follow the later

---

6. *The Works of Rev. John Wesley* (London: Wesleyan Methodist Book Room,
n.d.), IX.150; N. Curnock, ed., *The Journal of Rev. John Wesley* (London: C. H.
Kelly, n.d.), VI.117, entry for August 24, 1776.

G. C. Berkouwer[7] in casting anchor here. Third, some elucidate their claim that the Bible has authority by saying that though the text is no more than a fallible and sometimes fallacious human witness to God in history, God is pleased to use it as the means whereby He speaks to our minds and hearts today. That dialectical instrumentalism is a main motif in the bibliology of Karl Barth, Emil Brunner, and the neo-orthodox school of thought generally. Fourth, some are illuminists, holding that the Holy Spirit in our consciences uses the human material of Scripture to trigger real theological and spiritual insight that may have only a loose, nonlogical link with what the human writer meant the text originally to convey. That position agrees in principle with historic Quakerism, which trusts the inner light; it is the stance of various sorts of contemporary liberals and existentialists. Calvin's view, as we shall see, was in line with the first of the four positions, but he did not have the other three to contend with and so never stated it in antithesis to them as present inerrantists have to do.

Today, discussion of inerrancy is further complicated by the fears of some, based on things they have seen, heard, or read, that accepting inerrancy locks one into unscholarly exegetical practice, linked perhaps with the zany notion that belief in inerrancy makes one an inerrant interpreter.[8] When it is affirmed, as it sometimes is, that Calvin cannot have been an inerrantist because he was a brilliant scientific exegete, what is being said is that he did not conform to that stereotype. Indeed he did not, and it would be well for the world if no present inerrantists did either. The truth is (whatever some inerrantists' behavior may have suggested to the contrary) that the confession of inerrancy is no more, just as it is no less, than an advance commitment to receive as from God everything without exception that the text of the Bible proves to be telling its readers.[9] What the text is in

7. Berkouwer's final view (*Holy Scripture*, trans. and ed. by Jack B. Rogers [Grand Rapids: Eerdmans, 1975]), is analyzed sympathetically by Rogers and McKim, pp. 426-37, and polemically by Henry Krabbendam in Norman L. Geisler, ed., *Inerrancy*, pp. 413-46.
8. Unshakable confidence in inerrantist exegesis is one of the traits criticized in James Barr's sour but perceptive polemic *Fundamentalism* (London: SCM, 1977).
9. See J. I. Packer, *God Has Spoken*, pp. 110-14; *Beyond the Battle for the Bible*, pp. 50-61.

fact saying must, however, be settled inductively and a posteriori by grammatical, historical, and theological exegesis into which no a priori commitments enter, except the knowledge that the human writer wrote to be understood and the message that he sent to his own readers in their situation is precisely the message that the Holy Spirit here and now directs and applies to us in ours.

But it does not follow that he who is resolved to take whatever Scripture says as instruction to him from God will therefore prove the best exegete. One's quality as an interpreter cannot surpass one's linguistic and historical skills. There is, to be sure, a type of popular piety, rooted in a somewhat problematical blend of fundamentalist rationalism and pietist illuminism, that insists that those who do not venerate the whole Bible as God's truth will never truly grasp any of the things it is saying. In fact, however, as conservative scholars know well enough, though those who have a loose view of biblical authority cannot but fail to realize how biblical teaching bears on their own lives, they may nonetheless discern its content from a historical standpoint very clearly; more clearly, perhaps, than their evangelical counterparts. The best exegete, therefore, other things being equal, will be the erudite eclectic who knows the original languages and backgrounds, who can pick up and follow a writer's train of thought, and who has no prejudice against the work of scholars whose overall theology differs from his own. Now that was Calvin's approach exactly. A man I knew who read and wrote copiously was once described to me as a "literary bloke." What one sees in Calvin is a "literary bloke" as believer, pastor, and ecclesiastic—a scholarly saint who saw it as central to his Christian vocation to be a saintly scholar. Calvin believed that everything in Scripture is from God to us— that Scripture is God's word of address to all Christians, indeed to all mankind, in every age. He also believed that the way into the mind of God is by way of the minds of the human writers, in and through whose thoughts and words the Holy Spirit was fulfilling his role as the church's teacher. As a humanist, Calvin already believed that the way to comment on any document was to follow and bring out the writer's flow of thought, and that we see him already doing with success in his first, prebiblical commentary, that on Seneca's *De Clementia*.[10] As a commentator on Scripture, Calvin's method was to do the same and present the result as the teaching of God, as instruction that the Holy Spirit had "dictated" to God's faithful "secretaries" (amanuenses) for the direction of Christian lives. The principle underlying Calvin's practice was that "if the expositor reveals the mind of the writer, he is revealing the mind of the Spirit."[11]

T. H. L. Parker has traced the way in which Calvin crystallized his strategy and goals as a commentator.[12] He would not focus on topics (loci) like Melanchthon but write running expositions of the text and confine topical analysis to the *Institutes*, which would thus serve as a preparation for and an aid in Bible study.[13] He would not run to words like Bucer, but go for *perspicua brevitas*, lucid brevity, crystal clear terseness and relevance.[14] He started with Paul's letters, taking Romans first, and moved on to the rest of the New Testament and the major theological books of the Old. In the end, he wrote on all the New Testament except 2 and 3 John and Revelation (the last of which he claimed not to understand), and on the Pentateuch, Joshua, the Psalms, Isaiah, 1 Samuel, Job, Jeremiah, Ezekiel, Daniel, and the Minor Prophets.[15] Time has done nothing to invalidate the verdict that B. B. Warfield passed in 1909 on the significance of that achievement: "His expositions of Scripture . . . introduced a new exegesis—the modern exegesis. He stands out in the history of biblical study as . . . 'the creator of

10. F. L. Battles and A. M. Hugo, eds. and trans., *Calvin's Commentary on Seneca's De Clementia* (Leiden: E. J. Brill, 1969).
11. T. H. L. Parker, *Calvin's New Testament Commentaries* (London: SCM, 1971), p. 59.
12. Ibid., pp. 26-68.
13. John Calvin, *Institutes of the Christian Religion*, trans. F. L. Battles, ed. J. T. McNeill (Philadelphia: Westminster, 1960), "John Calvin to the Reader," I.4f.; better translated from the 1539, rather than the 1559, wording by T. H. L. Parker, p. 53.
14. Parker, pp. 50-54.
15. The commentaries on the Pentateuch, Joshua, Psalms, and Isaiah were written as such; the rest of the Old Testament material is lecture-sermons at a level and in a style similar to the commentaries. The material on 1 Samuel and Job was not included in the Calvin Translation Society's forty-five volumes (reprinted by Eerdmans in 1948). Parker, pp. 76-78, doubts the authenticity of Calvin's reported acknowledgment that he did not understand Revelation and points out that he cited it forty times, quoting from fourteen of its twenty-two chapters.

genuine exegesis.' The authority which his comments immediately acquired was immense . . . Richard Hooker—'the judicious Hooker'—remarks that in the controversies of his own time, 'the sense of Scripture which Calvin alloweth' was of more weight than if 'ten thousand Augustines, Jeromes, Chrysostoms, Cyprians were brought forward.' Nor have they lost their value even today. Alone of the commentaries of their age the most scientific of modern expositors still find their profit in consulting them."[16] Calvin's contributions to exegesis were of epoch-making excellence because of the quality of insight that his knowledge of Greek, Hebrew, ancient history, and classical rhetorical technique, allied to his natural intelligence, gave him into the human writers' flow of expressed meaning. Yet Calvin presupposed throughout all his work both the divine origin and the inerrancy of all Scripture, as we shall see more fully in a moment.

The reputation of modern inerrantists for crude and unnatural exegesis rests on the idea that (1) they construe biblical statements about natural facts as teaching science, in the sense of answering the "how" questions about the phenomena of the created order that are the natural scientist's concern, (2) they claim to find in prophetic Scriptures allegorically couched but currently recognizable predictions of specific present and impending world events prior to Jesus' return, (3) they impose on Scripture rationalistic theological grids that scale God down to the capacities of human minds (humanize Him, we might say) and thus eliminate the mystery of His being and acts, (4) they deprecate enquiry into the human origins, backgrounds, and sources of the biblical books, and (5) they harmonize apparently inconsistent texts in ways that are not plausible from a literary or a historical standpoint. This is not the place to discuss those allegations. Suffice it to say that Calvin was no less an inerrantist for being certainly free of the first

---

16. B. B. Warfield, *Calvin and Augustine* (Philadelphia: Presbyterian & Reformed, 1956), pp. 9ff. Calvin's New Testament commentaries have been retranslated under the editorship of D. W. and T. F. Torrance (Edinburgh: Oliver & Boyd and St. Andrew's Press, 1959-72). Older testimonies to Calvin's excellence as a commentator are collected in the Calvin Translation Society's version of the *Commentary on Joshua*, trans. Henry Beveridge (Grand Rapids: Eerdmans, 1948), pp. 376-464.

four lapses and arguably of the fifth,[17] from which we may conclude that there is nothing necessarily unscholarly about inerrantist exegesis and that it darkens counsel to assume otherwise.

APPROACHING CALVIN

Since publication of the fifty-nine volumes of Calvin's works in the *Corpus Reformatorum* series was completed,[18] Calvin research has become a lively, international cottage industry among Christian scholars.[19] Out of that research has come an in-depth picture of Calvin in his own age that shows him to have been an even more outstanding literary man, churchman, pastor, and theologian than previous generations thought he was. The Calvin of time-honored caricature—Calvin the misanthrope, the power-hungry dictator of Geneva, the obsessive predestinarian speculator, the sadist who demonized God—has vanished,[20] and in his place, clear to view, stands a man of towering intellect and enormous mental energy, endowed with a magnificent memory, formidable elo-

17. H. Jackson Forstman, *Word and Spirit* (Stanford: Stanford U. Press, 1962), ch. vii, pp. 106-23, argues that Calvin would on occasion "overlook or deny the natural meaning of the inspired text in order to uphold its unity" (p. 123), but the evidence he produces (some of which he seems to misunderstand) fails to prove his point.
18. *Ioannis Calvini Opera quae supersunt Omnia*, ed. N. W. Baum, E. Cunitz, E. Reuss, P. Lobstein, and A. Erichson (Brunswick and Berlin: C. A. Schweiske, 1863-1900). That edition, cited as *CO*, comprises vols. 29-87 of the *Corpus Reformatorum.*
19. Bibliographies: W. Niesel, *Calvin-Bibliographie 1901-59* (Munchen: Chr. Kaiser Verlag, 1961); D. Kempff, *A Bibliography of Calviniana 1959-74* (Leiden: E. J. Brill, 1975); T. H. L. Parker, "A Bibliography and Survey of the British Study of Calvin, 1900-40," *Evangelical Quarterly* 18 (1946): 123-31; J. T. McNeill, "Fifty Years of Calvin Study (1918-68)," in Williston Walker, *John Calvin: The Organizer of Reformed Protestantism 1509-64* (New York: Schocken, 1969), pp. xvii-lxxvii; E. A. Dowey, "Studies in Calvin and Calvinism since 1948," *Church History* 24 (1955): 360-67; "Studies in Calvin and Calvinism Since 1955," *Church History* 29 (1960): 187-204; J. N. Tylenda, "Calvin bibliography 1960-1970," *Calvin Theological Journal* 6 (1971): 156-93; Peter DeKlerk, Calvin bibliographies for each year, 1972-78, *Calvin Theological Journal* 7 (1972): 221-50; 9 (1974): 38-73, 210-40; 10 (1975): 175-207; 11 (1976): 199-243; 12 (1977): 164-87; 13 (1978): 166-94. On Calvin's view of Scripture, the most useful bibliography is that of Richard Stauffer, *Dieu, la creation et la Providence dans la predication de Calvin* (Berne: Peter Lang, 1978), p. 72 n. 1.
20. Cf. Basil Hall, "The Calvin Legend," in G. E. Duffield, ed., *John Calvin* (Abingdon: Sutton Courtenay Press, 1966), pp. 1-15; J. I. Packer, "Calvin the Theologian," p. 150.

quence both analytical and satirical, learning as wide, exact, and deep as that of any man of his day, unflinching moral courage, scrupulous fair-mindedness in applying his principles, and utter devotion to his God. As to his personal crest—a burning heart held by a huge hand, with the French motto *prompte et sincere* and the Latin legend *cor meum quasi immolatum tibi offero, Domine* [I offer you my heart, Lord, as a sacrifice] speaks volumes. A child of Renaissance humanism as well as a child of God, he was reared on the recognized humanities—grammar, logic, rhetoric, history, poetry, and what we would call moral philosophy, as set forth in Greek and Latin classics—plus legal studies for the juristic career planned for him by his father.[21] To that multiple expertise he later added biblical geography and Hebrew[22] and also historical theology, both patristic and medieval. He seems to have known the Bible like the back of his hand, just as he did the theological world of his time. Most of his biblical insights first reached him, it appears, through the writings of Luther and Bucer, and the many controversial encounters that bulked-up the final version of the *Institutes* show that nothing of significance from professional, Latin-writing theological circles had escaped him. The combination of academic knowledge, mental skills, shrewd argument and good judgment, profundity of analysis, and absolute convictional consistency[23] that we see in Calvin over the thirty years of his literary career mark him out as one of the best minds ever. He was a moral, intellectual, and spiritual marvel, whose stature fresh study continues to enhance.

21. Rogers and McKim, pp. 93-98, summarize that well, drawing on an unpublished paper by the late F. L. Battles.
22. H. J. Kraus, *Interpretation* 31 (1977) pp. 14ff., "For his training in Hebrew Calvin was primarily indebted to Conrad Pellicanus's book *De Modo Legendi et Intelligendi Hebraea*, which appeared in 1503 . . . the Reformer used such exegetical works as those of David Kimchi, Abraham ibn Ezra, and Raschi . . . there is scarcely a Reformed exegete of the sixteenth century who did not have a good knowledge of Hebrew."
23. Cf. Packer, *God Has Spoken*, p. 152, "He never changed his mind on any doctrinal issue. The only alteration in his published views that has been demonstrated to date is that whereas in *Psychopannuchia* [Calvin's first theological work, 1534] and the 1536 *Institutio* he ascribed the apocryphal book of Baruch to Baruch, he later concluded it to be pseudonymous. . . ." That statement should have read: "He considered the apocryphal book of Baruch canonical, he later concluded it was not so." For details on Baruch, cf. Warfield, p. 55, n. 19.

Calvin's *Institutes*[24] (fifth and last edition in Latin, 1559, in French, 1560) was his crowning achievement before he died, worn out at fifty-four, in May 1564. It won unqualified admiration in his own day and remains one of the world's great books.[25] It is a vast integrated web of catechetical, kerygmatic, confessional, apologetic, moral, devotional, and polemical theology, all based on what Calvin called grammatical (and what we would call theological) exegesis of texts in their literary and canonical context.[26] Organized around the concept of knowing God (Book 1 on knowing God the Creator, Book 2 on knowing God the Redeemer in Christ, Book 3 on knowing the grace of Christ by faith through the Spirit, Book 4 on the church's life and ordinances as the means of that knowledge), the *Institutes* follow roughly the order of topics In the Apostles' Creed and Paul's letter to the Romans.[27] In his preface to the second and subsequent editions, Calvin spoke of the book as, among other things, an overview of biblical faith to prepare the way for study of the Scriptures themselves and of Calvin's own commentaries, whose *perspicua brevitas* would assume acquaintance with that, his basic work.[28] The widespread idea that the Calvin of the commentaries differs from and is somehow more authentic than the Calvin of the *Institutes* is a mistake; there is only one Calvin, and his *Institutes* and commentaries belong together, complementing each other in the manner described.

24. "Institutes" as a rendering of Calvin's word *Institutio* goes back to the translation by John Allen (1813), superseding the excellent Elizabethan version by Thomas Norton (1561; last printed 1762), which was titled *The Institution of Christian Religion. Institutio* means "instruction."
25. Cf. the excellent "Introduction" by F. L. Battles to his translation of the *Institutes*, I.xxix-lxxi.
26. "Theological" is Barth's word for exegesis that focuses on the witness-content of Scripture as proclamation of the living God. More recently, Brevard S. Childs has spoken of "canonical" exegesis in the same sense.
27. Cf. Packer, *God Has Spoken*, p. 157.
28. Cf. note 13 above. Calvin announced in the preface to the second and each subsequent edition of the *Institutes*: "If I shall hereafter publish any commentaries on Scripture, I shall always condense them and keep them short, for I shall have no need to undertake lengthy discussions on doctrines. . . . By this method the godly reader will be spared great trouble and boredom, provided he approaches the commentaries forearmed with a knowledge of the present work as his necessary tool."

Calvin offered the *Institutes* as Christian philosophy.[29] We tend
to think of it as his systematic theology (a term that did not exist
in his day); we should note, however, that its scope is wider than
that of most systematic theologies, for the life of faith (ethics and
spirituality) is no less its theme than is the substance of faith (articles and dogmas). We should remember that its title is *Institutes of
the Christian Religion*, which is more than Christian theology, and
also that knowing God in Scripture embraces all aspects of our
relationship with God, over and above our professed belief-system.
The *Institutes* transcend any supposed dichotomy between the
intellectual and moral aspects of Christianity and has the status of
a devotional, no less than a theological, classic.

CALVIN'S APPROACH TO SCRIPTURE

Calvin's concerns in bibliology (another word that he did not
know) were not, as was said earlier, identical with ours. In his day
the divine authorship of Scripture went unquestioned, and what
was in debate was only its interpretation and authority as instruction from God through men. Hence Calvin centered his interest
on the message-content of Scripture (when he spoke of Scripture
as the Word of God, he always had in view its message-content)
and on the function of Scripture in creating and sustaining faith
and obedience. In the *Institutes*, as elsewhere, we find him fighting
about Scripture on four fronts. First, there was his running battle
against medieval and Renaissance natural theology, with its
assumption that reason (meaning, for practical purposes, thoughts
lifted uncritically from Aristotle, Plato, and the Stoics) establishes
things about God that Scripture does not say, which things then
become a frame of reference that relativizes and blunts things that
Scripture does say. Second, Calvin attacked various additions to
biblical faith (diminishings of it, from one standpoint, since they
diminish Christ) that rest only on postbiblical tradition. Third, he
challenged the idea that the church gives Scripture its authority,
insisting that the divine authority intrinsic to all that it says
becomes known to us through the Spirit's inner witness (I.viii).

29. Rogers and McKim, pp. 92ff. and notes; *Institutes*, trans. Battles, I.6 and
note 8.

Fourth, I.ix was a broadside against "fanatics"[30] who appealed to the Spirit in themselves in disregard of and sometimes against the Spirit's instruction in the Word.

The main sources for studying Calvin's view of Scripture are three sections of the *Institutes*. In I.vi-ix, the basic passage, Calvin dealt with the necessity of Scripture for knowledge of God (vi) and its self-evidencing divine authority (vii)—authority that rational arguments fortify, though they cannot themselves convince us of it (viii), and authority from which God's Spirit will never lead us away (ix). In III.ii, especially sections 6-7 and 29-32, Calvin explained that true, God-given faith (defined as knowledge of God's gracious favor in and through Christ) is confidence based on and correlative to God's promises in Scripture. In IV.vlii, Calvin argued that the church's teaching should always be subject to the biblical Word of God. In addition to those passages, Calvin's views appear in his comments on relevant biblical texts, though as we saw he did not draw out the full dogmatic implications of those texts in the commentaries themselves, believing himself to have done that in the *Institutes*.

Calvin's approach to Scripture has perplexed some modern scholars. Parker analyzes the perplexity as "a question of relating the numerous passages where [Calvin] speaks of the Holy Spirit 'dictating' the Scriptures to the prophets and apostles, his 'amanuenses,' and the no less frequent places where he treats the text as a human production and, as such, sometimes incorrect on matters of fact." (We shall see reason to doubt whether Parker's last eight words are happily chosen, but let that pass for the present.) "Some scholars," Parker continues, "emphasize the one side, some the other. Doumergue will distinguish between the form and content of Scripture and say with Gallican (*sic*) fervour: 'It is not the words that are important, it is the *doctrine*, the *spiritual doctrine*, the *substance*.' But Professor Dowey considers that Calvin 'believes the revelation to have been given word for word by the Spirit.' Both

---

30. Probably against the "Libertines," Quintin Thieffry and Antoine Pocquet and their followers, rather than against Anabaptists, as has often been supposed. Calvin distinguished between Libertines and Anabaptists. See *Institutes*, trans. Battles, I.93 and note 1; W. Balke, *Calvin and the Anabaptist Radicals* (Grand Rapids: Eerdmans, 1981), pp. 10, 98f., 330.

views are quite right and can be supported easily by quotations from Calvin's writings."[31] What should be said about that?

That perplexity reflects the unfortunate way in which Calvin has been interrogated by modern scholars. It is a fact that some scholars have felt unhappy with the doctrine, supposed to go back to Calvin, of the "verbal inspiration" or "verbal inerrancy" of Scripture, according to which God so overruled the mental and physical actions of the writers who produced the original Hebrew, Aramaic, and Greek documents that every single word they wrote should be seen as God-given, and every assertion they made on matters of fact, whether natural, historical, or theological, should be received as God-taught truth. Such scholars have come to entertain a restricted view of God's overruling that makes it impossible that biblical documents should be *both* divine instruction in the sense affirmed *and* authentically human products, bearing the marks of each author's human idiosyncracies and limitations. They have then brought their disjunction (*either* inerrant divine words *or* genuinely human reaction and expression, *but not both*) to Calvin and asked which alternative he embraced. They have recognized that for Calvin biblical doctrine (*doctrina*, Latin for teaching) is from God. But their question has been, How far did he go in distinguishing between divine doctrine and its human formulations, and in particular, was he prepared to find factual, logical, and conceptual slips in the writers' proclamation of God? Observing that Calvin certainly exegeted Scripture as human reaction and expression (witness, as we would say) and that he notes prima facie inconsistencies in the text and limitations of knowledge and attitude on the writers' part, they jump to the conclusion that in the back of his mind was a distinction, implicit if

---

31. Parker, p. 57. J. K. S. Reid, *The Authority of Scripture* (London: Methuen, 1957), pp. 54ff., lists authorities on both sides. Emile Doumergue's discussion is in *Jean Calvin: Les Hommes et les Choses de son Temps*, 7 vols. (Lausanne: G. Bridel, 1897-1927), 4:70-82. The problem is discussed from different standpoints by E. A. Dowey, *The Knowledge of God in Calvin's Theology* (New York: Columbia U. Press, 1952), pp. 99-105; John Murray, *Calvin on Scripture and Divine Sovereignty* (Philadelphia: Presbyterian & Reformed, 1960), pp. 11-31, especially pp. 20-27; Reid, pp. 43-45; R. E. Davies, *The Problem of Authority in the Continental Reformers* (London: Epworth, 1946), pp. 113-16. The attempt to find Calvin acknowledging factual errors in Scripture goes back into the nineteenth century, cf. Warfield, p. 65, n. 46.

not explicit, between God's message in Scripture (His Word) and the sometimes defective form of human words in which we find it embodied. They thus, in effect, find Calvin reflecting their own views back to them, and sometimes they have praised him on that account.

But Calvin does not merit their praise. Having a clear concept of God's absolute sovereignty in foreordaining and overruling free (that is, psychologically self-determined) human acts, so that people say and do things of whose place in God's plan they are quite unaware,[32] Calvin could not with consistency have found any problem with the idea of verbal inspiration; it would have been an unprecedented lapse from his own theology had he done so, and there is not the least evidence that he ever did so. He did not work with the concept of nondecisive divine influence in human action, as Arminians and process theologians do; he was, after all, a Calvinist, and all the evidence suggests that at that point, as at all others, he thought like one. So, though in exposition and debate he never stressed the thought that every single word of the text is from God (he did not need to; nobody in those days doubted it), and though, unlike some since, he always used the phrase *the Word of God* to signify the *doctrina* contained in Scripture or Scripture viewed as the bearer of that *doctrina*, rather than the uninterpreted text as such (which is only to say that he reproduced the ordinary usage of *ho logos tou theou* in the New Testament), and though he made much of the thought that God accommodates Himself in the phraseology of Holy Scripture to our limited understandings (see below), never did he describe or treat the text as anything less than a flow of words that came from the Holy Spirit, carrying meaning that is God-given and that we learn as we enter into each human writer's expressed mind. What the writer says, God says.

And when the text appears to say something incorrect or unworthy, Calvin labored to show that, rightly understood, it was both less and more than an error—less, because no mistake due to ignorance was actually made, and more, because the odd form of the statement itself yields us instruction in some way. If we ask

32. See *Inst.*, I.xvi-xviii.

why Calvin always took that line, rather than posit human error in the modern manner, the answer seems to be that since it was axiomatic for him that the text as given was the work of the Holy Spirit, he saw himself required by his very reverence for God as the author to try to show how at every point Scripture bears the marks of divine wisdom. The idea that at any point it really does not bear those marks would have seemed to him irreverent to the point of blasphemy and in fact no less impossible than it was intolerable.[33] If we then ask how Calvin found it credible that sinful, fallible human beings should freely, spontaneously, and with all their idiosyncrasies showing, nonetheless have written material that was error-free and marked by divine wisdom in that way, his answer, drawn from prophecy as the paradigm case, is: "They put forward nothing of their own;"[34] "they dared not announce anything of their own, and obediently followed the Spirit as their guide, who ruled in their mouth as in his own sanctuary."[35] That God the Spirit had effectively overruled and guided their conscious obedience to His own prompting was Calvin's complete explanation of how it was that they genuinely "spoke from God" (2 Pet. 1:21).[36] Gerrish's account of Calvin's approach to Scripture is thus entirely right.

> For Calvin, in fact, the whole Bible is the "Word of God." The expressions "Scripture says" and "The Holy Spirit says" are used synonymously (*passim*). In the Scripture God "opens his own sacred mouth" (I.vi.1). We are sure that the Scriptures came to us "from the very mouth of God" (*ab ipsissimo Dei ore ad nos fluxisse*: I.vii.5). Hence Calvin can introduce his exposition of the Decalogue with the invitation: "Let us now hear God speaking in His own words" (*Nunc Deum ipsum audiamus loguentem suis verbis*: II.viii.12). . . . The human agents . . . are "amanuenses" (IV.viii.9), "organs of the Spirit" (*Comm.* on 2 Tim. 3:16), "ministers"

33. Therefore, Calvin vigorously (and successfully) opposed the admission of Sebastion Castellio to the Geneva pastorate, for Castellio regarded the Song of Solomon as a secular love poem and not canonical Scripture. See Warfield, pp. 52ff., and notes 70 and 71 below.
34. *CO*, 54:286, from the twenty-fourth sermon on 2 Timothy.
35. Commentary on 2 Pet. 1:20, cf. Stauffer, p. 64.
36. Cf. R. C. Prust, "Was Calvin a Biblical Literalist?" *Scottish Journal of Theology* 20 (1967): 321ff.

(*hominum ministerio*: I.vii.5). The writers did not speak *ex suo sensu*, nor *humano impulsu*, nor *sponte sua*, nor *suo arbitrio* [by their own understanding, human impulse, their own initiative or decision] (see on 2 Tim. 3:16 and 2 Pet. 1:21). The real "author" of Scripture is God Himself (*authorem eius esse Deum*: I.vii.4). The writings of the apostles are to be regarded as the oracles of God (*pro Dei oraculis habenda sunt*: IV.viii.9). The Scripture comes from God alone and has no human "admixture" in it (*ab eo solo manavit nec quicquid humani habet admixtum*: IV.viii.6). In a word, Scripture is produced by the dictation of the Holy Spirit (*dictante Spiritu sancto*: IV.viii.6) ... Calvin is obliged by his view of inspiration to think of the Scriptures as inerrant ...[37]

Some have thought that Calvin's frequent reference to the Spirit "dictating" Scripture reflects a belief that in the process of inspiration the writers were psychologically passive, so that they wrote mechanically, like automata, without their own individuality finding expression.[38] But that is quite unplausible, for many reasons. (1) Calvin never said anything like it; the hypothesis is built on the alleged implications of just the one word, (2) he did in fact regard the recording of God's revelations and the recounting of the events that surrounded them as part of the writers' active and conscious obedience to God, as we have seen, (3) his conviction that God sovereignly orders the psychologically free, spontaneous workings of men's minds everywhere and all the time made it needless for him to posit the suppressing of human spontaneity in that instance to guarantee divine content expressed in divinely chosen words; that we have also seen,[39] (4) his exegesis consistently highlights the writers' individuality no less than it stresses that

37. B. A. Gerrish, "Biblical Authority and the Continental Reformation," *Scottish Journal of Theology* 10 (1957): 353ff.
38. O. Ritschl, *Dogmengeschichte des Protestantismus*, vol. 1 (Göttingen: Vandenhoeck und Ruprecht, 1908), p. 59, is one authoritative scholar who took the term that way.
39. So, when R. W. Davies, p. 114, writes, "We are forced to conclude, with Seeberg, Bauke, Warfield and Binns, that Calvin committed himself to a completely verbal and mechanical theory of inspiration," the proper comments are: verbal—yes; mechanical—no; theory—*confession* would be a better word; Warfield—a challenger, not an exponent, of the idea that Calvin's view of inspiration was mechanical; see note 43 below.

God the Holy Spirit says for our learning all that they say,[40] (5) elsewhere he used "dictate" metaphorically, speaking of experience, natural law, reason, and will "dictating" conclusions and actions,[41] and there is no a priori unlikelihood that the meaning is metaphorical still when it is the Holy Spirit who dictates (but if that is so, then *dictates* means only "suggests" and carries no implications about the psychological mechanics of the process), and (6) his contemporaries used "dictate" in the same metaphorical way (the Council of Trent, for instance, said *dictante Spiritu Sancto* of the unwritten traditions that the Spirit was held to have given), so that if Calvin had wanted his readers to understand him as affirming something about the psychological mode of the biblical writers' inspiration, he would have had to say more than simply that the Spirit dictated (and it is hard to doubt that he was a good enough rhetorician, or "communicator," as we would say) for them to know that. So the fact that in the course of his frequent assertions that the Spirit gave the Scriptures he never did say more becomes decisive evidence against the idea that he meant us to gather more.[42] Calvin was not telling us what it felt like to be God's penman or how God made His messengers aware of what they had to pass on in His name; he was just telling us, over and over again, that the God-givenness of Scripture is a fact we must reckon with and should never lose sight of. Gerrish is again on the right track when he says:

---

40. Of Gal. 5:12, "I wish those who unsettle you would mutilate castrate themselves!" Calvin said in a sermon, "Let us fear this sentence, as if we are hearing heaven's thunder against all those who trouble the church; for it is certainly St. Paul who has spoken, but yet the Holy Spirit guided and governed his tongue" (*CO*, 51:15). Again, in *Inst.*, I.v.13, biblical material is introduced by the following series of formulae: "The Holy Spirit pronounces ... Paul declares ... Scripture, to make place for the true and only God, has condemned ... there remains the firm teaching of Paul ... the Holy Spirit rejects. ..." It is natural to treat that alternation between human and divine as not merely elegant but also explanatory; Calvin was reminding us that what God says in Scripture, man says; what man teaches in Scripture, God teaches also.
41. See *Inst.*, I.v.3, III.xxv.7, etc.
42. It is observable that in *Inst.*, I.vi.2, Calvin pleads ignorance of "whether God was known to the patriarchs through oracles and visions or put into their minds through men's labour and ministry what they should then hand on to posterity."

the term *dictare* scarcely supplies Calvin with a fully-articulated "theory of inspiration." Neither Luther nor Calvin devote much space to the "mechanics" of inspiration: they are far more interested in the *results*. The real problem of the Reformers' teaching on this theme lies in their apparent assumption of an inerrant text: it is less [than] just to accuse them of holding to a mechanical view of inspiration. Several scholars have maintained that Calvin did not intend "dictation" to be understood literally at all. This may be true: in any case, Warfield is surely right in saying that "What Calvin has in mind is, not to insist that the mode of inspiration was dictation, but that the result of inspiration is as if it were by dictation, viz., the production of a pure word of God free from all human admixtures."[43]

So far, we have been focusing Calvin's approach to Scripture in terms of his concept of inspiration. We are certainly not false to him when we do that, as his comment on 2 Timothy 3:16 ("all Scripture is inspired by God and profitable for teaching, for reproof, for correction, for training in righteousness") shows:

He [Paul] commends the Scripture, first, on account of its authority, and second, on account of the usefulness that springs from it. In order to uphold the authority of Scripture, he declares it to be divinely inspired [*divinitus inspiratam*]; for if it be so, it is beyond all controversy that men should receive it with reverence . . . Whoever then wishes to profit in the Scriptures, let him first of all lay down as a settled point this, that the law and the prophecies are not teaching [*doctrinam*] delivered by the will of men, but dictated [*dictatam*] by the Holy Spirit . . . Moses and the prophets did not utter at random what we have from their hand, but, since they spoke by divine impulse, they confidently and fearlessly testified that, as was actually the case, it was the mouth of the Lord that spoke [*os Dei loguutum esse*] . . . We owe to the Scripture the same reverence which we owe to God, because it has proceeded from him alone, and has nothing of man mixed with it [*nec quicquam humani habet admixtum*].

That passage shows how important the idea of inspiration was

43. Gerrish, p. 355, n. 2. The Warfield quote is from *Calvin and Augustine*, pp. 63ff.

for Calvin. Yet perhaps a fuller grasp of his approach to Scripture emerges from exploring his concept of *doctrina*—"doctrine" in the sense of God's teaching conceived from the standpoint of God its teacher, in other words truth divinely revealed in history and now set forth for our learning in Scripture.[44]

There is, said Calvin, one single divine *doctrina* that was given through the Son, God's personal Word, with more or less fullness at different times to different recipients.[45] It is known more fully and clearly under the gospel than it was before,[46] but it was no less truly embodied in the Old Testament than it is in the New.[47] Its content, first to last, concerns God's covenantal relationship with men, with all its gifts of grace and claims upon man's worship and service. In its final, New Testament presentation, as was indeed the case clearly enough before, *doctrina* focuses on Jesus Christ, in and through whom this relationship is now a reality for those who believe. *Doctrina* in its original form was specific revelations given to individuals; now it takes the form of Holy Scripture, where all the revelations that God wanted to be passed on stand recorded. Scripture, in its character as *doctrina*, is in effect God preaching, teaching, promising, admonishing here and now, for what is written is interpreted and authenticated to present readers by the Holy Spirit, who makes them aware that it is God's Word to them. Observe how Calvin used the concept of *doctrina* (the teaching) in the following key passage.

> Whether God was known to the patriarchs through oracles and visions or put into their minds through men's labour and ministry what they should then hand on to posterity, it is beyond doubt that firm certainty of *the teaching* (i.e., certainty that it was God's teaching) was engraved on their hearts, so that they were convinced and knew that what they had learned came from God. For by his word

44. Prust, pp. 317-26, perceives the importance of *doctrina* as the concept in terms of which the God-givenness of Scripture is most adequately understood, though he does not make the best use of his own insight. His idea that *doctrina*, as Calvin conceived it, is essentially nonpropositional, preverbal, and incomprehensible is certainly a mistake.
45. *Inst.*, IV.viii.5.
46. Ibid., II. 20-22; commentaries on Isa. 25:9; 2 Cor. 3:14-17; 1 Pet. 1:10f.
47. See the quotation from Calvin's comment on 2 Tim. 3:16 in the previous paragraph.

God has always made faith to be beyond doubt [*indubiam*], and thus superior to all (mere) opinion. At length, so that his truth might survive in the world forever as *the teaching* (i.e., God's communicating of revelation) constantly went forward *continuo progressu doctrinae*, he willed that those same oracles which he had given to the patriarchs should be recorded as it were on public placards [*tabulis*]. For this purpose the law was published, and the prophets were thereafter added as its interpreters . . . it was particularly laid upon Moses and all the prophets to teach the way of reconciliation between God and men, whence Paul calls Christ the end [*finem*, which Calvin takes to mean "goal, end in view"] of the law (Rom. 10:4) . . . yet I repeat that beside that particular *teaching* of faith and repentance, which sets forth Christ the mediator, Scripture picks out by sure marks and signs the one true God who created and governs the world, lest he be confused with the crowd of false gods . . . We must hold that for true religion to shine on us we have to make our start from the heavenly *teaching*, and that no one can get the tiniest taste of right and sound [*sanae*, healthy] *teaching* unless he is a pupil of Scripture. So the source [*principium*] of true understanding emerges when we reverently embrace what God willed to testify there about himself. For not only perfect, that is, fully equipped [*numeris suis completa*] faith, but all right knowledge of God is born of obedience (sc., to God's testimony in Scripture).[48]

From that we see that Calvin's doctrine of divine *doctrina* was indeed the larger whole to which his assertions about the origin and nature of Scripture belong. Now we see that those assertions were part of Calvin's total presentation of God the Creator speaking in human language down the centuries to bring us sinners to know Him through knowing Jesus Christ. We miss the overall thrust of Calvin's view of Scripture unless we see it in that frame of reference.

48. *Inst.*, I.vi.2. Battles translates *continuo progressu doctrinae* as "with a continuing succession of teaching," meaning apparently that once the oracles were made permanently available in writing, they could be taught to each succeeding generation. But *progressus* always signifies "advance" in some sense, never "succession," and *doctrina* in Calvin, as we have seen, ordinarily means the substance of God's teaching, not teaching as a human activity.

CALVIN'S DOCTRINE OF SCRIPTURE

We have now reached the point from which we can view Calvin's account of Scripture as a whole. It is an impressive construct. Its theme is kerygmatic; it proclaims God graciously communicating with us so that we may commune with Him. Its thrust is religious; it seeks to lead us into humble acceptance of God's instruction and obedient response to Him by faith, repentance, worship, righteousness, and godly living. Its perspective, to achieve that pastoral goal, is polemical; Calvin developed it in contradiction to naturalistic paganism, authoritarian Romanism, and varieties of subjectivist (his word is *fanatical*) Protestantism, seeking to guide his readers into sounder ways. Its key points, briefly, are these.

The necessity and sufficiency of Scripture. *Institutes* I.vi is titled: "Scripture is needed as guide and teacher for anyone who would come to God the Creator." Chapters iii and iv are respectively titled: "The knowledge of God has been naturally implanted in the minds of men" and "This knowledge is either smothered or corrupted, partly by ignorance, partly by malice." Those titles together point up the first reason Calvin held that we all need Scripture, namely, that the sinful perversity and blindness of heart that mark our fallen state are such that, left to ourselves, we constantly twist our Creator's self-disclosure in His works of creation and providence into some kind of lie. God's "general" or "natural" revelation (to use the terms of later theologies) never of itself produces true apprehensions of God or due worship; our minds, however sharp in other ways, always tend to distort, more or less, those inklings and flashes of insight concerning God that come through to us from the outshining of revelation in the ongoing processes of the cosmos, which Calvin declares to be the theater of God's manifested glory. And so the explicit verbal instruction of Scripture has to be brought in to set us straight.[49] Second, knowledge of God as redeemer was set forth in history long past—history that began with the patriarchs and reached its climax and conclusion with Christ and the apostles—and to the revelation given in that history Scripture, and Scripture alone, affords trustworthy access.[50]

49. Ibid., I.vi passim.
50. Ibid., IV.viii.6.

Scripture, then, comes to us from God so that it may function as (to use Calvin's own images in I.vi) the thread that leads us out of the maze of our confusion about God,[51] the spectacles that enable us to see our maker clearly,[52] and the schoolmaster that ministers to our ignorance.[53] "Scripture is the school of the Holy Spirit, in which, as nothing is omitted that is needful and useful to know, so nothing is taught but what is expedient to know."[54] The Scriptures, though not offering answers to all the idle questions that might occur to us, are thus sufficient for their designed purpose; "everything that relates to the guidance of our life is contained in them abundantly."[55] Through them the Spirit leads us into "all truth," and to suppose that they need supplementing from other sources is "to do grievous injury to the Holy Spirit."[56]

The necessity and sufficiency of Scripture are the two bases on which Calvin's theological method rests. No reliance may be placed on the speculations and fancies of fallen men, Christians though they be; all our theology should find explicit validation from the Word or be judged illegitimate and false. The use of traditional ideas is to suggest questions to put to Scripture—no more—for such ideas have no intrinsic authority. But from Scripture the Spirit shows and teaches us all that we need to know for life and godliness, in fact vindicating older traditional ideas (patristic, as distinct from medieval scholastic) a great deal of the time.

The clarity and limits of Scripture. Scripture is clear, said Calvin, in the sense that those who persevere in humble, prayerful study of the text, who "do not refuse to follow the Holy Spirit as their guide,"[57] and who look to official ministers to illuminate the Word by their teaching[58] will find that they come to understand it more

51. Ibid., I.vi.3.
52. Ibid., I.vi.1.
53. Ibid., I.vi.2.
54. Ibid., III.xxi.3. "Whatever, then, is set down in Scripture, let us labour to learn; for it would be an insult to the Holy Spirit, if we should think that he has taught anything which it is irrelevant for us to know" (commentary on Rom. 15:4).
55. Commentary on Isa. 30.1.
56. Commentary on John 16:13.
57. Commentary on 2 Pet. 3:16.
58. In his commentary on Zech. 1:21, Calvin explained that we should learn to depend on the ministers of the Word to open to us the meaning of Scripture, just as Zechariah had to depend on the angels to interpret to him his visions.

and more. Here, however, everything depends on one's spiritual disposition, whether one is impatient, self-willed, and self-reliant, or (to use one of Calvin's favorite words) docile.

> When we come to hear the sermon or take up the Bible, we must not have the foolish arrogance of thinking that we shall easily understand everything we hear or read. But we must come with reverence, we must wait entirely upon God, knowing that we need to be taught by his Holy Spirit, and that without him we cannot understand anything that is shown us in his Word.[59]

For clarity's sake, God in giving Scripture accommodated Himself to our capacity (*captus*), condescending not only to talk man's language but to do so in an earthy and homespun way, sometimes "with a contemptible meanness of words [*sub contemptibili verborum humilitate*]."[60] "God lowers himself to our immaturity [*se ille ad nostram ruditatem demittit*]. . . . When God prattles to us [*balbutit*] in Scripture in a clumsy, homely style [*crasse et plebeio stylo*], let us know that this is done on account of the love he bears us."[61] It is a sign of love for a child to accommodate to his language and to be willing to use baby talk in conversing with him, and so it is, said Calvin, when God in Scripture speaks to us in a simple, not very dignified way. It helps us to understand Him, and the very fact that He does it assures us of His affection and goodwill. Following Origen and Augustine, Calvin developed the thought that in Scripture God scales Himself down, condescending to our limited capacity in the manner described. Calvin used that thought for a threefold purpose: apologetic and defensive, to counter the criticism that the biblical idiom and thought forms are not always worthy of God; exegetical and didactic, to explain what is and is not meant when the infinite, eternal, immutable Creator is said, for instance, to have a mouth, a nose, eyes, ears, hands, and feet,

---

59. Sermon on 1 Tim. 3:8-10 (*CO*, 53:300). Calvin spoke constantly of the Holy Spirit as the giver of spiritual understanding to our sin-darkened minds, cf. Forstman, pp. 74-79.
60. *Inst.*, I.viii.1. As a Renaissance humanist, Calvin took for granted, as the Corinthians had done before him (cf. 1 Cor. 1:17—2:5; 2 Cor. 10:10), that unadorned, unrhetorical expression was always poor style.
61. Commentary on John 3:12.

to rest, remember, yearn, laugh, and repent (change His mind); and pastoral and edificatory, to strengthen faith in the love of God who stoops to put Himself on our level linguistically so that we may know Him well.[62]

But the insight that God adapts His speech to our limitations, though assuring us that Scripture mediates to us real knowledge of Him, reminds us also that we do not and cannot know Him as He is in Himself. What frames and surrounds God's self-revelation is the mystery, utterly dark or overwhelmingly bright (Calvin says both from time to time), of that which in God remains unrevealed, namely His incomprehensible life, power, and activity, as those are known to Himself. God constantly warns us to stay within the bounds of revelation, not to stray outside the circle of God-given light into the darkness that lies beyond, not to try to penetrate by guesswork (what Calvin calls speculations, born of curiosity) into places where Scripture offers no thoughts for us to think. Often Calvin reminds us, echoing 1 Timothy 6:16, that God dwells in unapproachable light where no man can see Him, so that any speculative venture going beyond what He Himself tells us in Scripture is a sort of Promethean presumption foredoomed to disaster. For instance, Calvin's introduction to the study of predestination is as follows.

> First let [curious persons] remember that when they enquire into predestination they enter the shrine of God's wisdom, where any who rush in with blithe self-confidence [*secure ac confidenter*] will not gain satisfaction for their curiosity and will enter a labyrinth from which they will find no way out. . . . If this thought prevails with us, that the word of the Lord is the only road that can lead us to track down what is rightly to be held about him, and the only light that will illuminate us for discerning what ought to be seen concerning him, it will readily hold us back and keep us from all presumption [*temeritate*]. For we shall know that the moment we go past the limits [*fines*] of the word our course is off the path and in

---

62. See F. L. Battles, "God Was Accommodating Himself to Human Capacity," *Interpretation* 31 (1977): 19-38. Battles quotes Calvin's words in his commentary on 1 Pet. 1:20 about the incarnation as marking the acme of divine accommodation: "In Christ God so to speak makes himself little [*quodammodo parvum facit*] in order to lower himself to our capacity [*ut se ad captum nostrum submittat*]."

the dark, where we are bound again and again to go astray, slip and come a cropper [*impingere*]. Let this, then, be the first thing before our eyes, that to seek any knowledge of predestination save that which is unfolded by the Word of God is as mad as to seek to travel where no road is or to see in the dark. Nor let us be ashamed to lack some knowledge about it when there is such a thing as well-taught ignorance [*aliqua docta ignorant*]. Rather let us gladly eschew that quest for knowledge, the craving for which is stupid, dangerous and even destructive. . . .[63]

For Calvin, Wallace says, "adoration rather than curiosity is the fitting attitude when searching out the secrets of revelation,"[64] and the humility of wisdom counsels us to keep most conscientiously within the bounds of what Scripture says.

The authentication and authority of Scripture. Here we explore that correlation of Word and Spirit that is rightly seen as methodologically decisive in all Calvin's theology. Calvin spelled it out in *Institutes* I.vii and ix. His basic claim was that the Spirit of God who "dictated" Scripture also leads us by His own secret inward witness [*arcano, interiore Spiritus testimonio*] to acknowledge Scripture as the divine teaching that it truly is.[65]

The same Spirit who spoke by the mouth of the prophets must enter into our hearts to persuade us that they faithfully proclaimed what was divinely commanded. . . . Let this then stand as a fixed point, that those whom the Spirit has inwardly [*intus*] taught rest firmly upon Scripture, and that Scripture is self-authenticated, and that it is not right for it to be made to depend on [human] demonstration and reasoning, for it is by the Spirit's witness that it gains in our minds the certainty that it merits.[66]

The divinity of Scripture becomes evident to us as we become aware of the presence of God with us and realize that He is saying to us all that Scripture says. But because of sin's blinding and

63. *Inst.*, III.xxi.1,2.
64. R. S. Wallace, *Calvin's Doctrine of the Word and Sacrament* (Edinburgh: Oliver & Boyd, 1953), p. 99, n. 2.
65. *Inst.*, I.vii.4. The later phrase, *testimonium Spiritus Sancti internum*, means the same, but Calvin did not seem actually to use that set of words.
66. Ibid., I.vii.4,5.

deafening effect, we remain unaware of the presence and utterance of God in and through Scripture until the Spirit restores to us mankind's lost ability to discern God's reality. But once that happens,

> enlightened by his [the Spirit's] power [*virtute*] we believe that Scripture is from God, not on the basis of our own judgment nor that of others; but, rising above human judgment, we conclude with absolute certainty, as if we saw God's own majesty [*numen*] present in it, that it came to us by the ministry of men from God's very mouth. . . . It is a conviction which does not call for rational proofs [*rationes*]; a knowledge with which the best reasoning agrees, in which indeed the mind rests more securely and steadily than in any rational proofs, an awareness which can only be born of heavenly revelation. I speak only of what every believer experiences, save that my words fall far short of a just account of the matter.[67]

The secret inner witness, then, is not the Spirit privately revealing to individuals information not publicly available but the Spirit renewing and actualizing that capacity to recognize God that man was made with but lost through sin. The dynamism of divinity that characterizes Scripture—known by the light that shines from it, the power that it exerts, the presentation of God that it offers, the presence of God that it communicates—is, so to speak, intrinsic to it, and what the Spirit does is to open the eyes of our understanding, so that we "see" (that is, perceive and know) what is already there, objectively evidencing itself to us in the same immediate way in which, at a lower level, colors, sounds, and tastes also do.[68] *Witness* in Calvin's phrase thus signifies not so much driving out ignorance by communicating information as eliminating doubt and double-mindedness by imparting certainty.

Calvin's concept of the Spirit's authenticating witness was his

67. Ibid., I.vii.5.
68. Ibid., I.vii.2, "As to their question, How can we be assured that it [Scripture] has come from God, if we do not have recourse to the church's decision?—it is like asking, Whence shall we learn to tell light from darkness, white from black, sweet from bitter? Scripture actually [*ultro*] displays as clear evidence [*sensum*] of its truth as white and black things do of their colour, or sweet and bitter things do of their taste."

counter to the idea that the authority of Scripture strictly and properly depends on the say-so of the church. (The title of I.vii is: "By what witness Scripture should be ratified, namely that of the Spirit: so that its authority may stand sure; and that it is an ungodly falsehood to suspend faith in it on the church's judgment.") He dismissed, as making the Holy Spirit a laughingstock [ludibrio], the supposition that the church must decide for us which books should be received as canonical,[69] and that would seem to show (though he does not discuss the matter further) that to his mind authenticating the canon as such was part of the Spirit's witnessing work.[70] Criticism of that view as impossibly subjective

69. Ibid., I.vii.1.
70. For discussion of the relation between historical attestation in, to, and by the church and the Spirit's immediate authenticating witness in making known to us the divine authority of Scripture, see Warfield, pp. 48-57, 90-103; Packer, God's Inerrant Word, pp. 110ff.; R. E. Davies, pp. 108ff., 141-46. Calvin's key thoughts here seem to have been: (1) The evidence that the canonical Scriptures are from God is objective in the sense of being intrinsic, public, and to anyone whose mind works properly, unmistakable. "Though learned and most judicious men should rise up in opposition, and bring all their strength of mind into play in this debate, unless they have become hardened to that point of shamelessness which marks the lost [ad perditam impudentiam] they will have to confess that in Scripture clear signs of God speaking [it] are seen, from which it is evident that its teaching [doctrinam] is from heaven" (I.vii.4). The fact that some do not confess that argues a defect in them, not in the evidence. (2) The interior witness of the Holy Spirit is an enlightening of minds darkened to spiritual realities, a restoring of perceptive powers atrophied by sin, so that the objective evidence that the words and contents of Scripture are being spoken by God is received and responded to. Stauffer, pp. 66ff., catalogues Calvin's images for that in his sermons: the Spirit "pierces [opens] the ears," "softens the heart," "engraves the doctrine [la doctrine] presented by Scripture on our hearts," "writes in our hearts the doctrine of salvation," "signs and seals God's truth, which Scripture attests, in our hearts," "opens the eyes," and gives a "spiritual view" of the light that shines from God's word. Warfield was right to say that the Spirit's witness as Calvin saw it "was directed to making men Christians" and right to characterize it as "what we in modern times have learned to call 'regeneration' considered in its noetic effects," pp. 102ff. (3) It is frivolous for any present individual to challenge any of the church's historic judgments about canonicity, based as they are on earlier testing and enquiry, and confirmed as they have been by the consensus of many generations of Christians in whose hearts the divine authentication has been a reality. One should rather seek humbly to be better taught by God at the point of one's personal eccentricity. That attitude appears in Calvin's report of the Geneva ministers' exchange with Castellio (see note 33 above): "We conjured him first of all, not to permit himself the levity of treating as of no account the constant witness of the universal church; we reminded him that . . . this [book] is one which has never been openly repudiated. We also exhorted him against

assumes that Calvin thought in terms of anatomic individualism, as if each Christian had to verify the canon for himself by the light of his own experience. That would indeed be a hazardous view to hold. Who on that basis could end up equally confident of each of our sixty-six books, neither more nor less?[71] But Calvin, though he made much of personal Christian experience, thought theologically in terms of biblical corporateness, and plainly for him the shape of the question was, Can anyone justify rejecting the canonicity of any of the historically attested and accredited books, which over so many centuries have spoken to the church corporately with the accents of God and continue to do so today? Maybe the question merited more analysis than Calvin gave it, but that his final appeal on canonicity questions is to the historic witness of the Spirit in and to the church as a whole seems to be beyond doubt.

The authority of canonical Scripture has in modern times been construed in various ways: as the authority of the witnessing church, expert religious opinion, saving history, mystical intuition, honest experience, and so forth. None of those categories, however, was Calvin's. For him, the authority of Scripture was formally (as we should say) the authority of God instructing us and materially (our word again, not his) the authority of what God teaches—that is, of God's *doctrina*, which Scripture presents to us embedded in and illustrated by the flow of events of which God's particular verbal revelations were part. The narrating and the theologizing of which Scripture consists together constitute God's authoritative Word.

It should be noted here that Calvin showed a vivid sense of the historical progress of revelation and of the historical experience of Old Testament Israel, the first-century church, and the individuals whose personal story Scripture records. He was, of course, untouched by our present "historical consciousness" (as some would call it), which tells us that the mentality and experience of former generations, especially in other cultures, was so different from our own as to be largely incomprehensible to us. Arguably,

---

trusting unreasonably in his own judgment. . . ." (*CO*, 11:674-76, cited in Warfield, pp. 52ff.
71. Had that been Calvin's position, he could never have objected to Castellio on the grounds that he did (see previous note).

that was to his advantage since that modern idea has been taken to such extremes by certain sociologists and anthropologists that it has become a real blockage to any understanding of the past.[72] But Calvin, being free from those sophisticated inhibitions, treating the nature of man, like the nature of God, as a constant, and viewing the historical facts of Scripture in the light of its revealed theological teaching, found *doctrina* in both the content and the manner of the Bible's historical narratives, as his commentaries and transcribed sermons abundantly show. Nor does the fact that verbally he distinguished revelations of truth from their historical matrix give any basis for supposing that those historical facts, and the factuality of the Bible narratives of them, were of less importance to him than were the revelations of theological truth that the apostles and prophets set forth. Everything in Scripture—narrative and theology together—was for him verbally God-given and substantively part of God's Word, the *doctrina* under whose authority Christians should live.

God's Word, then, functions as God's scepter,[73] the emblem and instrument of His government over men. But that government is itself both the rule of the Spirit, who reigns by interpreting the Word to us and molding our lives in obedience to it, and also the rule of Jesus Christ, whom the Word proclaims as incarnate Mediator, risen Savior and enthroned Lord, and whose reign is an effective reality just so far as the Word of God is heeded. Of the Spirit in that connection Calvin wrote:

> The Holy Spirit so joins himself [*inhaerere*] to his truth which he expressed in Scripture that he shows his power in action precisely when reverence and respect for him come to be attached to the Word . . . as the sons of God see themselves bereft of all the light of truth without the Spirit of God, so they know that the Word is the instrument by which the Lord bestows the illumination of his Spirit on the faithful.[74]

72. Cf. Packer, "Infallible Scripture and the Role of Hermeneutics," in D. A. Carson and J. D. Woodbridge, eds., *Scripture and Truth* (Grand Rapids: Zondervan, 1983).
73. The phrase is Calvin's, *Inst.*, trans. Battles, I.12, "To the King of France."
74. *Inst.*, I.ix.3.

Of Christ he wrote, "Wherever the doctrine of the gospel [a phrase that for Calvin was equivalent to the full message of Scripture] is preached in purity, there we are certain that Christ reigns; but where it is rejected, his government is set aside."[75] Thus the authority of the Word, the Spirit, and Christ belong together; indeed, they are one in the sense that if you do not acknowledge all three you do not in reality acknowledge any single one of them.

Preached in the last quotation is a reminder of Calvin's belief that oral instruction in the *doctrina* by duly accredited pastors and teachers is God's appointed way of ruling the church. The word also indicates the importance for Calvin of Scripture being competently interpreted (exegeted and applied). As Berkouwer said (and Calvin would have agreed), "to confess Holy Scripture and its authority is to be aware of the command to understand and interpret it,"[76] for without proper interpretation, its authority is nullified. That leads to our next section.

The understanding and unity of Scripture. To say that Calvin subscribed to the Reformation tag "Scripture interprets Scripture" [*scriptura scripturae interpres*] is true, but more than just that must be said. Interpretation of Scripture was for Calvin a scholarly discipline of some complexity. It is convenient to follow the listing of Calvin's eight ideals as an interpreter that H. J. Kraus gives.[77]

Clarity and brevity—"a clarity of explanation that corresponds to the clarity of Holy Scripture"[78]—should be sought. The interpreter should not allow himself to lose sight of the wood among the trees.

The human author's intention (his *point*, as we would say) should be determined and kept in constant view. To make clear why the text says what it says is the main job of the commentator on any document, secular or sacred. Exegesis has to be directionally as well as grammatically correct. The way to enter into the mind of God is via the minds of the biblical writers, for both the substance and thrust of what each says are from God.

75. Commentary on Isa.11:4.
76. G. C. Berkouwer, p. 137.
77. Kraus, pp. 12-18.
78. Ibid., p. 13. That and the next ideal are spelled out in Calvin's letter dedicating his first New Testament commentary, that on Romans, to Simon Grynaeus. Parker discusses the contents of the letter, pp. 26f., 50f.

To that end the *historical, geographical, cultural, and situational background* of each document must be determined. In his commentaries Calvin did that most assiduously.

Linguistic knowledge should be added to knowledge of the background to determine the "real," "true," "original," "literal," "simple" meaning (Calvin used all those terms) of each passage. As a good humanist, his aim was to read out of passages all that was in them and not to read into them what was not there. Calvin's linguistic knowledge embraced not only the grammar of Greek and Hebrew but also the classical theory of rhetoric (that is, effective ad hominem speech) as set forth by men like Cicero and Quintilian, and that enabled him to fix the flow of meaning in documents in the same way that modern linguistic and communication theory tells exegetes today to do.[79] (Indeed, a great deal of what current linguistic and communication theory tells exegetes Calvin already knew.)

The *context* of each biblical statement [*peristasin, hoc est complexum, vel . . . circumstantiam*[80]] should be taken account of to see precisely what is and is not implied by (and what does and does not follow from) the things that are actually said.

Idioms and implications involved in the form of expression must also be reckoned with or we shall miss some of what is meant. Idioms like *synecdoche* (putting the part for the whole, or the whole for the part) are frequent in biblical language, as in all language, and should be identified where they occur.[81] The Decalogue, in particular, is evidently synecdochic throughout and should be interpreted accordingly.

There is always more in the commands and prohibitions than is expressed in words . . . in just about all the commands synecdoches are displayed so plainly, that anyone who wants to limit the meaning of the law to the narrow confines of its words will rightly be laughed at. So it is plain that a responsible [*sobriam*] interpretation

79. Cf. A. C. Thiselton, "Semantics and New Testament Interpretation," in I. Howard Marshall, ed., *New Testament Interpretation* (Grand Rapids: Eerdmans, 1977), pp. 75-104; G. B. Caird, *The Language and Imagery of the Bible* (Philadelphia: Westminster, 1980).
80. *Inst.*, III.xvii.14; cf. IV.xv.18, xvi.23.
81. Cf. Forstman, pp. 107-9.

of the law goes beyond the words . . . in each commandment we must look to see what it is about; then we must seek out its goal [*finis*] . . . an argument to the opposite must be drawn out . . . like this: if *this* pleases God, the opposite displeases him; if *this* displeases him, the opposite pleases him; if he commands *this* he forbids the opposite; if he forbids *this*, he commands the opposite.[82]

Calvin was here thinking in character as a professional jurist and man of letters; he was as far as possible from the unnatural wooden literalism that equates the verbal form with the meaning itself.

Other figures of speech should be recognized when they occur. *Metonymy*, for instance, a use of one word for another reflecting a link between the things to which the words refer (e.g., effect for cause, container for thing contained, material for thing made), is frequent in biblical as in all speech. It is neither to be literalized nor allegorized but explained as calling attention to the link that produced it. The total flow of thought of which it is part will fix its precise force. *Metaphor*, again, is metonymy of a particular kind: it encapsulates a comparison with and thereby illuminates that to which it refers. An example of Calvin finding metaphor is his argument that the fiery trial of 1 Corinthians 3:12-15 refers to divine testing here, not literal purgatory hereafter.[83] An example of his finding metonymy in another form[84] is his argument against Lutheran and Zwinglian extremes that the eucharistic "this is my body" is one of many biblical phrases in which

> on account of the affinity that the things signified have with the symbols of them, the name of the thing was given to the symbol . . . though in essence the symbol differs from the thing signified, the one being spiritual and heavenly while the other is physical and visible, yet inasmuch as it does not just picture in the manner of a bare and empty token the reality it was consecrated to

82. *Inst.*, II.viii.8. Cf. rule 4 for interpreting the Decalogue in the Westminster Assembly's Larger Catechism, answer 99: "That as, where a duty is commanded, the contrary sin is commanded: so, where a promise is annexed, the contrary threatening is included; and, where a threatening is annexed, the contrary promise is included."
83. *Inst.*, III.v.9.
84. Not a metaphor, *pace* Kraus, pp. 16ff.

represent, but also truly holds forth that reality, why may not the name of the reality rightly attach to it?[85]

Those are typical examples of Calvin's care not to mishandle figures of speech that we can appreciate whether we accept the details of his exegesis or not.

Jesus Christ, the personal divine Word through whom all revelation and knowledge about God came and always will be given, should be regarded (Calvin often said) as the "scope" [*scopus*] of all Scripture—that is, its main subject, focal point, and center of theological reference. "We must read the Scripture with the purpose of finding Christ in it. If we turn aside from this end, however much trouble we take, however much time we devote to our study, we shall never attain the knowledge of the truth."[86] For, as Calvin saw, the New Testament books identify themselves and the Old Testament Scriptures with them as witness to Jesus Christ and build up their account of Jesus in narrative and theology largely by displaying Him as the fulfillment of Old Testament promises, prophecies, and types. So "the Christological interpretation in Calvin's Old Testament commentaries looks to the future for the fulfillment of promises and prophecies, and his New Testament commentaries have as the determining factor for exegesis a movement toward Christ."[87] Though Calvin was careful not to read Christ into texts that did not certainly refer to Him,[88] the commentaries and sermons are as a whole "Christward" expositions to a very marked degree.

One further ideal reflected in Calvin's exegesis should be mentioned here. The interpreter should always show the *naturalness* of his choice between competing interpretative options. There should

---

85. *Inst.*, IV.xvii.21.
86. *CO*, 47:125, cited from W. Niesel, *The Theology of Calvin* (London: Lutterworth, 1956), p. 27.
87. Kraus, pp. 17ff.
88. Kraus, p. 15, notes how Calvin, in expounding the traditional "Protoevangelium"(Gen. 3:15), declined to take *seed* as a specific reference to Christ, and declares: "Calvin always reveals himself as an unusually careful interpreter of the Old Testament when it comes to christological interpretations. On Psalm 72:1 he observes, 'We must always be careful not to give the Jews any reason to claim that we split hairs in order to find a reference to Christ in passages not directly related to him' " (*CO*, 59:664).

be no arbitrary refusal on a priori grounds of what appears as the plain meaning when the a posteriori criteria of scientific interpretation (those embodied in the eight ideals listed above) are applied. H. J. Forstman, having rightly said that for Calvin "it is a foregone conclusion that all exegesis must uphold the divinity and, therefore, the unity and perfection of Scripture," then states that "because of this, Calvin as an exegete was free to read into a passage whatever might be necessary to arrive at the foregone conclusion."[89] But that is wrong. The truth is that Calvin not only declined to read into biblical passages anything that was not certainly there, he also argued *to* the unity of Scripture as much as *from* it, by showing over and over that common sense and disciplined care in exegesis can resolve seeming discrepancies with astonishing success. In other words, it seemed clear to Calvin that the *natural* meaning was also regularly and demonstrably the *harmonious* meaning and vice versa.

That needs stressing, for those conditioned by conventional modern scholarship are likely at first to find it hard to believe that Calvin seriously thought that, just as they may well find it hard to take the idea seriously themselves. Forstman, for instance, at one point looks away from the evidence that he himself has produced on Calvin's exegetical sensitivity to tell us that in pursuit of Bible harmony "at times he (Calvin) had to depart from what seems to the contemporary reader the natural meaning of the text."[90] With that opinion at least one contemporary reader, namely the present writer, totally disagrees, and he is confident that he is not alone in his disagreement. Take as an example Calvin's *Harmony of the Gospels*.[91] Anyone who works through it cannot but come to respect Calvin's honesty, intelligence, and alertness in facing the many superficially awkward problems that arise from differences of detail, wording, and order among the evangelists. More than that, however, he will in addition have to acknowledge that, though contemporary scholars doubt the usefulness of even trying

89. Forstman, p. 109.
90. Ibid.
91. Translated by William Pringle (Grand Rapids: Eerdmans, 1948); A. W. Morrison and T. H. L. Parker, 3 vols. (Edinburgh: Saint Andrew Press, 1972).

to harmonize the gospels, Calvin actually showed that once it is recognized that the evangelists let themselves disrupt chronology for topical reasons and reproduce more or less of Jesus' words for didactic reasons, simple, natural solutions for every apparent inconsistency suggest themselves. Calvin's introductory claim that "the Holy Spirit has given (the evangelists) such wonderful unity in their diverse patterns of writing that this alone would almost be enough to win them authority if a greater authority from another source did not supply it"[92] is impressively substantiated by the *Harmony* as a whole. Here, as in all his commentaries, Calvin's constant contention, expressed both by his actual arguments and by the rhetoric with which he clothed and presented them, is that it shows either perversity or stupidity or both to deny that the Bible, when naturally interpreted, is factually, theologically, and didactically self-consistent, for the evidence, point by point (so he urged), does in fact refute that denial. Thus Calvin earned himself the right to claim "the beautiful agreement of all its parts with each other" as one of the arguments that are "most suitable aids" to support faith in Scripture as the Word of God.[93]

CALVIN AND INERRANCY

It must seem obvious from what has been said that Calvin could never have consciously entertained the possibility that human mistakes, whether of reporting or of interpreting facts of any sort whatever, could have entered into the text of Scripture as the human writers gave it. Nor did he. As Dowey says, "To Calvin the theologian an error in Scripture is unthinkable. Hence the endless harmonizing, the explaining and interpreting of passages that seem to contradict or to be inaccurate."[94] Calvin would fault an apostle for poor style and bad grammar but not for substantive

92. *Harmony of the Gospels*, trans. A. W. Morrison, I.xiii.
93. *Inst.*, I.viii.1. The whole sentence reads: "It is wonderful how much confirmation comes from pondering with keener study how well ordered and arranged the economy of the divine wisdom appears there, how consistently heavenly is its doctrine, savouring of nothing earthly; how beautiful is the agreement of all its parts with each other; and the other such qualities which conspire to impart majesty to writings."
94. Dowey, p. 104.

inaccuracy.[95] When Scripture and secular sources diverge, Calvin held to Scripture, and the attribution to him by Emile Doumergue,[96] J. T. McNeill,[97] and Rogers and McKim,[98] among others, of willingness to admit errors of detail and form in the biblical text (what Rogers and McKim call "technical errors") rests on a superficial misreading of what he actually said.[99]

The handful of passages in Calvin's commentaries that have sometimes been taken to show that he thought particular biblical writers had gone astray prove on inspection to fall into the following categories.

Some are reminders of points at which God accommodated Himself to the rough-and-ready forms of human speech that simple people can understand. All that Calvin said about them is that in such cases God is evidently not concerned to speak with a kind or degree of accuracy that goes beyond what those forms of speech would naturally convey. The classic case is Calvin's handling of

95. Thus, for instance, Calvin commented on Rom. 5:15 as follows: "Although he [Paul] frequently mentions the difference between Adam and Christ, all his repeated statements . . . are elliptical. Those, it is true, are faults in his language, but in no way do they detract from the majesty of the heavenly wisdom which is delivered to us by the apostle" [*The Epistles of Paul the Apostle to the Romans and Thessalonians*, trans. David and Thomas Torrance (Grand Rapids: Eerdmans, 1960), p. 114]. Rogers and McKim thus mislead when, attempting to show that Calvin acknowledged minor errors in Scripture, they echo J. T. McNeill's article "The Significance of the Word of God for Calvin," *Church History* 28 (1959): 131-46, and claim that Calvin was "critical of the 'defects of the discourse' of the *original text* as for example at Acts 4:6 and Romans 5:15 where he speaks with reference to the actual biblical writers themselves—Luke and Paul—not just of the 'errors' in the text's transmission by careless copyists" (p. 142, n. 254, referring to McNeill, pp. 144ff. [italics theirs]). The "defects" are of style only, not substance, and Calvin saw divine wisdom in them, for the comment on Rom. 5:15 continues: "On the contrary, the singular providence of God has passed on to us these profound mysteries in the garb of a poor style, so that our faith might not depend on the power of human eloquence, but on the efficacy of the Spirit alone." On Acts 4:6 all that Calvin said was that it is *mirum* (remarkable) that Luke said Annas was high priest when Josephus says that officially Caiaphas, his son-in-law, held that office. Modern commentators suppose that the two men shared the jurisdiction. Calvin's remark notes an oddity that raises a question of fact, but it does not by any stretch of the imagination detect or allege a "defect."
96. Doumergue, iv.70-82.
97. McNeill, pp. 144ff.
98. Rogers and McKim, pp. 109-14.
99. The following paragraphs are based on what I wrote in *God's Inerrant Word*, pp. 105-7.

Genesis 1, where he described Moses as "accommodating himself to the simplicity of ordinary people [*vulgi ruditati*]" and "speaking popularly [*populariter*],"[100] and declared that he "wrote in a popular style things which, without instruction, all ordinary persons endowed with common sense can understand. . . . Had he spoken of things generally unknown, the uneducated might have pleaded in excuse that such subjects were beyond their capacity."[101] On that basis Calvin defended Moses for speaking about created things as they appear rather than in scientific terms (when, for instance, he called the sun and moon "two great lights," though astronomers had since discovered that Saturn is a greater light than the moon). "As befitted a theologian," wrote Calvin crushingly, "he had respect to us rather than to the stars."[102]

Other passages state that particular texts show signs of having been changed—corrupted, as textual critics say—in the course of transmission. Thus for instance, commenting on Matthew 27:9, where the words of Zechariah 11:13 are ascribed to Jeremiah, Calvin wrote that "by mistake" [*errore*] Jeremiah's name has somehow "crept in" [*obrepserit*]. The verb is Calvin's regular word for inauthentic textual intrusions. Again, comparing Acts 7:16 with Genesis 23:9, he wrote, "As for Luke's addition that they were laid in the tomb which Abraham bought from the sons of Hamor, it is plain that there is a mistake [*erratum esse*] in the word Abraham . . . hence this place must be emended [*corrigendus est*]." The roundabout "there is a mistake," with the use of *corrigo*, the ordinary word for emending a text corrupted in transmission, indicates that here also Calvin was talking about a copyist's error

---

100. *Inst.*, I.xiv.3.
101. Commentary on Gen. 1:16.
102. Commentary on Gen. 1:14-15. Rogers and McKim, p. 112, having correctly concluded from those words that for Calvin "Moses' comments on the natural world were . . . an example of accommodated communication from God," then say: "There was no reason to suppose that Moses knew any more or thought any differently about the natural order than other people of his time and culture"—as if to say: God's accommodated communication was partly a matter of not letting any of Moses' mistaken notions about the natural order get on paper! But the two extracts from Calvin's Genesis commentary that they quote before and after that remark show that Calvin thought Moses knew what he was doing in deliberately declining to talk about the cosmos technically and above people's heads, which Calvin evidently assumes he could have done.

rather than an author's lapse. Rogers and McKim misread the latter comment, as J. T. McNeill did before them, and accuse Calvin of ascribing the error to Luke, but that is unwarrantable.[103] Similarly, having quoted Calvin's comment on Matthew 27:9, they go on to say, "For Calvin, technical errors in the Bible that were the result of human slips of memory, limited knowledge, or the use of texts for different purposes than the original were all part of the normal human means of communication"[104]—as if Calvin had been saying that Matthew made a "technical error" here. But that reading of Calvin is also unwarrantable, unnecessary, unnatural, and altogether unlikely. Neither of those passages is evidence for their generalization, for which, in fact (to anticipate our conclusion), there seems to be no evidence at all. *Technical error* is not a concept that Calvin knew or used.

Other passages deal with cases where apostolic writers, appealing to Old Testament texts as proof or confirmation of New Testament truth, cite them loosely and paraphrastically. Calvin, however, stated over and over that when they did that, they never falsified the text's main point. Here is one generalized statement of his principle, occasioned by Matthew's report of how Micah 5:2 was quoted at Herod's court.

> We must always observe the rule, that whenever the Apostles quote a testimony from Scripture, though they do not render it word for word and in fact may move quite a way from it, they adapt it suitably and appropriately for the case in hand. So readers should always take care to note the object of the Scripture passages that the evangelists use, not to press single words too exactly, but to be content with the one message which they never take from Scripture to distort into a foreign sense, but suit correctly to its real purpose.[105]

Rogers and McKim say that Calvin thought Paul "misquoted" Psalm 51:4 in Romans 3:4 and affirmed in his comment on Hebrews 10:5 (which they cite as 10:6—a "technical error") that

103. Rogers and McKim, p. 110; McNeill, p. 143.
104. Rogers and McKim, pp. 110ff.
105. *Harmony of the Gospels*, on Matt. 2:6.

the saving message of Scripture is "adequately communicated through an imperfect form of words."[106] *Misquoted* and *imperfect* are, however, unjustified. Rogers and McKim are fathering onto Calvin the view (their own?) that quotations that are not verbatim are not correct, but what Calvin said in the passages they cite, as in many others too, is that quotations that genuinely apply at the level of principle are entirely correct, even when they are verbally loose. It is an odd freak that those two authors, who are elsewhere so insistent that Calvin's concern for Scripture focused on its intent, content, and function, rather than its verbal form,[107] should here accuse Calvin of criticizing the apostles' Old Testament quotations from an entirely verbal and formal standpoint. But their book contains several odd things.

Other passages deal with points of what Rogers and McKim might wish to call formal error or technical inaccuracy, by explaining that in those cases no assertion was intended and therefore no error can fairly be said to have been made. The inference is clearly cogent if its premise can be established, for where no assertion is attempted the question of falsehood and error cannot arise. One example is Calvin's insistence that the evangelists never intended to present all that they reported about Jesus in an order that is chronologically exact but held themselves free to follow, on occasion, a topical or theological arrangement. From that it follows that they cannot be held to err or to contradict each other when they narrate the same events in a different sequence. Another example (that John Murray, perhaps rightly, thought unhappy and "ill-advised,"[108] but that clearly comes in that category) is Calvin's suggestion that in Acts 7:14 (the seventy-five souls) and Hebrews 11:21 (Jacob's staff) the writer may have chosen to echo the Septuagint's mistranslation of the Hebrew of Genesis 46:27 and 47:31 rather than correct it, lest he disconcert his readers and so distract them from the point he was making, which was not affected by the mistranslation one way or the other. In those cases, so Calvin appears to imply, alluding to the incidents in the familiar words of the Greek Bible would not involve asserting either

106. Rogers and McKim, p. 109.
107. Ibid., p. 99.
108. John Murray, p. 31.

that the Septuagint translation was correct or that it expressed the facts at the point where it parted company with the Hebrew. On neither issue would the New Testament writer himself be asserting anything, and hence his formal inaccuracy in echoing the substantial inaccuracy of the Septuagint would not amount to error (false assertion) on his part. Whether that line of explanation is accepted or not, it is clear that so far from admitting that biblical authors fell into error, Calvin's concern in his treatment of all those passages was to show that they did no such thing, and that is what matters for us at present.

At the start of this chapter we noted that Calvin was not the sort of inerrantist who held that: (1) Scripture teaches science, in the sense of giving us concepts about nature that are logically alternative to those of the empirical disciplines, (2) biblical prophecy details future world history in a crackable pictorial code, (3) biblical theology dispels the mystery of God's essence and transcendence, (4) books of Scripture should not be looked at as human compositions at all, or (5) reasonableness is an irrelevant criterion when devising harmonistic hypotheses. What we have seen has confirmed those negative points and has also indicated what kind of inerrantist Calvin was when it came to interpreting God's written Word. He was a humanist exegete for whom every book and text of Scripture was a fully human piece of writing, a product of careful thought, often of hard study, and always of obedient attention to God on the writer's part. He was also a theological exegete for whom every passage was a divine oracle, dictated by the Holy Spirit. In explaining Scripture he took note of both the cultural and historical factors that anchor each book in its own time and also the universal truths about God and men that make each book part of God's message for all time. He was a literary exegete, weighing, evaluating, and sometimes dissenting from the biblical elucidations of all his predecessors—from Origen, Chrysostom, and Augustine to his friend and peer Martin Bucer. He was also a churchly exegete, interacting throughout with the varied understandings of biblical faith that had at different times established themselves, more or less, in the Spirit-taught, though often fallible, fellowship of the people of God. He was in no way a naive expositor, for his academic equipment was outstanding for his or any day, and he saw already a remarkable number of the questions that modern exegetes have raised and worked through them with consistent academic rigor. At the same time he was a clear, down-to-earth Bible teacher, alert to the realities of religion no less than of theology and as far as can be imagined from the arcane subtlety that tends to afflict knowledgeable academics today. Calvin was, quite simply, a magnificent interpreter, and we may properly cite as one confirmation among many of the viability of an inerrantist view of Scripture the fact that it can yield exposition that by ordinary rational standards is as coherent and penetrating as was his.

POSTSCRIPT: A FLAWED ACCOUNT

All that remains of our agenda is to say something directly about the presentation of Calvin's approach to Scripture that Rogers and McKim offer on pages 89-116 of their book as part of a chapter called, very properly, "Concentration on the Bible's Saving Function during the Reformation."

Much that those authors tell us about Calvin's humanistic education and orientation in theology, his contextual method of exegesis, the influence of his rhetorical training on his outlook, and his Christological and soteriological interest in the Bible is well informed and helpful. However, their book is a tract for the times with a case to make and an axe to grind, and their desire to claim Calvin as being on their side makes them squeeze him into the alien mold of their own mind-set, particularly in relation to two alleged antitheses that Calvin never contemplated and could not have accepted. They are as follows.

Antithesis number one is between concern for the *form* of Scripture and concern about its *function*, that is between stressing and vindicating the God-givenness and factual truth of every word and phrase of the original text on the one hand and on the other hand accepting and using Scripture as God-given instruction for leading us to Christ, feeding our souls, and teaching us to see life as it is under God and to worship God as Lord of all. Rogers and McKim, whose own explicit concern is with the latter matter rather than the former, deal with those as rival interests and present the major Reformed theologians as if each in resolving to highlight one had thereby resolved to downplay the other. Put that way, their historical thesis sounds unbelievably silly. So indeed it is. Only special pleading sustains it, and when they deal with Calvin, it leads them to ascribe to him, as a man like themselves, a recognition of "technical errors" that is simply false to the facts, as we have seen already and shall in a moment see again.

But Calvin would have thought the antithesis itself absurd. As a literary man, he knew very well that it is through the particular words used and the particular nuances that their arrangement expresses that language fulfills its function of communicating the precise meaning that the speaker or writer has in mind; its function depends directly on its verbal form. For Calvin, Scripture was able to fulfill its God-given function precisely by virtue of its God-given form, and the Holy Spirit, through whose agency that function is fulfilled, was directly responsible for producing the words in that particular form. The Spirit teaches from a textbook that in effect He wrote Himself. For Calvin, therefore, anyone who set the form and the function of Scripture, its givenness and its usefulness, in antithesis to each other, treating them as alternative rather than complementary theological concerns, would be talking a kind of nonsense, just as one would if one set food in antithesis to eating. The antithesis, Calvin would have said, is not a real one, and no one who is attending to Scripture itself would ever think of positing it.

We should note here that a further aspect of the antithesis as Rogers and McKim intend it is that those whose concern centers on the form of Scripture will attempt to show that God's book contains no historical or scientific inaccuracies, and those whose concern centers on its function will leave that question open or even allow that historical and scientific errors are actually there. By that criterion, however, Calvin was every bit as concerned about the form of Scripture as he was about its function, as we have already seen. Why should that be? We ask why Calvin should have had an interest here that Rogers and McKim make a point of not sharing? The pressure of that question brings us to the second antithesis, which for Rogers and McKim is really the fundamental one.

Antithesis number two is between *accommodation* and *inerrancy* in Scripture. The writers try to make Calvin party to their own view that God's gracious condescension in accommodating to our limitations the language in which He speaks to us in Scripture entailed features in the text for which "technical errors" is the only proper name. They distinguish between "technical errors"— nonverbatim quotations, nonexpository quotations in which Old Testament words are used in an altered sense,[109] verbal slips, and evidence one way or another of limited factual knowledge—and intentional untruths and claim Calvin with Augustine as their authorities for allowing that Scripture contains the former, though not the latter.[110] To say that, they think, does justice to the religious concern that lay behind historic affirmations of biblical trustworthiness and evades unnecessary problems about biblical phenomena. So they embrace the thesis as their own. But leaving aside the question of whether Augustine is being fairly reported and whether in any case that is an acceptable view in itself, what is the evidence that Calvin took the position ascribed to him? As we saw, Rogers and McKim are prima facie wrong in supposing that Calvin ascribed an erroneous assertion to Matthew in Matthew 27:9 and to Luke in Acts 7:16 and thought of paraphrastic quotation from the Old Testament as error. And there seems to be no other evidence that Calvin's thoughts about the human phenomena of Scripture included any concept of error, "technical" or otherwise.

In fact, the evidence points the other way. Calvin's concept of the unity of human and divine expression in the God-given Scriptures reaches further than Rogers and McKim and their mentor

109. Rogers and McKim, p. 109f. They cite Calvin's reply in his comment on Heb. 2:7 to the complaint that the author uses the phrase "a little lower than the angels" in a sense different from that in which David in Psalm 8 meant it. Calvin wrote: "It was not the purpose of the apostle to give an accurate exposition of the words. There is nothing improper if he looks for allusions in the words to embellish the case he is presenting." But why they should treat Calvin's words here or his recognition (p. 110) that in Rom. 10:6 Paul adapted the words of Deut. 30:12 to make them carry new meaning as acknowledgment of a "technical error" by a New Testament writer nowhere appears. If one is not trying to quote or expound exactly, what error is involved in the fact that one fails to quote or expound exactly? None, according to Calvin.

110. Ibid., pp. 109-14, especially p. 111.

G. C. Berkouwer[111] seem to see. Calvin would certainly have criticized the positing of technical errors in Scripture as implicitly blasphemous because thereby error would be ascribed to the Holy Spirit. Whereas Rogers and McKim and the later Berkouwer, with Barth and most moderns, draw the regular instrumentalists' distinction between Scripture as human witness to God and God's Word spoken through it, Calvin made no such distinction; to him the two were one. It is significant that immediately after the statement in the commentary on Genesis 1:16: "Had he [Moses] spoken of things generally unknown, the uneducated might have pleaded in excuse that such subjects were beyond their capacity"—an explanation that Rogers and McKim quote[112] to explain why Moses did not launch into a technical discourse on astronomy—Calvin's very next sentence (which they do not quote!) is: "Lastly, since *the Spirit of God* here opens a common school for everyone, it is not surprising that *he* should mostly select subject matter which would be intelligible to all." Evidently for Calvin, what Moses teaches the Spirit of God also teaches, actively, deliberately, explicitly, so that if Moses or any other biblical writer made a technical error, the Spirit would be making it too. With that concept of the unity and identity of divine and human teaching in Scripture in his mind, it is no wonder that Calvin should have labored to show the internal coherence and factual correctness of all that Scripture says. For him, the truthfulness and honor of God were directly involved in every single thing that Scripture expresses.[113]

There are other unreal and misleading antitheses in the mindset of Rogers and McKim, notably that between what they see as

111. Cf. Berkouwer, pp. 227ff.
112. Ibid., p. 112.
113. So, for instance, Calvin was not indifferent to the apparent discrepancy between 1 Cor. 10:8, where Paul mentions 23,000 being killed instead of 24,000, as in Num. 25:9. Rogers and McKim (p. 142, n. 252) quote only his statement that "it is not unheard of, where it is not intended to make an exact count of individuals, to give an approximate number." That alone might suggest that Calvin simply brushed the matter aside; in fact, however, he also said in that context: "But . . . it is easy to reconcile their statements . . . Moses gives the upper limit, Paul the lower." There is no question that Calvin, believing all scriptural statements of fact to be God-taught and therefore true, regarded harmonizing (i.e., demonstration of their truth and credibility, so far as one can do that) as part of the commentator's job.

the Augustinian-Platonist and Thomist-Aristotelian philosophical heritages, which also distort their presentation of the Calvin of history.[114] But enough, perhaps, has already been said to show that on this, as on other matters in their presentation of the Christian past, they are by no means reliable guides and that those who wish to understand Calvin's view of Scripture will on the whole be wise to look elsewhere.

114. Thus, for instance, to maximize Calvin's Augustinian-Platonist credentials, they assimilate his view of general revelation (a relational reality) to Plato's notion of innate ideas (a constitutional fact about man), and let the witness of the Spirit, which brings faith in Scripture, appear to be opposed to any idea of rational argument as a means whereby the Spirit induces that faith, which was certainly not Calvin's perspective.

6

John Owen on Authority and Scripture

Stanley N. Gundry

INTRODUCTION

"The problem of authority in religion can be stated as follows: Is there any accessible source of religious truth which is wholly authoritative? and, if so, what is it?"[1] The course of past and present theological debate testifies that this is a crucial theological issue; its solution will put all other problems of theology on a clearly defined level. The theological debates of the seventeenth century are no exception in that regard. As Cragg wrote, "for any thoughtful person in the seventeenth century the problem of authority was urgent. It was involved, directly or indirectly, in

1. Rupert E. Davies, *The Problem of Authority in the Continental Reformers* (London: The Epworth Press, 1946), p. 9.

STANLEY N. GUNDRY, B.A., Los Angeles Baptist College; B.D., Talbot Theological Seminary; S.T.M., Union College, University of British Columbia; and S.T.D., Lutheran School of Theology at Chicago, is Executive Editor, Academic Books for the Zondervan Publishing House, Grand Rapids, Michigan. He was previously professor of theology at Moody Bible Institute. In addition to publishing *Love Them In: The Life and Theology of D. L. Moody*, he has served as contributing editor to *Wycliffe Bible Encyclopedia* and coeditor for *Tensions in Contemporary Theology, A Harmony of the Gospels*, and *Perspectives on Evangelical Theology*.

every controversy of the age."[2] The centrality of the problem in the seventeenth century makes a study of the various answers proposed in that day especially instructive for ours.

The views of John Owen (1616-83), onetime vice-chancellor of Oxford University, leading Independent Congregational minister and key figure in the Savoy Assembly, and Puritan theologian par excellence, are of special interest. He was unexcelled as a theologian. However, it has also been claimed that he was a transitional figure in English Reformed circles between the "Reformation stance of the Westminster Divines and the Protestant scholasticism of his continental contemporaries."[3]

That assertion of Jack Rogers and Donald McKim is but one link in their understanding of the chain of development from Luther and Calvin to Princeton theology. Of course, the validity of their interpretation must be tested at a number of key points. If it can conclusively be shown that their interpretation of Calvin, continental Reformed orthodoxy, the Westminster Divines, or English Reformed orthodoxy is seriously defective, the question of whether or not Owen was a transitional figure tends to become irrelevant. Still, the accuracy of the Rogers/McKim interpretation needs to be tested at that point as at others. Thus we need to ask the larger question: What was Owen's approach to the problem of authority and Scripture? With the answer to this more comprehensive question in hand, we will not only be able to evaluate that particular link in the Rogers/McKim proposal but also be in a position to learn from Owen himself.

Owen is an ideal figure for such a case study, for no other theme is more pervasive throughout the volumes that came from his pen. He was convinced that in theological debates with Enthusiasts, Roman Catholics, Rationalists, Socinians, and Arminians the primary issue to be addressed was the question of authority. He wrote,

2. Gerald R. Cragg, *The Church and the Age of Reason: 1648-1789*, vol. 4 in *The Pelican History of the Church* (Harmondsworth, Middlesex: Penguin Books, 1960), p. 71. Cf. also Cragg's discussion in *Freedom and Authority: A Study of English Thought in the Early Seventeenth Century* (Philadelphia: Westminster, 1975), pp. 7-35.
3. Jack R. Rogers and Donald K. McKim, *The Authority and Interpretation of the Bible: An Historical Approach* (San Francisco: Harper & Row, 1979), pp. 219-20.

Until such men will return unto the only rule and guide of Christians, until they will own it their duty to seek for the knowledge of truth from the Scripture alone, and in their so doing depend not on anything in themselves, but on the saving instructions of the Spirit of God, it is vain to contend with them; for they and we build on diverse foundations, and their faith and ours are resolved into diverse principles,—ours into Scripture, theirs into a light of their own. There are, therefore, no common acknowledged *principles* between us whereon we may convince each other.[4]

A brief description of the life and career of Owen, especially as reflected in his writings, shows his intense concern for this subject.[5] Born in 1616 and educated at Oxford University, Owen began to come into the limelight in 1642 with the publication of his work *The Display of Arminianism.* That book showed Owen to be a Calvinist. Except for the fact that he moved from Presbyterianism to Independent Congregationalism, Owen's theological position underwent no significant change during his lifetime. In 1643 he published *The Duty of Pastors and People Distinguished.* Owen, a pastor at the time, occasionally was called on to preach before Parliament. He soon came to the attention of Oliver Cromwell. Cromwell was so impressed by Owen that in 1652 he nominated Owen vice-chancellor of Oxford University, which, in effect, placed him at the head of the university. He served with distinction in that position until he was forced to resign in 1657 for his part in opposing the crowning of the Lord Protector Cromwell. His time in the vice-chancellorship was a period of significant literary activity that included his *Vindiciae Evangelicae,* a refutation of Socinianism. That was soon followed by *Review of the Annotations of Grotius.* Two

4. William H. Goold, ed., *The Works of John Owen,* 24 vols. (Johnstone and Hunter, 1850-55), 4:159 (hereafter cited as *Works,* with volume and page numbers following). Italicized words in quotations from *Works* always represent Owen's own italics.
5. For more complete biographical information see: (1) William Orme, *Memoirs of the Life and Writings of John Owen,* vol. 1 of *The Works of John Owen,* ed. Thomas Russell (London: Richard Baynes, 1826); (2) "Life of John Owen," by A. Thomson, *Works,* 1.xxi-cxxi; (3) Peter Toon, *God's Statesman: The Life and Work of John Owen* (Grand Rapids: Zondervan, 1973); (4) Peter Toon, ed., *The Oxford Orations of John Owen* (Linkinhorne: Gospel Communication, 1971); (5) Peter Toon, ed., *The Correspondence of John Owen (1616-1683)* (Cambridge: James Clark & Co., Ltd., 1970).

other works from this period are characteristic of his interests and approach—*On Communion with God* and *A Discovery of the True Nature of Schism*.

After retiring from the vice-chancellorship, Owen remained involved in the affairs of his day. He participated in the Savoy Assembly (1658), a meeting of ministers and delegates from the Independent Churches for the purpose of preparing a confession of their faith and order. As a leading figure in the assembly, Owen was able to exercise considerable influence; indeed, he probably wrote the preface to the Savoy Declaration.

In 1659 two especially significant works came from Owen's pen: *The Divine Original of the Scriptures* and *A Vindication of the Greek and Hebrew Text*. The former of those presents his distinctive view of authority, and both of them taken together involved him in a controversy regarding the integrity of the available Greek and Hebrew manuscripts.

In 1662 Owen released *Animadversion on Fiat Lux*, a reply to *Fiat Lux*, written by a Franciscan friar named John Vincent Cane. Friar Cane replied with *Vindication of Fiat Lux*, and Owen in turn replied in 1664 with *A Vindication of the Animadversion on Fiat Lux*. In both works Owen dealt extensively with the matter of authority as it related to the church.

In 1668 the first volume of Owen's exposition of Hebrews appeared. In its exegetical method and incidental references to Scripture, that and the subsequent volumes contained valuable material concerning Scripture and authority. In 1677 Owen published another of his really important works, *The Reason of Faith*. It was an elaboration of a theme that had appeared throughout Owen's previous writings, the question of why people ought to and Christians do believe the Scriptures to be the Word of God. In 1678 *The Causes, Ways, and Means of Understanding the Mind of God as Revealed in His Word* appeared. In it Owen argued for the necessity of an illumining ministry of the Holy Spirit and the use of proper hermeneutics in the interpretation of Scripture. A year later he published a treatise on the person of Christ that eloquently proclaimed Christ as the sum, substance, and center of Scripture, yet maintained the necessity of an authoritative Scripture for a knowledge of Him. That work was followed in 1684, one year after Owen's death, by a similar volume entitled *Meditations on the Glory of Christ*.

Against the backdrop of that brief résumé of the life and writings of John Owen, we turn our attention to his view of Scripture. As both writer and reader, we should attempt to allow Owen to speak for himself within his own historical context. Though contemporary issues are similar to those of the seventeenth century, we should beware of pouring Owen into our own mold. We should stand ready to learn, to criticize, and to evaluate the transitional role that has been claimed for him by Rogers and McKim, a role that makes him a transitional figure from a Reformation stance to Protestant Scholasticism in England.

THE NEED FOR SCRIPTURE

Every rational creature is obliged to give honor and glory to God for the perfections and majesty of His person. However, "God in His own essence, being, and existence is absolutely incomprehensible." That is the logical starting point for Owen in his view of Scripture and authority.

> Therefore, we can have no direct intuitive notions or apprehension of the divine essence, or its properties. Such knowledge is too wonderful for us. . . . All the rational conceptions of the minds of men are swallowed up and lost, when they would exercise themselves directly on that which is absolutely immense, eternal, infinite.

Owen concluded "that our conceptions of God, and of the glorious properties of His nature, are both generated in us and regulated, under the conduct of divine revelation. . . ."[6] Originally, God revealed Himself by external means other than written words, but unwritten revelations had many disadvantages. "There being no *certain standard* of divine truth whereunto they might repair, they brake off the easier from God, through the imperfection of this dispensation. . . . Where the standard of the word is once fixed, there is a constant means of preserving divine revelations."[7]

6. *Works*, 1:65-67; cf. 4:7-8.
7. Ibid., 4:10-11.

Scripture is "the outward means for the preservation and propagation for the faith of the Church."[8] To preserve the safety of the church and to save her from delusions, Owen declared that

> there was a *standing rule* in the church, whereby whatsoever was or could be offered *doctrinally* unto it might certainly and infallibly be tried, judged, and determined on. And this was the *rule of the written word*. . . . This, in all ages, was sufficient for the preservation of the church from all errors and heresies or damnable doctrines; which it never fell into, nor shall do so, but in the sinful neglect and contempt hereof.[9]

THE PURPOSE OF SCRIPTURE

Owen did not insist on the necessity of a written revelation for its polemic value alone. The preeminent purpose of Scripture was soteriological. "The principal divine effect of the word of God," he wrote, "is the conversion of the souls of sinners unto God."[10] "The word is the seed of the new creature in us . . . and by the same word is this new nature kept and preserved."[11] Then he summarized by saying, "All the power which God puts forth and exerts, in the communication of that grace and mercy unto believers whereby they are gradually carried on and prepared unto salvation, he doth it by the word."[12] Writing concerning the new creation in another place, Owen noted, "This revelation is made unto us, not that our minds might be possessed with the notions of it, but that we may know aright how to place our trust in him, how to obey him and live unto him, how to obtain and exercise communion with him, until we come to the enjoyment of him."[13]

THE AUTHORITY OF SCRIPTURE

Scripture, then, functioned as "an everlasting rule of faith and

8. Ibid., 1:9.
9. Ibid., 4:471-72.
10. Ibid., 4:94.
11. Ibid., 4:95.
12. Ibid., 4:95; cf. 3:302.
13. Ibid., 3:158.

obedience unto the church."[14] "The Holy Scripture . . . is that which we profess to own as the rule of our faith in life. . . ."[15] "The revelation, then, and the dispensation of the mind and will of God in the word are to be considered as an *act of supreme, sovereign authority*, requiring all subjection of soul and conscience to the receiving of it."[16] Owen did not mean that it is simply *an* authority or even a *very important* authority. In reply to Socinian assertions that there were other subordinate rules that might be followed, Owen declared:

> It is the glory of the Scriptures, not only to be *the rule*, but the *only one*, of walking with God. If you take others in comparison with it, and allow them in the trial to be rules indeed, though not so exact as the Scripture, you do no less cast down the Scriptures from its excellency than if you denied it to be any rule at all. It will not lie as one of the many, though you say never so often that it is the best.[17]

The implications of Owen's position are far-reaching, and he did not hesitate to follow them out. Thus, all the principles and motives of our love to God and Christ are to be derived from Scripture.[18] Whatever is without precept or precedent in Scripture exceeds the direction of Scripture and is to be rejected.[19] Any supposed enthusiasms are to be rejected when they go beyond the precepts of Scripture, and thus enthusiasms are rendered useless and vain.[20] The church has no authority to judge, except by Scripture.[21] In fact, "the sole rule and measure of the government of the church" is the "law of Christ"; and "wisdom in the knowledge of the will of Christ as revealed in Scripture is that alone which is of use in the government of the church."[22] Owen meant

14. Ibid., 1:90.
15. Ibid., 8:497.
16. Ibid., 20:37.
17. Ibid., 12:84.
18. Ibid., 1:141.
19. Ibid., 1:142.
20. Ibid. The word *enthusiasm* in that usage refers to direct, extra-scriptural revelations to individuals.
21. Ibid.
22. Ibid., 16:133-34.

that all matters of worship, order, discipline, and doctrine are subject to the authority of the written Word only.[23]

Scripture, the sole rule of the church, should also be the sole rule of personal holiness and individual obedience to God.[24] That is so because

> the *pattern* which we ought continually to bear in our eyes, whereunto our affection ought to be conformed, is Jesus Christ and the affection of his holy soul. . . . To this purpose ought we to furnish our minds with instances of the holy affections that were in Christ, and their blessed exercise on all occasions. The Scripture makes a full representation of them unto us, and we ought to be conversant in our meditations on them.[25]

To appreciate the unique preeminence assigned to the authority of Scripture in Owen's thought and theological system is to appreciate a motif that runs through everything he wrote. He was jealous for the authority of Scripture at every turn and for the believer's right of access to it. He wrote:

> Our belief in the Scriptures to be the word of God, or a divine revelation, and our understanding of the mind and will of God as revealed in them, are the *two springs* of all our interest in Christian religion. From them are all those streams of light and truth derived whereby our souls are watered, refreshed, and made fruitful unto God. It therefore concerneth us greatly to look well to those *springs* that they be neither stopped nor defiled, and so rendered useless unto us. Though a man have pleasant streams running by his habitation and watering his inheritance, yet if the springs of them be in the power of others, who can either divert their course or poison their waters, on their pleasure he must always depend for the benefit of them.[26]

The source and ground of Scripture's authority was a very critical issue for Owen. He posed the question thus: "Now, when we speak of the authority of Scripture, and ask from whence it hath

23. Cf. ibid., 13:340; 15:143, 173, 449.
24. Ibid., 3:469.
25. Ibid., 7:467-68; cf. 3:370-71.
26. Ibid., 4:121.

it, we do but inquire whence it is that the Scripture persuades, convinces, or binds us to believe it, or commands us to assent to it, as the word of God; or wherein its power of doing so is founded. . . ."[27] In other words, how is the authority of Scripture to be known? On what basis is the authority of Scripture to be accepted? Owen asked, "What is the obligation upon us to believe the Scripture to be the Word of God? What are the causes and what is the nature of that faith whereby we do so? What it rests on and resolves into, so as to become a divine and acceptable duty?"[28] An assurance of the authority on which a revelation proceeds is as necessary to the benefit and comfort of that divine revelation as assurance of its fullness and infallibility.[29]

Owen said that basically there were two means by which the authority of Scripture could be known—on the authority of man or on the authority of God Himself. If the question is viewed thus, it becomes clear why the issue seemed so crucial to Owen. He summarized the matter well:

> It is, then, the wisdom of every Christian to inquire upon what account he receives this rule;—why he believes it and submits to it;—whether he be persuaded that it is of God by God himself, or only by man. For if he can find indeed that he receives it upon the authority of God, he may be secure of the truth and sufficiency of it; but if only on that of men, they being liable to mistakes, may lead them into error; and so he can never be sure that what he owns as his rule is indeed the right one, and of God's own prescribing.[30]

Owen regarded human authority to be an inadequate ground for the authority of Scripture and an inadequate means by which the authority of Scripture could be known. As he analyzed the problem, there were two types of inadequate human authority that pretended to serve as the ground for belief in Scripture.

One was to "prove" the authority, sufficiency, and infallibility of the Scriptures by the use of the "rational arguments." The so-

27. Ibid., 8:500.
28. Ibid., 4:5; cf. 16:306.
29. Ibid., 1:94.
30. Ibid., 8:497.

called rational arguments were external considerations that on rational grounds were supposed to prove that the Scriptures were from God. They included considerations such as the antiquity of Scripture, its preservation, fulfillment of prophecy, the holiness and majesty of its doctrine, miracles, the testimony of the church in all ages, the blood of the martyrs, and so on.

Owen allowed such considerations what he called "their proper place."[31] Indeed, he called them "unanswerable arguments."[32] They had their use when Scripture was attacked by atheism and may also be considered as inducements to belief, though their use as such had never been very successful.[33] But there was a more valuable use; they might serve as a means for strengthening the faith of those who had already believed.[34] That was as far as Owen was willing to go.

> To say that they contain the formal reason of that assent which is required of us unto Scripture as the Word of God, that our faith is the effect and product of them, which it rests upon and is resolved into, is both contrary to the Scripture, destructive of the nature of divine faith, and exclusive of the work of the Holy Spirit. . . . [35]

The crucial question in the matter of authority is, "Why do you believe?"[36] What is it that prevails upon one to believe? If the answer is that certain rational considerations have persuaded one to believe, then that faith is a faith that rests on human authority and arguments that are highly probable but nevertheless fallible. That was entirely unacceptable to Owen's concept of authority and faith. Saving faith is a divine, supernatural, and infallible faith in the self-evidencing voice of God in Scripture. Only divine revelation can be the proper object of divine faith. A faith resolved into the cogency of rational arguments for the divinity of Scripture is still a human and fallible assurance.[37] Such a reason for

31. Ibid., 4:5, 15.
32. Ibid., 1:470.
33. Ibid., 4:71.
34. Ibid.; cf. 4:47.
35. Ibid., 4:47.
36. Ibid., 4:46.
37. Ibid., 4:46, 49; cf. 21 for a summary statement.

believing is also to be rejected because it negates the need of the Holy Spirit to enable man to believe, no more being required than "a naked exercise of reason."[38]

The other type of inadequate ground for belief in Scripture, according to Owen, was the testimony of the church. Here he was primarily speaking against the claims of the Roman church. For him its authority was merely a human authority. The Roman church, he wrote, claimed

> to be the only sufficient ground of men's believing the Scripture to be the Word of God; and so tell us that the Spirit bears witness to the divinity of the Scripture by the testimony of the church, and makes use of that as a medium or argument by which he persuades men to receive the Scripture as the Word of God, and that without that testimony, or antecedently to it, men cannot know, nor be bound to believe, the Scriptures so to be.[39]

To Owen, that meant that authority would reside in the church. He rejected it because:

> *We have more certainty in our way than they have, or can ever have, in their way.* Our faith is built upon no worse a bottom than the infinite veracity of him who is the truth itself, revealing himself to us in the Scripture of truth, and not on the sandy foundation of any human testimony:—it leans upon God, not upon men; upon "Thus saith the Lord," not, "Thus saith the church." Though we despise not the true church, but pay reverence to all that authority wherewith God hath vested it, yet we dare not set it in God's place. . . . And so we believe it, not because men have ministerially led us to receive it, or told us it is of God; but because we ourselves have heard and felt him speaking in it. The Spirit shines into our minds by the light of this word, and speaks loudly to our hearts by the power of it, and plainly tells us whose word it is; and so makes us yield to God's authority.[40]

The interposition of any sort of human authority between

38. Ibid., 4:49; cf. 46, 107.
39. Ibid., 8:503; cf. 499.
40. Ibid., 8:537.

Scripture and the individual—whether that of a church or of external, rational arguments—destroys the authority of Scripture. Or, to put it another way:

> Our faith is not founded upon any revelation at all, if that revelation needs something else, which is not revelation, to give credit to it, or if that which is the first revelation yet needs another to make it manifest to us, it is not itself the first. . . . In the business of faith, either we must come to some first revelation, or we must go on from one to another without any end.[41]

All grounds of human testimony and argument are inadequate to produce faith in the authority of God speaking in Scripture. Owen saw only one viable alternative. The authority of Scripture is grounded in God himself. "The authority of God speaking in and by the penmen of the Scriptures is the sole bottom and foundation of our assenting to them, and what is contained in them, with faith divine and supernatural."[42]

But on what grounds or for what reason does one believe the Scripture to be the Word of God with such a faith that is divine and supernatural?[43] Not upon rational principles; not upon the authority of the church. "But I believe it so to be with faith divine and supernatural, resting on and resolved into the authority and veracity of God himself, evidencing themselves unto my mind, my soul, and conscience, by this revelation itself, and not otherwise."[44] The key words in that statement are "themselves" and "itself." Scripture, since it is the Word of God and grounded in the authority of God himself, has a self-evidencing power. Believers accept it

41. Ibid., 8:506.
42. Ibid., 20:38.
43. The way in which Owen answers the question colors his whole view of authority and Scripture. Though his viewpoint on the matter can be found in and permeates many of his writings, his most complete and systematic treatment is to be found in *The Reason of Faith; or, an Answer to that Inquiry, "Wherefore We Believe the Scripture to be the Word of God;" with the Causes and Nature of that Faith Wherewith we do so: Wherein the Grounds whereon the Holy Scripture is believed to be the Word of God with Faith Divine and Supernatural are declared and vindicated"* (ibid., 4:1-115). The title of the work is self-explanatory.
44. Ibid., 4:70.

as the Word of God because it is the Word of God. It is that simple.

In answer to the question "Why or on what account, do you believe the Scriptures, or books of the Old and New Testament to be the Word of God?" Owen answered:

> The Authority of God, the supreme Lord of all, the first and only absolute Truth, whose word is truth—speaking in and by the penmen of the Scriptures—evinced singly and by the Scripture itself—is the sole bottom and foundation or formal reason of our assenting to those Scriptures as his word. . . . His word is accompanied with its own evidence, and gives assurance unto us. His authority and veracity sufficiently manifest themselves, that men may quietly repose their souls upon them. . . .
>
> The Scriptures of the Old and New Testament do abundantly and uncontrollably manifest themselves to be the word of the living God; so that, merely on the account of their own proposal of themselves unto us in the name and majesty of God as such—without the contribution or help or assistance from tradition, church, or anything else without themselves—we are obliged upon the penalty of eternal damnation . . . to receive them, with that subjection of soul which is due to the word of God.[45]

THE INSPIRATION OF SCRIPTURE

Because Scripture as the Word of God carried a self-evidencing authority, Owen did not argue from either the fact of inspiration, the evidences of inspiration, infallibility, or inerrancy to scriptural authority. Nevertheless, he held that inspiration was necessary if Scripture was to have a unique and infallible authority.[46] Owen did not systematically elaborate a doctrine of inspiration, but from incidental references it is possible to discover his view.

First, Owen understood the efficient author of Scripture to be the Holy Spirit.[47] In fact, he emphasized this in such strong terms that one suspects he held to a dictation theory of inspiration. Concerning the apostles he wrote, "The word that came unto them

45. Ibid., 16:306-7.
46. Ibid., 2:236.
47. Ibid., 1:89-90; 4:77; 20:20.

was a book which they took *in* and gave *out* without any alteration of one tittle or syllable."[48] Scripture, then, only had the appearance of coming from human authors.[49]

The relationship of the penmen to the Holy Spirit would seem to be that of mechanical reproducers. But there are places where Owen tempered his statements, allowing for a more dynamic relationship between the Holy Spirit and the writers. Even in the context of the above citation Owen wrote:

> We may also grant, and do, that they used their own abilities of mind and understanding in the choice of words and expressions. . . . But the Holy Spirit, who is more intimate unto the minds and skills of men than they are themselves, did so guide, act, and operate in them, as that the words they fixed upon are as directly and certainly from him as if they had been spoken to them by an audible voice.[50]

A similar moderating tendency seemed to be present when Owen wrote that "the style of the holy penmen is, in a gracious condescension, *suited unto them, and their capacity.* . . ."[51]

Such statements allow for a more dynamic relationship between the human writer and the Holy Spirit than Owen usually suggested, but the exact relationship was left vague. However, the general relationship between the Holy Spirit and the human penmen, as Owen conceived it, was quite clear. The Holy Spirit was the efficient and actual author of Scripture, and the penmen were His passive instruments. The extent and manner of the contribution of those passive penmen, to the extent that it existed at all, was at the most slight, and it in no way adulterated the Scriptures with human error.[52]

Since the Spirit was the efficient author of Scripture, it followed that for Owen inspiration was verbal. He referred the verbal aspect of inspiration to Scripture as written in the original lan-

48. Ibid., 16:299; cf. 2:236; 3:129, 131-34, 143; 16:298, 304-5.
49. Ibid., 3:144-45.
50. Ibid., 3:145.
51. Ibid., 18:54; cf. 16:305.
52. Cf. especially ibid., 3:144-45.

guages.[53] But inspired words were not ends in themselves; they guaranteed the communication of inspired concepts. The believer was to be concerned with the originally inspired words to learn the inspired concepts God revealed. The words serve no other purpose and in and of themselves have no purpose other than that of being signs of ideas. "The majesty, holiness, and spirit of the Scriptures," wrote Owen, "lie not in words and syllables, but in the truths themselves expressed in them; and whilst they are incorruptedly declared in any language, the majesty of the word is continued."[54]

By virtue of its inspiration, Scripture was also perfect and infallible.[55] Alluding to the work of the Holy Spirit in inspiration, he wrote, "The word is come forth unto us from God, without the least mixture or intervenience of any medium obnoxious to fallibility (as is the wisdom, truth, integrity, knowledge, and memory, of the best of all men)."[56] Owen's usual word to describe the absence of human error from Scripture is *infallible*.

Perfection and infallibility involved fullness and perspicuity. Of what use would a perfect and infallible revelation be without the fullness and clarity of that revelation?[57] However, Owen did not mean that the believer could know everything about everything. He did not claim that God had revealed all that He might have revealed, nor did he claim that one could understand all that had been revealed in Scripture.[58]

THE HOLY SPIRIT IN RELATION TO SCRIPTURE

The Holy Spirit not only inspired Scripture but also sustains a continuing relationship to it whereby the Scriptures are preserved from being a "dead letter" and are "the living oracles of God." "They are accompanied with a living power."[59] The continuing relationship of the Spirit to the written Word is threefold.

53. Ibid., 3:144; 4:213; 16:300, 305.
54. Ibid., 14:134; cf. 4:213; 18:51.
55. Ibid., 3:144.
56. Ibid., 16:300; cf. 14:273-74.
57. Ibid., 1:94; 14:280.
58. Ibid., 4:193; 14:177, 491.
59. Ibid., 21:575.

First, Scripture is the "instrument whereby the Holy Spirit reveals unto us."[60]

> All things mentioned as wrought instrumentally by the word are effects of the power of the *Spirit* of God. The word itself, under a bare proposal to the minds of men, will not so affect them. . . . It is, therefore, the ministration of the Spirit, in and by the word which produces all or any of these effects on the minds of men; he is the fountain of all illumination.[61]

Second, the Spirit testifies in and to Scripture. It is the "Spirit of God" who "evidenceth the *divine original and authority* of the Scripture by the power and authority which he puts forth in it and by it over the minds and consciences of men."[62] Hence, in speaking of the self-evidencing power of Scripture, Owen said that it is accepted as divine revelation "solely on the evidence that the Spirit of God, in and by Scripture itself, gives unto us that it was given by immediate inspiration of God."[63] Such, then, is the "authority of its principal Author," "the seal and testimony which in the Scripture he gives unto it and by it to be his own work and word."[64] It is the "testimony of the Spirit of God in the word itself—witnessing it to be of God in the word itself, by that stamp," and that "is the immediate and principal, and a sufficient, reason of our believing it to be the word of God."[65] "The Spirit shines into our minds by the light of this word, and speaks loudly to our hearts by the power of it, and plainly tells whose word it is; and so makes us yield to God's authority."[66]

Third, the Holy Spirit is the illuminator of Scripture. "Hereby alone . . . can we know or understand the mind of God in the Scripture in such a manner as God requireth us to do."[67] All the mental and logical disciplines are useless without such an internal act of grace.

60. Ibid., 4:321; cf. 21:21.
61. Ibid., 3:235-36; cf. 3:197; 4:43; 23:495.
62. Ibid., 4:93.
63. Ibid., 4:20.
64. Ibid., 18:56-57.
65. Ibid., 8:503-4.
66. Ibid., 8:538; cf. 4:72-73.
67. Ibid., 4:130; cf. 187.

Although men may bear themselves high on their learning, their natural abilities, their fruitful inventions, tenacious memories, various fancies, plausibility of expression, with long studies and endeavours, things good and praise-worthy in their kind and order; yet unless men are made wise by the Spirit of God they will scarce attain a due acquaintance with his mind and will.[68]

Without the gracious operation of the Spirit, one may attain unto a "notional speculative apprehension and perception of the meaning and truth of the propositions contained in Scripture"; but a "gracious, saving, spiritual perception of them, and assent unto them with faith divine and supernatural is the especial work of the Holy Ghost in the hearts of the elect."[69]

THE CHRIST OF SCRIPTURE

A few hours before his death John Owen was told that his treatise *Meditations and Discourses on the Glory of Christ* had just gone to press. Hearing the news, Owen replied, "I am glad to hear that that performance is put to the press; but, O brother Payne, the long looked-for day is come at last, in which I shall see that glory in another manner than I have ever done yet, or was capable of doing in this world!"[70]

Those words were spoken in character, for, as James Moffatt wrote, "In his supreme passion for Jesus Christ, he stands apart not merely from many of his own party, but from the rational theologians who were the glory of Cambridge in the Seventeenth Century."[71] And, as Moffatt also pointed out, the preeminence of Christ occupied the central place in his thought and writings. Even his concern for the sole authority of Scripture was rooted in a deeply personal and thoroughly genuine love for Christ. The relationship, as Owen conceived it, between Christ and Scripture can be subsumed under three general topics.

First, Christ is the sum, substance, and center of Scripture. The

68. Ibid., 4:173.
69. Ibid., 14:276-77; cf. 4:14-15, 156-57.
70. Ibid., 1:274.
71. James Moffatt, *The Golden Book of John Owen* (London: Hodder & Stoughton, 1904), p. 48.

nature of the relationship between Christ and Scripture is based on the proposition that the chief end of man is to know God in order to be like Him. But what may be known of the nature and existence of God and of the counsels of His will can only be known in Christ. "The end of the Word itself, is to instruct us in the knowledge of God in Christ."[72] "Christ is the image of the invisible God, the express image of the person of the Father; and the principal end of the whole Scripture, especially of the Gospel, is to declare him so to be, and how he is so."[73]

Of course, Owen said, the Scriptures are also an external doctrinal revelation of the divine nature and properties. But such was not sufficient for the purposes of God in the manifestation of Himself. Consequently, "the whole Scripture is built on this foundation, or proceeds on this supposition—that there is a real representation of the divine nature unto us which it declares and describes." "All this is done in the person of Christ. He is the complete image and perfect representation of the Divine Being and excellencies." Thus is the "glory of God" represented unto us and "seen and known only in the face of Christ."[74]

That being the case,

> This principle is always to be retained in our minds in reading of the Scripture,—namely, that the revelation of the person of Christ and his office, is the foundation whereon all other instructions of the prophets and apostles for the edification of the church are built and whereinto they are resolved. . . . Lay aside this consideration hereof, and the Scriptures are no such thing as they pretend unto,—namely a revelation of the glory of God in the salvation of the church.[75]

Though every sacred truth of Scripture is a pearl whereby the believer is enriched, when he meets with the glory of Christ in Scripture, he has fallen upon the "pearl of great price"; and "this is that which the soul of a believer cleaves unto with joy."[76]

72. *Works*, 1:65.
73. Ibid., 1:74; cf. 18:48.
74. Ibid., 1:69-70.
75. Ibid., 1:314-15.
76. Ibid., 1:316.

Then do we find food for our souls in the word of truth, then do we taste how gracious the Lord is therein, then is the Scripture full of refreshment unto us as a spring of living water,—when we are taken into blessed views of the glory of Christ therein. . . . He is the sun and firmament of it, which only hath light in itself, and communicates it unto all other things besides.[77]

The believer understands Scripture only as much as he knows Christ in Scripture. Indeed, "truths to be believed are like believers themselves. All their life, power, and order consists in their relation unto Christ; separated from him they are dead and useless."[78]

Second, Scripture is the only glass in which to behold Christ. For that reason, Owen contended for the "possession of the Scriptures against all that would deprive us of it, or discourage us from a daily diligent search into it"; they were trying "to take from us the only glass wherein we may behold the glory of Christ."[79] "Our love to Christ ariseth alone from the revelation that is made of him in the Scripture—is ingenerated, regulated, measured, and is to be judged thereby."[80]

Third, Scripture is the Word of Christ. Scripture is all that it is as the Word of God "by virtue of its relation unto Jesus Christ, whose word it is. . . ."[81] Indeed, Owen asserted that the revelation that Jesus made by His Spirit is no less divine and immediate from Himself than what he spoke unto His disciples on earth.[82] Scripture, then, is to be regarded as the mind and will of Christ; and it therefore has an authority obliging the consciences of all who believe.[83]

---

77. Ibid.
78. Ibid., 20:19. I am tempted to go on indefinitely with such lyrical quotes, but I will be content to refer the reader to a few more: 1:74-75, 81-82, 84-87, 99, 343; 20:518-19.
79. Ibid., 1:316; cf. 157.
80. Ibid., 1:161.
81. Ibid., 21:351.
82. Ibid., 5:59.
83. Ibid., 15:246; cf. 6:545-46.

THE PRESERVATION OF SCRIPTURE

Textual criticism in Owen's time was not yet a highly developed discipline. Nevertheless, new and startling discoveries were being made, and theories about the history of the Greek and Hebrew texts were being proposed. Those were matters of grave concern to Owen, for as he viewed the matter they vitally affected the question of the authority of Scripture. He was no textual critic; indeed, by his own admission he had little knowledge of the facts of the case; but as a theologian he ventured forth into the field.

As scholars began to study the evidence, some conjectured that the ancient Hebrew letters had undergone a change (from Samaritan to Chaldean) and that the vowel points and accents of the Hebrew text were the invention of some late Masoretic scholars. Others argued that the Jews had corrupted the Hebrew text so that all that could really be known of the Old Testament text comes from the Septuagint. On the basis of the known Greek and Hebrew manuscripts, it was being asserted that there were variant readings in existence in both the Old and New Testaments. Owen's reaction to those developments was immediate. He held that to accept the validity of those assertions was to destroy all scriptural authority and that "there is nothing left unto men but to choose whether they will be Papists or atheists."[84] In fact, he suspected that such theories were usually the corrupt emanations of Socinianism and Arminianism on the one hand and popery on the other in an effort to destroy the authority of Scripture.[85]

The position that Owen took can best be understood when seen in the historical perspective of his debate with Brian Walton, editor and compiler of the *London Polyglott* (1652-58).[86] As Owen explained the succession of events, he had written a treatise in which he had strongly stated that divine providence had preserved in the known Greek and Hebrew manuscripts the very jot and tittle of the original manuscripts. Upon the completion of that

84. Ibid., 16:285-86.
85. Ibid., 4:217-18; 16:347-53.
86. Owen's explanation of the sequence of events may be found in ibid., 16:347-52.

work, a copy of the "Prolegomena" and "Appendix" to the *Biblia Polyglotta*, with its massive evidence of extant variant readings, came into his hands. He immediately suspected that those variant readings (he did not consistently admit to their validity) tended to discredit his claim. Hence, he asked:

> But what, I pray, will it advantage us that God did so once deliver his word, if we are not assured also that that word so delivered hath been, by his special care and providence, preserved entire and uncorrupt unto us, or that it doth not evidence and manifest itself to be his word, being so preserved?[87]

He then concluded that if the assertions of the *Polyglott* be granted, it would be almost impossible to know for certain whether any individual word or expression was from God or not.

Consequently, without further investigation of the facts as they were then available, Owen wrote a reply to the assertions of the Polyglott entitled *A Vindication of the Purity and Integrity of the Hebrew and Greek Texts of the Old and New Testaments; In Some Considerations on the Prolegomena and Appendix to the Late Biblia Polyglotta*. To that treatise Walton replied, and the battle was joined; it was the one occasion during Owen's long and illustrious career that he left the field of battle undeniably vanquished.

Owen granted that the autographs had in all likelihood perished. But he asserted that though the copyists were subject to error, their religious care and the providence of God had preserved the original autographs in their entirety.[88]

For Owen that meant that the vowels and accents of the Hebrew text were completed at least by the time of Ezra and his companions; they were not a late creation or addition to the text.[89] That he regarded as of the utmost importance, for "the words are altogether innumerable whose significations may be varied by an arbitrary supplying of the points."[90] He even rejected the theory that the Masoretes were merely putting into

87. Ibid., 16:350.
88. Ibid., 16:354-57.
89. Ibid., 16:371.
90. Ibid., 16:373.

writing the vocalization that had been universally used and recognized on the grounds that at that time the Jews were no longer custodians of the Hebrew text. They were unbelievers, biased and spiritually ignorant; their work could not be relied upon.[91]

Owen even went so far as to say that the *Keri* and *Ketib* cannot be cited as evidence of corruption of the text. They are part of the integrity of the text, though he confessed that he did not quite understand their real significance.[92]

Yet there is also ambiguity in what Owen said, even contradiction. In contrast to the above, he admitted that copyists were not always completely preserved from error. He said that he would believe that variant readings existed when he was shown that they do exist, and he admitted that possibility. In his *Exposition of the Epistle to the Hebrews*, he recognized and discussed textual variants and the possibility of different vowel points for a Hebrew word in the quoted Old Testament text.[93] Owen's words clearly show his inconsistency and contradiction:

> There is no doubt but that in the copies we now enjoy of the Old Testament there are some diverse readings, of various lections. . . . But yet we affirm, that the whole word of God, in every letter or tittle, as given from him by inspiration, is preserved without corruption. Where there is any variety it is always in things of less, indeed of no importance.[94]
>
> Nor is it enough to satisfy us, that the doctrines mentioned are preserved entire; every tittle and iota in the Word of God must come under our care and consideration, as being, as such, from God.[95]
>
> It is known, it is granted, that failings have been amongst them and that various lections are from thence risen. . . .[96]
>
> We are ready to own all their failings that can be proved. To assert in this case without proof is injurious.[97]
>
> *The whole Scripture*, entire as given out from God, without any

91. Ibid., 16:381-85.
92. Ibid., 16:401-6.
93. Ibid., 24:128-29.
94. Ibid., 16:301.
95. Ibid., 16:303.
96. Ibid., 16:355.
97. Ibid.

loss, is preserved in the *copies of the originals* yet remaining; what variations there are among themselves shall afterward be declared. In them all, we say, is every letter and tittle of the word. These copies, we say, are the rule, standard, and touchstone of all translations, ancient or modern, by which they are in all things to be examined, tried, corrected, amended; and themselves only by themselves.[98]

Notwithstanding what hath been spoken, we grant that there are and have been various lections in the Old Testament and the New. . . .

In their consideration of every letter, point, and accent of the Bible, wherein they spent their lives, it seems they found some varieties. Let anyone run them through as they are presented in this Appendix, he will find them to be so small, consisting for the most part in unnecessary accents, of no importance to the sense of any word, that they deserve not to be taken notice of.[99]

All that yet appears impairs not in the least the truth of our assertion, that every letter and tittle of the word of God remains in the copies preserved by his merciful providence for the use of his church.[100]

There is a basic contradiction running through almost all of what Owen has to say on textual preservation. Conflicting statements sometimes appear on the same page. The only viable conclusion is that Owen stated his position poorly, did contradict himself, and wrote in panic. He seems to have realized that there actually were variant readings but feared that his theological presuppositions were being undermined. But whatever the inadequacies and contradictions inherent in the language Owen used (and whatever conclusions may be reached, the fact of inadequacies and contradictions should be acknowledged), it is still only fair also to consider Owen's fears concerning the *London Polyglott*.

Though not necessarily harmonizing contradictory statements, one soon notices a basic objection running through all that Owen had to say about the *Polyglott*. He objected that it included conjectural emendations and listed them as though they were variant

98. Ibid., 16:357.
99. Ibid., 16:358-59.
100. Ibid., 16:359; cf. 363, 409-10.

readings in the manuscripts of the Greek and Hebrew. "Men," he wrote, "must here deal by instances, not conjectures."[101] Those conjectures were made on the basis of changing Hebrew vowel points, transposition of letters, possible mistakes caused by likeness of figure or sound, and variant senses derived from the Latin Vulgate and the Septuagint. According to Owen, such conjectures were being proposed and given equal status as variant readings even when no corresponding evidence from Greek and Hebrew manuscripts existed.[102] Owen felt that conjectures were being multiplied with a vengeance, particularly by those opposed to the authority of Scripture.

A more deliberate and careful investigation of textual studies would have enabled Owen to present a more accurate and harmonious defense of scriptural authority, forthrightly admitting the existence of variant readings and suspending his judgment on matters not yet conclusively settled. But the fact is that Owen did not follow the last alternative. Even so, it is only fair to remember the conditions of his day and the danger he saw in the admission of seemingly endless conjectural emendations. When that allowance is made, it is possible to understand why he reacted as he did.

THE INTERPRETATION OF SCRIPTURE

Owen did not devote any one treatise to the subject of the interpretation of Scripture. Nevertheless, it is possible to determine the principles that he thought should govern its reading and use.

First, one should resist the tendency to impose one's own meanings on another's words because of personal bias. Rather, one should go "nakedly to the word itself, to learn humbly the mind of God in it." Since the opinions of others can also unduly influence what the individual exegete sees in Scripture, Owen also warned against allowing the opinions of others to be imposed on it.[103] He wrote:

101. Ibid., 16:359.
102. Cf. ibid., 16:290-292, 301, 349, 359, 408-9, 420.
103. Ibid., 18:9.

And truly I must needs see that I know not a more deplorable mistake in the studies of the divines, both preachers and others, than their diversion from an immediate, direct study of the Scriptures themselves unto the studying of commentators, critics, scholiasts, annotators, and the like helps. . . . Not that I condemn the use and study of them, which I wish men were more diligent in, but desire pardon if I mistake, and do only surmise, by the experience of my own folly for many years, that many which seriously study the things of God do yet rather make it their business to inquire after the sense of other men from the Scriptures than to search studiously into them themselves.[104]

Second, the study of the Scriptures is best done in the original languages, for it is the words and phrases of the original languages that have the benefit of being directly and originally inspired.[105] However, Owen was far from saying that the Word of God cannot be known in translations; in fact, "the design of God was, that his word should be always read and used in that language which was commonly understood by them unto whom he granted the privilege thereof."[106] But the Scriptures in the original languages are the touchstone to which all translations and interpretations should be put.

In the translation and interpretation of the originals, particular attention was to be given to the usage of words, not only in the language as generally used, but also in the peculiar usages of the individual author whose writings were under consideration. Owen wrote, "In the interpretation of the mind of anyone it is necessary that the *words* he speaks or writes be rightly understood; and this we cannot do immediately unless we understand the *language* wherein he speaks, as also the idiotisms of that language, with the common intention of its *phraseology* and expressions." He also advised that a knowledge of the Greek of the Septuagint, as well as a sufficient knowledge of Hebrew and its concepts and manner of expression, would be a further aid in discovering the meaning of New Testament Greek.[107]

104. Ibid., 12:52.
105. Ibid., 4:213; cf. 210, 214.
106. Ibid., 4:210.
107. Ibid., 4:215; cf. 18:9.

Third, Owen recognized the importance of the syntactical relations and the general style of the passage. This involved due allowance for the figurative use of language.[108] The meaning of each word, phrase, and sentence should be related to its context; it should not be isolated and given a meaning other than that which it was originally intended to bear.[109]

Fourth, Owen realized the importance of reading Scripture in the light of each book's historical and geographical situation. This included an acquaintance with the geography of any of the places involved in each particular book, a knowledge of chronology, and an insight into the historical conditions of the time under consideration, especially the state and condition of those being written to.[110]

Fifth, Owen counseled to interpret in harmony with other Scripture and in harmony with the "analogy" or "proportion of faith." Whenever statements of Scripture seem to be in contradiction, one is to seek to reconcile them, giving the most weight to those passages that are most systematic, clear, and complete.[111] The analogy of faith might be loosely defined as the general tenor of Scripture. Owen defined it as "what is taught plainly and uniformly in the whole Scripture as the rule of our faith and obedience."[112] If the interpreter will always give appropriate attention to the analogy of faith, he will be preserved from serious errors. Adherence to this rule is especially important and helpful when interpreting obscure passages; for,

> Although a man should miss of the *first proper sense* of any obscure place of Scripture, which with all diligence, we ought to aim at, yet, whilst he receiveth none but what contains a truth agreeable unto what is revealed in other places, the error of his mind neither endangereth his own faith or obedience nor those of any others.[113]

The analogy of faith also was regarded by Owen as a good safe-

108. Ibid., 4:201; 19:64; 21:35-36, 167.
109. Ibid., 4:201, 209; cf. 12:62.
110. Ibid., 4:209, 219-22.
111. Ibid., 4:209; 5:384-85.
112. Ibid., 4:198.
113. Ibid.; cf. 194.

guard for those who were ignorant of the original languages and hence dependent on translations.[114]

Sixth, Owen warned against the imposition of alien philosophical categories and an artificial system on Scripture. In sum, he rejected scholastic methodology and notions. He wrote:

> God puts not such value upon men's *accurate methods* as they imagine them to deserve, nor are they so subservient unto his ends in the revelation of himself, as they are apt to fancy; yea, ofttimes, when, as they suppose, they have brought truths unto the *strictest propriety of expression*, they lose both their power and glory. Hence is the world filled with so many *life-less, sapless, graceless*, artificial declarations of divine truth in the *schoolmen* and others. We may sooner squeeze water out of a pumice-stone than one drop of spiritual nourishment out of them. But how many millions of souls have received divine light and consolation, suited unto their condition, in those *occasional occurrences* of truth which they met withal in the Scripture, which they would never have obtained in those wise, *artificial disposals of them* which some men would fancy ... Artificial methodizing of spiritual truths may make men ready in notions, cunning and subtile in disputations; but it is the Scripture itself that is able to "make us wise unto salvation."[115]

Owen explained why he believed God had not made a systematic proposal of doctrine in Scripture. "All that can be supposed of benefit thereby is only that it would lead us more easily into a *methodical comprehension* of the truths so proposed; but this we may attain, and not be rendered one jot more *like unto God* thereby."[116] He observed that the attempt to frame revelation

> in rigid confessions, or systems of supposed credible propositions, a Procrustes' bed to stretch them upon, or crop them unto the size of, so to reduce them to the same opinion in all things, is a vain and useless attempt, that men have for many generations worried themselves about, and yet continue so to do.[117]

114. Ibid., 4:216.
115. Ibid., 4:188-89.
116. Ibid., 4:189.
117. Ibid., 14:314.

He went on to declare:

> If those theological determinations that make up at this day
> amongst some men the greatest part of those assertions, positions,
> or propositions, which are called *articles of faith* or truth,—which are
> not delivered in the words that the Spirit of God teacheth, but in
> terms of art, and in answer unto rules and notions which the world
> might haply, without any great disadvantage, [have] been unac-
> quainted withal unto this day had not Aristotle found them out or
> stumbled on them,—might be eliminated from the city of God and
> communion of Christians, and left for men to exercise their wits
> about who have nothing else to do, and the doctrine of the truth
> which is according unto godliness left unto that noble, heavenly,
> spiritual, generous amplitude, wherein it was delivered in the
> Scripture and believed in the first churches, innumerable causes of
> strife and contentions would be taken away.[118]

Again, emphasizing the adverse results that may come from
preoccupation with systems of doctrine, Owen disapprovingly
wrote that "some learn their divinity out of the *late* and *modern*
schools, both in the Reformed and papal church; in both which a
science is proposed under that name, consisting in a farrago of
credible propositions, asserted in terms suited unto that philosophy that is variously predominant among them."[119] His conclusion was that he was no more happy with the results in the
Reformed churches than he was in the Papal church.

Therefore, though Owen was a systematic theologian himself,
he maintained in his work on the doctrine of justification, "I shall
as much as I possibly may, avoid all those *philosophical* terms and
distinctions wherewith this *evangelical* doctrine hath been perplexed rather than illustrated. . . ."[120] And then concerning the
way in which the doctrine had so often been developed he wrote:

> To carry it out of the understanding of ordinary Christians by
> speculative notions and distinctions, is disservicible unto the faith
> of the church; yes, the mixing of evangelical revelations with philo-

118. Ibid., 14:315.
119. Ibid.
120. Ibid., 5:8.

sophical notions hath been, in sundry ages, the poison of religion. Pretence of accuracy, and artificial skill in teaching, is that which giveth countenance unto such a way of handling sacred things. But the spiritual amplitude of divine truths is restrained hereby, whilst low, mean philosophical senses are imposed on them.[121]

As a whole, Owen's hermeneutical principles would be characterized as grammatico-historical. This was the only means by which the one true determinant sense of Scripture could be discovered.[122]

EVALUATION

The shape of John Owen's handling of the problem of authority and his view of Scripture are now quite clear. The time has come for evaluation. The major item on the agenda is evaluation of the claim by Rogers and McKim that John Owen was a "transitional figure between the Reformation stance of the Westminster Divines and the Protestant scholasticism of his continental contemporaries."[123]

They argue that his approach is like the Westminster Divines in some regards, though it moved his English Reformed constituency toward Scholasticism. In our sketch of Owen's views, it is obvious that he held to many of the elements commonly identified as characteristic of Reformation theology. One need only think of his views of reason, the self-evidencing, self-authenticating authority of God in Scripture, the testimony of the Spirit, and the relationship of Christ to the written Word to remember how prominent those elements were in his thought. Indeed, so all-pervasive are those themes in Owen's writings that they at least call into question any claim for so-called scholastic elements in his works. This is especially true in view of the Rogers/McKim statement that Protestant Scholasticism represented a spirit, a mood, and a mind-set—a shift of emphasis—rather than drastically different doctrines.[124]

121. Ibid., 5:10.
122. Ibid., 18:9.
123. Rogers and McKim, pp. 219-20.
124. Ibid., p. 185.

When one considers the scholastic emphases identified by Rogers and McKim, it is clear that few of them can seriously be considered characteristic of Owen. Consider the following:

> Owen's emphasis was not on the rational defense of a settled deposit of doctrine spelled out in Aristotelian fashion. Indeed, Owen ridiculed the scholiasts and followers of Aristotle (see pages 198, 212-13, 215-17 above).
>
> He was not preoccupied with metaphysical speculation (see pages 204-5, 215-17 above).
>
> He did not believe that reason was superior to faith (see pages 197-99, 204-5 above).
>
> He did not substitute philosophical speculation for growth in the Christian life as the goal of theological work (see pages 194, 215-17 above).
>
> He did not make faith primarily an act of intellectual assent (see pages 194-95, 197-99 above).
>
> He did not view the text of Scripture as atomistic units to be rearranged and fit into a logical system (see pages 204-5, 213-14 above).
>
> He repudiated the tendency to subject Scripture to inappropriate philosophical categories, and he largely avoided that himself (see pages 215-17 above).
>
> He did not subordinate the inner witness of the Spirit to rational arguments for the authority of Scripture (see pages 196-201, 203-5 above).
>
> He did not allow theology to become abstract speculation rather than a practical discipline for the salvation and sanctification of God's people. "Precision did not replace piety as the goal of theology" (see pages 204-7 above).

Rogers and McKim apparently would agree with most of those conclusions.[125] Still, they do identify several points in Owen that they believe were significant shifts away from a Reformation stance toward Scholasticism. Such shifts supposedly assisted in rigidifying doctrine in England.[126]

First, Rogers and McKim claim that in at least one treatise

---

125. Ibid., pp. 220-21.
126. Ibid., p. 221.

(*The Divine Original of Scripture*) Owen subjected scriptural material to inappropriate Aristotelian and Cartesian modes of presentation.[127] In that work Owen "supposedly adduced arguments to persuade people of Scripture's divine origin and thus divine authority." Rogers and McKim also claim Owen's arguments proceeded from "human reason and natural knowledge to the eventual perception of Scriptures as the Word of God, thus reversing the Augustinian order of faith seeking understanding."[128] But the evidence they cite is not convincing.

In fact, when one examines what Owen actually said in context, it is clear that Rogers and McKim seriously misrepresent his position. It is true that in the treatise Owen said he did not want to weaken those reasons and arguments usually used to prove the divine authority of Scripture. But the role of those arguments was one of confirmation.[129] He said he did not like to multiply arguments that conclude only in probability and can produce only a firm opinion at best. And then he wrote, "The principle intended to be evinced is *de fide*, and must be believed with faith divine and supernatural."[130] That is precisely the opposite of what Rogers and McKim claim Owen was arguing for! Even more remarkably, Rogers and McKim apparently did not perceive Owen's primary point in "the divine original [i.e., origin] of Scripture." It was that Scripture shows itself to be from God by its self-authentication.[131] It "hath such an impression of his [God's] authority upon it, as undeniably to evince it is from him."[132] Nothing else was needed or adequate to produce faith.

Second, Rogers and McKim cite Owen's tendency to treat the human authors as mere scribes recording divine words as a scholastic rigidifying of Reformation doctrine.[133] As evidenced above, Owen seemed to hold that view of the human writers. But just as clearly there are contrary elements in Owen, and one should temper any dogmatic and rigid claim that he viewed the writers as

---

127. Ibid.
128. Ibid., pp. 221-22.
129. *Works*, 16:312.
130. Ibid., 337.
131. See especially ibid., 306-12, 325-36.
132. Ibid., 312.
133. Rogers and McKim, p. 222.

mere scribes taking dictation. In any event, that is hardly a clear enough or a significant enough point to conclude that Owen was moving in a scholasticizing direction. Indeed, is Owen's language on that point any clearer or stronger than Calvin's references to the dictation of Scripture?[134]

Third, Owen supposedly followed the scholastic trend to press verbal inspiration to an unnecessary extreme by insisting that the vowel points were inspired.[135] Owen is properly faulted for insisting the vowel points were part of the original text of the Old Testament. But his real point was that the meaning of a word depended on the vocalization of its Hebrew consonants. If words are important as the bearers of meaning, obviously their spelling (including jots, tittles, and vowels) is also important. Can Owen be faulted on that point? Would Rogers and McKim have been content with less than accurate spelling in their own book? Still, as important as the words, including jots, tittles, and vowels were, Owen did not view them atomistically apart from their context and the concepts they were intended to communicate. Nor did he allow the words of Scripture to become ends in themselves or divorced from the Christ of Scripture.

Rogers and McKim seem to regard Owen's views of textual preservation and textual criticism as another indication of scholastic tendencies.[136] Again, it should be admitted that Owen's treatment of the subject was seriously deficient. But Rogers and McKim do not recognize that the evidence is that Owen's statements are self-contradictory. They are not evidence of a rigidifying Scholasticism but of a confused man, a man who had legitimate concerns and fears concerning arbitrary changes that might be made in the text by unfriendly critics. His concerns were real; his confusion concerning the textual evidence and its significance is obvious; his self-contradictory statements are open for examina-

---

134. For example see Calvin's *Institutes* 4.8.6,8,9; see also Calvin's comments on 2 Tim. 3:16 and 2 Pet. 1:20 in his commentaries. Those citations only scratch the surface of Calvin's "dictation language." For a more detailed discussion and documentation see Kenneth S. Kantzer, "Calvin and the Holy Scriptures," in John F. Walvoord, ed., *Inspiration and Interpretation* (Grand Rapids: Eerdmans, 1957), pp. 137-41.
135. Rogers and McKim, p. 222.
136. Ibid., p. 223.

tion. As confused and wrong as he was, that hardly makes him a transitional figure toward a rigid Scholasticism in England.

But it seems to me that the more serious and fatal flaw in the analysis and conclusions of Rogers and McKim (here as elsewhere) is the rigid dichotomy they posit between form and function. They regard the two as so incompatible that they cannot see them existing as two legitimate concerns in the same individual. In some cases this apparently blinds them to clear indications that concern for the form of Scripture does not preclude concern for its function and vice versa. In the case of Owen, the dichotomy between form and function in the thinking of Rogers and McKim leads them to conclude that in spite of Owen's concern for function, his concern for the form of Scripture is evidence that he was a transitional figure toward Scholasticism in English Reformed theology. But their premise should be challenged. It is not an adequate model by which to study Owen, or anyone else for that matter. Perhaps it is that premise that leads them to ignore Owen's express repudiation of both Roman Catholic and Reformed Scholasticism.

We should not be forced to an either/or choice between the form and function of Scripture as God's Word in our interpretation of Luther, Calvin, Turretin, the Westminster Divines, Owen, or the Old Princeton school. The crucial question is, Was the concern for form and function kept in proper balance?

And that question also confronts evangelicals today. In particular, noninerrantists need to be challenged with the importance of the form of Scripture as God's Word. But inerrantists must also be questioned: Have we tended to be so preoccupied with the form of Scripture as God's Word that we have lost sight of its function as God's Word?

For both his insights and shortcomings, John Owen is a model to be studied by both sides in the current debate.[137]

---

137. For a more detailed analysis of Owen's approach to the problem of authority, see my S.T.M. thesis, *John Owen's Doctrine of the Scriptures: An Original Study of His Approach to the Problem of Authority* (Union College of British Columbia [now the Vancouver School of Theology], 1967).

7

Infallibility, Wesley, and British Wesleyanism

Wilber T. Dayton

The purpose of this chapter is to identify John Wesley's and early British Wesleyanism's doctrine of the Scriptures. In the process attention will be given to the factors that contributed to those convictions and to the effect Wesley's approach had on British Wesleyanism.

It might come as a shock to many Wesleyans that anyone would waste ink on this subject. The absolute authority and total reliability of the Bible was taken for granted in early Wesleyanism as emphatically as motherhood has been assumed to be the principle for the survival of the race. Nothing would have been more repugnant to original Methodism than to cast doubt on the Word of God, the very source of life. Wesley explained his attitude toward the Bible and his method of arriving at truth. The familiar account is as follows.

WILBER T. DAYTON, B.A., B.D. Houghton College, M.A. Butler University School of Religion, M.R.E., Th.D. Northern Baptist Theological Seminary, is professor of biblical literature and historical theology at Wesley Biblical Seminary, Jackson, Mississippi. He was formerly president of Houghton College and has contributed to the *Wesleyan Bible Commentary*, *Zondervan Pictorial Encyclopedia of the Bible*, and the *Wycliffe Bible Encyclopedia*. He was also a member of the editorial committee of the *New International Version* of the New Testament.

To candid reasonable men, I am not afraid to lay open what have been the inmost thoughts of my heart. I have thought, I am a creature of a day, passing through life as an arrow through the air. I am a spirit come from God, and returning to God: just hovering over the great gulf; till, a few moments hence, I am no more seen; I drop into an unchangeable eternity: I want to know one thing—the way to heaven; how to land safe on that happy shore. God Himself has condescended to teach the way; for this very end He came from heaven, He hath written it down in a book. O give me that book! At any price, give me the book of God! I have it: here is knowledge enough for me. Let me be *homo unius libri*. Here then I am, far from the busy ways of men. I sit down alone: only God is here. In His presence I open, I read His book; for this end, to find the way to heaven. Is there a doubt concerning the meaning of what I read? Does anything appear dark or intricate? I lift up my heart to the Father of Lights: "Lord, is it not Thy word, 'If any man lack wisdom, let him ask of God?' Thou hast said, 'If any be willing to do Thy will, he shall know.' I am willing to do, let me know, Thy will." I then search after and consider parallel passages of Scripture, "comparing spiritual things with spiritual." I meditate thereon with all the attention and earnestness of which my mind is capable. If any doubt still remains, I consult those who are experienced in the things of God; and then the writings whereby, being dead, they yet speak. And what I thus learn, that I teach.[1]

It is that plain and simple. The Scriptures stood alone and adequate as the ultimate source of Wesley's belief and teaching. Oxford scholar that he was, there was only one book that he trusted as utterly reliable in the great issue of life. Though he read ten languages and published nearly four hundred pieces himself, it was only to understand better that one book. How could any doubt surround Wesley's view of the Scriptures or that of his followers? Whether the term is truth, reliability, infallibility, or inerrancy, it was taken for granted that Wesley and Wesleyanism had no reservations.

What has changed? We are now told that the idea of inerrancy

1. John Wesley, *The Works of John Wesley*, 14 vols. (Grand Rapids: Zondervan, n.d.), 5:2-4.

was spawned by "ailing evangelicals,"[2] particularly of the Princeton school. Battles says that the chief goal of Rogers and McKim's massive volume was to discover how "the defensive, intransigent position of inerrancy that marks the handling of Scripture among certain twentieth century children of the Protestant Reformation came into existence."[3] In their introduction the co-authors report that the key to that understanding of inerrancy is not found in Calvin or the Reformers but in a post-Reformation Scholasticism that was "almost the exact opposite of Calvin's own" approach.[4] To their minds, "certain features of the central church tradition regarding the authority and interpretation of the Scripture, which had been retained from the early church down through the Reformation, were lost in the post-Reformation reaction to the rise of scientific criticism of the Bible."[5]

The trouble was traced to Francis Turretin, who dared to assert that the authority of the Scripture "was based on its form of inerrant words." Rogers and McKim moan that the innovators showed "no trace of the central Christian tradition of accommodation."[6] "Rather, it was assumed that what the Bible told us was what God told us, down to the details. Inspired men thought God's thoughts after him and transmitted them in writing."[7] When Princeton Seminary was founded in 1812, Turretin's book was used as the principal text in systematic theology until Hodge's *Systematic Theology* replaced it and "continued Turretin's theological method."[8] It is the tradition of Turretin, Hodge, and Warfield that Rogers and McKim found unacceptable and "not historically correct."[9] They argue that such an allegedly new and extreme position prevailed over Briggs in a heresy trial and was declared to be the doctrine of the Presbyterian Church and the confessional position of the historical church.[10] Since the doctrine of inerrancy

2. Jack B. Rogers and Donald K. McKim, *The Authority and Interpretation of the Bible* (San Francisco: Harper & Row, 1979), p. xvi.
3. Ibid., p. xv.
4. Ibid., p. xvii.
5. Ibid.
6. Ibid.
7. Ibid., p. xviii.
8. Ibid., p. xvii.
9. Ibid., p. xi.
10. Ibid., p. xviii.

was carefully formulated and its implications explored in a way that could be defended, it was called scholastic. As such, that doctrine was strong enough to engage in the fundamentalist-modernist controversy, to establish a relationship with the denominational roots of various evangelical traditions, to reinforce the "scholastic" view of inerrancy in Lutheranism, and to spread its mischief down to the current "Battle for the Bible."[11] Rogers and McKim's purpose is to unscramble the eggs—to expose the error of inerrancy and to "restore" the accommodation view so that the church can again believe that God accommodated Himself to human frailty and error. At all costs, it seems, they are determined that the church must be delivered from the "uncritical" view that the Bible in its entirety is the inerrant Word of God.

Once an issue like that is drawn, such "critical" opinions are widely accepted uncritically. No one wants to be an inflexible "seventeenth century scholastic" or a "nineteenth century fundamentalist," when the "central church tradition" is supposedly "much richer and more flexible."[12] After the faithful for centuries have steered the ship of Zion between the rocks of mysticism and agnostic rationalism, one does not want to be called a mystic or a rationalist.[13] In any case, for whatever cause, there are those who claim to find support for their rejection of the verbal inerrancy of the Scriptures in their own evangelical heritage, as Dr. Timothy L. Smith affirms.[14] If that proves anything, it could simply be that not everyone's evangelical faith is scholastic. In the flexibility of human understanding, some believe more than others, and they often find that the faith of their saintly forebears is not so much a list of opinions or convictions as it is a relationship of deep commitment to God through Jesus Christ, as revealed in the Scriptures. Evangelical faith and fully orthodox views are not necessarily identical, though they tend to go together.

In any case, this chapter is about Wesley and British Wesleyanism, particularly in relation to the infallibility of the Scriptures.

11. Ibid., pp. xviii-xxiii.
12. Ibid., p. xxiii.
13. Ibid., pp. xxi, xxii.
14. Timothy L. Smith, "Determining Biblical Authority's Base," *Christian Century* 94 (1977): 198.

Whether or not the Princeton theologians correctly understood the history of Christian faith, it should not be necessary to prove that eighteenth-century Wesleyans did not borrow their view of Scripture from nineteenth-century Princeton scholars. And the burden of proof would be on those who argue that they were following "post-Reformation scholasticism, mysticism, or rationalism." It would be impossible here to trace and refute all the conjectures and allegations that have been made in the literature about Wesley and the Wesleyans or to examine in detail all the points at which one might disagree with Rogers and McKim in their interpretation of the Fathers. Consequently, we will focus our attention on a few questions that should help one understand Wesley's view of the Scriptures, how he came to his conviction, and what results followed his approach in his own ministry and in British Wesleyanism.

Fortunately, there is an abundance of data in Wesley's own words. The fourteen volumes of *The Works of John Wesley*,[15] the eight volumes of *The Letters of John Wesley*,[16] and the eight volumes of *The Journal of John Wesley*[17] cover a mountain of data. Add to that his three-volume *Explanatory Notes upon the Old Testament*,[18] his one-volume *Explanatory Notes upon the New Testament*,[19] and his own translation of the *New Testament*.[20] Wesley's *Works* include scores of sermons and treatises that set forth his beliefs and methods. And then there are the hundreds of books by and about Wesley and his times, as well as the archives of Methodism from the eighteenth century to the present.

One limitation should be noted in the scope of the present treatment. British Wesleyanism will be studied mainly in the eighteenth and nineteenth-centuries. As will be noted, the movement maintained its momentum on its founding principles with amaz-

15. *Works.*
16. *The Letters of the Rev. John Wesley, A.M.*, ed., John Telford, 8 vols. (London: Epworth Press, 1931).
17. *The Journal of the Rev. John Wesley, A.M.*, ed., Nehemiah Curnock, 8 vols. (London: Epworth Press, 1909).
18. *Explanatory Notes upon the Old Testament* (Salem, Ohio: Schmul Publishers, 1975).
19. *Explanatory Notes upon the New Testament* (London: Epworth Press, 1966).
20. *The New Testament with an Analysis of the several books and chapters* (Philadelphia: John C. Winston Company, 1938).

ing consistency until near the end of the nineteenth century. Some of the changes that characterized the twentieth century were so drastic that one is, in many respects, dealing with a whole new world, or at least with a very different phase in the life of a major movement.

WESLEY AND INFALLIBILITY

Did Wesley believe that the Scriptures are the infallible Word of God? It would be hard to believe that any plain person in Wesley's day would deny or doubt what was so abundantly evident. If, on the other hand, one were trying to force Wesley's vocabulary and meaning into the terms of late twentieth-century debate, one might find ways of escaping the plain truth. Before attempting to understand Wesley, one ought to give serious consideration to the way in which he used words. He was not trying to be a philosopher; he was not even primarily a theologian. He was an evangelist. He sought plain truth. When he believed that he had found it, he passed it on as plainly as he understood it. His hope was that plain people would understand it and benefit from it. Philosophical opinions bore little weight with him. He sought certainty and dealt in convictions. In the preface to his published sermons, he wrote:

> I design plain truth for plain people: Therefore, of set purpose, I abstain from all nice and philosophic speculations; from all perplexed and intricate reasonings; and, as far as possible, from even the show of learning, unless in sometimes citing the original Scriptures. I labor to avoid all words which are not used in common life; and, in particular, those kinds of technical terms that so frequently occur in Bodies of Divinity; those modes of speaking which men of reading are intimately acquainted with, but which to common people are an unknown tongue.[21]

The present writer was so accustomed to that Wesleyan type of plainness for plain people that he remembers the culture shock he experienced when he was first asked his opinion in the debate

21. *Works*, 5:2.

about the infallibility of the Bible. If the question had been about the reliability, trustworthiness, genuineness, authenticity, integrity, or truthfulness of the Scriptures, there would have been an immediate and confident answer. But what particular "bone" was my friend trying to pick with that technical term? Was some "nice and philosophic speculation" hidden under a technical theological term? As a true disciple of Wesley, the writer opted for the plain and simple meaning of the word and affirmed his belief that the Bible is unfailing in all that it undertakes and affirms.

If one takes Wesley as meaning what he says and as saying in clear and sober terms what he means, there can be no doubt that he would affirm the complete infallibility and inerrancy of the Scriptures. And if anyone has ever earned credibility for his statements, certainly Wesley has by his long and consistent life and by his zealous proclamation of the Word.

While Semler was making distinctions between the Word of God and Holy Scripture and was saying that "by no means all parts of the Canon can be inspired,"[22] Wesley was saying the opposite with all candor and assurance.

Concerning the Scriptures in general, it may be observed, the word of the living God, which directed the first patriarchs also, was, in the time of Moses, committed to writing. To this was added, in several succeeding generations, the inspired writings of the other prophets. Afterwards, what the Son of God preached, and the Holy Ghost spoke by the apostles, the apostles and evangelists wrote. This is what we now style the Holy Scripture: this is that "word of God which remaineth for ever"; of which, though "heaven and earth pass away, one jot or tittle shall not pass away." The Scripture, therefore, of the Old and New Testament is a most solid and precious system of divine truth. Every part thereof is worthy of God; and all together are one entire body, wherein is no defect, no excess. It is the fountain of heavenly wisdom, which they who are able to taste prefer to all writings of men, however wise or learned or holy.[23]

22. Werner Georg Kümmel, *The New Testament: The History of the Investigation of its Problems* (Nashville: Abingdon, 1972), p. 63.
23. "Preface," *Explanatory Notes upon the New Testament*, p. 10.

Again, in the same preface, while Semler was saying that the books of the Bible were no different from any other books and were subject to all the same canons of criticism, Wesley wrote of the Bible without pausing to argue his case:

> All the elegancies of human composure sink into nothing before it: God speaks, not as man, but as GOD. His thoughts are very deep, and thence His words are of inexhaustible virtue. And the language of His messengers, also, is exact in the highest degree: for the words which were given them answered the impression made upon their minds; and hence Luther says, "Divinity is nothing but a grammar of the language of the Holy Ghost." To understand this thoroughly, we should observe the emphasis which lies on every word—the holy affections expressed thereby, and the tempers shown by every writer. But how little are these, the latter especially, regarded! though they are wonderfully diffused through the whole New Testament, and are in truth a continued commendation of him who acts or speaks or writes.[24]

The same candor and simplicity are seen in Wesley's note on John 10:35, "And the Scripture cannot be broken." He said, "That is, nothing which is written therein can be censured or rejected."[25]

To Wesley, being a Christian implied a belief in the full inspiration of the Scripture, and such inspiration implied inerrancy. In 1776 Wesley commented in his *Journal* on a tract entitled *Internal Evidence of the Christian Religion*, wondering whether the author, Jenyns, was a Christian, a deist, or an atheist. He wrote:

> If he is a Christian, be betrays his own cause by averring that "all Scripture is not given by inspiration of God, but the writers of it were sometimes left to themselves, and consequently made some mistakes." Nay, if there be any mistakes in the Bible, there may as well be a thousand. If there be one falsehood in that book, it did not come from the God of truth.[26]

For Wesley, the true view of Scripture was not acquired by dia-

24. Ibid., p. 12.
25. Ibid., p. 245.
26. *Journal*, 6:117.

logue with unbelievers. One is either a Christian believer or he is not. The Christian believer has a Bible that is the inerrant Word of God. The unbeliever does not. It is that simple. No amount of human dialogue could change that fact for Wesley. Some have tried to limit the sphere in which Wesley claimed inspiration and inerrancy for the Scriptures. They have said, for instance, that Wesley's concern was soteriological and that, therefore, he was referring only to the saving message of the Scriptures when he said they could be fully trusted. Since the Bible is not a textbook on history and science, they assume that inspiration does not cover statements of historical or scientific import. It is true, of course, that Wesley's primary concern in the Scriptures coincides with God's primary purpose in giving the Word—the message of salvation, the way to heaven. But Wesley saw no reason to believe that the rest of the Bible was an unaided human product, just because he believed that the Bible's theology, Christology, and soteriology were the inerrant Word of God. For Wesley, the Scriptures were the only infallible rule for faith and practice. But that did not discredit the truthfulness of all else that the Scriptures affirm. Daryl E. McCarthy well says that "in all his writings Wesley never once gave the slightest indication of a dichotomy between the inerrancy of 'spiritual' matters and the errancy of historical and other 'nonspiritual' matters."[27] As Skevington Wood says, "Whilst there may be room for further discussion as to how Wesley conceived the mode of inspiration, there can be no doubt as to what he took to be the effect of inspiration. He received the Bible as from God Himself."[28] In Wesley's own words, " 'All Scripture is given by inspiration of God;' consequently, all Scripture is infallibly true; 'and is profitable for doctrine, for reproof, for correction, for instruction in righteousness;' to the end 'that the man of God may be perfect, thoroughly furnished unto all good works.' "[29]

As has already been seen, Wesley expressed his confidence in the Scriptures as the infallible Word of God by explicit state-

27. A paper, "O Give Me That Book:—John Wesley and the Bible" (Kansas City College and Bible School, Overland Park, Kansas).
28. A. Skevington Wood, *The Burning Heart: John Wesley, Evangelist* (Grand Rapids: Eerdmans, 1968), p. 214.
29. *Works*, 5:193.

ments. All that was needed was an inquirer or an audience. Wesley was quick to give candid testimony to candid people. To him, God was the ultimate and only sure source of truth. What the Bible said, God said. And it was unthinkable that God could be in error in anything that He said in His Word, whether it directly concerned the central theme of salvation or whether the discussion was about human and temporal affairs more akin to history and science. If one takes Wesley's words seriously, it is impossible to deny that he professed to believe completely in the full truthfulness and inerrancy of the Scriptures.

The question naturally arises whether that profession of confidence was simply a set of traditional opinions held loosely and uncritically, perhaps as the expected "stock in trade" of an Anglican priest to give authenticity to his ordination, his ministry, his manse, and the "living." Tradition, indeed, there was. Whatever other claims the Church of England or any dissenting body made, the real focus of authority involved a reliable Word of God. Wesley was not alone in being nurtured in a tradition that held a high view of Scripture. C. J. Cadoux, the Oxford church historian and zealous promoter of liberalism, frankly says in *The Case for Evangelical Modernism*,

> The most signal of these abandoned beliefs is that in the inerrancy of Scripture—which was accepted by Christendom with practical unanimity from the second century to the nineteenth. A partial exception to this statement is to be seen in the liberty assumed by certain of the sixteenth-century Reformers, and in particular in the slap-dash expressions of Luther. In expounding the doctrine of justification by faith, Luther assumed a very free attitude to Scripture; but he had no consistent view, and his followers on the whole stood by plenary inspiration. Calvin as a scholar admitted the existence of small inaccuracies, and allowed himself here and there considerable freedom in critical exposition: but on the whole he too ranks as a supporter of belief in Biblical inerrancy. Brunner makes a great deal of what he considers the freedom of "the Reformers" from bondage to this belief; but it is impossible to credit them with any consistent freedom from it, or with anything at all resembling the critical attitude approved by the modern Barthian. The fact that belief in Biblical inerrancy was not incorporated in any for-

mal creed was due, not to any doubt as to its being an essential item of belief, but to the fact that no one challenged it. The view held by the late Dr. Gore and some other Catholics that Catholicism (in the broad sense) was not committed to belief in the inerrancy of the Bible, but that this belief was introduced by Protestants at the Reformation—a view based on the fact that no Church-Council had authoritatively declared the belief obligatory—had been exposed as quite erroneous (by Dr. J. V. Bartlett in the *Hibbert Journal*, April 1932, 460-462). Such difficulties as the belief raised were dealt with, for the most part, not by denying Biblical accuracy, but by liberty of interpretation.[30]

The fairness and accuracy of Dr. Cadoux's analysis is remarkable indeed in view of the fact that he does not share the belief that he shows to be so predominant and normative throughout most of the history of the Christian church. In fact, he said all of that to show what powerful considerations were necessary to abolish such well-established traditions and to establish what he considered the true orthodoxy of "Evangelical Modernism." Whatever his motives, he does make it clear that the "central church tradition" was, at its core, a confidence in an inerrant Bible as the fully reliable Word of God. If Dr. Cadoux misinterpreted the case at all, the fault was probably in underestimating the confidence of Luther and Calvin in the Word of God. If one follows their deeds as well as their words, they were both "captive to the Word" in a very true sense.

Cadoux is certainly right that the tradition of an inerrant Scripture did not begin with Turretin (as opposed to Calvin) or in the elaborations of the Princeton School but started no later than the early church (second century), of which it was the "most signal belief." It was first seriously challenged by modern liberals. In fact, Cadoux mentions in the next sentence what happened in the eighteenth and nineteenth centuries. It was not the birth of inerrantism and its espousal by an "ailing evangelicalism." Though Cadoux spoke too confidently of the victory of liberalism over the church traditions, he did identify the most serious threat to the

---

30. Cecil John Cadoux, *The Case for Evangelical Modernism* (London: Hodder & Stoughton, 1938), pp. 64-65.

gospel of Jesus Christ that has appeared in many centuries. He wrote, "The coming of Higher Criticism has abolished that particular belief for all traditionalists (including Barthians), other than Roman Catholics and Fundamentalists."[31] Now, of course, the more common term is historical criticism, a term that suggests that men are to judge the Scriptures, to determine what part, if any, is the truly inspired and reliable Word of God.

By word and deed, Wesley and his stalwart successors of the nineteenth century made clear that they would have no part in such an approach of doubt and unbelief. They went to the Word to be judged, not to judge it. To them, there was no authority equal to that of the Scripture. Even "the church, in all cases, is to be judged by the Scripture, not the Scripture by the church."[32]

But it is not in words alone or even in words primarily that Wesley gave expression to his confidence in the Scriptures. It is even more, if possible, in the way that the Bible became the source of his spiritual life, the guide of his conduct, the authority of his ministry, the sole standard of truth, and the ultimate judge of human destiny and of human institutions.

It is not surprising, then, that John and Charles Wesley and two other young Anglicans, when they became zealous about spiritual matters, began to spend evenings together in Bible study with their Greek Testaments. Their zeal and regularity of life soon earned them the name *Methodists*. Wesley said later,

> They were all zealous members of the Church of England; not only tenacious of all her doctrines, so far as they knew them, but of all her discipline, to the minutest circumstance. They were likewise zealous observers of all the University Statutes, and that for conscience' sake. But they observed neither these nor anything else any further than they conceived it was bound upon them by their one book, the Bible; it being their one desire and design to be downright Bible-Christians; taking the Bible, as interpreted by the primitive Church and our own, for their whole and sole rule.[33]

31. Ibid., p. 65.
32. *Works*, 10:142.
33. Ibid., 8:348.

In another reference, Wesley fixed on the year 1729 as the time (nine years before his Aldersgate conversion experience) when he "began not only to read, but to study, the Bible, as the one, the only standard of truth, and the only model of pure religion."[34] The climax of assurance of salvation that occurred at Aldersgate was in the context of searching the Scriptures to find God's way of salvation and life. And then he found a new power in proclaiming the Word that had brought life to him. Preaching was not philosophizing and announcing opinions. It was the proclamation of the Word of God. As those early Wesleyans had "resolved to be Bible-Christians at all events," so they determined "wherever they were, to preach with all their might plain, old, Bible Christianity."[35] As Skevington Wood says,

> Wesley went out of his way to make it clear that the basis of his work from the beginning was the Word of God. It was by accepting this standard that he himself had entered into the knowledge of salvation and it was from this fountain that he derived all his refreshing, soul-converting messages. The sermons which changed a nation came straight from the Book of books.[36]

If one wonders why Wesley so seldom dialogued with negative criticism, it was probably because he was so busy preaching the Word as the ultimate and only revealed truth. He wrote, "My ground is the Bible. Yea, I am a Bible bigot. I follow it in all things, both great and small."[37] Again, "The Scriptures are the touchstone whereby Christians examine all, real or supposed, revelations."[38] With the assurance of revealed truth, Wesley's heart was aflame with the love of God that made him a tireless evangelist. And all his other labors were to further his central task of saving souls. He showed his faith in the Scriptures by devoting his life and his all to bringing life and light from the Word of God to those who sat in darkness. Wesley did not opt for an opinion. He was sold out to a conviction. God had spoken, so he must speak.

34. Ibid., 11:367.
35. Ibid., 8:349.
36. Wood, p. 210.
37. *Works*, 3:251.
38. *Letters*, 2:117.

James S. Stewart once wrote, "The first axiom of effective evangelism is that the evangelist must be sure of his message."[39] Wesley had that "clear conviction of revealed truth and of its power to save."[40] As Woodrow Wilson said in an address at Wesleyan University in 1903, the bicentennial of Wesley's birth,

> Neither men nor society can be saved by opinions; nothing has power to prevail but the conviction which commands, not the mind merely, but the will and the whole spirit as well. It is this, and this only, that makes one spirit the master of others, and no man need fear to use his conviction in any age. It will not fail of its power. Its magic has no sorcery of words, no trick of personal magnetism. It concentrates personality as if into a single element of sheer force, and transforms conduct into life.[41]

Wesley, no doubt, did have gifts and some degree of genius, but his power was in the Word he preached. The infallible Word of God is the gospel of Jesus Christ. It was and is the power of God unto salvation. Wesley's view of the Scriptures was demonstrated even more in his powerful ministry than in his own affirmations.

WESLEY AND THE PLACE OF SCRIPTURE

In essence, the place of Scripture in Wesley's faith and ministry has already been affirmed. But the question of consistency must be raised concerning his principle. Millions in his day and since have professed (and tried) to live by principles that they only partially understood. Did Wesley really succeed in making the Scriptures the final source and authority of all that he believed and taught? Or was that primarily a rhetoric to encourage himself and others in a quest for certainty and authenticity? Did not Wesley believe in reason? Was he not sensitive to the scientific method of experimentation, observation, and reflection? Was he not influenced by the opinions of scientists and those engaged in historical research? Wesley was indeed a balanced person. He was constantly aware of

39. *A Faith to Proclaim* (1953), p. 12, quoted by Wood, p. 209.
40. Woodrow Wilson, *John Wesley's Place in History*, a bicentennial address at Wesleyan University on June 30, 1903 (New York: Abingdon, 1915), p. 46.
41. Ibid.

his human limitations and the numerous faults and imperfections even of those who, he believed, enjoyed the grace of "Christian Perfection." He wrote,

> They are not perfect in knowledge. They are not free from igno-rance, no, nor from mistake. We are no more to expect any living man to be infallible, than to be omniscient. They are not free from infirmities, such as weakness or slowness of understanding, irregu-lar quickness or heaviness of imagination. Such in another kind are impropriety of language, ungracefulness of pronunciation; to which one might add a thousand nameless defects, either in con-versation or behaviour. From such infirmities as these none are perfectly freed till their spirits return to God; neither can we expect till then to be wholly freed from temptation; for "the servant is not above his master." But neither in this sense is there any absolute perfection on earth. There is no perfection of degrees, none which does not admit of a continual increase.[42]

Wesley's awareness of his own defects made him reckon with the possibility of error even in what he thought he understood best. Wesley considered his translation of the New Testament his most important work. It was a product of more than twenty-five years of diligent and devout study in which he examined minutely every word of the New Testament in the original Greek. But in the preface to his *Explanatory Notes upon the New Testament* he said, "I cannot flatter myself so far as to imagine that I have fallen into no mistakes in a work of so great difficulty" (p. 9). He and his human sources, using the greatest care, had to admit human imperfection of knowledge and communication. But he would not grant the same imperfections to the Word itself. Of the Scriptures he wrote on the next page:

> The Scripture, therefore, of the Old and New Testament is a most solid and precious system of divine truth. Every part thereof is wor-thy of God; and all together are one entire body, wherein is no defect, no excess. It is the fountain of heavenly wisdom, which they who are able to taste prefer to all writings of men, however wise or learned or holy.

42. *Works*, 11:374.

There was a clear distinction in Wesley's ministry. He proclaimed the perfect and infallible Word of God, but he did not proclaim it perfectly and infallibly. He had "the book of God; here is knowledge enough." He was never able to get beyond that one book. But that did not make him independent of all human help. Nor did it make human diligence unimportant. He wrote:

> I sit down alone: Only God is here. In his presence I open, I read his book . . . Is there a doubt concerning the meaning of what I read? . . . I lift up my heart to the Father of Lights . . . I am willing to do; let me know, thy will. I then search after and consider parallel passages of Scripture, comparing spiritual things with spiritual. I meditate thereon with all the attention and earnestness of which my mind is capable. If any doubt still remains, I consult those who are experienced in the things of God and then the writings whereby, being dead, they yet speak. And what I thus learn, I teach.[43]

That is as near to certainty as a man can come. He had God's book—the true and reliable Word of God. And he had God's own help in understanding and obeying it. He diligently applied himself to knowledge and obedience, and he used all the human help available to find the meaning. That was not a lazy mysticism; it was a most authentic ministry in the Word of God. It even went beyond German pietism in its use of the Bible. As McGiffert said,

> In German pietism the Bible was employed chiefly as a devotional book. But in evangelicalism its significance as a divine revelation, authenticating the orthodox faith over against deism and scepticism, became especially prominent. Interpreted evangelically, it was made a doctrinal and moral authority of the most binding character. To venture to criticize its statements, to question its authority, to raise doubts as to the authenticity of any part, to set one's own judgment above it, to treat it as in any way ill-adapted to present conditions, all this was intolerable to a genuine Evangelical.[44]

43. *Works*, "Preface to Sermons," 5:3-4.
44. Arthur Cushman McGiffert, *Protestant Thought Before Kant* (New York: Scribner's, 1915), pp. 172-73.

That attitude on the part of Wesley and the Wesleyans was strongly opposed to the rationalism and deism of the times. How could they help but denounce and belittle the idea of "the sufficiency of human reason" as presumptuous and irreligious?[45] Naturally, the charge was made that Wesley was against reason. Why else would he denounce rationalism and espouse revelation? His answer to Dr. Rutherford was clear and to the point.

> You go on: "It is a fundamental principle in the Methodist school that all who come into it must renounce their reason." Sir, are you awake? Unless you are talking in your sleep, how can you utter so gross an untruth? It is a fundamental principle with us that to renounce reason is to renounce religion, that religion and reason go hand in hand, and that all irrational religion is false religion.[46]

Wesley was ever reasoning to refute error and to support truth and righteousness. His was a logical and scientific turn of mind. He experimented in the medical use of electricity and had a keen interest in the world about him—in the biological and physical sciences. Political, social, and economic theory were also objects of his concern to promote the welfare of people. The difference was that he recognized the limits of human wisdom. In his sermon on "The Imperfection of Human Knowledge" Wesley wrote:

> Therefore it is, that by the very constitution of their nature, the wisest of men "know" but "in part." And how amazingly small a part do they know, either of the Creator, or of his works! This is a very needful, but a very unpleasing theme, for "vain man would be wise." Let us reflect upon it for awhile. And may the God of wisdom and love open our eyes to discern our own ignorance.[47]

Wesley was deeply committed to reason and wrote much about it.[48] And in his sermon "The Case of Reason Impartially Considered," he pointed out that it is "reason (assisted by the Holy Ghost) which enables us to understand what Holy Scriptures

45. Ibid., p. 172.
46. *Letters*, 5:364.
47. *Works*, 6:338.
48. Ibid., 8:1-247.

declare concerning the being and attributes of God" and the great variety of matters revealed in the Scripture.[49] He said,

> Let reason do all that reason can. Employ it as far as it will go. But, at the same time, acknowledge it is utterly incapable of giving either faith, or hope, or love; and, consequently, of producing either real virtue, or substantial happiness. Expect these from a higher source, even from the Father of the spirits of all flesh. Seek and receive them, not as your own acquisition; but as the gift of God.[50]

The infallible Scriptures held the central place in Wesley's faith and ministry, not because he lacked commitment to reason, scientific method, or the values of research, but because there was a higher and more reliable source of knowledge and power than the wisdom and works of man. In the matters where the Bible has spoken, God has spoken. God cannot be wrong. Therefore, anything in scientific theory or reason that contradicts the Scripture is not to be received. The Bible is at the center. Human wisdom goes as far as it can, but God alone is completely true and completely efficacious.

Many have misunderstood Wesley at that point. It is not uncommon for one to observe his close reasoning, his scientific interest, his critical skill, his broad concerns, and his great erudition and draw the inference that if he were here today, he would be an expert critic of the Old and New Testaments after the pattern of Wellhausen and Bultmann, that he would admit significant error in the Scriptures, or that he would certainly believe in organic evolution. An example of reading such tendencies from a later context into Wesley's viewpoint is taken from Stolz's volume *The Psychology of Religious Living*.[51] Stolz wrote:

> John Wesley, the outstanding religious reformer in England of the eighteenth century, voiced an appreciation of speculative science, of which the majority of people called Methodists are as yet una-

---

49. Ibid., 6:354-55.
50. Ibid., 6:360.
51. Karl R. Stolz, *The Psychology of Religious Living* (Nashville: Abingdon-Cokesbury, 1937).

ware. . . . His work entitled *A Survey of the Wisdom of God in Creation, or a Compendium of Natural Philosophy* merits a larger circle of readers than it has hitherto attracted. In this work Wesley, leaning heavily for his science on John Francis Buddaeus of Jena, Germany, expounded a form of theistic evolution about eighty years before Darwin published *The Origin of Species.* . . . He describes the gradual progression of the works of God from vegetation to the polypus, from the bird to the quadruped, from ape to man. . . . He considers the ape a rough draft of man and interposes a prodigious number of connecting links between the two.[52]

That brief discussion in an otherwise good and helpful book puzzled the present writer. In the light of all that was known of Wesley, that data seemed preposterous and impossible. Fortunately, it was possible to obtain the two volumes from the Library of Congress.[53] True, Wesley had borrowed heavily from the Latin work of John Francis Buddaeus of Jena. What Dr. Stolz did not notice was that Wesley said that he quite largely rewrote the volumes according to his own purposes. He wrote, in part,

> But I have found occasion to retrench, enlarge, or alter every chapter, and almost every section. So that it is now, I believe, not only pure; containing nothing false or uncertain; but as full as any tract can be expected to be, which is comprised in so narrow a compass: and likewise plain, clear, and intelligible to one of a tolerable understanding. . . . It will be easily observed, that I undertake throughout not to account for things; but only to describe them. I undertake barely to set down what appears in nature; not the cause of those appearances.[54]

In other words, Stolz was right that Wesley produced remarkable volumes on science (formerly called natural philosophy, as Wesley understood it). He did indeed borrow heavily from Buddaeus of Jena. And it is true that Buddaeus used the carefully arranged categories of animal life to show some sort of evolutionary progression. There Stolz's scholarship ends and his prejudices

52. Ibid., pp. 116-17.
53. John Wesley, *A Survey of the Wisdom of God in the Creation, or A Compendium of Natural Philosophy*, 2 vols. (New York: N. Banas and T. Mason, 1823).
54. Ibid., 1:4-5.

take over. The obvious reason is that neither Stolz nor his advisers had read Wesley's volumes beyond part of the preface. As a result, he misunderstood the import of Wesley's introductory remarks.

Wesley did give credit to Buddaeus for much of the basic data of the work. The German scholar had made elaborate lists of categories of biological life from simple plants up to man. Wesley borrowed those valid descriptions of what existed, but specifically rejected the "speculative science" of Buddaeus by which he sought to account for the origin of those diversities. Wesley saw nothing contrary to the creation account in listing the categories in an order convenient for comparison, especially when the order was the same as in the Genesis account. But he specifically refused to draw the evolutionary conclusions to account for the similarities. To Wesley, the collection of scientific data was a legitimate function of a rational mind. But the speculative theory that contradicted the Bible in accounting for origins was without warrant. Worse than that, the creature was contradicting the Creator. Wesley would have none of it. It was Buddaeus's books, not Wesley's, that "expounded a form of theistic evolution about eighty years before Darwin." Or, more likely, the evolution was all in Buddaeus and the theism was all in Wesley. Wesley's volumes have no trace of the evolutionary hypothesis; it was read into it by Stolz, who assumed that a man as learned as Wesley would not use data from an evolutionist without himself being one.

Wesley was very explicit. To make the work of Buddaeus useful, he had "to retrench, enlarge, or alter every chapter, and almost every section" to make it "not only pure, containing nothing false or uncertain; but as full as" could be expected. And Wesley was very specific about the thing he edited out—the speculative theories about origins. He said, "I undertake barely to set down what appears in nature; not the cause of those appearances."[55]

That is in perfect harmony with Wesley's dictum "Let reason do all that reason can. Employ it as far as it will go."[56] But it was not human observation and reflection that held the central place

55. Ibid.
56. *Works*, 6:360.

in Wesley's faith and ministry. It was Scripture—the one infallible rule. Whatever allowance others made for error in the Bible in matters of science and history, Wesley was not caught in that inconsistency. It would have violated the integrity of his whole ministry to publish a volume of "speculative science" that disagreed with his one valid authority, the Bible.

WESLEY AND THE BATTLE FOR THE BIBLE

In a sense it is not always fair or wise to guess what a man would have done in a historical context different from his own. But in Wesley's case, it may be legitimate to speculate on the probabilities on the basis of his abundant testimony in word and deed.

There are aspects of the question that seem quite clear. Wesley would not have shrunk from the reproach of being called a Bible bigot. He would have been as candid and clear as he was two centuries ago on the source of his life and ministry. It is never popular to affirm that the Bible is the infallible Word of God. If deism, rationalism, formalism, and the rise of negative biblical criticism could not silence Wesley in the bleakest days of the eighteenth century, it is quite likely that he would still "lay open to candid reasonable men what have been the inmost thoughts of his heart."[57]

The questions of method, times, and circumstances of affirming his faith would be harder to predict. Wesley was first of all a man of conviction. And he had the courage of his convictions, whether he was preaching from the Oxford pulpit, his father's tombstone, in the streets, the fields, at the foundry, or at the mines. Closing the churches and pulpits to him early in his ministry only made him more persistent and effective. At the same time, he hated controversy, especially when it tempted Christians to speak and act unworthily. That was so important to him that he waited until after the death of his good friend George Whitefield before he began to edit the *Arminian Magazine*. For forty years he had turned aside such requests—until he himself was about seventy-four years

57. Ibid., 5:2-4.

old.[58] That delay is generally attributed to a love for people that transcended disagreements and a desire to avoid controversy. Wesley showed his attitude toward controversy when he answered criticism in the preface to his precious *Explanatory Notes upon the New Testament.*

> But my own conscience acquits me of having designedly misrepresented any single passage of Scripture, or of having written one line with a purpose of inflaming the hearts of Christians against each other. God forbid that I should make the words of the most gentle and benevolent Jesus a vehicle to convey such poison! Would to God that all the party names and unscriptural phrases and forms which have divided the Christian world were forgot, and that we might all agree to sit down together, as humble, loving disciples, at the feet of our common Master, to hear His word, to imbibe His Spirit, and to transcribe His life in our own![59]

But Wesley was also a man of action. If he believed that a standard should be raised against an error that he feared would weaken the authority of the Word of God, he would most certainly speak out. In a way it was easy in Wesley's time. Those who did not believe in an inerrant Word of God were, for the most part, deists or rationalists. To Wesley, they were hardly distinguishable from agnostics and Muslims. He did not so much argue with them as warn his hearers against falling into the same unbelief. The only genuine and authoritative Christianity Wesley knew was a scriptural Christianity. It is hard to know how Wesley would have classified professed Christians of a generation ago who had doubts about an infallible Bible or, for that matter, evangelicals who now say so many things that were once said only by liberal Christians or unbelievers. We only know that Wesley would have serious problems with any Christianity that did not have at its very heart the touchstone of an infallible Bible.

It might well be that he would like the approach of the International Council on Biblical Inerrancy. He might like to witness as reasonably as possible to the divine nature and quality of the

58. Ibid., 4:113.
59. Ibid., 4:9.

Scripture. He might be happy to avoid any unnecessary unchristianizing of believers. At the same time, the trumpet of faith would have no uncertain sound. If it took a battle to witness to the truth of God, Wesley was not unfamiliar with the smell of smoke. Nor was he unaccustomed to the labors of study and publication. In spite of an amazingly heavy schedule, from 1733 to 1791 he published an average of six volumes a year (until his death).

But whatever part Wesley would take in the "Battle for the Bible," his heart and his thrust would be in what J. I. Packer calls *Beyond the Battle for the Bible*.[60] More important than how we phrase our beliefs and doubts and the matter of who wins plaudits in debates is the fundamental question of the gospel itself. It would do no good to define faith in glowing terms if the life-giving message of the gospel was lost in endless debates. It is the power of God's Word to transform life that is the crux of the matter. And it was Wesley's proclamation of that Word of God that made enough people new creatures in Britain that McDonald credits him with a major part in demonstrating the high estimate of the Bible.[61] As Laurence Wood said, "The Wesleyan hermeneutic implied the primacy of infallible Scripture supported by history, reason, and tradition."[62] Wesley's concern was not speculative or philosophical. It was practical. His position was not less than the battle for inerrancy. It was beyond that battle. One cannot afford to win a battle and lose the war.

WESLEY AND HIS SOURCES

Though Wesley was born when the practice of true religion was at a very low ebb in England, there was still much in the traditions that could lead one to the paths that he trod. It was not that there was no form of godliness. It was simply that so few knew the power of a life transformed by grace. Indeed, few admitted any real deed of grace, to say nothing of an assurance of salvation

60. J. I. Packer, *Beyond the Battle for the Bible* (Westchester, Ill.: Cornerstone Books, 1980).
61. H. D. McDonald, *Theories of Revelation* (London: George Allen & Unwin, 1963), p. 196.
62. Presidential address at the Wesleyan Theological Society meeting at Kansas City, Missouri, November 7, 1980.

based on an ancient revelation. Even at Oxford, it was novel in the eyes of all when a small group of young men methodically set about finding a real salvation, understood as the way to heaven. Sources there were, once one searched in faith and obedience. Mention has already been made of Cadoux's sober judgment that "the inerrancy of Scripture was accepted by Christendom with practical unanimity from the second century to the nineteenth." No effort was made to exclude the Church of England, in spite of the inroads that had been made by deism and rationalism. The inference is that the Anglican doctrinal formularies were still there and ready for one who was serious about turning to God. And in Wesley's own family over the past several generations, it would have been hard to account for the difficult and conscientious decisions, often costing the employment of the head of the family, if there had not been some clear reference to a sure Word of God and to a degree of evangelical insight into doctrine. McDonald, in fact, affirms that

> prior to 1860, the idea of the infallibly inerrant Scripture was the prevailing view. What has been stated as the characteristic estimation of the Bible throughout an earlier era could with equal exactness be referred to the years down to the middle of the nineteen hundreds. Apart from the Quakers, the doctrine of unerring literal inspiration was almost everywhere held in strictest form. Such indeed was the view of the Bible before the change of Zeitgeist brought about by the appearance of Darwin's evolutionism.[63]

The orthodoxy was there, whether or not there was a correspondingly earnest spirit and obedience to the truth. And there were orthodox apologists who attacked the deists, "moving on the assumption of a Bible at once verbally infallible and inerrant."[64] It is remarkable, but apparently true, that "there was certainly a climate of opinion in favor of the orthodox apologists. The Bible was by general consent regarded as an inspired book, which, as such, must be inerrant and infallible."[65] Wesley appears to have

63. Ibid., p. 196.
64. Ibid.
65. Ibid.

assumed the validity of that tradition. He did not argue the case. He only searched the Scriptures, determined to believe and obey, with God's help.

The living tradition of an adequate and infallible Scripture sprouted in the soil of Wesley's heart and was watered by the testimony of the Fathers. It needed only to be confirmed in a vital experience of grace through faith, and Wesley was well on his way of discovery in the book of God.

WESLEY AND HIS METHOD

Was Wesley a scholastic or, indeed, the father of a scholasticism in his doctrine of the Scripture? By now it should be said categorically that he was neither. Wesley's convictions about the Scripture were not received as the product of neatly argued syllogisms. Nor was he interested in building a "system" or "school" by which disciples could memorize the arguments for his position. Instead, his experience of saving grace through faith warmed his heart. He then proclaimed the word of grace to others so that their hearts, too, could burn within them. There was and is a Wesleyan movement. But let none call it scholastic. There are scholasticisms in both Catholicism and Protestantism, and there is a certain value in the scholastic method. We simply deny that the Wesleyan view of the Bible is one of them. If one is to use the term in a pejorative sense, it applies much more accurately to (negative) historical criticism than to the belief in inerrancy. The dogmatism of men like Semler, Bauer, Wellhausen, Bultmann, and many others is much more restrictive concerning what one may observe and believe, as well as how one may handle his data, than any conservative system that supports inspiration and infallibility. Arbitrary denials of the miraculous and the supernatural, curious definitions of myth, excessive dependence on form, and prejudgments on possibility and impossibility have distorted so much of biblical criticism that one has to abandon the system to find a true historical setting. That, not inerrancy, is a scholasticism that represses and oppresses the scholar in his quest for truth. If evangelicalism is ailing, there are other approaches that are more ailing.

Nor was rationalism the method of Wesley. True, no one tried harder than Wesley to be reasonable. As has been noted, reason was a necessary ingredient of his religion. But his ultimate dependence was not on human reason. Revelation from God was all that he trusted completely. The mere fact that Wesley and others tried to make sense of their data, "comparing spiritual things with spiritual," does not make them rationalists. Their seat of authority was not human reason but the God of truth. Nor was Wesley a mystic. He had an interest in what could be learned by direct experience, but he never entrusted himself to his feelings apart from the Word. Mysticism, before conversion, was a disappointing experience for Wesley. The written Word was used to bring comfort and assurance to the troubled soul. The seat of authority was not in feeling or mystical contact. As has been said, Wesley was skeptical of speculative philosophies and patterns. He cried, "O give me that Book." He was a man of the book—one book, the Bible. There he found life. And that book was central to the life he shared with many thousands. In simple terms, he was a believer and an evangelist. In any final sense, that is all he wanted or needed.

WESLEY AND THE EFFECT OF HIS APPROACH

Volumes have been written on conditions in England before and after Wesley. Some believe that the Wesleyan movement averted a revolution comparable to the French Revolution. Others believe that England's social conscience and humanitarian reforms were a direct result of the Wesleyan revival. The waves of evangelism and missions that affected the nineteenth and twentieth-centuries in much of the world have been credited, in part, to Wesley's leadership. Certainly, a vast number of people were changed and moved heavenward. Society has not ceased to feel the impact of its encounter with God and His Word through God's Oxford don turned evangelist.

Though there is neither time nor space to discuss other effects at length, we should note Wesley's influence on the belief in inerrancy. In his excellent historical study of revelation, McDonald says:

And apart from the dogmatisms of the orthodox in this respect, had not this high estimate of the Bible been demonstrated by the preaching of Wesley as creatively effective in the experiences of thousands? It was Wesley who had vindicated the reality of the Bible's inspiration, and he, too, had maintained its inerrant infallibility.[66]

Though the primary function of every movement toward God is "to serve the present age," one wonders what later tragedies to faith were averted by the demonstration and proclamation of inspiration and inerrant infallibility. In the nineteenth-century onslaughts of Darwinism and negative historical criticism, one wonders if there would have been a near eclipse instead of a band of stalwarts like Spurgeon, Liddon, Parker, Moule, and Ryle who rose up and, under God, kept faith alive in England, insisting on the "inerrancy of the Bible and the infallibility of its truth."[67]

WESLEYANISM AFTER WESLEY

The historical question of Wesleyanism after Wesley deserves more time and space than is available. However, it can be said, in brief, that the Wesleyan movement in Britain did continue for another century after Wesley with amazing vigor and consistency. Dr. Elden Dale Dunlap tells the story with good insight in his doctoral dissertation at Yale entitled *Methodist Theology in Great Britain in the Nineteenth Century*.[68]

The following observations of Dunlap put the matter in focus and provide a basis for comment.

> Methodism in the nineteenth century was a continuing manifestation of eighteenth century Methodism. . . . John Wesley's Model Deed was still the foundation stone of Methodist Polity and doctrine. . . . Wesley's death did not alter Methodist theology in any obvious or radical manner. Methodism did not go into the nineteenth century in either theological poverty or bankruptcy, but in full possession of a rich heritage provided and bequeathed to her

66. Ibid.
67. Ibid., p. 205.
68. Elden Dale Dunlap, *Methodist Theology in Great Britain in the Nineteenth Century* (New Haven: Yale U. Press, 1956).

by the founder of the movement. Without a fairly clear conception of its theological heritage no sensitive interpretation of Methodist theology in the nineteenth century is possible. The theology of John Wesley will provide a standard of comparison by which to measure subsequent Methodist thought.[69]

Those statements are justified in the light of the outstanding followers of Wesley who dominated the nineteenth century. To Adam Clarke and Richard Watson belonged the first half of the century and to William Burt Pope the second half.

Adam Clarke, who traveled with Wesley as a young man, has been called the greatest name in Methodism in the generation that succeeded Wesley. Dunlap quotes Maldwyn Edwards as saying, "He had not the sparkling eloquence of Samuel Bradburn nor the theological acumen of Richard Watson, but in combination of gifts he surpassed them all. He was not only the greatest scholar in Methodism, but amongst the greatest of his age."[70]

Though Clarke is best known today for his *Commentary* and for other scholarly and intellectual attainments, "he thought of himself and his work primarily as a preacher and a churchman. All of his writing was looked on as serving this end."[71] As an earnest lad of about twenty, he left Ireland for England in 1782 and placed himself at Wesley's disposal. He was in turn an evangelist, missionary in the Norman Isles, circuit rider, and superintendent. By special exception he was allowed to remain in the London area for a long time to promote his scholarly projects, but he never lost the intensely evangelistic concern that commanded the interest and energies of the Methodists in the years following Wesley's departure. He expressed his own passion for saving souls in "A Letter to a Preacher on His Entrance into the Work of the Ministry." He wrote: "Your call is not to instruct men in the doctrines and duties of Christianity merely: but to convert them from sin to holiness. A doctrine can be of little value that does not lead to practical effect:

---

69. Ibid., pp. 16-17.
70. Ibid., p. 11.
71. Ibid., p. 95.

and the doctrine of Christianity will be preached in vain to all who have not the principle of obedience."[72]

For all of Clarke's accomplishments, he takes second place to Richard Watson as a systematic theologian. Watson has been recognized as the first great theologian among the Methodists. His *Institutes* was standard theological fare for Methodist preachers until the days of W. B. Pope.[73] Watson was also an eloquent pulpit figure and advocate of foreign missions. As was true of Wesley and Clarke, the practical work of evangelism consumed his strength. There were souls to be saved. Though there was need for system in theology,

> There was neither much time nor inclination to enter into the arid and unprofitable theological joustings of the time or to do battle with the rising scientific spirit. . . . There is insight in the fact that the two men in all of Methodism during this time whose names were synonymous with scholarship and theology, Adam Clarke and Richard Watson, were equally and in all probability more affectionately—known as the champions of the missionary movement both at home and abroad.[74]

Both men shared the attitudes and labors of their founder and served with the same motivation and passion. The Holy Scripture was still the basic foundation on which Methodist theology rested.

> Throughout the whole of Richard Watson's writings, particularly the *Institutes*, it is apparent that final appeal is always made to Scripture and in the face of the testimony of Scripture all rational conclusions must give way. Adam Clarke . . . insisted—as was typical of the Evangelicals of his time—that "the WORD OF GOD alone contained his creed" (*Old Testament Commentary*, 3:725). The great doctrines of justification by faith, the witness of the Spirit, and sanctification were not taught to him by men but were revealed to him in the study of the Bible. . . . The doctrines of Protestantism rest on the Bible alone. The Holy Scriptures can be afforded this position of authority because they are the divine reve-

72. Ibid., pp. 90-91, quoting Adam Clarke, *Detached Pieces* (London: Thomas Tegg, 1844), 3:140.
73. Ibid., p. 11.
74. Ibid., p. 90.

lation of God (Watson, *Works*, 6:11-17; Clarke, *Detached papers* 3:132).[75]

That was not to decry reason.

> Since both reason and revelation come from the same source it is impossible that there should be anything in the one contrary to the other, although revelation may contain that which is above the reason of man [Clarke, *Works*, 8:420ff; *New Testament Commentary*, 2:1070]. It is even God's way that He gives man understanding and reason and then places a revelation of Himself before that reason which is able to receive and understand it [Clarke, *Old Testament Commentary*, 3:519]. Revelation and reason go hand in hand; faith is the servant of the former, and the friend of the latter; while the Spirit of God, which gave the revelation, improves and exalts reason, and gives energy and effect to faith [*New Testament Commentary*, 2:1070].[76]

In the last half of the nineteenth century William Burt Pope dominated Methodist thought and "next to John Wesley himself, did more to provide Methodism with a systematic standard of doctrine than anyone else."[77] Even so, his theological greatness lay in conserving theology, not in innovation. Though he remained active in the affairs of the Conference, he became a theological professor, serving at Didsbury College from 1866-86, until failing health forced his retirement.

The starting point of theology in Pope's three-volume *Compendium of Christian Theology*[78] was revelation. Clarke and Watson had begun with atonement, as known by revelation. All, of course, are oriented toward redemption. For Pope, since the action of God is divine action rather than human action, man can know the purpose of God only as He discloses it to him (1:36). The Christian Scriptures constitute that disclosure (1:38). As revelation, they refer to God the revealer; as received by man they are the Chris-

---

75. Ibid., p. 155.
76. Ibid., p. 161.
77. Ibid., p. 266.
78. William Burt Pope, *A Compendium of Christian Theology*, 3 vols. (New York: Phillips & Hunt, n.d.).

tian faith (1:35f., 42). Thus at a time when the authority of the Scripture was being assailed by both biblical criticism and evolution, Pope interpreted Christianity as uniquely a religion of revelation based on Scripture as its authority.[79]

It is clear, then, that the strong confidence of Wesley in the Scripture as the sure Word of God was still central in Methodist theology as long as Clarke, Watson, and Pope were the stalwart leaders. No wavering was seen in the leadership, and there was an amazing unanimity among those who accepted the discipline of the Methodists. There may have arisen questions as to the best way to explain the manner of God's operation in inspiring the Scriptures, but confidence was strong that the result of that inspiration was an infallible Word of God. We do not judge it; it judges us.

That confidence in the full authority of the Scripture and in its life-giving power was what held British Wesleyanism together on its founding principles to the end of the nineteenth century. It has been said that "without the Bible there is no Christianity." At any rate, it is certain that without full confidence in the infallible Word of God, there would have been no dynamic Wesleyan revival in the eighteenth century, with vigor extending through the nineteenth century. They had to be "Bible bigots" to survive and propagate their kind.

From the standpoint of such a "Bible bigot," the twentieth century in British Methodism is different in both cause and effect. The dam did break. Scripture, for many, ceased to be the infallible authority that it had been. What Dunlap says of American Methodism became also the problem in Britain.

> It may be noted that many of these tendencies which characterize such a large part of contemporary American Methodist theology came in through the German idealism imported into Methodism by scholars who studied in Germany around the turn of the century. We are only beginning to discover how alien this was to the evangelical Anglicanism of John Wesley.[80]

79. Dunlap, p. 273.
80. Ibid., p. 4.

As Dunlap says again, "These themes of current Methodist theologizing, with their semi-Pelagian, quasi-Abelardian, idealistic-rationalistic, and humanistic emphases, provide a thought-provoking contrast to the orthodoxy which is characteristic of John Wesley."[81]

One gains the impression that the indulgent pluralism in twentieth century Methodist theology is not working well in Britain. Why else are most of the seminaries closing, and why are so many of the churches for sale? And why is church attendance at such a low ebb? Where is the soul-saving message of evangelism? Is there a famine of the Word of God, and, as a result, is real Wesleyanism a vanishing species in many parts of Britain? May it not be so!

81. Ibid., p. 3.

Part 2

The Tradition of the Infallibility of Scripture in American Christianity

8

Jonathan Edwards and the Bible

John H. Gerstner

Never in history did a finer philosophical mind than that of Jonathan Edwards give its sustained and almost undivided life-time attention to the Bible.[1] Examining it in its exegetical detail, historico-redemptive sweep, theological system, and above all in its evangelistic use and effects, Edwards preached without ceasing (vacations were unheard of). He commented on virtually every text—often entering the critical arena—and tied it all together, beginning with election and Adam and reaching, via the book of Revelation, into his own time and beyond. He was always escha-

---

1. For an expanded treatment of this chapter, see "Jonathan Edwards and the Bible," *Tenth* 9 (1979): 2-71. The collected *Works* used are the Worcester reprint of 1879, unless otherwise noted. *Miscellanies* are cited by their letter or numbers following *M*. Sermons are indicated by text and doctrine. If they are printed, that is usually also indicated. *Notes on The Scriptures* and other works are usually quoted from the manuscripts and often located, if in print. All manuscripts are quoted in a form as close to the original as feasible for a modern reader.

JOHN H. GERSTNER, B.A. Westminster College, B.Th., M.Th. Westminster Theological Seminary, Ph.D. Harvard University, is professor-emeritus of church history at Pittsburgh Theological Seminary, Pittsburgh, Pennsylvania. He has written *Calvin's Political Influence in America*, *The Epistle to the Ephesians*, *The Gospel According to Rome*, *An Inerrancy Primer*, *Reasons for Faith*, *Steps to Salvation: The Evangelistic Message of Jonathan Edwards*, and *Theology of the Major Sects*. He is a member of the International Council on Biblical Inerrancy.

tologically oriented.[2] Edwards worked the Bible into the greatest possession of orthodoxy, defended its fundamental doctrines by the deepest analysis of the human will ever produced, examined its doctrine of religious affections definitively, and all the while that he majored in God's book of special revelation, so far from neglecting His book of nature, he actually grounded the Bible in natural theology while vindicating natural theology by it.

Basic to any discussion of Edwards's view of revelation is his understanding of reason. Reason came first in his thinking, just as it did in his existence. Revelation was subsequent in thought as well as in being.[3]

REASON AND REVELATION

It is a false contrast to polarize reason and revelation. They are not contradictories, contraries, or even comparables. They are like apples and oranges. Revelation is a means of communication (and secondarily, that which is communicated); reason is the means of apprehending what is communicated. The only means by which anything is communicated is revelation (unfolding or disclosing). The only way anything revealed is apprehended, grasped, or understood is by reason. There is no other way of communication but revelation. There is no other way of apprehension but reason. Without revelation there would be no knowledge; without reason there would be no apprehension of knowledge.

WHAT REASON CAN DO IN RELATION TO REVELATION

Though Edwards wrote that "the light of nature is in no sense whatsoever sufficient to discover this religion" (Christianity),[4] he also wrote that "there is perfect harmony"[5] between reason and

---

2. The fifth volume in the Yale U. Press edition of *The Works of Jonathan Edwards*, ed. Stephen J. Stein, is devoted to *Apocalyptic Writings*, appropriately celebrating Edwards's "lifelong commitment to apocalyptic speculation."

3. By contrast Brunner found it essential to begin his theologizing with revelation, as the very title of one of his major works indicates: Heinrich Emil Brunner, *Revelation and Reason: the Christian Doctrine of Faith and Knowledge*, trans. Olive Wyon (Philadelphia: Westminster, 1946).

4. *M*, 1337.

5. Ms sermon on Rom. 3:11.

revelation. That "perfect harmony" was not spelled out in any one work, but scattered indications are everywhere. We may mention eight areas of harmony. First, reason must prove the existence of God, the revealer. Second, reason anticipates that there would be a revelation. Third, reason alone can rationally grasp any "pretended" revelation. Fourth, only reason can demonstrate the rationality of revelation. Fifth, reason must verify any "pretended" revelation as genuine. Sixth, reason argues revelation's dependability. Seventh, reason, having anticipated mysteries in any genuine divine revelation, defends them, refuting any objections to their presence. Eighth, though the "divine and supernatural light" does not come *from* reason, it alone comprehends what that light illumines. Of those eight areas of harmony, number five is especially significant.

REASON MUST VERIFY THE SUPERNATURALNESS OF REVELATION

Reason must verify a "pretended" revelation as genuine. It is not enough to understand the revelation and declare it free of contradiction; reason must determine its credibility. That is the *judicium vereficationis*: "It is the prerogative of reason to judge of the credibility of a revelation." Reason could declare something "credible" but not verified as what it purports to be. It may be conceivable that the Bible is the Word of God, yet it may not be rationally necessary so to believe. One cannot rationally believe something "is" (in distinction from "may be") unless there is evidence (though one could know that something "is not" because of contradiction). Particularly, one could never believe a book to have supernaturally come from God simply because that is not inconceivable. It must not only be conceivable; it must be mandatory so to believe as well. That also is for reason to determine, and reason does so determine. The evidence for the supernaturalness of the Bible is in! And the evidence is overwhelming, according to Jonathan Edwards.

Internal evidence. The internal evidence for scriptural revelation is basic with Edwards. He preached that "God gives men good evidence of the truth of his Word."[6] The evidence is internal ("evident stamp") especially but external as well. In fact, "there is as much in the gospel to show that it is no work of men, as there is in the sun in the firmament."[7]

Arguing internally for divine inspiration, Edwards suggested that one consider the immediate source of the revelation—the words of the human teachers. Could any divine thing come out of human sources as such? For example, how could the Jews, who were not learned in science or philosophy and were as prone to idolatry as the nations around them, produce their refined and advanced doctrine of God? How does one explain Moses' knowledge, for example?

> Who should contrive that God should send Moses with such a message, "I AM hath sent me unto you"? Who can believe that those plain simple persons in that most unphilosophical age, should so much surpass Socrates, Plato, or Tully, as this most certainly doth? The third and sixth chapters of Exodus as strongly and as irresistibly prove themselves by their own powerful light to be of divine authority, as the meridian light of the sun proves it to be in our hemisphere.[8]

Perhaps nowhere did Edwards better state his view of the internal evidence of Scriptural inspiration than in the early *Miscellany 333*: "The being of God is evident by the Scriptures, and the Scriptures themselves are an evidence of their own divine authority." That is after the analogy of our knowing human minds "by the motions, behaviour and speech of a body of human form and contexture." From those "motions" we infer a rational mind. So "such stamps everywhere of exalted and divine wisdom, majesty and holiness" in the Scriptures show that they "are the word and work of a divine mind." As an infant who at first does not distinguish between human motions and those of inanimate things until "its comprehension increases," so men at first see no evidence of

6. Ex. 9:12-16, "They that will not yield to the power of God's word shall be broken by the power of his hand," July 1747.
7. Eph. 3:10, "The wisdom appearing in the way of salvation by Jesus Christ is far above the wisdom of angels," *Six sermons*, March 1733, *Works*, 4:133-68.
8. *M*, 22.

the divine mind in the Scriptures because "they are so little acquainted" with them and "have not comprehension enough to apprehend the harmony, wisdom, etc." The greatest American "fundamentalist" is arguing that it is the unbeliever, not the believer, who is naive; the "cultured despisers" are unsophisticated; the emperors have no clothes.

To put the whole matter more succinctly, the Bible "shines bright with the amiable simplicity of truth."[9] Not only is all that is found in Scripture true, but there are no sound views found outside that are not derived from the Bible.[10] "Where the Scriptures have come there has been light; all the rest of the world has remained in darkness. So 'tis now all over the world," he told his little Indian congregation on the edge of the wilderness.

External evidence. Though Edwards nowhere cited Locke's expression "credentials of a messenger,"[11] he clearly shared that viewpoint. That is, he too held that God's certifying a messenger as His establishes that person's right to propose divine doctrine and to be recognized by his hearers. The certification that God gave His commissioned messenger was the power to do miracles in His name. When God reveals Himself, He does not merely leave us to deduce His presence from the inadequacy of the human writers as sources of such revelation; He certifies them by miraculous attestation as well. It is especially clear that Jesus' miracles attest a divine messenger.

Miracles are sometimes in view when they are not specifically mentioned. When, for example, Edwards observed that the Bible prevails though the mighty of the world are often against it,[12] he apparently saw the survival of Scripture itself as a miracle—a kind of literary burning bush. Thomas Chubb may have thought miracles improbable and John Toland thought them impossible, but for Jonathan Edwards, they had thoroughly established the Bible.

9. *Works*, 7:474.
10. *Six sermons*, *Works*, 4:194, 2 Tim. 3:16.
11. John Locke, "A Discourse of Miracles," in *The Reasonableness of Christianity with a Discourse of Miracles, and part of A Third Letter concerning Toleration*, ed. I. T. Ramsey (Stanford, Cal.: U. Press, 1958), p. 81.
12. *Works*, 4:194, 2 Tim. 3:16, "The Devil and wicked men make against it. Another thing that shews [that it is] the Word of God is this: it has PREVAILED against such great opposition."

In fact, the miracle of its survival established the Bible so well that subsequent miracles could not compare with it. The testimony of Scripture was greater than one rising from the dead and returning to this world.[13] The Scripture is "surer than a voice from heaven"[14] because it has established the worldwide church that has a glory compared to which Moses' church had none.[15] Though miracles ceased with the apostolic age, the good obtained by the Bible lasts forever,[16] and God never fails His Word.[17] Though the internal evidence for the divinity of Scripture is overwhelming, God gave miracles also to prove that men wrote the Bible under supernatural inspiration.[18]

So, for Jonathan Edwards, believing is not seeing, but seeing is believing. Seeing the evidence, internal and external, is believing. At least, it is the basis for believing. A person may have the rational basis and not build faith on it. But if he is to build in true faith, there must be the intellectual or speculative foundation.

WHAT REASON CANNOT DO

There are indeed things that reason cannot do with reference to revelation. Indispensable as are the things it can and must do, those things that it cannot do are even more significant. Those things, which we will enumerate and develop—important and critical as they are, are also quite compatible with the things that reason can do. Edwards was no less reasonable when he limited reason than when he used it. In fact it was by the use of reason that he learned the limits of reason. As someone—it could have been Edwards—has written: reason is never more reasonable than when it refuses to reason about the things that are beyond reason.

13. Luke 16:31, "The warnings of God's word are more fitted to obtain the ends of awakening sinners and bringing them to repentance than the rising of one from the dead to warn them," n.d. *Works*, 4:330ff.
14. *Notes on Scripture*, No. 265, London, *Works*, 2:814.
15. Dwight, *Works*, 8:211-12.
16. Ps. 19:7-10, "The good that is obtained by the word of God lasts forever," n.d.
17. Matt. 24:35, "God never fails of his word," before 1733.
18. *Works*, 4:193, 2 Tim. 3:16, "When God told the wise and holy men to write the Bible He gave them power to work great MIRACLES, to convince men that it was His work."

Only, Edwards would say, that it is not beyond reason to recognize that some things are beyond reason.

There are at least four basic limitations of the human reason. First, it cannot make the knowledge of God "real" to unregenerate man. Second, it cannot yield a supernatural, salvific revelation or even ascertain it on reason's own initiative. Third, if it does receive a revelation, it cannot thereafter determine what that revelation may and may not reveal. Fourth, it cannot even "apprehend" divine revelation as divine revelation, though it may recognize its presence.

Edwards vindicated virtually every traditional argument for God. Concerning point number three, Edwards believed that though there must be evidence for revelation, that was not the same as saying that the revelation must be comprehensible. That it is revelation must be evident; precisely what the revelation in its entirety is may not be comprehensible, much less evident.

Speaking for himself, Edwards explained how it was that religion may be at once in a nonparadoxical way revealed and yet hidden.

> Some writers insist that for a thing to be revealed, and yet to remain mysterious, is a contradiction; that it is as much as to say, a thing is revealed, and yet hid. I answer: the thing revealed is the truth of the doctrine: so that the truth of it no longer remains hid, though many things concerning the manner may be so. Yet many things concerning the nature of things revealed may be clear, though many things concerning the nature of the same things may remain hid. God requires us to understand no more than is intelligibly revealed. That which is not distinctly revealed, we are not required distinctly to understand. It may be necessary for us to know a thing in part, and yet not necessary to know it perfectly.[19]

Thus there are apparent theological discrepancies in Scripture that Edwards could not reconcile and that he did not suppose that God expected men to be capable of reconciling.

So we have moved from reason to revelation. Rather, we have moved from natural revelation to supernatural revelation—the

19. *Works*, 3:542.

Bible. But that is not the acme of revelation that comes when the God who revealed Himself in nature and then savingly in Scripture brings the Word of God alive in the souls of the redeemed by none other than the Spirit of God. From creation to revelation to re-creation—all is from God, all of it apprehended by the reason of man as the light of God's transcendent glory shines into elect man's darkness and a new day is born.

THE NATURE OF INSPIRATION

Does Edwards's view of revelation, for which he showed the necessity, evidence, and reasonableness, imply a divine dictation? If God spoke through human agents, would He have had to dictate His message? Given Edwards's well-known respect for his Reformed fathers, how else would one interpret these words of his: "Ministers are not to preach those things which their own wisdom or reason suggests, but the things that are already dictated to them by the superior wisdom and knowledge of God."[20] The word *dictate* and its cognates occur throughout that ordination sermon. Nevertheless, there is no laboring of it. No use of the correlative *amanuensis*, or secretary, occurs. In fact, apart from the word itself, there is no hint of mechanical inspiration. On the other hand, Edwards assumed that the words of Scripture are the very words of the Holy Spirit. They could not be more so *if* they were literally dictated.

Peter's words in 2 Peter 1:20 are not merely Peter's words. The "one's own interpretation" of "no prophecy of Scripture is a *matter* of one's own interpretation" is thus interpreted by Edwards: "It is not men's speaking their own sense of things or interpreting their own minds but the mind of God. That which is their sense is not always the sense or interpretation of Scripture, but that which was the sense of the Holy Ghost. The prophets did not always perceive the meaning of their own prophecies."[21] The reasoning seems to be: the words of the text are the words of the Spirit, and the forbidden, private interpretation is a substitution of one's own wisdom for the wisdom of God. Edwards was not opposed to private interpre-

20. 1 Cor. 2:11-13, Ordination of Mr. Billing, appointed May 7, 1740.
21. *Blank Bible*, 2 Pet. 1:20, p. 878.

tation in the historic Protestant meaning of *private judgment,* in fact he was practicing it. It was his own private judgment that private interpretation of the text did not refer to a proper interpretation that is expected of every individual who reads the words but to a substitution—conscious or unconscious—of that individual's opinions for the opinions of the Holy Spirit. So, Edwards was saying, we should interpret what the infinitely wise Holy Spirit said through Peter and not what we think He should have said.

Edwards also frequently spoke of the "penmen" of the Bible and said that the Holy Spirit used the expressions attributed to the human writers.[22] Nevertheless, Edwards obviously did not believe in mechanical inspiration. The way in which he supposed inspiration to have come about can best be seen in a statement in *The Mind* and a later one in the *Miscellanies*. The first shows how the inspired person himself encountered the deity, the second how he went about communicating the message received from the deity.

First, we see how inspiration actually came to pass.

> The evidence of immediate inspiration that the prophets had when they were immediately inspired by the Spirit of God with any truth is an absolute sort of certainty and the knowledge is, in a sense, intuitive—much in the same manner as faith and spiritual knowledge of the truth of religion. Such bright ideas are raised and such a clear view of a perfect agreement with the excellencies of the divine nature that it is known to be a communication from him. All the deity appears in the thing and in everything pertaining to it. The prophet has so divine a sense, such a divine disposition, such a divine pleasure, and sees so divine an excellency and so divine a power in what is revealed, that he sees as immediately that God is there as we perceive one another's presence when we are talking together face to face. And our features our voice and our shapes are not so clear manifestations of us as those spiritual resemblances of God that are in the inspiration are manifestations of Him. But yet there are doubtless less various degrees in inspiration.[23]

22. *Notes on the Scriptures,* No. 328, London, *Works,* 2:747. Cf. Jer. 17:16-18 in the *Blank Bible,* where reference is made to Jeremiah "and other inspired penmen of the Old Testament."
23. *Mind,* No. 20; Townsend, *Philosophy of Jonathan Edwards,* pp. 33-34.

Those "bright ideas" are so naturally-supernaturally or super-naturally-naturally given that anything like dictation seems out of the world of inspiration. Such inspiration and dictation would seem to be opposites rather than correlatives or synonyms. When dictation is mentioned, one—at least in the twentieth century—thinks of shorthand note-taking or the clanging of the keys of a typewriter, not "intuitive," "spiritual knowledge" that affords a "clear view" of excellency.

But second, notice how the revelation once so naturally-supernaturally communicated by God is naturally-supernaturally articulated by man. In the case of Solomon's writing of his *Song of Songs*, that was the way Edwards described it.

> I imagine that Solomon when he wrote this song, being a very philosophical, musing man and a pious man, and of a very loving temper, set himself in his own musings to imagine and to point forth to himself a pure, virtuous, pious, and entire love, and represented the musings and feelings of his mind that in a philosophical and religious frame was carried away in a sort of transport, and in that his musings and the train of his imaginations were guided and led on by the Spirit of God. Solomon in his wisdom and great experience had learned the vanity of all other love than of such a sort of one. God's Spirit made use of his loving inclination, joined with his musing philosophical disposition, and so directed and conducted it in this train of imagination as to represent the love that there is between Christ and his spouse. God saw it very needful and exceeding useful that there should be some such representation of it. The relation that there is between Christ and the church we know, is very often compared to that that there is between man and his wife; yea this similitude is abundantly insisted on almost everywhere in the Scripture; and a virtuous and pious and pure love between a man and his spouse is very much of an image of the love between Christ and the church so that it is not at all strange that the Spirit of God which is love, should direct a holy amorous disposition after such a manner, as to make such a representation, and 'tis very agreeable to other the like representations.[24]

It would appear that Jonathan Edwards taught a very

24. *M*, 303.

nonmechanical dictation. The dictation referred to the end product, the very words that God intended and from which the faithful minister should not depart. The manner of that dictation was mechanical only in the sense that it was natural to the human vehicle of inspiration. Solomon went about the writing of his *Song* just as he would, apparently, had he no divine inspiration. Nevertheless, the supernatural divine inspiration produced the very words God intended and would have produced had Solomon received mechanical dictation. So far from Edwards's view being unique, it was the common understanding of almost all the Fathers of the church in all ages,[25] though we see here a characteristic uniqueness and profundity of argument, analysis, and articulation.[26]

However God moved His agents of revelation to write Holy Scripture, the end result was verbal inspiration. Not only was the *Verbum* of God present but the *verba* as well. The Bible is the very Word of God, as inerrant as if it were mechanically dictated (though it was not) and as unified as if it were written by the divine Author only (though it was not).

If Edwards was an inerrantist in the classic tradition, how did that affect his biblical criticism? All but the inerrantists seem to assume that inerrancy destroys criticism. It is taken as axiomatic that a person cannot believe a document to be inerrant and then seek to find errors in it. Of course, it is axiomatic that a person cannot believe a document to be without error while seeking for errors in it, unless he is refuting persons who charge errors in the document or the document he now has (not being the original) may have had errors creep into it that the inerrantist is anxious to detect and remove, thus restoring it as closely as possible to the original. That explains why inerrantists have been the most interested of all in detecting errors in the Bible!

Jonathan Edwards was no exception. That Edwards was keenly interested and active in biblical criticism is quite evident. He was

25. Cf. my "The Church's Doctrine of Inspiration," in *The Foundation of Biblical Authority*, ed. J. M. Boice (Grand Rapids: Zondervan, 1978) pp. 23-60; and J. I. Packer, *Fundamentalism and the Word of God* (1958).
26. Samuel Hopkins's words seem justified: "We know of no writer, since the days of the apostles, who has better comprehended the word of God," London, *Works*, 1:239.

sensitive to critical problems. He did something with all of them and considerable with some of them. Many of them he addressed at great length. He dealt with authorship problems, for example the Mosaic authorship of the Pentateuch. He wrote no less than forty-four sophisticated pages in his *Notes on Scripture*[27] defending the Mosaic authorship.

Edwards also dealt with alleged errors in fact, such as the apostles' prediction of the return of Christ in their generation. He set forth no less than nineteen acute arguments against the critical notion, widely held even today, that the apostles taught the return of Christ in their lifetime.[28] He addressed alleged discrepancies in historical details, as in the accounts of the resurrection of Christ.

Nor did he ignore vital ethical problems such as the imprecatory Psalms and Jephthah's vow. Ethical issues were of special concern to Edwards. He gave a lengthy discussion of Jephthah's vow, arguing that, properly interpreted, the narrative does not teach that the famous Old Testament judge killed his daughter out of respect for an evil vow to sacrifice the first thing that came out of his house to meet him upon his return in victory.[29]

Many entries deal with the more acute ethical problem of imprecations by saints in the Bible. Edwards did not deny that in both testaments the saints were known to have justifiably called for God's curses on their enemies.

Even doctrinal differences in the Bible were not sacrosanct, and Edwards faced them frankly and critically. He gave himself to the reconciliation of Paul and James, whom even Martin Luther thought to be irreconcilable. The apparent discrepancy between James and Paul on justification by faith alone caused Edwards no such trouble as it gave Luther. Edwards treated the subject at fair length in his published sermon on Romans 4:5.[30] James, Edwards explained, was simply using the word *justify* in the sense of *vindicate*, so that works vindicate the reality of Abraham's faith but

27. No. 416.
28. London, *Works*, 2:468-70.
29. *Notes on the Scriptures*, No. 223, London, *Works*, 2:734-37.
30. "We are justified only by faith in Christ, and not by any manner of goodness of our own," Nov. 1734, *Works*, 4:64-132. "Works are here spoken of as justifying as evidences," p. 125.

have nothing to do with being the meritorious ground of Abraham's justification.

By way of summary, we note that Edwards saw the Bible as the inerrantly inspired Word of God. He conveyed that conviction, not shrinking even from the word *dictation*. However, his understanding of dictation left the writers free to follow their customary ways of thinking and expressing themselves, while at the same time producing the very words of the Holy Spirit. Reverence for that Word, which should control all the preaching of ministers, was not incompatible with wrestling with biblical problems, something Edwards did himself, as well as relying on such labors by others.

THE CANON OF SCRIPTURE

Having seen that Edwards's Word of God extended to each critically ascertained word of the Bible, we now ask how far those words extended—the canonical question. That leads us to consider the Old and New Testaments as constituting the one canon, the closing of that canon, and its historical and ecclesiastical determination.

THE OLD AND NEW TESTAMENTS CONSTITUTE THE CANON

The unity of revelation runs through all Edwards's discussions of the Bible. "Christ did not give to the world any new moral precepts that were not either expressed or implied in the precepts of the Old Testament and in the Ten Commandments. He did not, as some have supposed, make by His rule some things duty which before were not duty but only revealed some things more fully."[31]

Edwards's *Harmony of the Genius, Spirit, Doctrines and Rules of the Old Testament and the New*,[32] unfinished though it was, demonstrated the profound and extensive unity of the two testaments. The first part of that work compared the two testaments on specific

31. Matt. 5:44, "That men ought to love their enemies," before 1733.
32. Manuscript, Beinecke Library and Rare Book Room, Yale University.

teachings.[33] Edwards later shifted to a consideration of various texts of the Old Testament, in canonical order, and compared their doctrines with those of the New Testament. That part, which ran through the Psalms, was entitled "Particular Texts in the Old Testament which Harmonize with the Doctrines, Precepts, etc. of the New."[34]

THE CLOSING OF THE CANON

Granted that inspiration extends to the very words of Scripture, what, we now ask, are the canonical limits of those words? Though Edwards nowhere to our recollection lists the sixty-six books of the Protestant canon, there can be no doubt that he had the very list in mind that was enumerated by his favorite creed, the Westminster Confession.[35]

How did Edwards know and prove that the canon ceased with the sixty-six books? He was far more concerned with locating the biblical revelation than with fixing its limitations. He had preached a whole series of sermons on 1 Corinthians chapter 13,[36] but later realized that the last five verses had to receive special treatment because they dealt with the closing of the canon. That sermon series has never been published, though it is as important historically as theologically.[37] Edwards's view was that the charismata have permanently ceased, never to reappear even in the Millennium, though claims were made for them in the age follow-

33. Faith (pp. 1-5), Love to Enemies (pp. 6-8), Humility Toward Men (pp. 9-10), Selling All for Christ (pp. 11-13), Weeping with Those That Weep (p. 15), Honoring All Men (p. 16), and A Being Without Anxiety or Carelessness (p. 17).
34. That part is separately paginated (pp. 1-194): Genesis (pp. 1-13), Exodus (pp. 13-18), Leviticus (pp. 18-22), Numbers (pp. 23-28), Deuteronomy (pp. 28-38), Joshua (pp. 29-41), Judges (pp. 42-44), Ruth (pp. 44-45), 1 Samuel (pp. 46-52), 2 Samuel (pp. 54-58), 1 Kings (pp. 59-61), 2 Kings (pp. 61-63), 1 Chronicles (p. 65), 2 Chronicles (pp. 66-67), Ezra (p. 67), Nehemiah (p. 68), Esther (p. 69), Job (pp. 70-82), Psalms (pp. 82-194).
35. *Works*, 1:2.
36. Later published by Tryon Edwards (with many rhetorical embellishments) as *Charity and Its Fruits; or Christian Love as Manifested in the Heart and Life* (New York: Robert Carter & Brothers, 1852).
37. 1 Cor. 13:8-13, "The extraordinary influences of the Spirit of God imparting immediate revelations to men were designed only for a temporary continuance while the church was in its minority and never were intended to be statedly upheld in the Christian Church," May 1748.

ing the Reformation and in Edwards's own time. That cessation of charismata marked the cessation of miracles, and that marked the cessation of biblical revelation—in a word, the closing of the canon.

The later, separate sermons on 1 Corinthians 13:8-13, though dealing with the temporary character of the charismata, took the same position with reference to spiritual graces that is virtually the main theme of the earlier, now published series on 1 Corinthians 13—graces are much superior to gifts. We see, then, that for Edwards charismata are "extraordinary," "common" gifts not to be confused with mere bodily effects (which may be good or bad), for with spiritual graces that are always good and the true goal of the charismata.[38]

Miracles for Edwards were proofs or seals of divine revelation. People in his day, as in ours, were beginning to offer an apology *for* miracles rather than *with* them. He found it necessary to say that spiritual persons were not really above the need for proof of their religious declarations. Even Christ, he observed, had urged His disciples to believe Him for His works' sake.[39] When Christ commissioned His apostles, He sent them out equipped with power to produce miracles. That was necessary and especially appropriate at the beginning of a new dispensation.[40] If miracles were not necessary, why were they so considered by Christ? Miracles, then, are proof of revelation. Revelational claims, apart from miracles, cannot be proved completely. There were many such alleged revelations in his own day, said Edwards, but few miracles. In the absence of miracles, claims were mere pretensions. The reason there are so many pretended revelations and so few pretended miracles is, the Yankee skeptic conjectured, because miracles are not so easy to fake.[41]

Speaking specifically of the charismatic miracles, Edwards said that those, too, were proofs of revelation. They were especially designed for that purpose, not for the edification of saints so much

38. Cf.*M*, 31, 236, 313, 444, 518, 584, 1026, 1190, 1223, 1306, 1341, 1342.
39. He cited John 5:37; 10:25, 37-38; 14:11.
40. Sermons on 1 Cor. 13:8-13.
41. Ibid.

as for the convicting of sinners.[42] They were to prove divine revelation and thus establish the ultimate means of grace, which is the
Bible. In other words, the purpose of gifts is grace (Eph. 4:11).
Charismata are not necessary for anything else. The gift of prophecy, in particular, made up what was lacking in the childhood of
the church until the canon was complete. When it was complete,
those charismatic attestations were no longer necessary; the canon
became the complete rule of faith. Having said that, Edwards
launched into his lengthy proof that the canon indeed is complete
and the function of the charismata accomplished.

While the canon was still incomplete, immediate revelations
were in order and were demonstrated by the continuing miraculous activity of God in giving further chapters to the book of
Scripture. That observation led Edwards to an important conclusion about biblical history; the charismata climaxed in the "era of
miracles"—the century from the birth of Christ to the death of the
apostle John. "But soon after that, the canon of Scripture being
completed, . . . these miraculous gifts were no longer continued in
the church."[43]

As was intimated in the sections cited above, when the canon
was closed, the charismata proper were over for Edwards. Their
function was to call attention to revelation. When that revelation
was fully given, they would and did naturally cease. It is evident,
therefore, that the concept of a closed canon was vital for Edwards
(though it may be said in passing that miracles did not immediately end with the closing of the canon but gradually ceased, as
those who had that gift gradually died).[44]

42. That and many other assertions in this section are drawn from the Ms sermons on 1 Cor. 13:8-13.
43. "*All these other fruits of the Spirit are but for a season and either have already ceased or
at some time will cease.*—As to the miraculous gifts of prophecy and tongues,
etc., they are but of a temporary use and cannot be continued in heaven.
They were given only as an extraordinary means of grace that God was once
pleased to grant to his church in the world. But when the saints that once
enjoyed the use of these means went to heaven, such means of grace ceased,
for they were no longer needful. There is no occasion for any means of grace
in heaven, whether ordinary, such as the stated and common means of God's
house, or extra-ordinary, such as the gifts of tongues, and of knowledge, and
of prophecy. . . ." Again, Edwards referred to Eph. 4:11ff. (*Charity and Its
Fruits*, pp. 444-49)
44. 1 Cor. 13:8-13.

The closed character of the canon was so important to Edwards that he devoted no less than twenty-six pages and nine arguments to that theme in his most important discussion of the cessation of the charismata.[45] First, the Bible itself never foretells any further revelation. Second, the church is founded on the prophets and apostles. Third, the words of the apostles were given as the rule for all succeeding ages. Fourth, the conclusion of the Bible in John's revelation indicates that the canon is closed. Fifth, no church has ever since claimed any further canonical revelation. Sixth, miracles have ceased and have not been revived. Seventh and eighth refer specifically to Daniel 9:27 and Hebrews 1:1-2 as textual indications of a closed canon. Ninth, alleged postapostolic miracles have failed to convince.

Edwards closed and sealed the canon at the sixty-six books. At least if any other inspired books were ever given, the church could not certainly recognize them because no miraculous test has been forthcoming and will not be even in the halcyon latter days. Edwards could never imagine God giving an addition to the inspired canon after He had already closed it, because there was no way by which His people could see that He had reopened it. We turn now to the way the church recognized the completion of the canon.

It was not until *M*, 1060, surprisingly late in Edwards's life, that he turned to a rather full scrutiny of the history of the canon. If he did not do that earlier, it was probably because he was doing it implicitly. That is to say, in determining the biblical revelation internally and externally he was fixing the canon. If the criteria can be determined, the extent is ipso facto determined. If we know what defines the revelation, we know what confines the canon. We need not discuss *M*, 1060 here; it is rather conventional as the argument for closing the canon (discussed above) was not. Rather, we conclude with another aspect of the canonical issue, that of levels of inspiration within the canon.

Granting that for Edwards the sixty-six books of the Bible constituted the divinely inspired and inerrant canon, were there no varieties or levels of inspiration? "There are doubtless various

45. Ibid.

degrees of inspiration." There is a difference between things written by those under immediate inspiration of the Spirit and those under His direction. Writing in his interleaved Bible, Edwards approached Luther's type of scriptural evaluation; the epistles of Paul and those of John are the most important. He also noted Perkins's advice to read Romans from chapter twelve to the end and then go to the beginning. Justification and predestination he considered the most difficult themes. In general, Romans and the fourth gospel were the most important parts of the Bible. Though for Edwards all of Scripture was given by divine inspiration, God accomplished that in at least two different ways, "immediate inspiration" and "divine direction."

> We ought to distinguish between those things which were written in the sacred books by the immediate inspiration of the Holy Spirit and those which were only committed to writing by the direction of the Holy Spirit. To the former class belong all the mysteries of salvation, or all those things which respect the means of our deliverance taught in the gospel, which could not be known from the principles of reason, and therefore must be revealed. But to the other class those things belong which either are already known from natural religion, but are of service to inculcate duty on man and to admonstrate the necessity of a revealed means of salvation, or are histories, useful to illustrate and to assure us of the doctrines revealed and which point out the various degrees of revelation, the different dispensations of salvation, and the various modes of governing the church of God; all of which are necessary to be known in the further explanation of mysteries.[46]

Finally, for Jonathan Edwards, "All Scripture says to us is certainly true. There you hear Christ speaking."[47] That is what inerrancy means.

INTERPRETATION AND ILLUMINATION

We now have a divine, supernatural revelation that is miraculously inspired, so that every word is inerrant and its canonical

46. *Works*, 3:544.
47. No. 96.

limits defined as well. There remains the all-important purpose for which it was given—understanding and applying it. That is the hermeneutical question to which we turn in concluding our discussion of Jonathan Edwards and the Bible.

THE INTERPRETATION OF THE BIBLE

In a sense Edwards was dealing with the interpretation of Scripture almost every day of his life. All his notes in all his writings were directly or indirectly involved in that enterprise. We have never encountered a sermon that did not begin with a text of Scripture and expound and apply it throughout.

Probably the most straightforward, comprehensive statement Edwards ever made about the Bible, its interpretation, and its divinity is found in a *Miscellany* written shortly after he had begun his preaching career. We have referred to it before but we now quote in full.

> *Scriptures.* When one enquires whether or not we have Scripture ground for any doctrine, the question is whether or not the Scripture exhibits it any way to the eye of the mind or to the eye of reason. We have no grounds to assert that it was God's intent by the Scripture, in so many terms, to declare every doctrine that he would have us believe. There are many things the Scripture may support that we know already. And if what the Scripture says, together with what is plain to reason, leads [us] to believe any doctrine, we are to look upon ourselves as taught this doctrine by the Scripture. God may reveal things in Scripture, which way he pleases; if by what he there reveals the thing is any way clearly discovered to the understanding or eye of the mind, 'tis our duty to receive it as his revelation.[48]

Several things seem worthy of note. First, no specific hermeneutical principle is advocated, whether literal, allegorical, eschatological, or analogical. The question is only "whether or no the Scripture exhibits it *any way* to the eye of the mind. . . ." Presumably,

48. *M*, 426.

any type of interpretation is valid if reasonable.[49] No special disposition, regenerate or unregenerate, is insisted on. Second, what "is plain to reason," together with what Scripture teaches, justifies doctrine. That seems to be more than the usual "just and necessary consequence," which Edwards would surely regard as appealing "to the eye of the mind." What is plain to reason would seem to include not only the implicit but the self-evident and soundly-reasoned extrabiblical data as well. In *Freedom of the Will* Edwards had justified metaphysics as virtually the only way of understanding and justifying any cardinal biblical teaching, specifically the five points of Calvinism.[50] Third, whatever the Bible is found to teach, " 'tis our duty to receive it as his [God's] revelation." *Whatever* is an omnibus term that carries authority for every single item that the understanding sees the Bible to affirm. No room for restriction to the "normative," the "essential," to matters pertaining to "faith and morals" here. That is an absolute equivalent for the classic formula "What the Bible says, God says." Finally, it is a matter of "duty" to receive, and for Edwards that meant preach and practice. That sentence can explain his entire life and career.

ILLUMINATION

Though the internal evidence and the corroborative external

49. Stephen Stein, "Jonathan Edwards and the Rainbow: Biblical Exegesis and Poetic Imagination." *New England Quarterly* 47 (1974): 440-56, finds Edwards free to give vent to his imagination, not being restricted to the rational meaning of the words. The imagination could only operate under that aegis. Typology, for example, was no exercise of the imagination. On the other hand, there are things revealed in the Word of God and that God has "as it were bounden duty to believe that are above our comprehension. They have difficulties in them that we cannot explain. And God is not pleased to explain them to us but to let them stand as trials and exercising of our faith and humility." That is no way inconsistent with his statement about the meaning of Scripture "in the eye of the understanding." The mind grasps the biblical truth but does not comprehend it—cannot explain it. It is to be received and believed, however, as God's Word. That is not unlike Aquinas's things that are evident to reason and therefore accepted in contrast to things not capable of rationalization and are to be accepted as articles of faith. The illustration that Edwards gave in that context (after mentioning God's answering Job out of the whirlwind) was God's sovereignty in determining the state of the souls of men "where the answer given is to remind the protester of his presumption" (Ms sermon on Rom. 9:22).

50. 4:6; 13.

evidence prove the Bible to be the Word of God, that fact is brought home to the individual by divine illumination. The way to know that the Spirit of God was given to Christ is to have Him given to you.[51] No other book but the Word of Christ reaches the heart.[52] That fact shows that the internal miracle of illumination is a kind of external evidence also. Only the Word can "subdue the heart."[53] Edwards obviously agreed with the Westminster Confession of Faith, which after listing many biblical "arguments whereby it doth abundantly evidence itself to be the Word of God," carefully adds the significant reminder that "yet, notwithstanding, our full persuasion and assurance of the infallible truth, and divine authority thereof, is from the inward work of the Holy Spirit, bearing witness by and with the Word in our hearts."[54]

Illumination is dependent on knowledge. Knowledge is not dependent, in the same sense, on illumination. Illumination does powerfully promote knowledge. Once God has made the knowledge come alive spiritually, the saints develop an eager desire for more of such knowledge, in order that a more enlivening experience may be possible. The sense of the heart promotes the interests of the head.

> Spiritual saving knowledge of God and divine things greatly promotes speculative knowledge; as it engages the mind in its search into things of this kind, and much assists to a distinct understanding of them; so that, other things being equal, they that have spiritual knowledge are much more likely than others to have a good doctrinal acquaintance with things of religion. . . .

But Edwards hastened to add that "such acquaintance may be no distinguishing characteristic of true saints."[55] Mere speculative knowledge should *never* be confused with saving heart knowledge.

---

51. Luke 4:18, "Shew you how the Spirit of God was given to Christ. . ." St. Ind., July 1755.
52. Sermon on 2 Tim. 3:16, p. 194: "No word is as powerful to change the heart"; p. 196, "Scripture gives light . . . gives life."
53. Jer. 23:29, "Prop. 1. The hearts of the children of men are naturally like a rock. 2. That the word of God subdues and dissolves the rocky hearts of the children of men. 3. That herein it is like a fire and a hammer," April 1749.
54. Chapter 1, Sect. 5.
55. *True Grace Distinguished from the Experience of Devils, Works*, 2.13.

Though there is a divine illumination that marks the moment of conversion, those visions are given intermittently throughout the life of the Christian. They are usually brief disclosures of glory comparable to the sun coming from behind clouds. The beloved is like a roe on the mountains.[56] That glimpse is, however, reassuring. It is not the length of time but the nature of the view that guarantees the presence of the beloved. A contemporary Scottish minister, Ebenezer Erskine, spoke much of "blinks," an apparent reference to such enriching but infrequent views of the divine glory. As Erskine became older, he relied less on them, an indication perhaps of the truth of Edwards's statement that they are infrequently given. The purpose of those views, discoveries, or blinks is not that the beholders should stay on the mount of transfiguration or stand gazing into heaven, but radiate the light to others. Thus, Edwards appealed to "those that have lately been enlightened—don't only be enlightened but shine."[57]

JONATHAN EDWARDS AND THE BIBLE

What shall we say? For him it was nothing other than the verbally inspired and inerrant Word, and he always, as Isaiah advised, trembled at that Word. It had free course in him as he studied it day and night and preached it throughout his ministry. It was certified internally and confirmed by external credentials as well. It was an "awful book,"[58] with its dread warnings to the wicked and wondrous promises to the humble penitent. So Edwards, boxed in as he was by its authority, preached it in season and out, laboring to make its unique and saving message plain and powerful, fully aware that no sinner in Northampton or anywhere would ever see and receive it as God's very Word until God Himself cast His divine and supernatural light upon its pages and its proclamation.

56. 2 Cor. 13:5.
57. Song of Sol. 6:10, "First, I would show how the saints are said to look forth as the morning. 1. They are lightsome. . . . They receive light. . . . They shine forth by reflecting that light," Feb. 1741/42.
58. Rom. 2:5, "Unawakened and impenitent sinners do heap up to themselves wrath against the day of wrath as men are wont to heap up treasures," n.d.

9

Inerrancy in American Wesleyanism

Daryl E. McCarthy

American Wesleyanism is rooted deeply in British Methodism. Though there were some changes in polity, British Methodist theology was wholly embraced by early American Methodism. That is especially true for the doctrine of the inspiration of Scripture. As late as 1919, the Methodist Episcopal church's basic sources of theology were the Bible, Wesley's *Standard Sermons*, his *Notes on the New Testament*, and Richard Watson's *Theological Institutes*.[1] The unequivocal stand for biblical inerrancy by John Wesley, Adam Clarke, and Richard Watson—the triumverate that formed the fountainhead of Wesleyanism—has continued as the traditional

---

1. Emory Stevens Bucke, *The History of American Methodism*, 3 vols. (New York: Abingdon, 1964), 2:593; cf. 2:381. Most early American Methodist attempts at systematic theology "meant an American rewriting" of Watson's *Institutes*. The *Institutes*, especially until the last quarter of the eighteenth century, "not only provided a norm for subsequent doctrinal studies, but gave direction to the whole theological enterprise within American Methodism."

DARYL E. MCCARTHY, B.Th., Kansas City College and Bible School, M.A., Trinity Evangelical Divinity School, M. Div., Nazarene Theological Seminary, is professor of philosophy, apologetics, and practical theology at Kansas City College and Bible School, Overland Park, Kansas. He also serves as director of church growth programs for the Church of God (Holiness) Home Missions Department. He has contributed to the *Wesleyan Theological Journal*.

Wesleyan doctrine of Scripture throughout most of the history of American Wesleyanism.

We will examine the doctrine of Scripture held by several major Wesleyan theologians during the 1800s and then examine the fate of that doctrine in several Wesleyan-Arminian denominations during the 1900s.

SAMUEL WAKEFIELD 1799-1895

The first major Wesleyan systematic theology to appear following the lengthy domination of Watson's *Institutes* was Wakefield's *Complete System of Christian Theology* (1869).

Wakefield presented a thoroughly Watsonian defense of God's revelation, the Bible, as well as a more thorough explication of the doctrine of inspiration. Divine inspiration was the "extraordinary influence of the Holy Spirit upon the human mind by which men are qualified to communicate to others religious knowledge without error or mistake." Inspiration was absolutely essential because without it the Scriptures could not command our "entire confidence as an infallible standard of religious truth." Inspiration enables us to believe that by God's power the Scriptures were "infallibly preserved from all error."[2]

There are three degrees of inspiration: (1) the Holy Spirit *superintended* the writing of some sections, such as history, that contained material the authors basically knew on their own, but that supervision by the Spirit was important in that it prevented the "possibility of error in their writings," (2) at times the Holy Spirit *elevated* and enlarged their thoughts and understanding beyond their normal abilities, as in the apostles' recording of conversations and details related to Jesus' ministry, years after their occurrence, and (3) the highest degree of inspiration is found at the level of *suggestion* by the Holy Spirit of the exact thoughts and even words the writer was to use, such as in prophetic passages.[3]

The Scriptures are plenarily inspired; every part of the Bible is divinely inspired to varying degrees. However, not all parts of

2. Samuel Wakefield, *A Complete System of Christian Theology* (Cincinnati: Cranston and Stowe, 1869), pp. 71, 73.
3. Ibid., pp. 72, 78-82.

Scripture are verbally inspired in the strict sense of the word. At the level of superintendence, the Spirit did not tell the authors every word to write down but rather oversaw the writing process to make sure they made no mistakes or errors. On the other hand, there were some sections that were verbally, i.e., word for word, inspired.[4]

The doctrine of "occasional inspiration" should be rejected because it would allow for the possibility of errors and mistakes in the Scripture. "But if it is once granted that they are in the least degree alloyed with error, an opening is made for every imaginable corruption."[5]

Thus the Bible was "written by persons who were moved, directed, and assisted by the Holy Spirit, and who were, therefore, infallibly preserved from error."[6]

THOMAS RALSTON 1806-91

Ralston's *Elements of Divinity* delineated several points in the doctrine of Scripture. First, "inspiration is so full and complete that the sacred writers are not the real authors of the books they penned. . . . The Scriptures are the Word of God as really as were the 'Ten Commandments,' which were written by his own finger. In the one case God chose to write with his own finger, and in the other case he selected the sacred writers . . . as his amanuenses; but in both cases it is really God's writing—God's book—God's Word."[7]

Second, inspiration included the guidance, direction, and control of the writers by the Holy Spirit. That insured that Scripture would be "free from error, and just as God would have it." However, the Holy Spirit's control did not do away with differences in the preferences, abilities, or education of the writers.[8]

Third, inspiration does not guarantee that the writers were infallible at all times; they were infallible only when they were

4. Ibid., pp. 78-79, 82.
5. Ibid., p. 77.
6. Ibid., p. 81.
7. Thomas N. Ralston, *Elements of Divinity* (Nashville: Methodist Episcopal Church, South, 1876), p. 597.
8. Ibid.

serving as spokesmen for God in Holy Writ. They may have held to mistaken ideas in philosophy, science, or other areas. But it makes no difference as long as "they were preserved from all error, as official teachers of the doctrine of God."[9]

Fourth, the individuality of the writers was not destroyed by the Spirit's inspiration. "They were not used by the divine Spirit as mere machines."[10]

Fifth, the Scriptures were verbally inspired. "The very *words*, as well as the *thoughts*" were inspired by the Holy Spirit. "The Bible is the 'Word of God.' What the Bible says, God says, what the Bible declares to be true, is true."[11]

Sixth, all genre of literature in the Bible—whether historical, didactic, or poetic—are inspired by God. Regardless of the genre, inspiration had the effect on the writers of "freeing them from the possibility of mistake or error."[12]

From a historical perspective, Ralston noted that until the middle of the sixth century—at the time of Theodore of Mopsuestia—plenary inspiration was attacked only by "notorious heretics." For the next several centuries there were many who joined the attack, i.e., Jewish Talmudists, Maimonides, and others. In the sixteenth century Socinus and his followers attacked inerrancy, "asserting that the sacred writers sometimes failed in memory and were liable to error in some of their statements." But such a view is clearly infidelity.[13]

MINER RAYMOND 1811-97

Raymond, a professor of systematic theology at Garrett Biblical Institute for thirty-three years, published his *Systematic Theology* in 1877. He devoted the beginning section to an apologetical defense of revelation and inspiration. The Bible was an accurate record of the words, actions, feelings, thoughts, and circumstances of the

---

9. Ibid., p. 598.
10. Ibid. It was rather common for early Methodists to speak in quite mechanical terms, yet they clearly repudiated any mechanical theory.
11. Ibid., pp. 598-99.
12. Ibid., pp. 600-603.
13. Ibid., p. 596.

inspired authors. "The events they record are events of real history."[14]

Raymond linked the genuineness, the authenticity ("what it affirms is true"), and the inspiration (the direction, guidance, assistance, or control by the Spirit) of the Bible. "To prove the one is to prove the other. If the Bible be inspired, since God does not inspire men to speak falsely, of course, it is both authentic and genuine. If it be authentic, if what it says is true, it must be inspired, since it claims inspiration."[15]

He also clearly affirmed inerrancy. The Bible "is pure from any admixture of error and is an authoritative rule of faith and practice."[16] The Bible is "a complete and perfect rule of faith and practice."[17] Truly, the Bible is God's Word—"what it says, God says." It is a "God-given volume," as it professes to be.[18]

DANIEL D. WHEDON 1808-85

Whedon, the noted Methodist professor, editor, and theologian, was "a major factor in diverting the mind of nineteenth-century American Methodism away from an unqualified appeal to the doctrinal positions of Richard Watson." He was "a formative influence in the emergence of an indigenous theological tradition within American Methodism."[19]

Whedon emphasized the authority of the Word vis-à-vis its inspiration. The authority of the New Testament was established by the authority of Christ Himself. It was then upon the authority of the New Testament that the authority of the Old Testament was established. The New Testament should be recognized as the official, infallible record of Christ and His work. "Every New Testament writer is a witness chosen by Christ; and if every line and

14. Miner Raymond, *Systematic Theology*, 3 vols. (Cincinnati: Cranston and Stowe, 1877), 1:64-65.
15. Ibid., 1:116-17.
16. Ibid., 1:180.
17. Ibid., 3:86.
18. Ibid., 1:207.
19. Bucke, 2:382. Chiles called Whedon "the most important Methodist theological figure in the second half of the nineteenth century." Robert E. Chiles, *Theological Transition in American Methodism: 1790-1935* (New York: Abingdon, 1965), pp. 34-35.

word which such witnesses have left us is not reliable, then Christ pitifully failed in his attempt to give us his real system of holy truth." But no, the New Testament is *"Christ's own canon"* and "is in every part and particle binding on our Christian faith." On that basis, then, we can place a firm "reliance upon every part and particle of the true text in matters of faith and doctrine."[20]

Whedon believed that such a view of the plenary authority of the Bible was consistent with the admission of the possibility of mistakes in the inspired product. "We can easily conceive, indeed, a high state of spiritual inspiration, circumscribed within religious limits highly and perhaps perfectly authoritative within its sphere, yet perfectly consistent with mistake regarding a secular or historical fact." The prime example of that would be the historical errors of Stephen in his Acts 7 address.[21]

But what about mistakes, not on the part of speakers quoted in the canon, but mistakes by inspired canonical writers themselves? "When an unquestionable instance can be adduced of one of the inspired canonical *writers* having made a statement irreconcilable with truth, undoubtedly we must in that instance admit the limitation to his inspiration." Whedon hastened to add, *"But we wait for that instance to be* adduced [emphasis added]. The *authority* of the true text still stands over our religious faith. The Bible, the whole Bible, is the standard of ultimate appeal."[22]

In spite of all the controversy over biblical criticism and the momentary doubts one might have about the Bible's authority, it carried "a great *positive power* which holds the believer firm in his faith."[23] The Bible carries its own self-authenticating authority. The Scriptures "are sanctioned by God, as the veritable revelation from God, and as true in every part and proposition when interpreted in the intentional sense of the writer." When we read the Bible, we can assume "the perfect truth to the letter of all its declarations."[24] "We believe in the divinely sanctioned truth and

20. Daniel D. Whedon, *Statements: Theological and Critical*, ed. J. S. and D. A. Whedon (New York: Phillips & Hunt, 1887), p. 196.
21. Ibid., p. 194.
22. Ibid.
23. Ibid., p. 196.
24. Ibid., p. 197.

authority of every genuine syllable of these records."[25] In fact, we should still accept them as true in the face of alleged difficulties, even when there is simply the *possibility* that the difficulty could be solved with more knowledge of the facts.

Thus, with Whedon came the first crack in the dam. Though he accepted the plenary and absolute authority of the Bible and refused to admit that there were, in fact, any errors in it, he held that errors would not be inconsistent with the nature of divine revelation and inspiration. But he so totally accepted the fact of inerrancy that he did not follow through in examining the difficulties that would arise if one posited an errant revelation from an unerring God of truth.

RANDOLPH S. FOSTER 1820-1903

Foster, the saintly bishop and Drew Seminary professor, published *Evidences of Christianity*, the third volume in his six-volume *Studies in Theology*, in 1889. He argued that there were varying degrees of inspiration. Some parts were dictated verbally but others were either superintended or else the ideas were inspired. The writers were "amanuenses" of God in that "God spoke by them." But the Bible in no sense was mechanically dictated by God.[26]

Though all the Bible was sacred, it was not all of equal value or importance because of the varying degrees of inspiration and types of content (Foster seems to be the first Wesleyan theologian to stress the fact that there are varying degrees of value within Holy Writ). "But all the parts must be true, and must in some way serve the revelation."[27] Even in the parts that seem to be "mere human recitation" of commonly known facts, those are "still true, and a part of divinely-authenticated truth."[28]

Foster forthrightly admitted that there are problems in our modern translations. Even though our Bibles are "substantially authentic and accurate . . . some inaccuracies and mistakes may

25. Ibid., p. 198.
26. Randolph S. Foster, *Studies in Theology*, vol. 3: *Evidences of Christianity* (New York: Eaton & Mains, 1889), pp. 33, 333-36.
27. Ibid., p. 41.
28. Ibid., p. 2.

have occurred" in the process of copying and translation. Not every word or statement in our Bibles "is divinely inspired, or even divinely authorized, or certainly true." Yet those errors do not "impair the substantial accuracy of the record, or in any degree diminish its credibility and authority in matters of doctrine and history."[29]

Foster affirmed biblical inerrancy repeatedly and in the clearest terms.

> If the Bible be from God, it can contain nothing but truth in its original deliverances. If there be any thing in it false, so much must be eliminated, and if we find it false in respect of matters about which we know, and which we are able to test, it is impossible that we should rationally accept it in respect of matters which are required to be accepted on its authority: *falsus in uno, falsus in omnibus.*[30]
>
> We must claim for it, therefore, that it is true in its original deliverances, its recitation of facts, and its historical statements from beginning to end; and true in its doctrines and ethics assumed, implied, and enunciated on a fair rule of interpretation.[31]

The Bible is "a true history from beginning to end."[32] "It has not been possible to convict it of a single falsehood or error."[33]

> Any evidence that would invalidate any of these facts [the genuineness, authenticity, and credibility of the Bible] would put in jeopardy the whole volume, and would be absolutely fatal to so much of the contents as come under the invalidation. The truth of the entire contents must be sustained, or, at least, be invincible to the charge of error or falsehood.[34]

There is no contradiction between the Bible and science. But

29. Ibid., pp. 3-4. Later, Foster made this statement concerning the transcription errors: "They do not effect a single fact; they do not confuse a single doctrine; they do not overthrow a single statement" (p. 345).
30. Ibid., p. 248.
31. Ibid.
32. Ibid., p. 42.
33. Ibid., p. 44.
34. Ibid., p. 6. Similar statements are made on pp. 46, 50, and 330.

admittedly the Bible speaks in popular terms concerning natural events (e.g., the sun is rising).[35]

Thus, Foster emerged as the most thorough and explicit defender of inerrancy in late nineteenth-century Methodism.

JOHN MILEY 1813-95

The publication of Miley's *Systematic Theology* (1894) has been called "a major point of theological transition" within American Methodism.[36] Miley advocated a rather loose, dynamic theory of inspiration in which the Holy Spirit works in and through the human agent without reducing him to a mere implement. "Through the agency of the Holy Spirit he [the human agent] is so enlightened and possessed of the truth, and so guided in its expression, that the truth so given forth, whether by the spoken or written word, is from God."[37] "Inspiration is thus the divine warrant of truth in the Scriptures."[38]

Miley lodged several problems against the verbal theory of inspiration, which he equated with mechanical dictation: (1) there are obvious human elements in Scripture, (2) there are verbal differences at times between the writers in stating the same facts (e.g., Matt. 27:37; Mark 15:26; Luke 13:38; John 19:19), (3) we no longer have any of the original autographs. Since there are textual variants, we cannot possess a *true* revelation now, so (4) verbal inspiration is unnecessary. "An exact set of words, dictated by the Spirit, is not necessary either to the truthful expression of the divine mind or to the divine authorship of the Scriptures."[39] There can be changes in the wording without changes in the meaning. That is illustrated by the fact that Jesus and His apos-

---

35. Ibid., pp. 39, 248-49.
36. Frederick A. Norwood, *The Story of American Methodism* (Nashville: Abingdon, 1974), p. 2. Chiles asserts that Miley was the first Methodist theologian to more fully work out the complete implications of Whedon's theology. Chiles *Theological Transitions*, p. 35.
37. John Miley, *Systematic Theology*, 2 vols. (New York: Hunt & Eaton, 1894), 2:486.
38. Ibid., 2:488.
39. Ibid., 2:486-87.

tles often quoted from the Septuagint in an inexact manner, though one that still captured the meaning of the text.[40]

Within the milieu in which Miley wrote, it is significant that he was careful *not* to affirm any type of inerrancy.

MILTON S. TERRY 1840-1914

The professor of Hebrew and Old Testament exegesis at Garrett Biblical Institute, Milton Terry, provides us with an interesting study in the journey of a scholar from adherence to inerrancy and infallibility to a total reversal and bitter rejection of those doctrines. In most respects, Terry's doctrine of inspiration in the first edition of his classic *Biblical Hermeneutics* was traditional Wesleyan doctrine. He claimed that in some sense the writers "were used mechanically." At other times they were "inspired dynamically" by the Holy Spirit's supervision and direction. There was verbal inspiration in that God spoke His words to the authors (Jer. 1:9; 1 Cor. 2:13). That inspiration was plenary in that it "furnished an all-sufficient fullness, a revelation of the mind and will of God."[41]

In what form was divine inspiration given? Terry claimed he had no "technical theory" of inspiration.[42] But there was no support whatsoever for a strictly mechanical process, according to which God picked out every word for the writers all the time. But inspiration did affect the words, thoughts, feelings, and style of the writers. Four degrees of inspiration can be delineated: (1) suggestion—all the truth was communicated by the Spirit, (2) direction—the writer's style was directed by the Spirit, (3) elevation—additional strength and energy were provided by the Spirit, and (4) superintendency—the writers were kept from writing anything that might be "derogatory to the revelation" that was given.[43]

It was undeniable that God was concerned with both the style and form of the written Word. The theory that God inspired only the ideas and not the words denied too much of the divine ele-

40. Ibid., 2:483-87.
41. Milton S. Terry, *Biblical Hermeneutics* (Grand Rapids: Zondervan, 1950), p. 138.
42. Ibid., p. 150.
43. Ibid., p. 145.

ment. But it could be affirmed that "the wisdom and power of God secured, without any violation of individual freedom, the writing of the Holy Scriptures in their original form, and preserved the writers from vital error."[44]

Several objections concerning inspiration were treated by Terry. Variations in wording between parallel accounts do not refute divine inspiration because the writers were not trying to give the *ipsissima verba*. After all, the original words were in Aramaic, not Greek. The Spirit directed each writer in his choice of words. Each evangelist reported in his own way the substance of what the Lord had said. But "in all these varying reports there is no error, no real discrepancy."[45] Nor did the thousands of textual variants destroy verbal inspiration. "The denial of verbal inspiration logically diminishes one's devout interest and zeal in the critical study of the Scriptures . . . for if those words [in the autographa] were not divinely inspired we would naturally attach less importance to them."[46] But why bother with verbal inspiration when we do not have the autographa? Accurate and reliable translations are based ultimately on the fact that the original manuscripts were from God and were the "ultimate source of all appeal."[47]

"As for alleged discrepancies, contradictions, and errors of the Bible, we deny that any real errors can be shown." Spelling errors, inaccurate grammar, minor inaccuracies, or obscurity in expression are not incompatible with divine inspiration, nor are they to be considered as real errors.[48] For example, the fact that Stephen in his final address seems to have made a historical misstatement (though it is not certain) did not hinder the effectiveness of his message. Maybe the Holy Spirit permitted him to make such a mistake to show "how irresistible plenary inspiration is not conditioned 'in the wisdom of man, but in the power of God' (1 Cor. 2:5)."[49]

Most of the alleged discrepancies in the Bible are due to copyists' errors: a variety of names for the same person or places, dif-

44. Ibid., p. 146.
45. Ibid., p. 140.
46. Ibid., p. 148.
47. Ibid.
48. Ibid., p. 149.
49. Ibid., pp. 149-50.

ferent means of calculating time, varying historical or geographical perspectives, the particular purpose of each book, and the peculiarities of Oriental logic and expression.[50]

Does science contradict the Bible? Some try to escape the question by asserting that the Bible was not designed to teach science. Therefore, a contradiction of the Bible by science should not disturb us. Terry responded that a true, undisputed contradiction *would* prove the Bible "spurious." "Truths of whatever kind can never be in real conflict with each other."[51] He denied any real contradictions between the Bible and science. He defended biblical miracles. He explained the Bible's use of popular language to describe natural phenomena. However, at times in the process of reconciling the Bible and science, Terry surrendered far more of the literalness of the Bible than most Methodists had been willing to give up. For instance, both the creation account and the Noahic deluge were said to have been local and limited. He understood Joshua 10:12-14 as poetic or as an optical miracle (i.e., illusion).

Terry's gradual move away from inerrancy became more apparent in the second edition of *Biblical Hermeneutics* (1890).[52] He eliminated the chapters on divine inspiration and scientific contradictions. There was no discussion or mention of the inspiration of Scripture—not in the entire 511 pages of a text devoted to, of all things, biblical hermeneutics.

In 1901 Terry published *Moses and the Prophets*. He called it "An Essay Toward a Fair and Useful Statement of Some of the Positions of Modern Biblical Criticism."[53] In the essay he stoutly defended the documentary hypothesis and most of the other tenets of rationalistic higher criticism.

Terry's departure from orthodox Wesleyan doctrine was fully realized in his *Biblical Dogmatics* (1907). At the outset of his discus-

---

50. Ibid., pp. 514-32.
51. Ibid., p. 533.
52. Terry *Biblical Hermeneutics*, 2d ed. (New York: Hunt & Eaton, 1890), 511 pp. It should be noted that there was an 1885 second edition of *Biblical Hermeneutics* that was basically a reprint of the 1883 first edition. It is not clear why the 1890 shorter edition was called a "second edition," when in reality it was a third edition.
53. Milton S. Terry, *Moses and the Prophets* (New York: Eaton & Mains, 1901).

sion of "The Question of Inspiration," Terry announced that we should "oppose and drive away, so far as we are able, the dogma of verbal inerrancy of the records." Verbal inerrancy has no scriptural support. He never defined *verbal inerrancy* but seemed to interchange the term with *mechanical control.*[54]

What does the Bible claim for itself? The highest claim to be found in the Old Testament is by Isaiah in chapter 6 concerning his vision. But Terry claimed that "there is not a line of evidence that what was afterward written out as Isaiah's oracles was anything other than the prophet's own composition, prepared in the full exercise of all his personal faculties, and within the limitations of his own human thought."[55] Even when the psalmist claims God was speaking through him (2 Sam. 23:2—"The Spirit of the Lord spoke by me. And His word was on my tongue"), he was merely speaking in "the impassioned language of sacred poetry." Such verses are not confirmation that "the writer was an impassive machine, controlled by another Person, and miraculously secured against the utterance of any and every kind of error or mistake."[56]

The New Testament as well lacks any claim to "infallible dictation."[57] The most that can be said concerning the books of the Bible is that the

> Holy Spirit of God cooperated with their authors, and the result is a volume immeasurably more profitable, as a whole, for instruction in spiritual things than all the other religious writings of the world. . . . They embody and inculcate all the great religious truths which are anywhere known among men.[58]

Inerrancy is "a dogma of necessitarian philosophy" of human action. Mechanical inspiration is the natural result of the denial of human freedom and the belief in monergistic theology. With such a theology "our thoughts, words, and deeds become as mechani-

54. Milton S. Terry, *Biblical Dogmatics* (New York; Eaton & Mains, 1907), p. 18.
55. Ibid., p. 19.
56. Ibid., p. 20.
57. Ibid.
58. Ibid., p. 23. The Milton S. Terry Collection in the Garrett-Evangelical Theological Seminary Archives indicates in many lecture notes and other papers that in his later years he became quite enthusiastic about the field of comparative religions and indicated a universalistic tendency.

cal and necessary as the movements of the planets and tides."
Opposed to that as the only viable alternative is synergistic theology. Terry concluded that "the dogma of verbal inerrancy is inconsistent with existing facts, extravagant in its assumptions, and mischievous in its tendency to provoke continual controversy in the church . . . and is a positive hindrance to the rational study of the Bible."[59]

Infallibility as well was destroyed by the "numerous discrepancies in the Bible." In spite of the efforts to harmonize those discrepancies, "their very existence is a fatal witness against the unanimity of the Biblical writers." In the light of 2 Peter 3:16 and the never-ending biblical disputes, "obviously there is no such infallibility among men or books."[60] The fact that God is absolutely true says nothing about the Bible. "The Bible is not God."[61] No human production—not even the Bible—can ever be inerrant or infallible.

According to Terry, we should reject the popular shibboleth that "the Bible *is* the Word of God." That is true "only in a loose and inaccurate way of speaking" and is only a synecdoche, a mere rhetorical figure. The Bible never speaks of itself as a whole as being "the word of God."[62] Thus Milton Terry ended his journey.[63]

CONTROVERSY IN METHODISM

The turn of the century found Methodism embroiled in a bitter struggle between those who held to the traditional Methodist doctrines and those who advocated a more rationalistic, critical approach. Innuendoes were cast, linking Milton Terry and other liberal theologians with the well-known infidels Thomas Paine and Robert Ingersoll, who held similar views. Protest meetings of Methodist Episcopal ministers were called. Resolutions denounc-

59. Ibid., p. 23.
60. Ibid., p. 25.
61. Ibid., p. 26.
62. Ibid., pp. 32-33.
63. Holographs and typewritten notes in the Terry Collection in the Garrett-Evangelical Archives contain many statements very similar to a number in *Biblical Dogmatics*. Those are undated, but they seem to manifest the development of Terry's thought, which culminated in *Biblical Dogmatics*.

ing the liberal scholars were passed. Warnings were issued that the Methodist seminaries and colleges had sold out to the liberals and higher critics.[64] Entire periodicals were issued that denounced the forsaking of Methodist theology. Higher critics were charged with being apostate enemies of the Christian church and as belonging "among unbelievers and infidels."[65] There were vitriolic personal attacks from both sides.[66]

The theological ferment was directly linked in the minds of many Methodists with the other problems of Methodism, such as a general decline in spiritual life, worldliness in the church, the demise of class meetings, the neglect of the poor, and the lack of church growth.[67]

But the drift was irreversible. In the first twenty years of the new century, official Methodism moved away from many traditional Wesleyan doctrines. The Bible was understood merely as *Heilsgeschichte*. Inerrancy was inessential. In 1916 and 1918 there were extensive changes in the official course of study of the Methodist Episcopal Church and the M.E., South. By that time the liberals were firmly entrenched in official Methodism. The years

64. L. W. Munhall, *Breakers! Methodism Adrift* (New York: Charles C. Cook, 1913), pp. 47-87. Munhall documented in detail the attack on the Bible in the colleges and seminaries of Methodism. He cited vivid testimonials, often from parents of students whose faith was destroyed at those institutions. Munhall quoted the great Bishop Charles H. Fowler as saying, "The schools and universities of the Methodist Episcopal Church belong more to the devil today than they do to our Church," p. 64.

65. *The Methodist Outlook*, 1 (1902). Munhall also wrote another book, *Highest Critic versus the Higher Critics* (New York: Revell, 1892), in which he detailed the controversy within Methodism.

66. Even the *Chicago Evening Post* (n.d., copy in Terry Collection, Garrett-Evangelical Archives) published a denunciation of Terry by L. W. Munhall and a subsequent reply by Terry. Terry referred to Munhall with such phrases as "vociferous and pessimistic cur," "inflated pugilist," "illiterate evangelist," "mongrel Calvinist," and spoke of his "amazing stupidity," "obfuscated cerebration," and "malignant innuendo and misrepresentation." Terry attacked Munhall's claim that verbal inspiration and inerrancy are indispensable doctrines. According to Terry, such conclusions could only be made by a necessitarian Calvinist. He denounced Munhall's appeal to Calvinists such as Spurgeon, Hodge, Warfield, and Kuyper. "Being himself a mongrel Calvinist, and so leavened with the necessary pessimism of literalistic Second Adventism, he is thereby probably incapacitated for perceiving that necessitarian inspiration is a necessary corollary of . . . Calvinistic necessitarianism." All that in the *Chicago Evening Post*! Without a doubt, there were similar attacks from the opposing side as well.

67. Munhall *Breakers*, pp. 36-46.

1919-34 have been characterized by one historian as an era of "rampant liberalism." There was an almost total acceptance of the German style historical-critical approach to Scripture. Genesis was certainly folklore; creationism was taboo; evolutionism was in.[68]

The writings of men like Olin Curtis, Borden Parker Bowne, Albert Knudson, and Harris Franklin Ralls helped continue the liberal trend. By 1940 Ralls was denying that Christianity was a "supernatural, authoritative, and unchanging set of rules." By 1959 the Methodist laity had been so firmly indoctrinated that only 8.4 percent affirmed the infallibility of the Bible.[69]

Out of the ferment within Methodism, however, arose a new movement that would continue to promote Wesleyan theology—the Holiness movement. During the late 1800s and into the early 1900s, as Methodism declined, many Methodists began forming new denominations, associations, and schools. Revivals that swept across many regions brought new people into the folds of the growing Holiness movement. That movement was destined to reassert the traditional Wesleyan affirmation of biblical inerrancy. An examination of some of the Holiness denominations and seminaries will reveal their efforts to maintain that doctrine.

ASBURY THEOLOGICAL SEMINARY

Asbury Theological Seminary's founder, Henry Clay Morrison, wanted a seminary that would be "absolutely true to the teachings of the Holy Scriptures."[70] Throughout its history, in its official statements, Asbury has stood for biblical inerrancy. The seminary affirms of the Bible that "as originally given, ITS MANUSCRIPTS WERE FREE FROM ACTUAL ERROR

---

68. Bucke, 2:593-99; 3:248, 261-62. S. Paul Schilling, *Methodism and Society*, vol. 3: *Society in Theological Perspective* (New York: Abingdon, 1960), pp. 95-100, 120.
69. Schilling, pp. 100, 120. The survey statement Methodists responded to was as follows: "Every word is true [in the Bible] because it came directly from God."
70. "A Statement of Purpose," prepared by the faculty of Asbury Theological Seminary, n.d., rev.

OF FACT IN ALL REGARDS."[71] Thus the Bible is the "inerrant and authoritative Word of God."[72]

THE WESLEYAN CHURCH

The Wesleyan Methodist Church always held to a high view of Scripture. Their *Discipline* was based (as are most Wesleyan denominations) on the "Thirty-Nine Articles of Religion of the Church of England." But the church increasingly felt that its position needed to be stated even more clearly, since the original terms in the "Articles" did not seem to carry the same meaning that they did earlier. At the 1951 General Conference, the statement of faith was amended to affirm that the Scriptures are "the inspired and Infallibly written Word of God, fully inerrant in their original manuscripts and superior to all human authority."[73] Historians of the Wesleyan Church assert that the strong loyalty of the people to the Bible as the inerrant Word of God helped to guard the church against liberalism and modernism.[74]

Houghton College, a Wesleyan Church school, makes the following statement of faith in its catalog: "We believe the Scriptures of the Old and New Testaments are fully inspired of God, inerrant in the original writings, and that they are the supreme and final *authority* for matters of faith and practice."[75]

THE CHURCH OF THE NAZARENE

The Church of the Nazarene was forming and beginning to grow during the final years of theological ferment that had been shaking American Methodism for decades. Many of the early Nazarene leaders came out of the Methodist church during that

71. An undated brochure, Asbury Theological Seminary.
72. Asbury, "Statement of Purpose."
73. *The Discipline of the Wesleyan Church* (Marion, Ind.: Wesleyan Publishing House, 1968), pp. 26-27. Cf. Ira Ford McLeister and Roy S. Nicholson, *Conscience and Commitment*, 4th rev. ed. by Lee M. Haines, Jr., and Melvin D. Deiter (Marion, Ind.: Wesley Press, 1976). The ordination candidates are required to confess "faith in the inerrancy of the Holy Scriptures" (pp. 226-27).
74. McLeister and Nicholson, p. 642.
75. Houghton College catalog, quoted by Harold Lindsell, *The Bible in the Balance* (Grand Rapids: Zondervan, 1979), p. 108.

conflict. They were all staunch opponents of liberalism and the destructive aspects of higher criticism and stood unequivocally for biblical inerrancy. That is evident during the early years of the *Herald of Holiness*, the official Nazarene periodical. From 1912-19 there are frequent references to the infidelity and higher criticism so prevalent in the old denominations. References were frequently made to that "poisonous scepticism," the "illogical conclusions," and the "pernicious and disastrous effects" of the new theology and higher criticism.[76] Numerous affirmations were made of the plenary, verbal inspiration and inerrancy of the Bible.

> Verbal inspiration is the only theory of inspiration which furnishes us an absolutely restful and reliable basis for confidence in the precious Book. . . . The Bible ought to be absolutely reliable, for it is the basis and the book of authority of the only pure and undefiled religion known to human history. . . . This inspiration is verbal in the most acute, intense, literal, all inclusive sense.[77]

For the early Nazarene, the reliability of the whole Bible was inextricably related to the reliability of all the parts of the Bible. "It can not be relied on anywhere if it be false in one place. Here is our challenge—all or none. Proof of falsity or untrustworthiness established as to one chapter or one great historic fact . . . loses to us the whole Bible."[78]

In an editorial defense of verbal inspiration, B. F. Haynes stated: "There was an inexplicable power of the Holy Spirit put upon the authors and writers of these books of the Bible, in order to their guidance even in the employment of the words they used, and to preserve them alike from all error and from all omission."[79]

76. *Herald of Holiness*, 30 Oct. 1912, p. 4. The following issues also dealt with higher criticism: June 12, 1912, p. 4; July 17, 1912, p. 4; Sept. 4, 1912, p. 2; Sept. 25, 1912, p. 2; Nov. 20, 1912, p. 3; Dec. 11, 1912, p. 5; Feb. 5, 1913, pp. 1-2; Apr. 2, 1913, pp. 1-2; Apr. 9, 1913, p. 41; May 14, 1913, p. 3; June 4, 1913, p. 4; June 25, 1913, p. 5; Aug. 13, 1913, p. 4; Sept. 17, 1913, pp. 3-4; Sept. 2, 1914, p. 2; Oct. 21, 1914, p. 1; June 28, 1916, p. 2; Sept. 27, 1916, p. 4; Oct. 11, 1916, p. 4; Feb. 6, 1918, p. 1; Mar. 27, 1918, p. 2; Aug. 29, 1917, p. 1; Feb. 5, 1919, p. 2; May 14, 1919, pp. 6-7.
77. B. F. Haynes, "Verbal Inspiration," *Herald of Holiness*, 15 Oct. 1913, p. 1.
78. B. F. Haynes, "Does It Matter," *Herald of Holiness*, 1 Dec. 1915, p. 1.
79. Haynes, "Inspiration of the Scriptures," *Herald of Holiness*, 20 Feb. 1918, p. 2.

During those early years, the *Herald* featured many editorials and articles on the battle over inspiration. Editor Haynes made "no apology for the frequent reference to this pernicious work of these enemies of an inspired Bible."[80]

The *Herald* featured a thoroughgoing article by Andrew Johnson, demonstrating that the Bible was a "divine-human book."

> If God had any hand in the Bible at all, He would doubtless take enough interest in it to preserve it from error. . . .
>
> If there are errors, God is more responsible for them than man, for His eye was on every word, His presence was ever near, His commands were implicitly obeyed, therefore it was His prerogative to prevent any error from creeping into the original record.
>
> The critic . . . must choose between an errorless Bible or an errorless God. . . . If there is error in the Bible, there is error in God. If there is no error in God, then there is no error in the Bible.
>
> The only way . . . the ideal God of the Bible can be fully vindicated and truly glorified is to affirm an inerrant Bible.
>
> If God does not tolerate error, if God does not commit error, if God can prevent a divinely inspired prophet from error while recording the words of a divine revelation, then we have an infallible Bible.[81]

The union of the Church of the Nazarene and the Holiness Church of Christ in 1908 (considered to be the birth of the Nazarenes as a national denomination) was celebrated by the

80. Haynes, "A Warning Voice from the World," *Herald of Holiness*, 30 Apr. 1913, p. 3. Other *Herald* editorials dealing with the inspiration issue appeared in the following issues: Oct. 22, 1913, pp. 1-2; Apr. 8, 1914, pp. 2-3; May 13, 1914, p. 2; July 15, 1914, p. 1; Jan. 6, 1915, p. 2; Apr. 21. 1915, p. 2; May 19, 1915, p. 4; June 9, 1915, p. 4; Sept. 1, 1915, p. 2; Nov. 3, 1915, p. 1; Nov. 10, 1915, p. 1; Dec. 1, 1915, p. 1; Dec. 29, 1915, pp. 1-2; July 5, 1916, p. 3; May 23, 1917, pp. 4-5; Sept. 5, 1917, p. 2; Dec. 26, 1917, pp. 1-2; Feb. 20, 1918, p. 2; Apr. 2, 1918, p. 2; Sept. 11, 1918, p. 61; June 4, 1919, p. 1. Miscellaneous articles dealing with inspiration also appeared in the following issues: May 8, 1912, p. 7; Oct. 9, 1912, p. 3; Nov. 13, 1912, p. 6; Oct. 27, 1915, p. 5. It is interesting to note that as early as that, *inerrancy* was a term that was used frequently and was considered to be closely related to the whole issue of inspiration and infallibility. It was not a question of infallibility *or* inerrancy. Cf. 28 Oct. 1914, p. 4, editorial entitled "Inerrancy."

81. Andrew Johnson, "The Confusion of the Higher Critics," *Herald of Holiness*, 4 Aug. 1915, pp. 5-6.

publication of E. P. Ellyson's *Theological Compend.* It was a much-used handbook for the fledgling denomination for many years. Ellyson emphasized the infallibility of Scripture as well as verbal inspiration and the inerrancy of the original manuscripts.[82] In a later work Ellyson responded to claims that the Bible taught only religious matters and that it had scientific errors in it. "The Holy Spirit knows all the truths of nature, and would not inspire an untruth." "Logically and morally we are as much bound by the geological writings of Moses as by the theological writings of Saint Paul."[83] Certainly, the Bible is not the sole source of scientific knowledge, but it *is* a reliable source.

The 1915 General Assembly heard the General Superintendents declare that all Nazarenes were agreed on "the great fundamentals."[84] One of those "great fundamentals" was certainly the infallibility and inerrancy of Scripture.

During the 1920s the Nazarenes maintained and even intensified their defense of the Bible, especially in the pages of the *Herald.* In 1920 a series, "Is the Bible Inspired?" by Warren Slote was featured. Slote made the following observations, among others. First, there was disagreement concerning whether inspiration came in thoughts, with the authors using their own words, or whether the Spirit "supervised" the choice of words as well. Slote argued strongly for verbal inspiration in which the Holy Spirit selected or censored the words of Scripture.[85] Second, even though the Bible is not primarily concerned with scientific matters, its "language is always accurate" and "wonderfully correct."[86] Third, Slote argued for the authority of Scripture on the basis of Christ's view of the Old Testament.

There is no record anywhere that He ever criticized any part of

82. Edgar P. Ellyson, *Theological Compend* (Chicago: Christian Witness, 1908), pp. 77-78.
83. Edgar P. Ellyson, *The Bible in Education* (Kansas City: Pentecostal Church of the Nazarene Publishing House, 1913), pp. 101-2, 148; cf. pp. 91, 144.
84. *Proceeding of the Fourth General Assembly of the Pentecostal Church of the Nazarene* (Kansas City: Pentecostal Church of the Nazarene Publishing House, 1915), p. 53.
85. J. Warren Slote, "Is the Bible Inspired?" *Herald of Holiness,* 10 Mar. 1920, p. 8. Cf. Section 6 of the same series, 7 Apr. 1920, p. 10.
86. Ibid., 24 Mar. 1920, p. 6.

them. This argues most conclusively for their absolute accuracy, for if there had been any errors in them, or if any of the parts had been spurious, He who rebuked sin wherever He found it and corrected error as it came to His notice would surely have made some mention of these mistakes.[87]

Basil Miller charged in the *Herald* that the lack of spiritual power in the church world was due to the "doubting of the inspiration and inerrancy of the Bible."[88] Editor J. B. Chapman reasserted the interdependence of the doctrines of "the Word of God, the blood of Jesus and the operation of the Holy Spirit." When "men begin to question the inerrancy of the Bible," they will later change their beliefs concerning the blood and the Spirit.[89] Donnell Smith asserted that the Spirit kept the Scriptures "free from all error."[90] C. W. Ruth declared the Bible to be "absolutely reliable."[91] Sam Curtis declared that "the suggestion that the Bible is not the unerring Word of God . . . is a most wicked thrust at morality, law, and government. If the story of Jonah and the great fish is not true, then many would argue that the Ten Commandments may not be true."[92] Numerous other articles were written about the conflict with higher criticism and the doctrine of inspiration.[93]

87. Ibid., 31 Mar. 1920, p. 8. Paul Bassett, "The Fundamentalist Leavening of the Holiness Movement," *Wesleyan Theological Journal* 13 (1978): 73, commented on the point by Slote that "this side of the controversy, Slote's reasoning appears to be quite naive, even circular."
88. Basil Miller, "The Crisis of Christianity," *Herald of Holiness*, 28 Oct. 1925, pp. 4-5.
89. J. R. Chapman, "The Word, the Blood, and the Spirit," *Herald of Holiness*, 18 Feb. 1925, p. 1.
90. Donnell J. Smith, "The Inspiration of the Bible," *Herald of Holiness*, 30 July 1924, p. 7.
91. C. W. Ruth, "If Modernism Were True: What?" *Herald of Holiness*, 21 July 1926, p. 1.
92. J. Sam Curtis, "God and the Bible," *Herald of Holiness*, 5 Mar. 1924, pp. 4-5.
93. *Herald* articles on higher criticism include the following, among others: Jan. 7, 1920, pp. 4-5; June 16, 1920, pp. 1-2; June 23, 1920, p. 3; Sept. 22, 1920, p. 11; July 28, 1920, p. 3; Feb. 2, 1921, p. 6; Mar. 2, 1921, p. 3; Aug. 3, 1921, p. 2; Sept. 21, 1921, pp. 1-2; Feb. 2, 1922, pp. 4-6; May 31, 1922, pp. 5-6; Aug. 23, 1922, p. 11; Sept. 13, 1922, pp. 3, 5; May 2, 1923, p. 5; May 14, 1924, pp. 3-4; Aug. 13, 1924, p. 6; May 27, 1925, pp. 4-5; July 8, 1925, p. 5; Aug. 12, 1925, pp. 4-5; Feb. 10, 1926, pp. 2-3; Feb. 24, 1926, p. 6; Apr. 7, 1926, p. 3; Aug. 25, 1926, pp. 6-8; Dec. 22, 1926, pp. 10-11; July 20, 1927, pp. 7-8; Nov. 28, 1928, pp. 6-8; Jan. 15, 1928, pp. 5-7. *Herald* articles

Increasingly, the controversy was described in terms of fundamentalism versus modernism. One of the great fundamentals was the inspiration of the Word. The Christian world was divided into two opposing camps, fundamentalists and modernists.[94]

The rejection of the Bible was understood as tantamount to or worse than modernism. Chapman declared, "When one has rejected the Bible as the inerrant standard of truth he has opened the door for the incoming of theosophy, Christian Science, spiritualism, and every form of error of human or diabolical invention."[95]

Nazarene leaders did not hesitate to quote non-Wesleyan scholars to support their traditional doctrine of inerrancy. Sometimes the term *fundamentalist* was used to designate *all* those who held to such fundamentals as inerrancy—Wesleyans, Calvinists, and others.[96] But more often Nazarenes viewed fundamentalists as a group of Calvinists with whom they sympathized on several major doctrines. Chapman declared, "Of course, our sympathies are entirely with the Fundamentalists and we rejoice in their boldness for God and truth. . . . May God bless and prosper all who stand up for God and His Holy Book!"[97] Haynes, in an earlier editorial, had affirmed, "Our sympathies are naturally with the fundamen-

on the inspiration of Scripture include the following, among others: June 8, 1921, pp. 1-2; Feb. 22, 1922, p. 6; June 7, 1922, p. 3; Dec. 27, 1922, pp. 5-6; Feb. 7, 1923, p. 51; Apr. 4, 1923, p. 4; Sept. 12, 1923, p. 5; July 16, 1924, pp. 1-2; Apr. 8, 1925, p. 2; June 3, 1925, p. 11; July 1, 1925, pp. 3-4; July 29, 1925, p. 1; Sept. 30, 1925, p. 1; May 5, 1926, pp. 10-11; May 12, 1926, pp. 10-11; June 22, 1927, p. 141; Feb. 29, 1928, p. 5; Sept. 26, 1928, p. 13; Oct. 2, 1929, p. 17.

94. J. B. Chapman, "Fundamentalism versus Modernism," *Herald of Holiness*, 31 Oct. 1923, pp. 1-2. Cf. A. M. Hills, "A Creedless Christianity Impossible," Oct. 17, 1923, pp. 3-4. Other similar articles: Nov. 5, 1924, p. 1; Sept. 23, 1925, p. 5. In the Feb. 20, 1924 issue (p. 14) an advertisement for *The Battle Over the Bible*, a debate between John Roach and Charles Francis Potter claimed the "fundamentalist controversy" is "agitating the entire Christian church."

95. *Herald of Holiness*, 31 Oct. 1923, pp. 1-2.

96. Cf. July 6, 1921, p. 2; Sept. 20, 1922, p. 4; Aug. 29, 1923, p. 3; Oct. 29, 1924, pp. 5-6; Nov. 5, 1924, p. 7.

97. J. B. Chapman, "The Victories of the Fundamentalists," *Herald of Holiness*, 7 Feb. 1923, pp. 2-3.

talists" and spoke of the bitter opposition of others to maintaining "the infallible correctness of every word contained in the Bible."[98]

Editor Chapman realized that the term *fundamentalism*—a common noun—had become a proper name—*Fundamentalism*. Most of the "self-named Fundamentalists" were Calvinists and taught as fundamental certain doctrines that Wesleyan-Arminians viewed as unbiblical. Yet those Calvinistic fundamentalists failed to emphasize some important truths, such as entire sanctification.

> It follows, then, that if we are asked whether we are a Fundamentalist or not, we must know whether the word is used as a common noun or as a proper name. If it is used in the former sense, we answer in the affirmative, but if it is used in the latter sense our answer is "Yes, with reservations." In our own category of Fundamentals we would include nothing that is not positively necessary to life in Christ Jesus. . . . Our list then would include: The Inspiration of the Scriptures, The fallen state and condition of man, The Virgin Birth and deity of Jesus Christ, The personality, and office work of the Holy Spirit, regeneration and entire sanctification.[99]

Even though the early Nazarenes were frank in admitting their several doctrinal differences with their fundamentalist brethren, there was not the slightest hint during all those years of controversy of any basic differences in the Wesleyan view of inerrancy vis-à-vis the Calvinistic view.

The *Preacher's Magazine*, in its very first issue, featured the fundamentalist controversy. In the lead article, "Modernism and Christianity," F. M. Messenger averred, "If the Bible cannot be taken at its face value, it should be discredited altogether, for it claims too much to be authentic only in part." Either "accept the revelation which God has given" or declare yourself an agnostic.[100]

---

98. May 24, 1922, p. 1. Cf. Henry Rell, in "The Impending Church Split," Sept. 19, 1923, p. 5, who also sympathized strongly with the fundamentalists but viewed them as a separate group. Chapman did the same thing, Oct. 13, 1926, pp. 3-4.
99. J. B. Chapman, "What Is Fundamentalism?" Oct. 6, 1916.
100. *Preachers Magazine* 1 (1926), p. 5. Other early references to the controversy appear in the following issues, among others: Feb. 1926, pp. 6-9; May 1929, p. 133; Oct. 1926, pp. 12, 20-21; June 1926, p. 1; Aug. 1926, pp. 4-6.

Even in those stressful years of conflict, some leaders spoke clearly and without bitterness, advocating a balanced, calm approach even to one's opponents. Floyd Nease pointed out in an outstanding article in *Preacher's Magazine* that though the term *higher criticism* was usually used as "an introduction to a discussion of infidelity and as a precursor for the vehement utterance of certain stock phrases decrying the justly condemned rationalism," the term properly "deserves better treatment at our hands." There is a "reverent" and "scholarly" use of the term, designating "the study of the historic origins, the dates, and authorships of the various books of the Bible." That type of critical work is an invaluable, indeed indispensable, aid to preachers of the Word.[101]

Conversely, in the hands of antisupernaturalists, it becomes "destructive higher criticism." Nease traced the roots and development of destructive higher criticism and its relationship to the theory of evolution. Ultimately, such criticism aims to destroy "faith in an infallible and inerrant book, 'the Bible.'" With the historical reliability of the gospels discredited and significant doctrines removed, "the New Testament is devitalized and shrinks to the status of an Elizabethan drama." To such a philosophy, the "evangelical minister can have but one attitude, that of unalterable opposition."[102]

But in all of that controversy there should be fairness. Our attitude and spirit should exemplify our doctrine. "Is it basically more fair to the representatives of fundamentalism to assume that the literalists are a set of knaves than for the latter to assert that the fundamentalists are ignoramuses and fools?"[103]

In the mid-1920s the first major Nazarene rebuttal to destructive higher criticism and infidelity appeared—Basil Miller's *Cunningly Devised Fables*. It was frequently advertised with "enthusiastic testimonials" in the *Herald of Holiness*. The book (with an introduction by J. B. Chapman) spoke repeatedly of the "inerran-

---

101. Floyd W. Nease, "The Preacher's attitude Toward the Critical Study of the Bible," *Preacher's Magazine* 2 (1927), pp. 23, 25.
102. Ibid.
103. Ibid., p. 26.

cy" of the Bible.[104] Miller asserted that "the *Bible itself* affirms that it is the inerrant, infallible, inspired, and completed Word of God."[105]

Among all the quite adamant statements during that era, there was no endorsement of the mechanical dictation theory or of the inerrancy of the translations. It was commonly granted that there were some errors in our translations. But the character of God and the Bible itself demanded inerrant autographs.[106]

During the 1920s there seemed to be an increasing awareness of the threat that modernism posed to the life of the young, growing denomination. Warnings were issued to Nazarenes. Chapman editorialized:

> Our own Church of the Nazarene must be always vigilant to keep the Bible destroyers out (for, thank God, they are out until now) of the pulpit, out of our schools, out of our general boards, out of our missions and out of our books and literature; for in this way, and in this way only we will be able to keep them out of our homes and out of our pews.[107]

Cornell issued a similar alert—"Nazarene ministers, beware! Stick to the Old Book from cover to cover: Let no trace of doubt or unbelief impregnate your nature."[108]

At the 1923 General Assembly the General Superintendents rejoiced in the fact that though many denominations were debating and dividing over the basic doctrines of the church, the Nazarenes could say that "on the great fundamental truths of

104. Basil Miller and U. E. Harding, *Cunningly Devised Fables* (n.d.), pp. 8, 12, 20, 27, 31, 34, 38-39, 41-42, 44. One *Herald* advertisement of the book appeared on July 22, 1925, p. 16.
105. Ibid., p. 36. He cited as support for that point the following Scriptures: Matt. 5:18; John 10:35; Ex. 4:10-12; Deut. 5:32; 2 Sam. 23:2; and Isa. 1:10. On p. 37, R. A. Torrey is approvingly quoted as saying that on the authority of Christ, "I am compelled to accept the entire Book which He endorsed as being the inerrant Word of God, as being in reality such."
106. *Herald of Holiness,* 23 Aug. 1922, p. 1; 29 July 1925, p. 1. That is not to say that some of the less educated Nazarenes might not have held to mechanical dictation or the inerrancy of translations.
107. *Herald of Holiness,* 1 Mar. 1923, p. 2.
108. C. E. Cornell, "Uncovering the Cess Pool and Letting Out the Stink," *Herald of Holiness,* 29 Aug. 1923, p. 3.

God's Word and of the Church we stand today without a single exception."[109]

By 1928 there was clearly a need to declare with even more distinctness the Nazarenes' stand on inspiration. In the 1908 *Manual* the article on Scripture was basically borrowed from the Thirty-Nine Articles of Americanism and the Twenty-Five Articles of Methodism.

> By the Holy Scriptures we understand the canonical books of the Old and New Testaments given by Divine inspiration, revealing the will of God concerning us in all things necessary to our salvation; so that whatever is not contained therein, and cannot be proved thereby, is not to be enjoined as an article of faith.[110]

There were only minor changes in that article until 1928, when major revisions were made. In an earlier day it was sufficient to declare one's belief in the inspiration of the Bible. There was a basic understanding of what inspiration entailed. But later there were those who arose and declared their belief in inspiration but not in inerrancy or infallibility. And thus, the church should continually define its position in the light of present controversies. The Nazarenes stated:

> We believe in the plenary inspiration of the Holy Scriptures by which we understand the sixty-six books of the Old and New Testaments, given by divine inspiration, inerrantly revealing the will of God concerning us in all things necessary to our salvation; so that whatever is not contained therein is not to be enjoined as an article of faith.[111]

Throughout their 1928 address to the General Assembly, the General Superintendents made clear their stand for the Bible.

> We must stand for the whole Bible. We do not as a movement

109. Church of the Nazarene, *Journal of the Sixth General Assembly* (Kansas City: Nazarene Publishing House, 1923), p. 183.
110. *Manual of the Pentecostal Church of the Nazarene* (Los Angeles: Nazarene Publishing Co., 1908), pp. 22-26.
111. *Manual of the History, Doctrine, Government, and Ritual of the Church of the Nazarene* (Kansas City: Nazarene Publishing House, 1928), p. 22.

believe merely that the Bible contains the Word of God. We
believe the Bible is the Word of God. We believe it from Genesis to
Revelation. . . . The Bible has received the bitterest attack of the
enemy for centuries, but today the Old Book stands as impregna-
ble as the Rock of Gibraltar. . . . The church must stand first, last
and all the time for the whole Bible, the inspired, infallible,
revealed Word of God. . . .

Every man in this body is a fundamentalist and so far as we
know there is not a modernist in the ranks of the Church of the
Nazarene. We believe the Bible and accept it as being the revealed
Word of God, immutable, unchangeable, infallible and sufficient
for every human need. A modernist would be very lonesome in this
General Assembly.[112]

In 1931 the first major Nazarene systematic theology was published—A. M. Hills's *Fundamental Christian Theology*.[113] The chapter
on "Revelation and Inspiration" has caused confusion as to what
Hills actually believed concerning the inerrancy of the Bible.[114]
An examination of Hills's manuscript of the book, comparing sections written in 1911 with additions he made sometime in the
twenty years that elapsed before publication, leads us to the following conclusion.[115] In 1911 Hills was basically an unqualified
inerrantist. By 1931 he seems to have modified his position to

112. Ibid., pp. 52, 58; cf. pp. 49, 63. It is interesting to note that *fundamentalist* is
not capitalized in those references.
113. A. M. Hills, *Fundamental Christian Theology*, 2 vols. (Pasadena: C. J. Kinne,
1931). Hills, a Congregationalist who was sanctified and later joined the
Nazarenes, began writing what he considered to be his "Master Work,"
while in New Mexico in 1911, trying to start a holiness college. There he
wrote the first half of that text (including his discussion of revelation and
inspiration). He had finished the entire work by the spring of 1915 in Great
Britain. However, it was not until 1931 that C. J. Kinne, a dedicated Nazarene lay leader, published it for Hills (at the urging of General Superintendent Chapman). A. V. Hills, "A Handwritten Autobiography," copy at
Nazarene Theological Seminary Library, pp. 190, 217.
114. Cf. Bassett, pp. 80-81.
115. An examination of Hills's handwritten manuscript of his *Theology*, in the
Church of the Nazarene Archives, Kansas City, Missouri, indicates that
major additions to the text (additions sometime after 1915, while living in
Pasadena, most likely) appear on 126*b* (paragraph beginning, "We have
stated the two strongest theories. . . .") through 127*b* (closing at the end of
the first full paragraph on p. 127). Another addition is to be found on pp.
132*c* (paragraph beginning with "We are compelled to conclude. . . .")
through 134*d* (addition ends with the last full paragraph on that page).

allow for errors and a denial of what he calls "universal plenary inspiration."

In the 1911 sections Hills cited several definitions of inspiration, all of which assumed inerrancy and infallibility as an integral part of inspiration. They all included such phrases as "communicate truth without error," "without error, infirmity, or defect," "without error or mistake," and "infallible communication." He cited without apology non-Wesleyans as well as Wesleyans. Apparently, he saw no basic difference in a Wesleyan view of inspiration and other views. He was careful to point out that such definitions applied only "to the original documents of Scripture as they came from the hands of their authors...."[116]

> The inspiration of the ordinary Christian which we by no means underrate, may co-exist with many errors, and crude notions; but the Divine inspiration of the authors of the Word enabled them to give us the mind of God without crudity or error.[117]
>
> Jesus and His Apostles ... treat all they quote from [of the Old Testament] as the Word of God. They also refer to all classes of facts as infallibly true.
>
> Not only great *doctrinal* facts, such as the creation and probation of man; his apostasy; ... not only great *historical* facts, as the deluge, ... but incidental circumstances, and things of minor importance ... are all mentioned with a childlike faith in their absolute truthfulness.[118]

One of the greatest proofs against the "occasional inspiration" theory is that the writers would not always be

> writing, under the influence of the Spirit which rendered their writings the unerring Word of God; and that consequently, when they were writing without it, they were liable to make mistakes like other men. So that, as a result, there is in the Bible, an admixture of error and truth, the human and the divine. The logical difficulty of this theory is that, if it be once granted that there is an alloy of

116. Hills *Theology*, 1:117-18.
117. Ibid., 1:118-19.
118. Ibid., 1:119-20.

error in the Word, an opening is made for the assumption of every imaginable corruption.[119]

By verbal inspiration the Spirit guided and assisted the writers as they exercised their own faculties so they would "convey 'the mind of the Spirit' in its full and unimpaired integrity."[120] "Such verbal inspiration is always affirmed of Jesus." From statements throughout the Bible "it is evident that very much at least of the Bible is verbally inspired, so that the authors recorded the very words God would have them use."[121]

Inerrancy was affirmed only of the original manuscripts. Because of the discrepancies in translations, we should admit that *we no longer have an absolutely inerrant Bible.* We may affirm, however, that all that does not militate against the original inspiration of the Holy Word.

> If we knew all the facts, these trivial discrepancies, could probably most of them be satisfactorily explained. But some of them would doubtless remain, as unexplainable. They are the human elements that have accrued in the transmission through the ages of our blessed Bible.[122]

By 1931 Hills had shifted to a limited inerrantist position. In the post-1915 revisions of his working manuscript, he claimed that "absolute inspiration" puts "too great a tax upon faith." The Bible does not claim "absolute inspiration," and it is an unproveable theory.

> To . . . claim the absolute accuracy of all minute statements of fact, or the absolute harmony of all these statements geographical, historical, and scientific with one another—this is a task which the broadest and most thorough scholarship would not undertake. But if the inspiration of the *original text* were absolute and complete, and were absolutely proved [Hills now seemed to assume it was

119. Ibid., 1:123.
120. Ibid., 1:124. Hannah, quoted by "Field's Theology," p. 74.
121. Ibid., 1:125-26.
122. Ibid., 1:131-32.

not], no one can maintain that we have that text in every minute particular.[123]

Hills preferred the "essential inspiration" of the Bible or a dynamic theory. "The Scriptures are inspired to such a degree as to present, with all required fullness and accuracy, the great truths which it is the purpose of Scripture to present." That approach avoids the "insuperable difficulties" of the plenary, verbal inspiration of all Scripture. He quoted Miley; an "exact set of words" is unnecessary to have a true statement. The two major proofs against "universal verbal inspiration" were the "inaccurate quotations" by New Testament writers of the Old Testament and the varying records of the Lord's words. That seems to point to the fact that "not always the *very words, but the man himself is inspired.*" "In the human element there is always room for inaccuracy."[124]

Hills concluded that "in spite of all discrepancies, and disagreements, and errors, and minor inaccuracies, the Bible still remains God's inspired and infallible book. But *infallible for what?* . . . It is infallible as a revelation of God's saving love in Christ to a wicked world." But we should not claim the literal accuracy of the Bible because it is not free from error.[125]

There was little apparent immediate reaction or recognition of the impact of Hills's shift on inspiration throughout the 1930s in the Nazarene movement.[126] But throughout the 1930s the attack on liberalism and higher criticism continued in the *Herald*, though with nothing of the frequency of the previous two decades.[127]

---

123. Ibid., 1:126, quoting Fairchild.
124. Ibid., 1:126-27, 132-33.
125. Ibid., 1:134, quoting Marcus Dodd's "The Bible,"etc., pp. 135-55.
126. Bassett mentions that some have suggested that the Nazarene Publishing House did not publish Hills's *Theology* because he was considered "too liberal with respect to the authority and inspiration of Scripture" (p. 80). Sources: conversations with Mildred Bangs Wynkoop, Oct. 27, 1977 and C. B. Widmeyer, summer 1972.
127. The following *Herald* articles deal with that controversy: Feb. 1, Feb. 8, and Feb. 15, 1933; May 31, 1933, p. 31; Apr. 12, 1935, p. 51; Oct. 5, 1935, pp. 898-99; July 2, 1938, p. 484; July 18, 1936, p. 546; Sept. 12, 1936, p. 814. Nov. 18, 1931, p. 14 carries a satirical poetical attack on liberal theologian Harry Emerson Fosdick.

There was also a marked move away from Nazarene identification with fundamentalists. Editor Corlett clearly repudiated it.

We have no desire to partake of the spirit generally manifested by the average Fundamentalist. It is absolutely impossible for us to accept their extreme positions on the verbal inspiration of the Bible as differing from the plenary inspiration as held by our Church, nor do we find ourselves in accord with their emphasis on eternal security, their radical Calvinistic Pre-Millennial position, or their allowance made for "sin in the flesh." They are too judgmental and defensive. . . . We are willing to go with the Fundamentalists as far as they travel our path or accept our doctrinal standards. But where our paths separate we will part peaceably [128]

Frequent defenses of the inspiration of the Bible continued to appear in the *Herald*. Editor Chapman declared:

When we are presented a Bible which is said to be a mixture of truth and error and we are left to judge which is the one or the other we are really no better off than if we had no Bible at all. . . . There is not a single *fact* of history or science which does not wholly agree with it.[129]

During that time the term *verbal inspiration* was increasingly identified with mechanical dictation by the opponents of a high view of Scripture. There was also greater stress laid on the experiential proofs of the authority of the Bible.[130]

The decade of the 1940s was inaugurated (as were the 1930s)

128. D. Shelby Corlett, "Nazarenes and the Fundamentalists," *Herald of Holiness*, 20 Apr. 1935, p. 132; cf. May 30, 1936, p. 331 and Oct. 2, 1937, p. 909.
129. J. R. Chapman, "April Gleanings," *Herald of Holiness*, 30 Apr. 1930, p. 5; cf. May 16, 1930, p. 11; Oct. 15, 1930, pp. 11-12; June 3, 1931, p. 11; July 22, 1931, p. 8; Sept. 9, 1931, p. 13; Nov. 18, 1931, p. 14; Dec. 29, 1934, p. 1294; Feb. 15, 1936, pp. 1514-15; Nov. 12, 1936, pp. 1132-33; Apr. 5, 1939, pp. 98-99.
130. *Herald of Holiness*, 28 Feb. 1934, p. 5; 29 Feb. 1936, p. 1580; 19 Jan. 1935, pp. 1378-79. In 1936 a revised edition of E. P. Ellyson's *Theological Compend* appeared as *Doctrinal Studies*. Even though a whole chapter was now devoted to the inspiration of the Bible, it was clearly not in the same spirit as the earlier edition. Little more than a vague spiritual inerrancy of the Bible was affirmed.

with the publication of a major Nazarene theology—H. Orton Wiley's classic *Christian Theology*. Wiley clearly affirmed inerrancy, but he laid greater stress on the primacy of Christ as the Logos and the Spirit as the primary witness to the Word than did most of his Nazarene predecessors.

> Both the revelation and the Christian faith are co-incident with the Scriptures. We do not say identical, for Christian Theology must ever make Christ, the Living and Eternal Word, the supreme revelation of God. But the Holy Scriptures as the true and inerrant record of the Personal Word, and the medium of continued utterance through the Holy Spirit, must in a true and deep sense become the formal aspect of the one true and perfect revelation.[131]

" 'The Oracle and the oracles are one.' The Scriptures, therefore, become the perfect disclosure and finished revelation of the will of God in Christ Jesus."[132]

Wiley warned against the danger of separating the personal Word from the written Word. That leads to mere formal knowledge without spiritual knowledge, creedalism without spirituality, and orthodoxy without life. He obliquely chided the fundamentalists for a "mere legalistic defense of Scripture," in response to liberalism.[133]

Wiley defined inspiration as "the actuating energy of the Holy Spirit through which holy men were qualified to receive religious truth, and to communicate it to others without error."[134] Three factors were involved in all revelation: (1) superintendence—"God so guides those chosen as the organs of revelation, that their writings are kept free from error," (2) elevation—"an enlargement of understanding," and (3) suggestion—direct suggestion from God of thoughts "or even the very words" the writer was to use. Inspiration is constantly "guiding the writer at every point, thus secur-

131. H. Orton Wiley, *Christian Theology*, 3 vols. (Kansas City: Beacon Hill Press, 1940), 1:125.
132. Ibid., 1:33; cf. 138-39.
133. Ibid., 1:141-43, 35-37, 148.
134. Ibid., 1:169; cf. 1:167-68.

ing at once the infallible truth of his material, and its proper selection and distribution."[135]

He also repeatedly affirmed biblical inerrancy. "Only as we are convinced that the writers were aided by a supernatural and divine influence, and this in such a manner as to be infallibly preserved from all error, can the sacred Scriptures become a divine rule of faith and practice."[136] He approvingly quoted Hannah's definition of inspiration as the enablement given by the Holy Spirit "to embrace and communicate the truth of God without error, infirmity, or defeat [sic, defect]."[137] One reason inspiration was necessary was so that "a true and inerrant account" could be provided of historical facts such as the creation and the Deluge.[138]

Wiley called his own view "dynamical inspiration" and cites it as being the same view as that of Pope, Watson, Wakefield, and Ralston (all inerrantists), as well as Wiley and others. He used *dynamical* vis-à-vis *mechanical*. His plenary, dynamic view was that "the whole and every part is divinely inspired."[139]

Through the 1940s the battle for the Bible was subsiding. But the few references in the *Herald* still maintained its inspiration and truth. Ross Price, writing on John 10:35, declared,

> Our Lord, in this argument, assumed the absolute truth of the Scripture, and its changeless, indestructible authority.... The Bible is correct astronomically, geologically, historically, medicinally, botanically, zoologically, meteorologically, prophetically, and spiritually. It is the final court of appeals on matters of faith and practice.[140]

Stephen White propounded a dynamic theory in which "the

135. Ibid., 1:171.
136. Ibid., 1:173. He also (p. 172) quoted Wakefield, the earlier Wesleyan theologian, as saying: "The more important the communication is, . . . the more reasonable it is to expect that God should make the communication free from every admixture of error" (Wakefield's *Christian Theology*, p. 72.).
137. Ibid., 1:167.
138. Ibid., 1:172.
139. Ibid., 1:177, 184.
140. Ross Price, "The Immutability of the Scriptures (John 10:35)," *Herald of Holiness*, 29 Nov. 1948, pp. 670-71; cf. Jan. 8, 1945, p. 613; Feb. 3, 1940, p. 1485; J. B. Chapman, *Nazarene Primer* (Kansas City: Nazarene Publishing House, 1949). Chapman defended the absolute veracity of the Word.

thoughts of the writers of the Bible were so dominated by the Holy Spirit that the truth recorded is an infallible rule of faith and practice."[141] But there is no clear affirmation of the inerrancy of the Word.

Throughout the 1950s there seems to have been a total absence of any unequivocal affirmations of inerrancy. The truth and authority of the Bible was affirmed in general terms of faith and practice but not in other areas such as history and science. There was room in the Church of the Nazarene for those who held a loose, dynamic view, as well as for those who held to a stricter view.[142]

In the 1960s it became clear that the Nazarenes were definitely moving away from the traditional Wesleyan doctrine of inerrancy. But there were still general warnings sounded about the dangers of rejecting the Bible.[143]

Exploring Our Christian Faith, a Nazarene introductory theology text, appeared in 1960. There is a very evident attraction to neo-orthodox thinkers such as Barth, Brunner, C. H. Dodd, and John Baillie, among others. Such stock terms as "salvation-history" and references to the Bible as "a record of revelation" were used.[144] "Historical act becomes a revelation of God when interpreted through the eye of faith."[145]

Inspiration was limited to providing an accurate and true record of the "Christ-event." Wiley's three factors of inspiration are referred to. The writers seem to opt for dynamic, plenary inspiration without inerrancy.

141. Stephen White, *Essential Christian Beliefs* (Kansas City: Beacon Hill, 1940), p. 92.
142. Stephen White, "The Question Box," *Herald of Holiness*, 7 May 1952, p. 207; cf. ibid., July 16, 1951, pp. 447-48; Nov. 9, 1955, p. 850; "The Spirit of Truth," Oct. 31, 1956, pp. 824-25; "What We Believe," Mar. 13, 1957, p. 33; "Mathematical Intolerance," Oct. 2, 1957, p. 792. An official Nazarene Old Testament survey text, *Exploring the Old Testament*, ed. W. T. Purkiser (Kansas City: Beacon Hill, 1955), basically quoted Wiley concerning the inspiration of Scripture, p. 24.
143. Stephen White, "The Question Box," *Herald of Holiness*, 20 Apr. 1960, p. 181; W. Purkiser, "The Answer Corner," 15 Nov. 1961, p. 758.
144. W. T. Purkiser, ed., *Exploring Our Christian Faith* (Kansas City: Beacon Hill, 1960), pp. 64, 66. The *Beacon Bible Commentary*, 10 vols., ed. A. F. Harper (Kansas City: Beacon Hill, 1964-69), also seems quite enamored with neo-orthodox scholars from whom it frequently and approvingly quotes.
145. Purkiser, *Exploring Our Christian Faith*, p. 63.

While it contains nothing, properly understood, which is unscientific or unhistorical, yet the Bible is not a book of science or history. Its purpose is to make known the will of God, not to answer questions about nature or to satisfy our curiosity about general human history. . . .

It is only when limited and arbitrary standards of judgment are set up that the Bible may be charged with error. When considered in the light of its own purposes and by reasonable canons of value and truth, the Scriptures will be found to be without material error. . . . It is perverse to insist that the Bible conform to modern attitudes and thought patterns.[146]

The first major history of the Church of the Nazarene came in 1962, *Called unto Holiness*, by the distinguished historian Timothy L. Smith. Though admitting that many of the early Nazarenes held to a high view of inspiration, Smith views such persons as inordinately infected by Calvinistic fundamentalism. Inerrancy is viewed as an alien doctrine in Nazarene circles. He speaks of "Wesleyan fundamentalism" and seems to view much of Nazarene history as an attempt to rid itself of old, narrow views.[147]

The 1970s found more Nazarene scholars denying their Wesleyan heritage of inerrancy. Seminary professor Kenneth Grider admits that though "some holiness scholars teach that the Bible autographs' inerrancy extends to such matters as science and history . . . almost all Nazarene scholars hold the positive confidence that the autographs were inerrant on matters of doctrine and practice." Though he himself has never found any "non-faith" errors on any subject in the manuscripts, he does not teach the fact or necessity of full inerrancy as an article of faith.

If I were to say that the Bible is definitely without error of any non-important sort, I would be expressing a more exclusive kind of faith in it than I do in Jesus Christ, my Savior and Lord. He might have erred in some slight way, as when he was six, about, say, where his "father" was. I do not know whether or not he ever

---

146. Ibid., p. 75.
147. Timothy L. Smith, *Called unto Holiness* (Kansas City: Nazarene Publishing House, 1962), pp. 293, 306-7, 316-21.

erred. But my faith-confidence is that he was sinless, as Scripture states; not necessarily that he was errorless.[148]

According to Grider, affirmation of autographic inerrancy is meaningless for several reasons. We do not have any original manuscripts. The Holy Spirit was not interested in precise accuracy of minute details. Christ is the aim of Scripture, not "wooden, indifferent matters." Allegories and metaphors (which tend to be inexact) were often used in Scripture. Old Testament Hebrew had no vowels and thus translations are not always as exact as inerrancy would require. Grider applauds the "historical sleuthing" of Fuller Seminary professor Jack Rogers and charges that Harold Lindsell's views are a departure from orthodoxy, not Rogers's.[149]

Herald editor W. E. McCumber stated that the Nazarene Articles of Faith are committed to "all things necessary to our salvation" but left untouched the question of whether Scripture is inerrant on all other matters. "Among evangelical and holiness scholars, opinion has always been divided on the meaning and extent of inerrancy." He observed that such affirmations of Scripture's authority as 2 Timothy 3:14-15 and John 10:35 relate only to extant manuscripts and not to the "original, indefectible manuscripts no longer extant."[150]

Nazarene Theological Seminary professor Paul Bassett views early inerrantist Nazarenes as infected with non-Wesleyan fundamentalistic "leavening." Bassett claims that such inerrantists as J. B. Chapman were by no means speaking for "a certain significant leadership" of the Church of the Nazarene.[151]

In the light of the abundant body of literature on the enormous controversy that engulfed Methodism concerning biblical authority and inspiration, it is interesting to hear Bassett claim that "Methodism and the holiness movement did not concern themselves more than very minimally with the issues being raised by the so-called 'higher criticism' in the period 1870-1914."[152]

148. J. Kenneth Grider, "The Biblical Inerrancy Issue" (n.d.), pp. 1-4.
149. Ibid., pp. 4-7.
150. W. E. McCumber, "The Answer Corner," *Herald of Holiness*, 15 Dec. 1978, p. 31.
151. Bassett *Fundamentalist Leavening*, pp. 76-81.
152. Ibid., p. 69.

In the face of the innumerable affirmations of the inspiration and inerrancy of the Bible throughout the history of Wesleyanism, Bassett asserts that the rationale for inserting affirmations of the full inspiration and inerrancy of the Bible into the Nazarene creed was found nowhere but "in the broader context of American Protestant wars over the Bible."[153]

The thrust of Bassett's article is to prove that Wiley did not believe in inerrancy. Bassett claims that because of the "fundamentalist leavening" of the church, Wiley "came in on cat's paws, and a generation or two of holiness preachers thought he was basically a Fundamentalist. The contrast between his position and the 'received' position of the great majority was not perceived, though the clues are ample and Wiley does not dissemble."[154] Many passages from Wiley's *Christian Theology* are quoted in which he seeks to maintain the supremacy of Christ and the proper relationship of the personal Word and the written Word.[155] Interestingly enough, none of the passages in which Wiley clearly affirms inerrancy is quoted or referred to.

Throughout the article, there is an implicit admission that most of the Nazarene ministers in the history of the denomination believed in biblical inerrancy. One cannot help but wonder, with all the historic Wesleyan affirmations of inerrancy and the affirmations of inerrancy by a historic majority of Nazarene leaders, what it takes to make a doctrine genuinely Nazarene.

On the one hand, we have overwhelming evidence that Nazarene leaders historically have held to inerrancy. On the other hand, some modern Nazarenes ask us to believe it was never an authentically Nazarene doctrine. We are left with a choice. At best, the Nazarene leaders actually believed what they said they believed. At worst they said they believed in inerrancy but in truth they did not. Thus they were guilty of duplicity. In the light of their godly lives' unquestionable integrity and spiritual power, one is hesitant to say that those great men of God purposefully deceived several generations of Nazarenes. Those men believed what they said they believed!

153. Ibid., p. 74.
154. Ibid., p. 65.
155. Ibid., pp. 66-67, 82-85.

A refreshingly new approach in modern Nazarene scholarship came in 1980 with the publication of noted theologian Richard S. Taylor's *Biblical Authority and the Christian Faith*. Taylor writes with a different outlook and a fresh approach to the problem of biblical inspiration. He freely criticizes (in a way few Nazarene scholars had done for years) neo-orthodox theologians and their tenets. He just as freely and without apology quotes non-Wesleyan inerrantists.[156] He charges that destructive higher criticism destroys the authority of the Bible and the teaching of its tenets renders men "unfit to serve the Savior," in the words of William Beck. He warns against "excessive exposure" to critics such as Bultmann.[157]

Taylor emphasizes the primacy of Scripture. "The ultimate authority of God himself is necessarily in the Bible."[158] Thus the issue of infallibility becomes most crucial. Is the Bible "unfailing and unerring in disclosing God's self-revelation to man?" (Taylor believes it is "semantically difficult" to distinguish infallibility and inerrancy). There are three types of inerrancy: (1) salvation inerrancy holds to inerrancy on matters of faith only (e.g., neo-orthodox and neoevangelicals), (2) total inerrancy holds that "to concede any error at all of any kind is fatal to the authority of the whole" (e.g., Harold Lindsell and John Wesley), and (3) qualified inerrancy holds to inerrancy in all salvation matters, cosmology, and anthropology, but not necessarily in "every chronological, numerical, and grammatical detail." René Pache is cited, as is the

---

156. Richard S. Taylor, *Biblical Authority and the Christian Faith* (Kansas City: Beacon Hill, 1980). He criticizes the purely existential view of biblical authority (p. 39), the view of the Bible as being merely a record of revelation (e.g., John Baillie and James Barr, p. 40). He quotes C. S. Lewis's criticism of Bultmann's form criticism (p. 42). He advises caution by evangelicals in using Oscar Cullman's term *Heilsgeschichte* since it "allows for a deviation between the facts of real history" and the biblical account (p. 65). He charges that Paul Jewett's hermeneutics (in *Man as Male and Female*) is dangerous in that it divides the organic unity of the Bible (p. 76). Some of the non-Wesleyan inerrantists he approvingly quotes include the following: Carl F. H. Henry (p. 20), John Gerstner's article in the International Council for Biblical Inerrancy volume, *The Foundation of Biblical Authority* (pp. 30, 33, 58), Grant Osborne (p. 43), Francis Schaeffer (p. 52), Harold Lindsell (p. 62), R. C. Sproul (p. 70), and J. I. Packer (p. 75).
157. Ibid., pp. 88-92.
158. Ibid., pp. 30-31.

Lausanne Covenant, which affirms inerrancy for the Bible "in all that it affirms."[159]

Taylor claims that Wiley worded the Nazarene creed "inerrantly revealing the will of God concerning us in all things necessary to our salvation" in order "to leave elbow room in there" (in Wiley's reported words). "The objective was not to limit inerrancy but to exclude tradition" (as in Catholic theology) from being a determining authority of dogma. Once the terms *plenary* and *inspired* are understood in their historical meaning, and especially as used by the early Nazarenes, Taylor declares there is no room for "serious error of any kind." Wiley's several affirmations of inerrancy are quoted to support the importance of that point.[160]

Taylor has not resolved the questions as to "whether (1) there is such a thing as *inconsequential* error, and (2) whether indeed such inconsequential errors were in the original autographs." Some of the variations in the gospel accounts might fit in the category of "error."[161] We do know that "every part of the Bible is divine and every part is human." The only way to reconcile that with the possibility of errors is "to say that the Holy Spirit (and He alone) would know whether a particular error was truly inconsequential, and therefore would permit it." The whole question remains "debatable" for Taylor. But he is "not assuming that such error existed in the autographs."[162]

One wishes Taylor would have explained his position more thoroughly. What exactly does he mean by "inconsequential errors?" The qualifying phrase he cites, "in all that it affirms," appears even in the Chicago Statement on Biblical Inerrancy. Most signers of that statement believe that inerrancy is compatible with phenomenalistic language, a lack of historical precision, approximate citations of the Old Testament by New Testament authors, free renderings of the words of Jesus, and a lack of comprehensiveness of historical accounts.[163] Are those what Taylor means by inconsequential errors? That seems to be the case. If so,

159. Ibid., pp. 33-34.
160. Ibid., pp. 34-36.
161. Ibid., p. 36.
162. Ibid., p. 80.
163. See Paul Feinberg, "The Meaning of Inerrancy," in *Inerrancy*, ed. Norman Geisler (Grand Rapids: Zondervan, 1979), pp. 299-302.

it is refreshing to hear such a distinguished Nazarene scholar reaffirming such a high view of Scripture.

WESLEYAN THEOLOGICAL SOCIETY

The Wesleyan Theological Society (WTS) began in 1965 as a society of Wesleyan-Arminian scholars strongly committed to the full inspiration and authority of the Word. The first doctrinal statement said this about Scripture: "We believe . . . that both Old and New Testaments constitute the divinely-inspired Word of God, inerrant in the originals, and the final authority for life and truth."[164]

At the 1967 WTS annual meeting, several papers were presented concerning the doctrine of Scripture. William Arnett (Asbury Seminary), in his presidential address, presented John Wesley's view of Scripture as supporting the infallibility and inerrancy of the Word. Arnett considered one's stand concerning Scripture to be "the watershed of present-day theology."[165]

Wilber Dayton (then of Asbury, now at Wesley Biblical Seminary) presented a strong, comprehensive defense of inerrancy. Inerrant Scriptures are implied in a "high view of God" and "in the authority of Jesus Christ."

> To deny or ignore Biblical inerrancy would be to pull out the keystone and let the whole structure of theology collapse. Certainty could not survive in any area of doctrine. . . .
> Doubt or denial of inerrancy is historically accompanied by doubt or denial of other basic doctrines, widespread unbelief, a sick church, and vigorous and triumphant anti-Christian movements.[166]

Ralph Thompson (then of Spring Arbor College) more freely admitted to problems with a "strict doctrine of plenary, verbal inerrancy," such as the apparent discrepancies between various

164. On the back cover of the *Wesleyan Theological Journal*, vols. 1-4, spring 1966-spring 1969.
165. William M. Arnett, "John Wesley and the Bible," *Wesleyan Theological Journal* 3 (1968): 3, 5-6.
166. Wilber Dayton, "Theology and Biblical Inerrancy," *Wesleyan Theological Journal* 3 (1968): 30-31.

gospel accounts, New Testament quotations of the Septuagint, and the free manner in which New Testament authors quote the Old Testament. But Thompson concludes:

> To renounce the doctrine of biblical inerrancy is to strip Scriptures of their status as an objective standard of divine truth. Since Christ and His apostles claimed complete inerrancy for the Scriptures, to renounce the doctrine is to cast serious doubts upon the Bible's statements about God, the world, the nature and duty of man, the way of salvation, and man's destiny. Although to accept the doctrine of biblical inerrancy, at this point at least, is to do so in the face of serious critical problems, the alternative to doing so is in effect to destroy Christianity itself.[167]

In a poll of WTS members in 1968, the majority of them took a strong stand for biblical inerrancy.[168] But at the 1969 annual meeting, there was a shift in leadership to those who favored a weaker stand on that doctrine. At the same time a revision of the doctrinal statement was passed.

> We believe . . . in the plenary-dynamic and unique inspiration of the Bible as the divine Word of God, the only infallible (i.e., "absolutely trustworthy and unfailing in effectiveness or operation"— RHD) sufficient and authoritative rule of faith and practice.[169]

Since that change, there has hardly been any support for biblical inerrancy in the *Wesleyan Theological Journal*.[170] On the contrary, there is a tendency to deny that inerrancy ever had a place in the Wesleyan-Arminian tradition.[171]

---

167. W. Ralph Thompson, "Facing Objections Raised Against Biblical Inerrancy," *Wesleyan Theological Journal* 3 (1968): 26-27.
168. Conversation with Dr. Stephen Paine, Dec. 27-28, 1979.
169. On the back cover of the *Wesleyan Theological Journal*, vols. 5-13, spring 1970-spring 1978. In vols. 14-15 (spring 1979-fall 1980), the parenthetical statement is deleted, further diluting an already weak statement. Cf. Stephen W. Paine, "The Bible: Its Relation to Fellowship Among Holiness People," *The Wesleyan Advocate*, 4 May 1970, pp. 8-9.
170. One of the only articles in recent years in favor of inerrancy was this writer's article, "Early Wesleyan Views of Scripture," *Wesleyan Theological Journal* 6 (1981): 95-105.
171. Cf. K. Jerry Shelton, "John Wesley's Approach to Scripture in Historical Perspective," *Wesleyan Theological Journal* 16 (1981): 23-50.

WESLEY BIBLICAL SEMINARY

In 1974 the Wesley Biblical Seminary was begun as a seminary committed to "historic Methodist theology." Its confessional statement (which each trustee and faculty member must adhere to) asserts the inerrancy of Scripture.

> We hold . . . the supreme authority of the Word of God which stands written in the sixty-six books of the Holy Bible, all therein being divinely inspired by Almighty God and therefore without error or defect in the autographs. Believing the Bible to be the Word of God written, the only infallible rule of faith and practice, Wesley Biblical Seminary asserts the authority of Scripture alone over the life of the Church and its individual members. We therefore believe that a reverent and loyal approach to the study of the Bible recognizes and affirms its full inspiration and its absolute trustworthiness as the divinely revealed and authoritative Word of God.[172]

The seminary is continuing to grow as it attracts faculty members and students committed to an inerrant Bible.

THE CONSERVATIVE HOLINESS MOVEMENT

One group of denominations in the family of the American Methodistic church bodies is known as the "conservative holiness movement." That movement is distinguished by an emphasis on piety (especially a carefulness in life-style), traditionalism, and adherence to what is seen as orthodox Wesleyan doctrine, with a strong emphasis on sanctification as a second, definite work of grace. There remains an unabated adherence to biblical inerrancy within that movement. Publications such as *Convention Herald* (by H. E. Schmul and the Inter-Church Holiness Convention) and the Church of God's (Holiness) *Church Herald and Holiness Banner* support and promote inerrancy without equivocation.

At the 1980 Annual Convention of the Church of God (Holiness), the delegates gave unanimous approval to a strong inerrancy resolution. Other denominations such as Church of the Bible

172. *Wesley Biblical Seminary Catalog 1980-82* (Jackson, Mississippi), pp. 16, 18.

Covenant, Bible Missionary Church, Wesleyan Holiness Church, Allegheny Wesleyans, New York Pilgrim Church, Midwest Pilgrims, and others stand without question for biblical inerrancy.

CONCLUSION

The case for biblical inerrancy must be, and has been, established on grounds more solid than historical affirmations of the doctrine. But when historical claims are made, they should be examined. A few modern Wesleyan scholars, who themselves question inerrancy, charge that biblical inerrancy is a Calvinistic dogma and has no part in authentic Wesleyan-Arminianism. The historical evidence clearly refutes such an allegation. It is in the best of Wesleyan tradition that modern Wesleyans affirm that, with their Calvinist and Reformed brethren, "The Bible is the inerrant and infallible Word of God."

10

Baptists and Scripture

Tom J.Nettles

INTRODUCTION

Baptists in England and America from the seventeenth to the nineteenth century developed and defended a comprehensive doctrine of biblical inspiration. They also experienced a strange metamorphosis in the protagonist-antagonist roles related to the debate of that doctrine. At least five stages in the bibliological evolution of the English Baptists can be discerned. The earliest emphasis saw English Baptists relate the doctrine of *sola scriptura* to religious liberty. Second, and almost contemporary with the first emphasis, English Baptists eagerly aligned themselves with mainline Protestantism against the Roman Catholic view of Scripture. Third, English Baptists labored earnestly to dissociate themselves from the so-called rantings of the Quakers and their

TOM J. NETTLES, B.A., Mississippi College, M.Div., Ph.D., Southern Baptist Theological Seminary, is the chairman of the department of church history at Mid-America Theological Seminary in Memphis, Tennessee. He is co-author of *Baptists and the Bible* (Moody, 1980), *Growth for God's Glory* (a history of Broadmoor Baptist Church, Shreveport, Louisiana), and editor and publisher of *Baptist Catechisms*.

claim for immediate inspiration. Fourth, English Baptists developed their understanding of the doctrine of inspiration in a more detailed manner through their confrontation with deism and Socinianism in the eighteenth and nineteenth centuries. The rise of higher criticism among English Baptists constitutes the final area (within the scope of this chapter) in which one finds extensive writing on the doctrine of inspiration. The American development, though encompassing some of the same factors, is not divisible as clearly as that of the English. Therefore, the development is treated chronologically. However, the American conflict with higher criticism preceded the English conflict and had different results. The issues involved in both confrontations will be discussed together. That discussion will focus solely on the epistemological problem discerned early in the respective controversies. John Broadus most succinctly analyzed the implications of C. H. Toy's methodology; C. H. Spurgeon's *The Sword and the Trowel* set forth the problems of the Downgrade tendencies in England. Subsequent interaction seldom produced more pertinent analysis than that which came forth from the beginning of the bibliological impasse.

ENGLISH BAPTISTS: PRE-DOWNGRADE DEVELOPMENT

THE BIBLE AND RELIGIOUS LIBERTY

Baptists in seventeenth-century England enthusiastically endorsed the Reformation principle of *sola scriptura*. The combination of that affirmation of Scripture as the sole authority of knowledge about God and salvation, and the belief in the perspicuity of Scripture, prompted Baptists into a position opposed to that of most of their orthodox contemporaries. They accepted and promoted liberty of conscience.

Baptist espousal of that tenet did not spring from any epistemological agnosticism. Rather, as far as Baptists were concerned, it was the only response consistent with the infallibility and clarity of Scripture. Man should not be forced to believe as the church believes, for all churches have erred, according to John Murton. If man is forced to believe as the church does, then "the scriptures are not the only rule of faith." However, if those in authority allow the people to read the Scripture and thereby to have their consciences enlightened and convinced, why will they not "suffer us to practice that we learn and know?"[1]

That same conviction was eloquently expressed by Roger Williams in his "Address to Every Courteous Reader," placed before *The Bloudy Tenet of Persecution*, published in England in 1644.

> In vaine have English Parliaments permitted English Bibles in the poorest English houses, and the simplest man or woman to search the Scriptures, if yet against their soules persuasion from the Scripture, they should be forced (as if they live in Spain or Rome itselfe without the sight of a Bible) to believe as the Church believes.[2]

THE BIBLE AND ROMAN CATHOLICISM

In the conflict with Roman Catholicism's tendency to annul scriptural authority, English Baptists spoke with one voice with other English nonconforming Protestants. The earliest Particular Baptist Confession of Faith (London, 1644) affirmed the doctrine of *sola scriptura* in unmistakable terms.

> The rule of this Knowledge, Faith, and Obedience, concerning the worship and service of God, and all other Christian duties, is not mans inventions, opinions, devices, lawes, constitutions, or traditions unwritten whatsoever, but only the word of God contained in the Canonical Scriptures.[3]

The phrase "contained in" should be understood to mean "limited to."

The Second London Confession,[4] based on the Westminster Confession, was much more detailed in its avowal of the Reforma-

---

1. John Murton, "A Most Humble Supplication," in *Tracts on Liberty of Conscience and Persecution*, ed. Edward Bean Underhill (London: J. Haddon, 1846), p. 209.
2. *The Bloudy Tenet of Persecution* (n.p., 1644), vol. 3 in *The Complete Writings of Roger Williams*, ed. Reuben Aldridge et al. (New York: Russell & Russell, 1903), p. 13.
3. William L. Lumpkin, *Baptist Confessions of Faith* (Pennsylvania: Judson, 1969), p. 158, Article VII.
4. Ibid., pp. 241-98.

tional understanding of the Scriptures. The first sentence of the article on Scripture states, "The Holy Scripture is the only sufficient, certain, and infallible rule of all saving Knowledge, Faith, and Obedience."[5] To reject the Roman Catholic teaching concerning the authority of oral tradition, their confession stated that the Lord had revealed Himself and declared His will to His church and had preserved both that revelation and declaration by committing "the same wholly unto writing." That the Bible is the very Word of God written was affirmed in other places by statements that God (who is truth itself) was the author of Scripture and that Scripture was "delivered by the Spirit."[6]

The Roman Catholic belief in the church's exclusive right to interpret Scripture was rejected in favor of the doctrine of the perspicuity of Scripture and the hermeneutical principle of the analogy of faith. Thus, the confession claimed that though all things in Scripture are not equally plain in themselves, "yet those things which are necessary to be known . . . [are] so clearly propounded, and opened in some place of Scripture or other" that any man "in a due use of ordinary means may attain to a sufficient understanding of them."[7]

The main principle of interpretation recommended in that article on Scripture is the analogy of faith. "The infallible rule of interpretation of Scripture is the Scripture itself." That principle assumes the full truthfulness and unequivocal nature of the entire canonical Scripture. Scripture, because God is its author, never contradicts itself any more than God could lie or deny Himself.[8] Therefore, the authority of Holy Scripture does not depend on the testimony of any man or church, but only on God Himself.

Thomas Grantham, a leader of the General Baptists, wrote *Christianismus Primitivus* in 1678. One of his purposes was to refute the Roman Catholic claim to the right of ecclesiastical arbitration in theological disputes. In rejecting that claim Grantham defended the premise that only Scripture could judge such disputes.

5. Ibid., p. 248.
6. Ibid., pp. 248-52.
7. Ibid.
8. Ibid.

That amongst all such parties of the Sons of Men, the only Infallible and Authoritative Judge of their controversies about Religion,
is the Lord Himself, as he speaketh by his Spirit in the Holy Scriptures; together with right reason; or thus, which is all one, The
Apostles and Prophets, as they speak in their Holy Writings, are
the only Infallible Authoritative Judge in these controversies.[9]

Grantham's rejection of the Roman Catholic claim makes several things clear. The words of Scripture are to be taken as the
words of the Lord Jesus Himself. Those words are infallible; they
are the exclusive judge of all theological disputes.

Baptists also rejected the Catholic assertion of the inspiration of
the Latin Vulgate. The Second London Confession stated that the
Old Testament in Hebrew and the New Testament in Greek,
"being immediately inspired by God," were the final appeal in all
controversies. John Smyth, the protobaptist, had said as much
when he claimed that "the Holy Scriptures viz. the Originals
Hebrew & Greek arc given by Divine Inspiration and in their first
donation were without error."[10]

John Gill (1697-1771), a major Baptist theologian of the eighteenth century, declared that the Catholic assertion of a divinely
inspired Vulgate was absurd since it "abounds with innumerable
errors and mistakes." Gill claimed that only the original languages could be considered inspired. All translations were to be
brought to the original to be examined, for if that were not the
case, "we should have no certain and infallible rule to do by."[11]

Assertion of the infallibility of the original manuscripts, however, in no way destroyed either the effectiveness or the necessity
of translations, Gill argued. On the contrary, only the absolute
purity of the autographs guaranteed either. A translation will be
effective for communicating God's revelation only if it arises from
a document that can be considered infallible. A translation will
certainly communicate no more truth than was contained in its

9. Thomas Grantham, *Christianismus Primitivus* (London: printed for Francis
Smith, 1678), 4:1-2.
10. John Smyth, *The Works of John Smyth*, 2 vols., ed. W. I. Whitley (Cambridge:
U. Press, 1915), 1:279.
11. John Gill, *Body of Divinity* (Reprint. Atlanta: Turner & Lasseter, 1950), p.
13.

source. Also, if one truly accepts the originals as a word from God, then it should be made available to all men, even though they may not be able to read the original tongue. The Second London Confession made that very clear in its eighth paragraph on Scripture.

> But because these original tongues are not known to all people of God, who have a right unto, and interest in the Scriptures, and are commanded in the fear of God to read and search them, therefore they are to be translated into the vulgar language of every Nation, unto which they come, that the Word of God dwelling plentifully in all, they may worship him in an acceptable manner, and through patience and comfort of the Scriptures may have hope.[12]

John Gill reaffirmed that teaching; he gave assurance to those who could only read translations that the skill and piety of translators guaranteed that the translations were trustworthy and that no momentous article of faith was affected by any slight inadequacy.

The writers of the *Orthodox Creed*, a General Baptist confession of 1678, confirmed the view of Scripture advocated by the Second London Confession. They were not hesitant to align themselves completely with Protestantism in their submission to biblical authority.

> And no decree of popes, or councils, or writings of any person whatsoever, are of equal authority with the sacred scripture. And by the holy scriptures we understand, the canonical books of the Old and New Testament, as they are now translated into our English mother-tongue, of which there hath never been any doubt of their verity, and authority, in the protestant churches of Christ to this day.[13]

THE BIBLE AND THE QUAKERS

The rise of the Quakers presented a problem for some Baptists, since there were many apparent similarities between the groups.

12. Lumpkin, p. 251.
13. Ibid., p. 325.

The freeness of style in worship services, a zealous lay ministry, and liberty of conscience were some beliefs and practices held in common. However, Baptists quickly discerned some basic differences and wasted no time seeking to demonstrate that on foundational points vital distinctions existed between the two groups. A republishing of the first London Confession in 1651 included a document called *Heart Bleedings for Professors Abominations*. The Quaker view of Scripture came up for specific examination and refutation. The Quaker practice of quoting Scripture with blatant disregard for context was exposed as empty, confusing, swollen, and vain. The claim that the authority of their "inner light" was equal to the authority of Scripture was rejected. Their spiritualizing of biblical passages was denounced as a mocking of "the holy Scriptures, those heavenly oracles of God, denying them to be the Word of God." Instead of the Quaker view, the Particular Baptists believed that the Bible presented "the whole Minde, Will and Law of God, for us and all Saints to believe and practice throughout all ages," and furthermore concluded that "the Scriptures which do declare this great mysterie of Jesus Christ and his gospel, be the holy Scriptures, and the infallible Word of God."[14]

Particular Baptists continued their disavowal of Quaker schemes of authority by including several phrases in the Second London Confession aimed directly at Quaker peculiarities. In the light of their claim to have Christ within, many Quakers rejected the necessity of having written Scripture; Baptists countered that since God's revelation was committed wholly to writing, the Holy Scriptures were "most necessary." The Quakers often acted on what they asserted to be direct revelation from the Spirit. The Baptist Confession stated that since "those former ways of God revealing his will unto his people" had ceased, nothing at any time was to be added to Holy Scripture, whether by (so-called) "Revelation of the Spirit, or traditions of men."[15]

General Baptists also faced the Quaker threat by affirming the authority of Scripture. John Griffith, an influential General Bap-

14. *Heart Bleedings for Professors Abominations*, appended to a 1651 edition of *The First London Confession*, pp. 16, 21.
15. Lumpkin, pp. 249-50.

tist pastor, prefaced a confession, *The True Gospel Faith*, with the following appeal for submission to Scripture.

> We therefore do desire that whosoever read (this confession) may weigh the Scriptures produced; and if it be according to the Scriptures, there is light in it, for its the Scriptures of the Prophets and Apostles that we square our faith and practice by, accounting that light within (not witnessed by the scriptures without) which some so much talk of to be deep darkness. . . . Let the Scripture therefore be the rule of thy faith and practice.[16]

Grantham also opposed what he called the "pernicious queries" of the Quakers. To the Quaker implication that Moses was not the author of the five books attributed to him, Grantham invoked the authority of the Lord Jesus Himself. He claimed that all five books of Moses were quoted by Christ and His apostles at least fifty times and they avouched "Moses as the Penman of the first Books of the Sacred Scripture." That fact clinched the argument for Grantham, for he abhorred "to think that our Saviour was either Unskillful, or Unfaithful, in recommending to us any supposititious Writings, instead of the sacred Oracles."[17] Critical inquiry should be subservient to the words of Jesus as recorded in Scripture, according to Grantham, or the coherence of biblical authority is exploded. In the context of answering a question related to the presence of words of Satan, liars, and imposters in Scripture, Grantham again asserted his full submission to the revelation from God that produced the Holy Scriptures.

> Yea this very passage [Genesis 3] I do affirm to be written by the Inspiration of God's Spirit, or the Motion thereof; and consequently all such like passages also. Otherwise this passage would be doubtful, and all the Historical part of the Scripture also which declares matter of fact. For either these things were written in the Book of God, by the Motion and Direction of his Spirit, or else they rest on Humane Authority, and Conjecture . . . but when God

16. Ibid., p. 191.
17. Grantham, pp. 44-45.

speaketh, we must submit our Reason; by Faith receive, what by Science we cannot understand.[18]

Grantham also opposed the Quaker claim to immediate inspiration from the Spirit. New revelation was unnecessary, in the first place, since no man can fully comprehend the depths of what is written in Scripture under the Spirit's guidance. Also, contrary to Quaker utterances, the Spirit would certainly not contradict Himself by giving information opposed to what He had already spoken in Scripture. The Spirit's authority cannot be separated from the authority of Scripture. Therefore, the voice of the Spirit speaking in Scripture ought always to be heard, rather than any supposed voice of the Spirit through a person who is not fully submitted to the absolute truthfulness of the Bible.

THE BIBLE AND THE RATIONALISTS

Socinianism and deism were the special objects of attention in late eighteenth- and early nineteenth-century England. Andrew Fuller, William Carey's close friend and secretary of the Foreign Mission Society, took an active part in opposing both movements. His discussion relates directly to the early nineteenth-century Baptist understanding of biblical authority.

In a written exchange with Mr. Priestly, a Socinian, Fuller approached the question concerning whether Socinian doctrine gave proper veneration to the Scripture. The principle Fuller assumed at the outset was this:

> If any man venerate the authority of Scripture, he must receive it as being what it professes to be, and for all the purposes for which it professes to be written. If the Scriptures profess to be Divinely inspired, and assume to be the infallible standard of faith and practice, we must either receive them as such, or, if we would be consistent, disown the writers as imposters.[19]

Fuller then briefly listed several claims the biblical writers

18. Ibid., p. 46.
19. Andrew Fuller, *The Complete Works of the Rev. Andrew Fuller*, 3 vols. (Philadelphia: American Baptist Publication Society, 1845), 2:196.

made for themselves with respect to the inspiration and authority of Scripture. He concluded that "nothing short of the most perfect divine inspiration could justify such language as this, or secure those who used it from the charge of bold presumption and base imposition."[20]

Priestly claimed that the biblical writers were, like other historians, "liable to mistakes with respect to things of small moment," because they may not have given sufficient attention to them. They must have been fallible, according to Priestly, simply because they were men. Such fallibility rests on the supposition, according to Fuller, that it is "impossible for God himself so to inspire a man as to preserve him from error without destroying his nature."[21] Fuller took the opposite course and believed that God had inspired men so as to preserve them from error.

Fuller further maintained that once fallibility at any point was imputed to Scripture, any argument quoting Scripture as its authority was inconsistent. One might seek to prove a point about the person of Christ from Scripture, but having before affirmed Scripture's fallibility even in "things of small moment"[22] would render the source of authority debatable and liable to err. Therefore, no absolute dependence could be placed on the decisions of the biblical writers in any instance.

Fuller maintained his confidence in the absolute consistency and truthfulness of Scripture throughout his ministry. Volume 1 of his works contains a section of thirty sets of Scripture passages in which there are apparent contradictions. His purpose was to demonstrate their actual harmony. In a sermon called "On an intimate and practical Acquaintance with the Word of God," Fuller admonished his readers to "seek the will of God in every part of the Bible."

> Do not take this part and leave that. Some people foolishly talk of Arminian texts, and Calvinist texts, as if Scripture were repugnant

20. Ibid., 2:197.
21. Ibid., 2:198.
22. Ibid., 2:200-201.

to itself! That system, whatever it be called, cannot be the right one that rejects any one part of Scripture whatever.[23]

In his conflict with deism, Fuller produced a book, *The Gospel Its Own Witness*. Part 2 of that book contends that the harmony of Scripture is an evidence of the divinity of Christianity. He defended the inspiration of Scripture because of the harmony between its prophecy and the events of history, between its picture of man and the morality it espouses and the dictates of an enlightened conscience, between what it claims for itself (divine inspiration) and the spirit and style in which it is written, as well as the consistency of the Christian doctrine of salvation through a mediator with sober reason, and the consistency of the doctrine of redemption with the magnitude of creation. After that entire discussion Fuller concluded, "Revelation is the medium, and the only medium, by which, standing, as it were, 'on nature's Alps,' we discover things which eye hath not seen, nor ear heard, and of which it never hath entered into the heart of man to conceive."[24] Earlier, he had concluded section 2 with a statement that may serve as an apt description of his understanding of the entire subject.

On the other hand, if [the Scriptures] speak of things as they are, if conscience echo to their charges, and fact comport with their representations, they must have been taken from life; and you must conclude them to be what they profess to be—a work of truth. And, since the objects described are many of them beyond the ken of human observation, you must conclude that they are not only a work of truth, but what they also profess to be—the true sayings of God.[25]

Fuller was not oblivious to the different literary genres in Scripture. To claim that the words of Scripture are the true sayings of God in no way diminishes the variety of literary devices that may have been used. Certainly, God is at least as imaginative and creative as the literary geniuses of world history, and is quite capable of communicating what He intends to communicate through

23. Ibid., 1:484.
24. Ibid., 2:97.
25. Ibid., 2:68.

many styles. The deists pointed to the popular language of Scripture as evidence that it was not revelation. Fuller thought otherwise.

The Scriptures are written in a popular style, as best adapted to their great end. If the salvation of philosophers only had been their object, the language might possibly have been somewhat different; though even this may be a matter of doubt, since the style is suited to the subject, and to the great end which they had in view; but being addressed to men of every degree, it was highly proper that the language should be fitted to every capacity, and suited to their common modes of conception. They speak of the foundations of the earth, the ends of the earth, the greater and less lights in the heavens, the sun rising, standing still, and going down, and many other things in the same way. If deists object to these modes of speaking, as conveying ideas which are inconsistent with the true theory of the heavens and the earth, let them, if they can, substitute others which are consistent: let them, in their common conversation, when describing the revolutions of evening and morning, speak of the earth as rising and going down, instead of the sun; and the same with regard to the revolution of the planets; and see if men, in common, will better understand them, or whether they would be able even to understand one another. The popular ideas on these subjects are as much "worked up" in the common conversation of philosophers as they are in the Scriptures; and the constant use of such language, even by philosophers themselves, in common conversation, sufficiently proves the futility and unfairness of their objecting to revelation on this account.[26]

In 1796 Fuller preached a message called "The Nature and Importance of an Intimate Knowledge of Divine Truth." For Fuller, divine truth was found only in Scripture, the Oracles of God. Though the phrase *oracles of God* is intensely strong and could border on blasphemous presumption if not used properly, Fuller did not shrink from applying the term to the Scriptures as "strongly expressive of their Divine Inspiration and infallibility."[27]

That message also advocated systematic presentation of biblical

26. Ibid., 2:88-89.
27. Ibid., 1:160.

doctrine, since there is "unity, order, arrangement, and fullness of design" in the teachings of Scripture, though they are scattered in lovely variety, much as the beauty of nature. The beauty of Scripture does not preclude systematization any more than the beauty of a rose precludes the study of botany.

The Bible answers man's need for a divine revelation, according to Fuller. If man is to know God, God must take the initiative in disclosing Himself. If we are to recognize that disclosure as such, it must be entirely truthful, or it cannot be judged to surpass the best wisdom of depraved human nature. The Bible claims to be just that kind of revelation. If it is not what it professes to be, then one can only conclude that it is a gross impostor. Therefore, Fuller affirmed that even in the recording of eyewitness events, the writer was superintended by the divine Spirit in such a way as to "preserve him from error, and from other defects and faults, to which ordinary historians are subject." Truths not empirically observable require an even higher degree of divine governance. But in whatever degree inspiration occurs, Fuller's main concern was not for the process but for the final product. "It requires that a book professing to be a revelation from God should contain truth, and nothing but truth: such particularly must be its history, its prophecies, its miracles and its doctrines."[28]

SUMMARY

By the middle of the 1800s, as a result of the many different types of conflicts, Baptists had developed a comprehensive understanding of the nature of biblical inspiration. They had investigated the implications of their view and had seen it weather the violent storms of traditionalism, enthusiasm, and infidelity. In brief, Baptists believed Scripture to be inspired by God. As a result of its inspiration, it was infallible. Its infallibility guaranteed its inerrancy, even in history and "things of small moment." Its inerrancy assured its pervasive consistency, and its consistency allowed the main principle of interpretation to be (second to the grammatical principle) the analogy of faith. Having gained doctrinal and

28. Ibid., 1:699.

numerical strength in the midst of attacks from outside, those foes of Scripture inflicted only minor pain compared to the hurt wrought from within by the Downgrade Controversy.

AMERICAN BAPTISTS: PRE-TOY DEVELOPMENT

Roger Williams stands at the fountainhead of Baptist life in America. In 1639 he was baptized by Ezekiel Holliman. Those two, along with eleven others, began the First Baptist Church in America at Providence, Rhode Island. Though he remained organically aligned with Baptist life only about three months, his theological sympathies remained Baptist throughout his life.[29]

Williams gave his most extended discussion of Scripture in a debate he held with the Quakers in 1672. In that debate he asserted that Scripture is the sole authority for all knowledge of God and ourselves; it should be studied in the original languages; it is infallible, for it has been penned by "the most holy and Infallible Spirit."[30]

In opposition to the Quakers' reliance on "inner light," Williams set forth Scripture as a "Declaration and Revelation of God's Will to his People and to the Whole World."[31]

Though Quakers insisted that "if the Scriptures were lost and burnt out of the world, the Spirit within them could give new Scriptures," Williams maintained otherwise. God had given the "Word Will or Mind of God written and pen'd by chosen Penmen as Pens in the hand of his holy Spirit."[32] He also argued that God had preserved Scripture miraculously through various attempts to destroy it. For Williams, the Bible stood as the canon by which all opinions should be tried. Therefore, a study of Scripture in the original languages was the sole answer to the pretensions of Quaker and Baptist alike in their advocacy of other authorities. Williams believed in the defensibility of the purity of the existing original manuscripts.

29. A. H. Newman, *A History of the Baptist Churches in the United States* (New York: Christian Literature Co., 1894), p. 79-84.
30. Roger Williams, *The Complete Writings of Roger Williams*, 7 vols. (New York: Russell & Russell, 1963), 5:159.
31. Ibid., 5:140.
32. Ibid., 5:141.

We must with Luther and his Associates, Calvin and his followers maintain Learning, study the Scripture, search the Originals, Copyes and Translations, and vindicate their Purity and Perfection, their Authority and sole external Direction how to judge of all pretending Christian Prophets.[33]

From the beginning of Baptist life in America, the ultimate authority and infallibility of the *autographa* was accepted. Williams denied that the "weak, lame, and Childish" writings of the Quakers could be the work of the "most holy and infallible spirit,"[34] but unequivocally affirmed the Bible to be the work of men who were "but Pens of Heaven writing, and used by the hand of the holy Spirit."[35]

The inspired character of Scripture imparts greater certainty to its truthfulness than any one might claim for personal experience, said Williams. Even the miraculous events of the New Testament were not more certain than the words and prophecies of Scripture. Peter's reference to the transfiguration experience serves as evidence of the primacy of Scripture over experience.

Therefore how oft is it written concerning the Lord Jesus, "These things were done that the Scriptures might be Fulfilled" in which regard, (as to our satisfaction and belief) the written word of Prophecie of the Prophets are a more sure Word and Evidence to us concerning the Lord Jesus than the Miraculous Appearance from Heaven of Moses and Elias, and the voice from Heaven of which Peter here speaketh; though in it self a true Testimony, yet not so sure, so firm and pregnant as the Word that God spake by the mouth of his holy Prophets from the beginning of the World, etc. Hence the Answer of Abraham, and indeed of Christ Jesus: If they, hear not Moses and the Prophets, neither will they believe though one should rise from the Dead.[36]

Baptists who were contemporaries of Roger Williams shared his views. Though they wrote no extended treatment of the inspira-

33. Ibid., 5:142.
34. Ibid., 5:159.
35. Ibid., 5:137.
36. Ibid., 5:153.

tion of Scripture, their willingness to suffer for a point of doctrine arose directly from their belief in Scripture as the unerring, unalterable Word of God. John Clarke, arrested and jailed for preaching and baptizing in Massachusetts, wrote to the court at Boston and offered to debate the ministers of that city. His proposal demonstrates his view of Scripture.

> I might dispute that point publicly, where I doubt not, by the strength of Christ, to make it good out of his last will and testament, unto which nothing is to be added, nor from which nothing is to be diminished. If the faith and order which I profess do stand by the word of God, then the faith and order which you profess must needs fall to the ground; I would draw up the faith and order which I hold, which conclusions I will stand by and defend until he whom you shall appoint, shall, by the word of God remove me from them; I desire like liberty, by the word of God, to oppose the faith and order which he and you profess, thereby to try whether I may be an instrument in the hand of God to remove you from the same.[37]

Obadiah Holmes was with Clarke at the time of Clarke's arrest and was his fellow prisoner. His treatment was more severe than Clarke's. He was whipped severely, "the man striking with all his strength (yea, spitting in his hands three times) with a three corded whip, giving [him] therewith thirty strokes."[38] Holmes set forth his simple but strong faith in a thirty-five article "Confession of Faith." His confidence in Scripture is stated succinctly.

> I believe that they that are sent of God are not to declare a mission of their own brain, but as it is in the Scripture of truth, for holy men wrote as they were inspired by the Holy Spirit. Thus have I given you an humble and true account of my standing that you may consider the same, comparing what is written by the Holy Scriptures, which are our rule towards God and Man.[39]

37. David Benedict, *A General History of the Baptist Denomination in America and Other Parts of the World* (New York: Lewis Colby, 1848), p. 373.
38. Ibid., p. 376.
39. Isaac Backus, *A History of New England with Particular Reference to the Denomination of Christians called "Baptists,"* 2d ed. 2 vols. (Newton, Mass.: Backus Historical Society, 1871), pp. 208-9.

That confession was in accord with his view of Scripture presented in "On My Life," Holmes's testimony of the spiritual struggle that led to his conversion. In that testimony he wrote:

> I have seen that it is evil to make men the strength of counsel or help; and taking men's words in order to [find] a spiritual way of direction is not safe. For the way is to try the spirits, for every spirit is not of God, and he who speaks not according to the Holy Scriptures does so because he has no light in them. Whereupon, I have only them and them alone for my rule and direction, beseeching the Lord to give me understanding of them by His Holy Spirit which is the only revealer of secrets to my soul.[40]

In his instruction to his children he reaffirmed that same position on Scripture. Recognizing that only the sovereign will of God produces regeneration, Holmes admonished his children to attend to the means used by the Spirit that they might be "born again and ingrafted in the true vine."

> Wherefore, wait on Him with care and diligence; carefully read the Scriptures and mind well what is therein contained for they testify of Him. Let your hearty desires be to Him that He would effectually be your Teacher by His Holy Spirit. Beware that you hearken to any that shall speak contrary to the Scriptures, for if they do speak otherways it is because they have no light in them. Let your conversation and life be squared by the same, and they will direct you how to behave yourselves toward God and man.[41]

That same faith in the Scriptures was shared by Thomas Gould, founder of First Baptist Church, Boston, and his sympathizers. Gould endured years of harassment from the ecclesiastical and civil authorities because he rejected infant baptism. When they asked him to bring his child for baptism, he replied, "I durst not do it, for I did not see any rule for it in the word of God."[42] His absolute trust in Scripture was demonstrated on numerous

40. Edwin S Gaustad, ed., *Baptist Piety: The Last Will and Testimony of Obadiah Holmes* (Grand Rapids: Christian U. Press, 1978), p. 80.
41. Ibid., p. 103.
42. Benedict, p. 382.

occasions as he stood alone before the church officials and the magistrates. He was willing to be convinced only out of the plain teaching of Scripture. David Benedict recorded the following anecdote that illustrates Gould's insistence on biblical proof.

At last one of the company stood up and said, I will give you one plain place of scripture where children were baptized. I told him that would put an end to the controversy. That place is in the 2d of the Acts, 39th and 40th verses. After he had read the scripture, Mr. Sims told me that promise belonged to infants, for the Scripture saith, "The promise is to you and your children, and to all that are afar off"; and he said no more; to which I replied, "even so many as the Lord our God shall call." Mr. Sims replied that I spoke blasphemously in adding to the scriptures. I said, pray do not condemn me, for if I am deceived, my eyes deceive me. He replied again, I added to the scripture, which was blasphemy. I looked into my bible, read the words again, and said it was so. He replied the same words the third time before the church. Mr. Russell stood up and told him it was so, as I had read it. Aye, it may be so in your bible, said Mr. Sims. Mr. Russell answered, yea, in yours too if you will look into it. Then he said he was mistaken, for he thought on another place; so after many other words, we broke up for that time.[43]

John Russell, who succeeded Gould as pastor, in 1660 set forth a defense of Baptists in "A Brief Narrative . . . of a Church of Christ, in Gospel Order . . . for clearing their innocency from the Scandalous things laid to their charge." As well as defending Gould and Thomas Osbourne for refusing paedobaptism, "not seeing any light for it from the Word of God," he explained that the sole "moral evil" of Thomas Foster was the same: refusing infant baptism, "not seeing any light from the word of God for it." Nor was his church able to "convince him from the Word of God."[44]

When charged with disturbing the peace, Russell denied that

43. Ibid.
44. Nathan Wood, *The History of the First Baptist Church of Boston* (Philadelphia: American Baptist Publication Society, 1899), pp. 152-59.

the church or its members had ever been guilty of such violations and affirmed:

> Indeed after the way that is called Heresie, so worship we the God of our Fathers, believing all things which are written in the Law, and the Prophets; and have hope towards God of the Resurrection of the Dead, both of the just and unjust, and herein do exercise our selves always, to have a conscience void of offence towards God, and towards Man.[45]

Furthermore, we may legitimately assume that the Boston Baptists agreed with the article on Scripture in the Second London Confession, first published in 1677. The most eminent Baptists of London in 1660 wrote the preface to Russell's "Brief Narrative." They testified that "the Authors of this Apology have declared their perfect agreement with us both in matters of Faith and Worship, as set down in our late Confession." That they accepted Scripture as the "only sufficient, certain, and infallible rule of all faith and practice" was borne out in their willingness to suffer, so that they would break no "rule of the gospel."[46]

Eighteenth-century Baptists in America continued to understand Scripture as the oracular communication of an unerring God. The Philadelphia Association bore constant witness to that settled conviction. Founded in 1707, the first Baptist Association in America consisted of five churches. By 1800 the Association reported thirty-five churches and over 2,600 members. During that time a host of churches had been dismissed to form other associations that spread into the South and New England: the Charleston Association in South Carolina, the Warren Association in New England, and the Ketocton Association in Virginia.

The Centennial minutes of that Association, from 1707 to 1807, were compiled in 1846 and finally published in 1851.[47] Those minutes contain multitudes of historical and theological treasures that depict Baptist life in America. Their understanding of Scrip-

---

45. Ibid., p. 163.
46. Ibid., p. 150.
47. A. D. Gillette, *Minutes of the Philadelphia Baptist Association* (Philadelphia: American Baptist Publication Society, 1851), pp. 3-8 passim.

ture can be gleaned from a thorough reading; that understanding may be viewed under three headings.

First, one may observe that the method of exhortation, instruction, and giving of advice was consistently related to an acceptance of absolute biblical authority. Yearly, churches presented "queries" to the association. A study of the answers demonstrates the association's strong adherence to biblical authority.

Query from the church at Philadelphia. Suppose a gifted brother, who is esteemed an orderly minister by or among those that are against the laying on of hands in any respect, should happen to come among our church; whether we may allow such an one to administer the ordinances of baptism and the Lord's supper or no?

Answered in the negative; because it is contrary to the rule of God's word: see Acts xiii. 2, 3; and xiv. 23: compared with Titus i. 5; 1 Tim. iv. 14; from which prescribed rules we dare not swerve. We also refer to the Confession of faith, chap. xxvii., sect. 9.

Whether it be justifiable for our members to neglect our own appointed meetings, and at their pleasure go to hear those differing in judgment from us?

Answered in the negative. Heb. x. 25.

Whether to deny the foreknowledge of the eternal God, concerning all future evil as well as good, be not a fundamental error.

Answer. We look upon such an opinion to be directly repugnant to Scripture; therefore exceeding erroneous and pernicious. First because it supposes God imperfect, and so no God, Psalm cxlvii. 5; Heb. iv. 13. Secondly: If so, there would be no room for the divine Being to make provision for the redemption of mankind before the fall of man, which is contrary to express Scripture testimony, Prov. vii. 28, 35; 2 Tim. i. 9. Thirdly: It is an error, which, in its nature and consequences, doth oppose and tend to overthrow the whole Christian religion, Acts ii. 23; iv. 28; Titus iii. 10.[48]

The answer to the last query is especially significant. An opinion "directly repugnant to Scripture" was considered, on that account, to be "exceeding erroneous." The practice of answering questions directly from Scripture was adopted as the official methodology in 1774, when the following proposal was accepted:

48. Ibid., pp. 30, 35, 58.

"That suitable endeavors be made as heretofore, to resolve cases and questions proposed by the churches, to the best of our knowledge, according to the Scripture."[49]

Second, in extended discussions of theological or ecclesiological subjects, oblique and passing references to the nature of Scripture affirm the association's conviction of biblical infallibility. In admonishing the churches to holy living, the letter of salutation for 1746 stated: "Be diligent in reading the holy Scriptures, which are our only rule of faith and obedience, without which we can have no saving knowledge of God, or of Jesus Christ our Redeemer and hope."[50]

On occasion, the minutes identify the words of Scripture with the words of the Holy Spirit. When discussing the biblical teaching on the election of various church officers, the minutes say, "We must note that the Holy Ghost had no where limited or bounded the time." Seeking a remedy for spiritual lethargy, the association in 1759 wrote, "Our Mediator, after his ascension to the throne of his glory, has prescribed an infallible remedy, in the 2d and 3d of the Revelations. . . ."[51]

Giving instruction on justification by faith and acknowledging his hearers' thorough acquaintance with Scripture, William Rogers, pastor at First Baptist Church, Philadelphia, made two passing but firm references to inerrancy in 1785.

> Educated in the school of Jesus, and instructed by the unerring Spirit of the Most High, you are ready, dearly beloved, to anticipate us under his head, by exclaiming with an inspired apostle, "It is God who justifieth," Rom. viii 33. Is it then, dearly beloved brethren, as hath been represented? Supported by the unerring volume, we think this question may be fully answered in the affirmative.[52]

Also, "the instrument used in sanctification is the divine word, which has transforming effect." The Bible was called the "volume of inspiration," "the Scripture of truth," "the sacred oracles,"

49. Ibid., p. 136.
50. Ibid., p. 50.
51. Ibid., p. 64.
52. Ibid., pp. 208, 213.

"divine revelation," "the holy Scriptures," "the oracles of divine truth," and "the Word of God, our sacred guide." The Spirit, who inspired the Scripture, was called the "unerring Spirit of wisdom."[53]

Third, the bibliology of the Philadelphia Association is evident in specific discussions of the nature of Scripture. They offer strong evidence of the Philadelphia Association's adherence to infallibility.

The Second London Confession of 1689 concretized the theological position of Baptists in Pennsylvania as well as Baptists in London. In use no later than 1724, that confession was officially adopted by the Association in 1742, with slight alterations. Thirty-two years later, in 1774, Abel Morgan suggested that the general associational letter contain "observations and improvements of some particular article of faith, contained on our confession."[54] The first article concerned Scripture. Its initial sentence stated, "The holy Scripture is the only sufficient, certain, and infallible... rule of all saving knowledge, faith and obedience."[55]

Morgan expounded the article on Scripture in 1774. He affirmed the inspiration, certainty, and infallibility of Scripture "in all its parts, historical, doctrinal and prophetical."

> These holy writings are of God, divinely inspired, 2 Tim. iii. 16; the word of God, John x. 36; 1 Cor. xiv. 36, 37; the mind of Christ, 1 Cor. ii. 26; of Divine authority, Isa. xl. 8; the infallible ground of faith and certain rule of obedience, Isa. viii. 20; full and complete in all its parts, historical, doctrinal, and prophetical; every way useful and profitable: e. gr. to obtain the saving knowledge of the one only living and true God, Father, Son, and Holy Ghost, 2 Tim. iii. 15; the knowledge of his essential attributes and immutable counsels, Heb. vi. 17; also of his works, of creation, providence, and particularly of redemption by Jesus Christ, the eternal Son of God, the one Mediator, God-Man. In the Scriptures we are clearly informed of the offices which he executes; of his unparalleled con-

---

53. Ibid., pp. 143, 223, 384, 385-92, 397, 401, 457.
54. Ibid., p. 146.
55. *The Philadelphia Confession of Faith with Catechism* (Sterling, Va.: Grace Abounding Ministries, n.d.), p. 15.

descension and glorious exaltation, his approbation with the Father; and of his grace, love, merits, titles, and benefits.[56]

Morgan also affirmed the infallibility of Scripture in 1780, when he presented the circular letter on "The Fall of Man." That the historicity of the accounts of the creation and Fall were accepted is obvious.

> Such is the excellency and usefulness of divine revelation contained in that sadly neglected book, the Bible, that it affords us an infallible certainty respecting things past, present, and to come, which do so nearly concern us to know; among other articles, man's creation, who was made upright, righteous and holy, after the likeness, or image of God, happy in the favor of God, and communion with him, endued with power to fulfill the law, given him for the rule of his obedience to his Creator, in that perfect state.
>
> Moreover, by the same word of truth, we are assured of the sorrowful change which befell our first parents by their acting contrary to the command of God. . . .[57]

The witness of the Spirit was tied to the witness of Scripture to itself. The Spirit, though working in a personal objective way, did not perform His work of illumination apart from the actual words of Scripture. The Philadelphia Association had dealt with that idea in 1761, when it received a query from Oyster Bay.

> Whether it be entirely proper to call the scriptures the rule and the Spirit the guide?
>
> Resolved: The Holy Scriptures we profess to be our full, sufficient, and only rule of faith and obedience, and caution all to beware of every impulse, revelation, or any other imagination whatever, inconsistent with, or contrary to, the holy Scriptures, under the pretence of being guided by the Spirit. The word of the Holy Spirit, illuminates the understanding to know the mind of God, contained in the Scriptures, and may properly be called a guide.[58]

56. Gillette, pp. 170-71.
57. Ibid.
58. Gillette, p. 82.

In short, the churches of the Philadelphia Association and other associations in fellowship with them accepted the infallibility of Scripture. Scripture to them was an unerring volume for it was given by inspiration of the unerring God. Though they recognized that its purpose was salvific and theological, they never separated the historical from the theological; they perceived that the latter was dependent on the former.

Isaac Backus (1724-1806), in regular communication with the Philadelphia Association, shared their view of Scripture. He also saw himself in direct conformity to the view expressed earlier by Williams, Clarke, and the Boston Baptists. In his invaluable work *A History of New England*, Clarke recorded the theological position of those mentioned above and saw himself in accord with them.[59]

In 1782 Backus decided to answer the universalist heresy propounded by Elhanan Winchester. The fact that no one had ventured an answer to Mr. Winchester prompted Backus to "offer [his] mite in the affair; hoping that it may encourage and excite others to step forward in the cause of truth to better purpose."[60]

Backus characterized his antagonist's argument as "generally from the less *against* the greater"; e.g., "if I desire the salvation of all then God would be bad if he did not. But God is not bad. So he desires and will effect the salvation of all."[61] That was a lively specimen of mystic philosophy, according to Backus!

However, according to Backus, the scriptural method is from the lesser to the greater—a method even approved by the Savior. After demonstrating that assertion biblically, at least to his own satisfaction, Backus wrote, "What madness must it then be in fallen men, to set up reason against the word of God!"[62] The point is not whether one approves or disapproves of Backus's analysis of logical method, but that he sought to govern logic by Scripture.

Purposeful misinterpretation of Scripture, as well as erroneous philosophical method, was another of Winchester's faults that Backus pointed out. Such manipulation of truth was contemptible

59. Backus, *History*, 1:205-208, 298.
60. Isaac Backus, *The Doctrine of Universal Salvation Examined and Refuted* (Providence: John Carter, 1782), p. 3.
61. Ibid., p. 27.
62. Ibid., p. 29.

practice. According to Backus, "It is a mean piece of dishonesty for any to steal a finer dress than this for human wisdom, from the divine oracles, and then to use the same against the infallible inspiration of the book they took it from."[63]

Backus used the inerrancy of Scripture as a means to combat Winchester's implication that God would not be good if anyone were condemned eternally. The inerrancy of Scripture is simply reflective of the consistency, truthfulness, and goodness of the God whose word it is. Deeper commitment to its unerring nature brings deeper harmony and security to the believer and fixes in his mind the absolute goodness and justice of God, even when manifest in the eternal torment of the wicked.

> As the powers of thinking and choice are essential to all immortal spirits, they must necessarily define the knowledge and enjoyment of the best good; and as all finite knowledge is bounded by certain limits, they would ever be liable to err, if they had not some sufficient guard which we can conceive of, is to have the infinite excellency of all God's perfections displayed before us in the clearest light, so as fully to demonstrate, that every desirable good is to be enjoyed in the way of obedience; and that disobedience to him is infinitely hateful and dreadful. The more deeply these ideas are fixed, and the stronger the persuasion is that he cannot err and that all his requirements are holy, just and good, the more earnest will be the desire to know and do his will continually. As I take it, all the sacred volume, and every event that has ever happened in the universe, have been ordered so by infinite wisdom, as forever to fix these ideas in every believing mind, and the endless torments of the wicked answer the same end.[64]

So the "sacred volume" is the "sufficient guard" to keep us from error in our conception of God and His activity. The Bible convinces the believing man that the God of infinite excellence does not err in His disposal of all His creatures. Nor does He err in communicating to man His purposes. Later, Backus reinforced his dependence on and affirmation of the inerrancy of Scripture as he

63. Ibid., p. 31.
64. Ibid.

appealed to the unerring nature of Scripture to expose the error of Winchester.

> In a word, if anyone of the human race is finally lost, the scheme we oppose must be false. And he who cannot err says of one of them, "good were it for that man if he had never been born".... But as certain as the Bible is true, all things do work together for the good of all the objects of God's love.[65]

John Leland (1754-1841), one of the leading champions of religious liberty during and immediately following the revolutionary period, made no break with the view of Scripture affirmed by eighteenth-century Baptists. Reflecting the consensus of Baptists around him, he carried that view into the nineteenth century.

In 1810 Leland published *A Budget of Scraps*. That unusual publication included a short article on the Bible. After relating several interesting facts about the Bible, such as the number of chapters and verses in it and the number of times certain words are found, Leland closed with an affirmation of his conviction that the Bible meets the need for a written revelation from God.

> Oral revelation was first. In this, God revealed His will unto men; but as letters were not in use, men had no way of preserving those revelations, but by their memories; these records were so treacherous, that the revelations were greatly mutilated and perverted. . . .
> Whether the use of letters was taught at once, or whether the science was gradual, the result is equally amazing; that with twenty-two [sic], all the thoughts of the human heart can be expressed. After letters came in use, the Almighty directed the hands of men to write down those revelations of his will, which he made known unto them; and such writings are called written revelations. These writings, collected together in one book, form the Bible, or Holy Scriptures.[66]

In 1793 Leland presented a circular letter at the Shaftsbury Association in Vermont in which he discussed the divine inspira-

65. Ibid., p. 38.
66. John Leland, *The Writings of John Leland*, ed. L. F. Green (New York: Arno Press and the New York Times, 1969), p. 338.

tion of the Bible. The letter sought to demonstrate to the "deists and infidels" that the Bible was certainly the inspired Word of God. The Bible is the "only confession of faith that [Baptists] dare adopt," according to Leland, and served as the final umpire in any controversy. Leland thought it ironical that Baptists, who "facilitate ourselves with this infallible guide," found themselves attacked by deists and infidels who delighted in declaring what is not true, but never told what was true. Their negative approach was part of Leland's evidence that their views were false, for "it can hardly be credited, that the parent of the universe should leave his offspring in this dreary world to make their way to eternity without some guide—some sure word of prophecy, to direct their course."[67]

Leland, obviously following the lead of Baptists like Benjamin Keach, John Gill, and Andrew Fuller, produced twelve proofs that the Bible is the guide that man needs, "a revelation of God's will, written by men divinely inspired."[68] The arguments Leland presented include the antiquity of the writings and the events they record, the honesty of the penmen, the unity of thought within the canonical Scripture and content of the various writers, the fulfillment of prophecy, the sublimity of style, the effects on the hearts of those who read and believe, the sufferings of those who have believed the Bible to be a revelation from God, the care God manifested in keeping the writings in existence, the claims of the biblical writers to be writing by divine inspiration, the reflection of the transcendent honor on the character of God and its perfect system of morality, the judgments that have been inflicted on those who have sought to destroy the writings, and the miracles that were performed in verification of the message of the apostles.

Leland essentially affirmed the inerrancy of Scripture as he discussed the unity of the Bible's teaching. Problems with the Scripture arise from two sources: our own ignorance and the numerous transcriptions through which the Bible has gone. He affirmed that some allowance should be made for language differences, customs of the people, and various peculiarities of writing style.

67. Ibid, p. 196.
68. Ibid.

Many of the apparent mistakes that are in the sacred volume, no doubt, are made by our own ignorance, but if there are a few of them that have been occasioned by a multitude of transcriptions, and other causes, yet they only respect numbers and places, and in no wise affect our faith and practice.[69]

Following Leland, Baptist life in the nineteenth century continued to manifest the same deep trust in the absolute truthfulness of all the Scripture. Two men who exemplified that during the middle of that century were Francis Wayland in the north and John L. Dagg in the south. Wayland's treatment of the doctrine of inspiration was couched in the practical application of Scripture to questions of the time. In his *The Elements of Moral Science*, Wayland wrote, "A system of ethics will be true, just in proportion as it develops"[70] the meaning of the sacred Scriptures. Wayland dealt creatively with the subject of slavery as it confronted America during those days, and was instrumental in producing an ironic defense of the necessity for manumission.

Wayland also applied his understanding of Scripture to Baptist preaching during the nineteenth century. In a book called *Notes on Principles and Practices of Baptist Churches*, Wayland addressed the question "Why take a text in preaching?"

It proceeds upon the supposition that the Bible is the word of the living God; the only manifestation that has been made to us of the will of our Creator and our Judge, the only record of what he has done for our salvation; the only volume on whose pages are inscribed the conditions on which we may escape eternal wrath, and enter into the rest which remaineth for the people of God. It is this truth alone which God has promised to accompany with that energy of Holy Spirit, without which we know that no soul is ever made wise unto salvation.[71]

In his concern for doctrinal preaching, Wayland emphasized the

69. Ibid., p. 197.
70. Francis Wayland, *The Elements of Moral Science* (London: The Religious Tract Society, 1835), Preface.
71. Francis Wayland, *Notes on the Principles and Practices of Baptist Churches* (New York: Sheldon, Blakeman and Co., 1857), pp. 297-98.

necessity of proving doctrine from the text of Scripture. The reality of divine revelation essentially settled the question of the full truthfulness of Scripture for him.

> The proof of any truth of revelation must be essentially revelation itself. God has not made a revelation of that which has already been made by natural religion. The highest authority for our belief of any truth, is that God said it. . . . There seemed to me a growing disposition to omit the proof of a revealed truth from revelation, an attempt to prove from every other source than the Bible. Why should this be? The Bible be true, why should we ignore its evidence? Do we not thus practically lead men to the conclusion that there is a higher authority than the word of God, by which it is to be judged, and to which its teachings are to be subjected?[72]

John L. Dagg (1794-1884) was a contemporary and friend of Francis Wayland. During his lifetime Dagg was an outstanding pastor, school administrator, professor, and theologian. In addition, he wrote books that influenced the formative years of the Southern Baptist Convention. Two of his works relate directly to the issue of the infallibility of Scripture. In 1853 he wrote a pamphlet, "The Origin and Authority of the Bible."[73] The basic tenets of that pamphlet were expanded into a work called *The Evidences of Christianity*, published in 1869. Both of those works defended the Bible from the standpoint of miracles, fulfilled prophecy, its effect on the lives of those who believe it, and its internal consistency. Dagg was thoroughly convinced that a harmonization of apparent discrepancies in the Scripture was entirely valid for the Christian apologist. The correlation of those discrepancies Dagg called "undesigned coincidences." According to Dagg, they represented important evidence for the full trustworthiness of Scripture.

> A candid mind, after contemplating the overpowering evidences of Christianity, would decide that the alleged disagreements of the evangelists cannot furnish a valid objection to the divine origin of

72. Ibid., pp. 285-86.
73. John L. Dagg, *The Origin and Authority of the Bible* (Charleston: Southern Baptist Publication Society. Richmond: Virginia Baptist Sunday School and Publication Society, 1853).

the religion, even if the apparent disagreements could not be harmonized. But patient investigation converts these apparent inconsistencies into undesigned coincidences, and finds, in the very ground of infidel cavils, a firm foundation for Christian faith.[74]

Dagg strongly affirmed the inerrancy of Scripture. Discussing the relationship of the Spirit's activity in sanctification to His activity in inspiration, Dagg affirmed that though one is never complete in this life, the other was complete and without error at its first instance. Though sanctification was for the benefit of one person and was not intended to be complete until the return of Christ, inspiration was for the benefit of the entire church in understanding the truth of God and should be secured without error from its beginning.

> It is a fundamental error in this objection, that it contemplates inspiration as designed merely for the benefit of the inspired; whereas it is clear that God gave his word to be spoken and written by prophets and apostles for the instruction and benefit of other men, who are required to see that, not as the word of man, but as in truth the word of God, attested by miracles. Positively, it is divine truth; negatively, it is not human error.[75]

Dagg saw the relationship between the Old and New Testaments as an evidence of inerrancy. He claimed that the New Testament obviously was superior in both clarity and finality to the dispensation of the Old Testament. Therefore, the New Testament writings must be as truthful as those of the Old Testament, which Christ and the apostles accepted as infallible. Dagg contended, "But whatever may have been the superiority of the New Testament revelation at its outset, it could not have equalled that of the Old Testament in permanent advantage, if it had not been committed to writing without human error."[76] Thus, according to Dagg, the inerrancy of Scripture is a necessary affirmation.

Such a conviction was continued in Southern Baptist life

74. John L. Dagg, *The Evidences of Christianity* (Macon, Ga.: J. W. Burke, 1869), p. 230.
75. Ibid., p. 224.
76. Ibid., p. 216.

through the founders and first faculty of Southern Baptist Theological Seminary. J. P. Boyce, John A. Broadus, and Basil Manly, Jr., all stated without equivocation their confidence in the inerrancy of Scripture.

In his *Abstract of Systematic Theology*, Boyce, in his discussion of special revelation, stated certain minimal characteristics one should assume to be present. He wrote, "It must be secured from all possibility of error, so that its teachings may be relied on with equal, if not greater, confidence in those that reason." He further affirmed that special revelation must "come with authority, claiming and proving its claim to be the word of God."[77] Basil Manly, Jr., shared that view. Though stated in several places, his view was most clearly set forth in a book called *The Bible Doctrine of Inspiration*. Speaking of its composition as being both human and divine, though not mitigating the authority of Scripture, Manly summed up his argument succinctly.

> The Bible is truly the Word of God, having both infallible truth and divine authority in all that it affirms or enjoins.
> The Bible is truly the production of men. It is marked by all the evidences of human authorship as clearly and certainly as any other book that was ever written by men.
> This two fold authorship extends to every part of Scripture, and to the language as well as to the general ideas expressed.
> Or it may be summed up in one single statement: the whole Bible is truly God's word written by men.[78]

Manly discussed biblical inspiration and human frailty as they related to the higher criticism of the late nineteenth century and from the standpoint of the Bible's witness to its own inspiration. In his "presumptive argument" Manly assured his readers that regarding Scripture, they should naturally expect that God would "control, protect from error, authorize its utterance."[79] He also answered objections to the doctrine of plenary inspiration and had a section in which he sought to show the harmony of passages in

77. James P. Boyce, *Abstract of Systematic Theology* (Philadelphia: American Baptist Publication Society, 1887), p. 48.
78. Ibid, p. 90.
79. Ibid., p. 94.

which there are alleged discrepancies or mistakes. Throughout the whole work, one is convinced that Manly never moved from his firm conviction that God protected the writers of Scripture from error.

John Broadus, a member of that same faculty, shared the view of Boyce and Manly. In a catechism published in 1891 Broadus asked the student, "Does the Bible contain any errors?" The answer he gave: "The Bible records some things said by uninspired men that were not true; but it is true and instructive that these men said them."[80]

In a section called "advanced questions" Broadus asked, "Did the inspired writers receive everything by direct revelation?" The answer: "The inspired writers learned many things by observation or inquiry, but they were preserved by the Holy Spirit from error, whether in learning or in writing these things."[81]

Other questions that Broadus constructed show equally his commitment to full biblical authority.

> What if inspired writers sometimes appear to disagree in their statements? Most cases of apparent disagreement in the inspired writings have been explained, and we may be sure that all could be explained if we had fuller information.
>
> Is this also true when the Bible seems to be in conflict with history or science? Yes, some cases of apparent conflict with history or science have been explained quite recently that were long hard to understand.
>
> Has it been proven that the inspired writers stated anything as true that was not true? No; there is no proof that the inspired writers made any mistake of any kind.[82]

CONCLUSION

On the basis of the evidence we have seen, it is easy to see that Baptists in both England and America entertained no doubts concerning the full inspiration and inerrancy of the Scripture until

80. John A. Broadus, *A Catechism of Bible Teaching* (Philadelphia: American Baptist Publication Society, 1892).
81. Ibid.
82. Ibid.

the late nineteenth century. However, in 1879 that consensus began to crumble. The Toy controversy at Southern Seminary was merely the first of several controversies over the nature of Scripture within Southern Baptist life. It also heralded struggles that were to come within American Baptist life. Crawford H. Toy, who, when he came to teach at Southern Seminary, shared the view of Scripture expounded by Broadus, Boyce, and Manly, gradually moved away from that affirmation because of the influence of the German school of higher criticism. As Toy himself wrote, his divergence from the Baptist view "gradually increased in connection with my studies, from year to year, until it has become perceptible to myself and others."[83] That difference led to his resignation in 1879, which was sadly but dutifully accepted by J. P. Boyce and the trustees of Southern Seminary.

English Baptist life saw the same shattering of a consensus in the Downgrade Controversy, centered on several basic ideas Charles Spurgeon saw as the symptoms of a degradation of theology in the rejection of the central doctrines of Christianity.

A new religion has been initiated, which is no more Christianity than chalk is cheese; and this religion, being destitute of moral honesty, palms itself off as the old faith with slight improvement, and on this plea usurps pulpits which were erected for Gospel preaching. The Atonement is scouted, the inspiration of Scripture is derided, the Holy Spirit is degraded into an influence, the punishment of sin is turned into fiction, and the resurrection into a myth, and yet these enemies of our faith expect us to call them brethren, and maintain a confederacy with them![84]

The Toy controversy resulted in the dismissal of the one who was divergent, but the Downgrade Controversy resulted in the censure of the man who sought to maintain the former conservative position of Baptists.

Both of those controversies are significant for two reasons. They highlight the fact that in the nineteenth century an actual change

83. *The Baptist Courier* (Greenville, S.C., 27 Nov. 1879).
84. C. H. Spurgeon, *The Sword and the Trowel*, ed. C. H. Spurgeon (London: Passmore & Alabaster, 1887), p. 397.

in the view of Scripture occurred. No one familiar with Baptist materials could maintain seriously and consistently that either the Downgraders in England or Toy in America were carrying forth the historic Baptist view of Scripture. Nor could one seriously contend that Spurgeon, Boyce, and Broadus were not the true heirs of the continuing Baptist witness to the Bible.

Second, in both of those controversies the epistemological issue was seen clearly and stated succinctly. The basic import of that has neither been answered by its opponents nor improved on by its adherents. Broadus stated it this way.

> If the Darwinian theory of the origin of man has been accepted, then it becomes easy to conclude that the first chapter of Genesis is by no means true history. From this starting-point, and pressed by a desire to reconstruct the history on evolutionary principles, one might easily persuade himself that in numerous other cases of apparent conflict between Old Testament statements and the accredited results of various sciences the conflict is real, and the Old Testament account is incorrect. He [Toy] thought strange of the prediction made in conversation that within twenty years he would utterly discard all belief in the supernatural as an element of Scripture,—a prediction founded upon knowledge of his logical consistency and boldness, and already in a much shorter time fulfilled, to judge from his latest works. Some of us are persuaded that if any man adopts the evolutionary reconstruction of Old Testament history and literature, and does not reach a like attitude as regards the supernatural, it is simply because he is prevented, by temperament or environment, from carrying things to their logical results.[85]

Spurgeon's *Sword and Trowel* analyzed the situation in the following way.

> In the case of every errant course there is always a first wrong step. What is the first step astray? Is it doubting this doctrine, or questioning that sentiment, or being skeptical as to the other article of orthodox belief? We think not. The first step astray is a want of

85. John A. Broadus, *Memoir of James Petigru Boyce* (New York: A. C. Armstrong & Son, 1893), pp. 260-63.

adequate faith in the divine inspiration of the sacred Scriptures. This fact is apparent: that where ministers and Christian churches have held fast to the truth that the Holy Scriptures have been given by God as an authoritative and infallible rule of faith and practice, they have never wandered very seriously out of the right way. But when, on the other hand, reason has been exalted above revelation, and made the exponent of revelation, all kinds of errors and mischiefs have been the result.[86]

The continued divergence in Baptist life manifests itself in various shades and hues. However, those who adhere to a limited infallibility only cannot consistently maintain Baptists as their forefathers, but must find themselves foreshadowed in deism, Socinianism, Toy, and the Downgraders. Advocates of inerrancy may rejoice in a long list of faithful men who accounted every opinion that is "repugnant to Scripture exceeding erroneous and pernicious."[87]

86. C. H. Spurgeon, "The Down Grade," in *The Sword and the Trowel*, April 1887, p. 170.
87. Gillette, p. 58.

11

Princeton and Inerrancy: The Nineteenth-Century Philosophical Background of Contemporary Concerns

D. Clair Davis

THE SIGNIFICANCE OF THE STUDY

A consideration of the view of biblical inspiration and inerrancy presented in the Presbyterian institutions of Princeton University (originally the College of New Jersey) and Princeton Theological Seminary is of the greatest importance for understanding the present evangelical position on Scripture and the great debate now revolving about it. That is immediately obvious because of the enormous influence Princeton theologians, particularly Charles Hodge and Benjamin B. Warfield, had in formulating and developing the evangelical position—an influence that reached far beyond denominational or regional concerns. Indeed, to this day Warfield's *Inspiration and Authority of the Bible* serves throughout

D. CLAIR DAVIS, B.A., M.A., Wheaton College, B.D., Westminster Theological Seminary, further study at Georg-August Universität, is professor of church history at Westminster Theological Seminary in Philadelphia. At Westminster Seminary, he has served as editor of the *Westminster Theological Journal* and as chairman of the faculty. He is also a member of the Evangelical Theological Society and the American Society of Church History and is associate pastor of New Life Presbyterian Church in Jenkentown, Pennsylvania.

evangelical academia as the starting point for instruction in that area.

Precisely because of the prominence of the Princeton influence, it is especially important that close attention be given to its nature. Has the position of Hodge and Warfield unduly colored the Princeton and American evangelical views of the Bible? Specifically, have their views weakened the whole evangelical thrust of the approach to Scripture by introducing a philosophical base that, if not opposed to Christianity, at least does not express its Christian character in the most useful manner?

When the question is put that way, it is easy to see its close relationship to the even greater historical question of our day that relates to biblical inspiration, that of the connection between Reformation theology and seventeenth-century Protestant orthodoxy. Did orthodox Scholasticism betray the great insights of the Reformation? Has preoccupation with the Bible obscured God's self-revelation in Jesus Christ? The answers to those questions are beyond the scope of this discussion. Evangelicals have already struggled with them and no doubt will continue to do so. There is some overlap between those questions and the topic of this chapter, however, because of the influence the theology of the seventeenth-century Swiss theologian Francis Turretin and the creed largely fathered by him, the *Formula Helvetic Consensus* (1675), had on Princeton.[1]

Turretin's theology was directed largely against that of the French Reformed academy at Saumur, usually known as Amyraldianism. That academy had a dual emphasis as it attempted to interpret orthodox Calvinism in a more congenial fashion. First, it attempted to explain the origin of saving faith not just in terms of its ultimate source, the grace of God, but also in terms of human, psychological explanations of why some believe and others do not. Second, and for our purpose more significant, the Amyraldians tried to work on the text of the Old Testament, especially by making use of the ancient translations and by seeking to explore the possibility of utilizing different vowels between the inspired Hebrew consonants (a process called "repointing").

---

1. This creed is most easily accessible in A. A. Hodge, *Outlines of Theology* (many editions); here also Hodge's own judgment about the pivotal significance of that creed for Princeton may be found.

Turretin and his new creed rejected both of those emphases, believing that the attempts at psychologizing both supernatural conversion and supernatural inspiration in reality undermined both. The *Consensus* specifically rejected all attempts to amend the inspired Hebrew text from the translations or from conjectured repointing as an attack on the supernatural care and preservation God had given the Bible, and affirmed the inspiration of the (unwritten) vowels or their "power." It is not overstating the case to say that in 1675 Turretin was concerned that over-preoccupation with the mode of inspiration (the phenomena) might swallow up the reality of the fact of inspiration (the doctrine).

One of the distinguishing features of Princeton theology was its enthusiasm for the theology of Francis Turretin. Before Charles Hodge produced his own *Systematic Theology*, instruction at Princeton was based on Turretin's Latin *Institutes*, and the *Consensus* was regarded as the most "scientific and precise" of all the Reformed creeds. Though history (church history included) does not repeat itself that much, it is striking to notice how the apologetic concerns of Princeton, directed at the New England psychologizing of faith and its introduction of German rationalistic biblical criticism, could make so much use of Turretin's response to similar issues.

In the light of those facts, it is instructive to note Warfield's early attention to textual criticism. Though some of the problems associated with Princeton apologetics may have to be traced to undue trust in the scientific method, what other canons for textual criticism are available to the evangelical scholar than the scientific ones and their probabalistic conclusions? Certainly, Warfield knew how to coordinate textual issues with the issue of doctrinal inspiration.[2]

SCOTTISH COMMON SENSE REALISM

A much more modern influence on Princeton University and Seminary was that of the Scottish philosophy of common sense. Though it has its share of distinctive features, that viewpoint should also be seen

2. Any discussion of the value of an inerrant text that is now unavailable (the original) will have to take into account Warfield's labors in textual criticism and his judgment that no important doctrine was in doubt and that all significant variants together would constitute only half a page of the New Testament.

as one of the many reactions against deism and rationalism, that is, as an expression of romanticism. Eighteenth-century rationalism, in its desire to arrive at fixed, certain truth, not subject at all to the mutability of human experience, decided to follow the most unchanging example of all, mathematics. It was taken for granted that the certain propositions of that way of thinking must correspond to reality, and that by recognizing the limitations and deceptiveness of nonmathematical thinking (and, consequently, deliberately avoiding them) one could attain to truly reliable knowledge. Romanticism protested that there is more to life than mathematics; in particular, the mathematical or scientific understanding of causality is totally inadequate to express or account for the realities of art and emotion, of ethics and religion, and especially of history.

By the nature of the case, romanticism could not be proved either, if what was meant was mathematical proof, for the whole point of the new movement was that mathematical rationalism was inadequate or even irrelevant to the many dimensions of life. Romantics pointed out that mathematics itself was based on axioms that it regarded as unproveable, self-evident truths. It was therefore just as legitimate for the proponents of morality (Kant) and religion (Schleiermacher) to rely on their own necessary but unproveable axioms as it had been for the rationalists. But when the axioms of one discipline were apparently contradictory to those of another, when it became increasingly apparent that the approach to one dimension of reality was radically different from that to another, how was skepticism to be avoided? Was not the conclusion that there were many truths equivalent to saying that there really were no real truths at all but only extremely partial, fragmentary insights? It is particularly that difficulty that the new Scottish philosophy attempted to resolve.[3]

The philosophy of common sense made into a philosophical system what all had tacitly recognized in passing: that as a matter of fact all men, including the most sophisticated philosophers, do conduct their lives on the assumption that they are sure of their own previous existence, that other humans besides themselves

---

3. Probably the best short treatment is that of S. A. Grave, *The Scottish Philosophy of Common Sense* (Oxford: Clarendon, 1960). For a good introduction of its relation to Princeton, see George M. Marsden, *Fundamentalism and American Culture* (New York: Oxford U. Press, 1980), pp. 110-16.

really exist, that there are laws of cause and effect, and so forth. Within the ordinary practice of all men, then, is a unifying principle, in spite of the very disparate and conflicting perspectives of different theoretical approaches. Put positively, common sense united what was otherwise hopelessly torn apart; put negatively, it was eclectic, and naively and uncritically so at that.

That philosophical school continued the general romantic idea that many types of experiences represent reality. It was not other specialized areas of life, such as poetry, concerning which that was said but the general assumptions (hence *common*) under which all men operate. Furthermore, the common sense school was not content with a type of approach to science that would have made it harmless by making it relative; it rejected such Kantian notions (more properly, those of the Scot David Hume, whose skepticism concerning scientific "laws" had first aroused Kant) and continued to affirm the validity of science on the basis of the common practice of men in presupposing the truthfulness of memory, causation, and the like. Though everyone, Hume included, granted that no one could live in ordinary matters on the basis of skeptical assumptions, the common sense school could see no point in a technical philosophy that had no relation to ordinary living. As we shall see, there is a good deal of affinity between that point of view and American pragmatism.

Common sense soon became the dominant viewpoint throughout America in the last century, becoming the foundation for virtually every discipline, especially on the preparatory level. As a philosophy of education, it served admirably to unite disciplines that elsewhere were becoming so specialized and antithetical or irrelevant to each other that integrated education was practically impossible. It is easy to see why Princeton could link the advance of Christian principles with the popularity of common sense.

It is precisely the eclectic nature of the common sense approach that raises the question of its value as a Christian viewpoint. Is not the modern scientific universe, with its careful exclusion of outside interference into its explanations, a decidedly anti-Christian perspective? Does not the admission that knowledge is only probable undermine gospel certainty? Is it not hopelessly naive and misleading to present the Christian faith as having anything at all in common with disciplines that function in ways that make clear their dependence on human abilities and not on supernatural revelation? Those are the sort of concerns that students of the nineteenth century have expressed. Those questions have come not just from the opponents of the evangelical view of Scripture but also from many of its supporters, especially at the institution that considers itself to be the evangelical continuation of old Princeton, Westminster Theological Seminary. There, scholars such as Cornelius Van Til and Edward J. Young have given enthusiastic support to Princeton's view of Scripture, though rejecting its philosophical, apologetic base in common sense. Van Til has even characterized the Princeton apologetic as Arminian!

Perhaps a preliminary answer to the questions in the previous paragraph can be given. It seems that the philosophy of common sense and the men at Princeton contrasted the partial, still developing character of scientific knowledge with the character of biblical revelation. Princeton was not comparing a full-blown system of modern scientific thought with that of Christianity. Rather, it was taking seriously science's claim of tentativeness, assuming that uninterpreted, discrete conclusions could easily fit into the Christian faith and that Christianity's foundational character could then give meaning to scientific conclusions. In Warfield's hands the incomplete character of science was utilized to indicate that by the nature of the case it could never be sufficiently exhaustive in its conclusions to demonstrate a real contradiction between science and the Bible. Perhaps it was becoming increasingly clear that harmonization of modern thought with Christianity was not as easy as had been expected, but the continued attempt to accomplish it was not rejected out of hand.

That sketch of the common sense philosophy provides a framework for appreciating the otherwise confusing methodology of Princeton. John Witherspoon, the president of Princeton University and the original importer of the Scottish philosophy, wrote in the new *Presbyterian Form of Government* that the discipline of the church depended on "enlightened public opinion." Charles Hodge routinely added to the biblical proof of almost any doctrine the secondary evidence of the common agreement of human experience. Warfield asserted in his *Counterfeit Miracles* that, though in the first centuries of the church a supernatural, miraculous witness to Christianity was necessary, that was no longer the case since the faith had been so widely accepted.

Such optimism, focusing on the use of the scientific method, was not restricted to nineteenth-century common sense and Princeton. Of course, there had been a close alliance between Calvinism and science almost as far back as the Reformation. That was partly due to the banning of those who were Reformed from the traditional universities in England, Germany, and France. That resulted in an affinity on the part of the Reformed for nonuniversity higher education, to the founding of their own academies, and hence to the adoption of curricula that led to other than the traditional professions (that were in a large measure forbidden to them). In short, it was easy for Christians outside the cultural establishment to opt for turning to a new kind of scientific establishment. No doubt the tremendous impact of the Calvinist philosopher of education Petrus Ramus had a great deal to do with that alliance. Ramus was convinced that simplified logic, one that required continual rechecking of the empirical data with which one was dealing, would prevent the absurdities of medieval thought. Theologically, that meant that sinful self-deception was much less likely if one were forced to confront the data of God's creation and therefore prevented from spinning ethereal theories that were not connected with reality.

The affinity of that line of thought with the Protestant approach to the Bible is obvious. Protestantism was convinced that Scripture was clear and self-interpreting. If medieval tradition was removed from standing between the reader and the Bible, the gospel would come through in all of its power. It was only natural for Protestants to look on the revelation of God in creation in a similar way. Concentration on the facts as they stood, without a prior commitment to any conclusions whatever, was bound to produce the same certain results in science as in Bible study. The philosophy of common sense assisted in reaffirming that viewpoint, but in doing so it was hardly innovative or distinctively Princetonian.

OVERLY PRECISE INTERPRETATION?

Controversial today is the question of whether that "scientific" approach led to an overemphasis on precision in exegesis, a superimposing on the Bible of an interest in the kind of technical accuracy in which the Scripture itself has no interest. Some regard the doctrine of inerrancy as just such a misconception of the nature of Scripture.

No doubt there were areas of exegesis where our fathers found more in the Bible than was really there. But was that limited to Princeton and her followers? It would not be too difficult to show where overly technical social exegesis by those who want nothing to do with inerrancy or with Princeton has found more than was there. Certainly, that is a tendency as one considers recent attempts to discover biblical endorsement for the ordination of women elders. Merely indicating that others are guilty of the same error that Princeton and contemporary inerrancy advocates are accused of is not sufficient, though. The question is, Did the proponents of inerrancy commit that fallacy?

It is difficult to find any hard evidence. Certainly, the Princeton Old Testament department was very reluctant to draw conclusions from the Bible concerning the age of the earth or of man, for example. Armstrong, in New Testament, was one of the first American evangelicals to assert that the order of events in the gospels was just as likely to be topical as chronological. Machen's reluctance to write on evolution because he was not an authority is also a case in point. Indeed, Warfield's demand that anyone who asserts that there is an error in the Bible must prove conclusively that what the Bible teaches contradicts science goes far to speak against a naive, technical approach to the Scriptures. It is difficult to tell who was the first to define inspiration in terms of "what the Bible *intends* to teach," but that became part of the stock-in-trade of the Princeton statement of the doctrine.

DISPENSATIONALISM

A great deal of attention has been given to possible links between Princeton inerrancy and another great evangelical phenomenon of the last century, dispensationalism.[4] Certainly, J. N.

4. The alleged link between Princeton and dispensationalist literalism is advanced by Ernest R. Sandeen, *The Roots of Fundamentalism* (Chicago: U. of Chicago Press, 1970), pp. 103-31. Sandeen concedes the obvious differences but still manages to see a link, against all the real evidence.

Darby, the English founder of the movement, identified with American Calvinism of the Princeton variety. Certainly, C. I. Scofield (the editor of the *Scofield Bible*) was a Presbyterian minister, and probably a majority of his associate editors were Reformed in denomination. Certainly, when the issue was one's relationship to the evangelical view of the inspiration and inerrancy of Scripture, Princeton and dispensationalism made common cause in opposing those who would attack inerrancy. But in spite of all that, it has to be made clear that Princeton theology was predominantly postmillennarian or amillennarian and clearly opposed to the central emphases of the new movement. Even though dispensationalism insists that it is not merely an eschatological emphasis but a complete theological system, Princeton saw no substantive difference between itself and dispensationalism on inspiration and inerrancy and therefore could identify with it.

That is to say that Presbyterian evangelicalism of that day (fundamentalism) took its stand on a minimal doctrinal base that was not distinctively dispensational or antidispensational but was rooted in the basic supernatural character of evangelical Christianity. That supernaturalism, as expressed in the doctrine of Scripture, did not imply a commitment to the dispensational sort of literalness. That issue has become so widely discussed that some background study should be useful. First of all, it should be noted that in the whole history of biblical interpretation, *literalism* has been associated not with what Protestantism has come to call the grammatical-historical approach to interpretation, but with the allegorical approach. Historically, one either emphasized the meaning of the text in terms of ordinary canons of interpretation—in which case shifts of wording are not essential—or he approached the text as a code to be solved, as a writing whose meaning transcends ordinary usage; and he therefore concentrated his attention on the details of the text and how they differed from each other. Without prejudice to dispensationalism, it is striking how great an interest it displays in the distinction between *Kingdom of Heaven* and *Kingdom of God*, for example, to say nothing of its interest in biblical numerology. Again, Princeton understood herself as standing in the Reformed, antiallegorical tradition and so was not that interested in technical detail.

Nevertheless, there is a sense in which Princeton agreed with dispensationalism in being opposed to a "spiritualizing" of Scripture. It appears that *spiritual* has always been ambiguous. Does it refer to the new age of the Holy Spirit and therefore to seeing the key to the understanding of the Old Testament in the New Testament interpretation of the Old, or does it refer to the priority that the spiritual aspect of man has over the physical and material aspects? The latter understanding of that foundational distinction is as old as Gnosticism; it was picked up by the Anabaptist understanding of the presence of Christ in the Lord's Supper and, more directly related to this study, by nineteenth-century liberalism. Certainly, if spiritualizing meant the right of the autonomous human spirit to superimpose its own agenda on Scripture, then of course empiricist common sense and all who followed it, both Princeton and dispensationalist, were vigorously opposed and, as all evangelicals should be, united on the crucial importance of a literal approach to the Bible. For the men at Princeton, interpretation could be and was to be both spiritual and literal, i.e., based on a literal understanding of how the fulfillment of the new spiritual age is the key to the interpretation of the Old Testament.

Doubtless, further work should be done to discover the philosophical roots of dispensationalism itself, as has been done by so many for Princeton. It is likely, however, that much of the same motivation lay behind dispensationalism: the desire to clarify the historical character of the Christian faith and to rescue understanding of the Scripture from the clutches of the liberal spirit. Furthermore, whatever one thinks of dispensationalist ecclesiology and eschatology, it is clear that the Princeton appraisal of its thoroughly evangelical view of Scripture is completely correct. Still, in the final analysis, it leads only to confusion to attempt to see any essential continuity between common sense Princeton and subsequent hermeneutical developments within dispensationalism.

GRACE AND FREEDOM

We have already seen that the question of the applicability of the scientific model of cause and effect to the study of the Bible was a basic one. Can such a model be utilized in the aesthetic realm, including that of literature? Is it necessary that the literary world be separated from the scientific so that an emphasis on free, personal response to the revelation of God may be preserved? Kant, Schleiermacher, and the other Romantics had answered with a resounding affirmative. Was the attempt of common sense to see the two realms as related hopelessly naive and anachronistic or even so eclectic as to itself constitute a fundamental denial of the essence of Christianity? Or was there at Princeton something worthy of evangelical emulation even today?

It is plain that at this point the question has gone far beyond the older, more limited aspects of biblical interpretation. It is not merely a matter of following proper grammatical rules to understand sentences in their original meaning. Modern "dimensionalism" has entered the hermeneutical area. As is always the case, when questions become more basic, so also must the answers be. The nature of the entire Christian faith, in particular the relation of God's grace and man's response, is here brought into sharp focus; that is for the best. Certainly, there can and should not be much interest in looking at the nature of God's revelation in the Bible without at the same time being concerned with the content and purpose of that revelation. In traditional Protestant language, the formal principle of the Reformation (the sole authority of the Bible) and the material principle (justification by faith alone) are not independent of each other but are different ways of saying that we live by God's grace alone. To put it another way, without the illuminating work of the Holy Spirit, the inerrant Bible cannot bring men to salvation. So it is not surprising that, after the dark night of rationalism with its reduction of all reality (including God) to a mathematical principle, the nineteenth century would commit itself to asking whether all of reality could be experienced and enjoyed in a unified, integrated way.

As has already been suggested, Princeton had a dual agenda in the last century, an agenda that paralleled to a striking degree that of Francis Turretin and the *Consensus* of 1675. That agenda was to come to grips with both the human side of conversion and the human side of the inspiration of the Bible, primarily in opposition to the theology being developed in New England. The controversies over conversion are better known. Even after the great progress in doctrinal development under the direction of Jonathan Edwards in the Great Awakening, New Englanders were still centering their theological focus on the importance of a proper attitude as a necessary condition for supernatural regeneration. Almost inevitably, those discussions degenerated into such preoccupation with human preconditions for divine grace ("preparation for grace") that God's work of salvation became of little interest in the discussion. Hence, it was not surprising that New England theology collapsed into Unitarianism with amazing rapidity. At the same time Princeton managed to avoid most of that subjectivism and psychologizing with a substantially more balanced perspective on the relationship of God's grace and man's responsibility. Princeton rejected artificial distinctions such as that between natural and moral ability and was content to affirm that man could do nothing to save himself but must rely solely on God's grace; the men at Princeton did not get bogged down in discussions of the way in which the sinner was to do that. In short, Princeton was open to revivalism with its stress on the urgency of repentance and faith.

It is not surprising that a similar controversy transpired between Princeton's high view of biblical inspiration and New England's openness to German rationalistic criticism of the Scriptures. In fact, the reason that Charles Hodge thought further study in Europe was necessary for his preparation was precisely so that he might be equipped to answer that criticism. A really adequate analysis of the Princeton view of inspiration would have to include some treatment of E. W. Hengstenberg, the Old Testament professor at Berlin, whose work was essential not only for Hodge but even more so for the Princeton Old Testament professor J. A. Alexander. As far as that goes, Princeton's openness from the beginning to the consideration of all significant European theology, whether in appreciation or in repudiation, makes it very difficult to rely too much on any monolithic understanding of Princeton, even if it is that of common sense.

In brief, the German and New England stress was on the human aspects of Scripture, including the alleged development of its religious thinking. Or, to put it another way, interest in romantic literary theory, with its emphasis on the feelings of great personalities, had come to overshadow considerations of the factuality of what they reported on. Indeed, emphasis on the human was so great that it gave rise to the concept of myth, the expression of religious feelings in dramatic ɪfashion not to communicate facts but to display the depth of the writer's convictions and the impact those convictions had on his personality.

Princeton's response is instructive. As in the conversion debate, the men at Princeton refused to be sidetracked into paying undue attention to the subjective, psychological mode, the "how" of inspiration, but instead concentrated on the objective doctrine of inspiration as taught by Scripture, Christ, and His apostles. We have already noted that the men at Princeton could be as sensitive as anyone to the necessity of taking account of what the Bible actually taught and not superimposing on it what an apologetic scheme would like to find (e.g., by not demanding of the gospels that they supply precise chronology). One need only think of the motto of Robert Dick Wilson, the Princeton giant in Old Testament, that could have stood for the entire institution: "I have not shirked the difficult questions." Though Princeton did not avoid the difficulties that the diverse, historical, human character of the Bible presented, it refused to permit those elements and the solutions to critical problems to be of normative, definitive value in the formulation of the doctrine of inspiration. It was just as misleading to permit a psychological understanding of the process of inspiration to determine one's thinking about the result as it had been to allow psychological problems of conversion to undermine the Bible's teaching about that topic. It can hardly be overemphasized that Princeton saw no difference in kind between relying on the biblical doctrine of the Bible and trusting the Bible's teaching about anything else.

Further demonstration of that is readily available in Warfield's understanding of the relation between the doctrine of God's providence and that of inspiration. Inspiration is only a special case of providence. All Christians are aware that somehow God is able to accomplish His plans through human decisions. Surely, He is able to bring about an inerrant revelation, though the human authors wrote out of their own convictions, out of great concern or anger, and while they were engaged in religious growth. Warfield urged that one see the Bible from the same perspective that he sees all of the Lord's working in the world.

Obviously, when the implications of that view of the Bible are thought through, one can hardly escape the conclusion that denial of the Bible's doctrine of itself can hardly arise from a sincere analysis of religious genius and the like; it arises from a repudiation, a rejection, a denial of what God has said so clearly in the Scriptures. Hengstenberg had even drawn the conclusion that those who deny the supernatural in the world of history do so because they have no experience of supernatural grace in their hearts, i.e., they are unbelievers. Princeton avoided that kind of judgment but did insist on the necessity for those who taught in the church of being committed to biblical authority. In that connection some attention should be given to Warfield's use of the Presbyterian doctrinal standards, the Westminster Confession and Catechisms, as applied to the doctrine of Scripture. As has already been hinted, the *Consenus* was necessary because to a large measure it addressed itself to doctrinal questions that were not present at the time of the writing of earlier creeds. However great an opinion Princeton had of the *Consensus*, it could hardly appeal to it in discipline cases, for it was not part of the constitution of the church. In fact, one of the great opponents of Princeton within the church, Charles A. Briggs, later to be removed from the Presbyterian ministry because of his views on Scripture, charged repeatedly that Princeton was substituting the *Consensus* for the constitutional doctrine of the church. Warfield's response is particularly significant from the perspective of common sense. He argued that the church's commitment to the clarity of Scripture necessitated the rejection of critical theories of the Bible that required their acceptance to make the Bible understandable. That is, any theory that demanded acceptance of a sophisticated, technical body of knowledge prior to or as a precondition for understanding Scripture was a denial of the perspicuity of Scripture. It was in that same vein that J. Gresham Machen, a teacher of New Testament at Princeton who left to found Westminster Theological Seminary in 1929, could speak of the modern "tyranny of the expert." Whatever one is to make of the common sense background to Princeton, at least Warfield, who had done a great deal of work in the history of the Westminster Confession, was convinced that the Confession's own doctrine of the perspicuity of Scripture was a sufficient rebuttal to modern criticism.

THE FUTURE OF COMMON SENSE

For those opposed to Princeton's position on Scripture, the apologetic value in defining that view in terms of common sense seems to be twofold. First, the eclecticism of common sense can be made responsible for Princeton's capitulation to a scientific model rather than commitment to a theological one. This study has attempted to show that common sense was also a theological model that had a very definite and comprehensive theological agenda—the unifying of religious and factual concerns. Unless one is convinced that the whole romantic Kantian-Barthian bifurcation of faith and knowledge has been an unmixed blessing, or the least of all possible evils, it is doubtful that one should repudiate common sense (and with it the Princeton view of inerrancy) without reconsidering the intention of common sense and questions such as the New England alternatives and what value the doctrine of perspicuity has to a modern Protestant.

The other purpose for linking Princeton's doctrine of inerrancy and common sense is the assumption that since common sense has been repudiated, the evangelical case for inerrancy is just as weak. Of course, the only definitive determination of the inerrancy question is still a theological and exegetical one. Even if the philosophical framework for Princeton's view of inerrancy is shaky, that would hardly permit one to avoid the Princeton analysis of the teaching of the Scripture concerning itself. Nevertheless, the question of why common sense was repudiated is of great interest.

Everyone is aware that no major philosophical issue ever seems to be definitively settled. The disciples of Plato and Aristotle will war among themselves until the end. Bringing those labels up-to-date, the debate between German idealists and Anglo-American empiricists is not moving toward unconditional surrender by either side. Without claiming that contemporary philosophers are very interested in the names or works of the great Scottish common sense philosophers, it cannot be denied that the kind of questions they raised and the answers they offered are still on the agenda of today's philosophers, though such concerns are not as vitally related to popular debates on philosophy of education and the like as they were in the past century.

If one allows a broader definition of common sense, so that its concerns and not its argumentation are the significant elements, then in that sense that tradition is still very much alive. It informs both the American pragmatic tradition beginning with C. S. Peirce and also the British ordinary-language philosophies of G. E. Moore and Ludwig Wittgenstein. In those diverse approaches there is a dominating concern that men's thoughts as they are, not as someone thinks they should be, are proper objects of investigation. That is particularly true when such thoughts become plans that lead to actions that make a difference. From that perspective there is something dated about nineteenth-century idealism, with its facile conviction that man can stand in judgment on the realities of human experience and question their significance, instead of learning to make use of them. That means that man is to be understood as really existing in society, including especially the society of ordinary men of common sense.

Granted, it is just as dangerous to prematurely baptize Anglo-American philosophy as it is German. Certainly, the Anglo-American direction has produced the distinctly anti-Christian philosophies of John Dewey and Bertrand Russell. It is conceivable that modern common sense is the most subjective, psychologizing, skeptical approach of all. It is one thing to say, "Take ordinary language seriously"; it is quite another to say that that language has any intrinsic meaning to it. Perhaps it is the only game in town, but that doesn't prevent it from being crooked.

Theologically, evangelicals, with their rejection of anything resembling Roman Catholic natural theology, with all their zeal for recognizing the basic, fundamental antithesis between the kingdom of light and the kingdom of darkness, still find it necessary to come to grips with the fact of common grace. Not only does the Lord send the sun and rain upon the unbeliever, He sends into his heart some conviction of the meaning of that sun and rain, of the grace of God Himself behind it. All the radical misuse of God's good gifts will not frustrate His purpose in having

His truth known, even though fallen man attempts to repudiate it. Since that is the case, some kind of common sense philosophy should have a part in the Christian apologist's armory, though he may also need the weapons of idealism to demonstrate how totally absurd life and man are in a world that attempts consistently to live without the God of the Bible.

That line of reasoning goes beyond the proper scope of this chapter. It is instructive, though, to discover in the most contemporary discussions of secular and biblical hermeneutics a repudiation of narrow, overly specialized approaches to the understanding of reality. It is even more striking to discover Wittgenstein being used in support of Warfield's type of argumentation for the Bible. Anthony C. Thiselton has recently argued that the authority of the Old Testament is the kind of axiom whose opposite cannot be imagined, i.e., without which Christianity cannot be understood. He even employs Wittgenstein against the device of old deists and modern form critics that affirms that the testimony of Jesus for the authority of the Bible is essentially meaningless since Jesus was compelled by His culture to think in that way. He argues that since the church recognized that it was bound to Jewish tradition and elements of the law, consequently the acceptance of the Scripture could not have happened without critical reflection.[5]

One could imagine Thiselton pursuing that argument and arriving at even more explicitly Princetonian conclusions! It is also impressive that the argument appears within a book committed to relating the "two horizons" of the interpretative task, that of the Bible and the recipients; the tradition of common sense continues to defy definition as a narrowly technical "scientific" exegesis.

PRINCETON AND EVANGELICAL APOLOGETICS

Some attention needs to be given to the internal evangelical debate about apologetics and its relation to the inerrancy controversy. Both the nonevangelical and evangelical worlds are divided

5. Anthony C. Thiselton, *The Two Horizons* (Grand Rapids: Eerdmans, 1980), pp. 434-37; cf. pp. 295-97.

between empiricists and idealists. Princeton apologetics has been perpetuated primarily by J. Oliver Buswell, Jr., and Kenneth Kantzer. In brief, with respect to the Bible, that apologetic argues that one should begin with Scripture as an ancient source book and grant it a high degree of accuracy. Based on the evidence it contains, one concludes that the miracles and resurrection of Jesus Christ are highly probable, that Christ is therefore who He claimed to be, and that therefore His testimony concerning the Scripture and the accrediting of His apostles as authoritative teachers is to be trusted; the Bible is to be received as the inspired, inerrant Word of God. The highly reliable book at the beginning of the argument is discovered at the end of the argument to be the very Word of God, partaking of divine qualities that far transcend mere empiricist reliability. Others in the same Calvinist tradition have vigorously denounced the Princeton-Warfield approach. They include Gordon Clark, who repudiates empiricism because of its invalid argumentation, and Cornelius Van Til, who repudiates it because of its unbiblical character. Van Til and Clark have departed from Warfield's apologetic but not from Warfield's view of the Bible. If anything, Van Til's commitment to the inspiration and inerrancy of the Bible as a presupposition, a first principle, would seem to make his view even more rigorous than Warfield's.

Furthermore, Clark's or Van Til's approach becomes more attractive every day as the totality of the rejection of evangelical Christianity in contemporary culture becomes increasingly obvious. The world in which the common man shared Christian assumptions seems to have existed a very long time ago. No longer is it a matter of the circulation of anti-Christian opinions; the whole mind-set of Western civilization has altered.

The rational man and his interest in the continuity of his personality has turned out to be someone who wishes with all his being to destroy his mind with chemicals or at least to seek such instant gratification that any interest in cause and effect seems totally laughable. For modern man to be told that his life is meaningless no longer has any shock value—he has known that for a long time. Whatever the relation between evangelical Christianity and common sense may once have been, it has long since evaporated. To the extent that that is correct and will continue to be correct, to that extent any appeal to the way people live is a ridiculous one. Men will hardly be impressed by an apologetic that encourages them to see the basis for the meaningfulness and significance of their lives in the way they live. If that is correct, then the charge of eclecticism against common sense is well-placed. The apologetic that is needed today (as well as the preaching, counseling, and Christian education) will be one that speaks of the judgment of God, of His giving up of idolaters to lives of deepening self-deception and mutual deception, and then of the great patience and restraint of the Lord, who still communicates His love and provision of saving grace through His Word, which remains without error in a world built on sand.

And yet is there not something to be said for the social character of common sense? The Christian faith is not simply for individuals but for families and nations. There is bound to be something of significance in a viewpoint that stresses the fact that it is not just individual significance that is at stake but also the structure of human life together. That is the point in seeing modern language philosophy as building on the common sense tradition. Indeed, if hermeneutical questions are the foundational questions of our age, as is so frequently stated, then questions of how people understand each other will have a great deal to do with how they understand God. Perhaps, then, in good common sense, eclectical style, even a radical apologetic might incorporate a linguistic-sociological aspect. It cannot be totally accidental that John Frame, one of Van Til's successors at Westminster, makes such great use of the insights of language philosophy in general and of Wittgenstein in particular. Most likely, contemporary evangelical apologetics is still taking shape. It is just as easy for an antithetical apologist to make use of common grace in a society or linguistic community, as he has long since learned to do with individuals. As that happens, the common sense tradition will live on in a a new ministry to the evangelical world.

CONCLUSION

A word of summary is in order. The Princeton view of Scripture is to be understood from a variety of perspectives. Not only common sense, but also the implications of Turretin's criticism of Amyraldian psychologizing, Princeton's own similar criticism against New England theology, the general evangelical response (as embodied in Hengstenberg) to international liberalism, and, in particular, a straightforward exegesis of the Bible's own teaching concerning itself should be taken into account. Not taken into account should be the agenda of dispensationalism, even though that does not imply reading that movement out of the evangelical or even Presbyterian camp; it is only fair to recognize that it never was in the Princeton camp. Negatively, all of that means that there is no obvious, single reason for rejecting Princeton out of hand because of her strange companion; to repudiate Princeton on the basis of historical reasons involves being suspicious of the entire spectrum of evangelicalism. That is possible, but it borders on such radical surgery of evangelical history as to violate an axiom of church history.

Positively, it is striking how Princeton integrated its views on Scripture with the rest of its theology. If one of the basic concerns is investigating how the word of man is also truly the Word of God, then it is not surprising that the theology of Calvinism, which has devoted so much of its attention to learning to see the responsibility of man as rooted in the sovereign grace of God, could perform a yeoman service for the entire evangelical community by helping it to understand its doctrine of Scripture. That is true not only in Warfield's call to see inspiration under the rubric of providence, but even more basically in its rejection of the psychologizing of conversion as parallel to its warnings against making normative for the doctrine of the Bible observations relating to the mode of its inspiration. Particularly, that last point is of inestimable value for today's debate.

Perhaps the most abiding result of this study is the conclusion that far from Princeton's view of the Bible's being dated because of association with an outmoded framework of thought, Princeton on the contrary turns out to have been extremely alert to worldwide theological developments from the past as well as the present, as she did her best to interpret and use the Bible. There was nothing glib or complacent about Princeton. Perhaps that is the great example for the contemporary evangelical movement—a team of hard-working scholars, not shirking the difficult questions.

Part 3

The Tradition of the Authority of Scripture:
A Recent Change Within Evangelicalism

12

Berkouwer and the Battle for the Bible*

Carl W. Bogue

During the period 1920-70 Dr. Gerrit Cornelis Berkouwer achieved theological stature, both in the Netherlands and internationally, comparable to Kuyper and Bavinck before him. In 1974 he produced an interesting and significant book. It is an expansion of a survey given during the completion of his regular lectures at the Free University of Amsterdam, translated into English three years later under the title *A Half Century of Theology*. Berkouwer is candid about his own participation in that half-century. Significantly, he tells us, "We are wrestling today with questions put on the agenda a half century ago."[1] When one reflects on the questions "put on the agenda" regarding Scripture, Berkouwer's 1971 question is indicative of where he stands: "Is there room in the Reformed Churches for persons—and I reckon myself

* Much of this material was used previously in *A Hole in the Dike* (Cherry Hill, N.J.: Mack Publishing, 1977) and "Berkouwer: The Evolution of a Twentieth Century Theologian," *The Journal of Christian Reconstruction* 7 (1980): 135-74.
1. G. C. Berkouwer, *A Half Century of Theology*, trans. Lewis B. Smedes (Grand Rapids: Eerdmans, 1977), p. 9.

CARL W. BOGUE, Jr., A.B., Muskingum College, B.D., Pittsburgh Theological Seminary, Drs., Th.D., Free University of Amsterdam, is pastor of Faith Presbyterian Church, Akron, Ohio. His published works include *Jonathan Edwards and the Covenant of Grace* and *Hole in the Dike: Critical Aspects of Berkouwer's Theology*.

among them—who at this stage of their reflection have great hesitations concerning the historicity of Adam?"[2]

The relevance of Berkouwer's pilgrimage for American evangelicalism needs to be understood. His direct and indirect influence are both considerable. During this same half-century the American evangelical community has witnessed a profound transformation. Some respected evangelicals, whether willingly or not, began to be identified by the term *neo*-evangelical. A split was growing that was to become much more than a mere intramural struggle. Part and parcel of that struggle was a growing difference of opinion on the doctrine of Scripture, a difference popularized by Harold Lindsell's *The Battle for the Bible*. The focal point was inerrancy. So aggressive had the errantists become that the erosion among evangelicals was rampant. The situation had deteriorated to the point that by 1977 an evangelical counteroffensive had been launched in the form of the International Council on Biblical Inerrancy. Warfield versus Berkouwer, a distinction underlined by Berkouwer himself, has become a popular symbol of the battle.[3]

Whether disciple or critic, those referring to Berkouwer as a "Reformed" theologian feel a necessity to qualify the definition. Rogers, for example, wants to remove him from the "bad company" of Warfield or Protestant scholastics.[4] Van Til includes him

2. Quoted in Harold Lindsell, *The Battle for the Bible* (Grand Rapids: Zondervan, 1977), p. 135.
3. One of the papers presented at the 1978 "Summit" on inerrancy was precisely on that topic, cf. Hendrick Krabbendam, "B. B. Warfield vs. G. C. Berkouwer on Scripture," Summit Papers, ed. Norman L. Geisler, International Council on Biblical Inerrancy, Chicago, October 1978, hereafter cited as Summit Papers, pp. 15.1-31. Those papers are scheduled for publication in revised form in the near future.
4. Cf. Jack Rogers, *Confessions of a Conservative Evangelical* (Philadelphia: Westminster, 1974), especially pp. 134ff.; Jack Rogers, "The Church Doctrine of Biblical Authority," *Biblical Authority*, ed. Jack Rogers (Waco, Texas: Word, 1977), pp. 41ff.; and Jack B. Rogers and Donald K. McKim, *The Authority and Interpretation of the Bible: An Historical Approach* (San Francisco: Harper & Row, 1979). Rogers stretches generalities to the extreme in the blanket way he includes Kuyper and Bavinck with Berkouwer in opposition to "old Princeton theology." Rogers may be unknown to many readers, and some may question why we have not chosen a more prominent figure. The fact is that Rogers's growing hostility toward everyone's interpretation of The Westminster Confession except certain contemporary neo-orthodox and neo-evangelical writers, coupled with his vigorous allegiance to Berkouwer, has thrust him to the forefront of spokesmen for a Berkouwer-influenced neo-evangelicalism. His role will appear from time to time later in this article.

with the "bad company" of the neo-orthodox.[5] Berkouwer stands with one foot in a confessional heritage he refuses to abandon and another foot in the world of ecumenical ventures that frequently conflicts with his heritage. To some, Berkouwer represents a breath of fresh air, providing evangelicals with a way out of the dilemma between "conservative" and "liberal."[6] To others, his theology is at best frustratingly inconsistent and at worst a theological capitulation.

It is certainly beyond dispute that Berkouwer has made some significant departures from his heritage, and on the basis of those departures there is justification for seeing a line of development from Berkouwer to the neo-evangelical movement and the rejection of biblical inerrancy. As contemporary evangelicals wake up to the fact that they have been robbed of much of the heart of classical Reformed orthodoxy, the "Dutch connection" cannot be overlooked. Berkouwer is, of course, but one of many influences. He is however, a considerable influence.

EARLY AND LATER BERKOUWER

Among disciples and critics alike it is commonplace to distinguish between an early and a later Berkouwer. Whether one calls it maturity or capitulation, there is certainly change. Berkouwer believes he missed the "real intentions of Barth" in his 1932 dissertation on the new German theology.[7] His sympathy with Barth

5. Cf. Cornelius Van Til, *The Sovereignty of Grace* (Phillipsburg, N.J.: Presbyterian and Reformed, 1969) p. 32, where Van Til says of Berkouwer: "His love for the Reformed faith is unquestioned"; however, "concomitant with his more 'positive' attitudes toward both Barth and Rome in recent times goes an increasingly negative attitude toward historic Reformed statements with respect to Scripture and doctrine." Near the conclusion of the book (p. 86) he states: "Berkouwer now advocates principles similar to those of Barth and of neoorthodoxy as though through them alone we can defend the teaching of free grace."
6. Cf. Rogers and McKim, *Authority and Interpretation*, p. 437: "Berkouwer thus offered twentieth-century evangelicals the Reformation stance as an alternative between scholastic rationalism and liberal subjectivism." By "scholastic rationalism" Rogers and McKim mean anyone defending inerrancy, especially "old Princeton theology." The authors give no compelling evidence as to why their view is not "subjective," while all the time using the term *scholastic* in a pejorative and ad hominem sense against the inerrancy position.
7. Berkouwer, *Half Century*, p. 45.

had increased significantly a couple of decades later in *The Triumph of Grace in the Theology of Karl Barth*, and by 1974 he was defending Barth against the likes of Van Til and Pannenberg.[8] Berkouwer's two main works on Scripture (1928 and 1966-67) reflect that change as dramatically as any. Krabbendam sees Berkouwer's early views on Scripture as "practically identical" to Warfield, while the later Berkouwer is "critical of Warfield" and "endorses and adopts the neo-orthodox position."[9]

It is a fair assumption that the early/later evaluation of Berkouwer accounts for the fact that only in more recent years has there been a growing chorus of critics willing to question the orthodoxy of such an esteemed "Reformed" theologian. Many had become uneasy with Berkouwer but were not quite sure why. The absence of firm criticism of Berkouwer was no doubt due to to critics' charity toward a man of his stature and the style of his writing, which is circumlocutory.

The critical voices are on the increase, however. The appearance in 1975 of the English translation of Berkouwer's *Holy Scripture* brought a new wave of criticism. At a time of growing evangelical awareness that biblical inerrancy was the issue where the battle must be fought, Berkouwer's *Holy Scripture* was tried and found wanting. One need only read the papers from the ICBI's 1978 Chicago Summit to see Berkouwer attacked from a variety of quarters.

Paralleling such increasing criticism is the emergence of Berkouwer as a rallying point for the neo-evangelical and errantist movements. A person in the Reformed tradition who denies inerrancy but wants to affirm a "high view" of Scripture and its "infallible message" will probably model his doctrine of Scripture on Berkouwer. Because of his prominence in the battle, Jack Rogers has become a prime symbol of that influence. Editor of *Biblical Authority*, a book that attacks inerrancy and the "Hodge-Warfield . . . rationalistic defense of Scripture,"[10] Rogers had earlier written a doctoral dissertation on the doctrine of Scripture in the

---

8. Ibid., pp. 69, 71.
9. Krabbendam, Summit Papers, pp. 15.3, 28.
10. This particular quote is from David Hubbard, "The Current Tensions: Is There a Way Out," in *Biblical Authority*, p. 167.

Westminster Confession. In it he pushed credulity to its limit by trying to make the Westminster Divines' view of Scripture essentially the same as that of Berkouwer.[11] Such an unhistorical conclusion apparently is the fundamental credential by which Rogers has become a spokesman for the errantist movement among neo-evangelicals in this country. Such "revisionist" interpretation of the Westminster Assembly is perpetuated and expanded in the new work Rogers has co-authored with Donald McKim. In it they deny that inerrancy was the historic position of the church but assert instead that it is the product of "rationalistic scholasticism" that came to full flower in "Princeton theology," which substituted an inerrant Bible for the gospel!

Any discussion of an early and late Berkouwer should also take into account a significant article by Hendrikus Berkhof, a neo-orthodox theologian, entitled "The Method of Berkouwer's Theology." Berkhof finds three phases in Berkouwer's theology, the first of which acknowledges "the absolute authority of Scripture."[12] The second phase Berkhof calls "the salvation content of Scripture," which begins as early as the start of Berkouwer's *Studies in Dogmatics* in 1949.[13] That phase is less polemical and moves from the authority of Scripture in an absolute sense to the nature of that authority, namely its salvation content via Christ. The third phase is "the existential direction of Scripture" with its kerygmatic-existential correlation manifesting itself in Berkouwer's changed view on Dordt and his "asymmetrical" emphasis on election.[14]

That methodological analysis by Berkhof is a strong indictment to anyone from an evangelical perspective. Simply put, Berkhof is saying that Berkouwer went from traditional Reformed orthodoxy

11. Jack Bartlett Rogers, *Scripture in the Westminster Confession* (Kampen: J. H. Kok, 1966).
12. H. Berkhof, "De Methode van Berkouwers Theologie," *Ex Auditu Verbi*, ed. R. Schippers, G. E. Meuleman, J. T. Bakker, and H. M. Kuitert (Kampen: J. H. Kok, 1965), pp. 40-43.
13. Ibid., pp. 44-48. Rogers and McKim, *Authority and Interpretation*, pp. 427-28, give support for Berkhof's thesis. After the appearance of Berkouwer's recent work on Holy Scripture, Rogers and McKim note the "criticism from some evangelicals who had previously lauded Berkouwer's theology." To the question, Had Berkouwer changed? their answer is no. "In actuality he had simply described the approach to Scripture that had enriched his volumes on other doctrines for twenty-five years."
14. Ibid., pp. 48-53.

to existential theology via a form of neo-orthodoxy. Whether one agrees with that analysis or not, a theologian of Berkhof's stature writing in an academic *Festschrift* honoring Professor Berkouwer must have seen some radical evidence to draw such a far-reaching conclusion. I was in the Netherlands at the time and understood that Berkouwer protested vigorously to Berkhof, though I saw nothing in print. Recently, however, Hendrick Krabbendam has provided important input on this issue by citing a Dutch work by F. W. Buytendach to the effect "that Berkouwer has acknowledged the transition from the first to the second phase, but objected to the construct of a third phase."[15] Apparently, Berkouwer is willing to acknowledge a significant change, a change that resulted in seeing scriptural content as not necessarily bound to scriptural form. That change, according to Krabbendam, would have been impossible "without . . . the influence of the Barthian type of neo-orthodoxy."[16]

BERKOUWER AND THE BATTLE

If Lindsell is correct when he calls biblical inerrancy "the most important theological topic of this age," with the battleground being the evangelical community, then Berkouwer's significance must not be underestimated. His influence on the shift in the doctrine of Scripture manifesting itself among neo-evangelicalism is considerable. Krabbendam sees Berkouwer as "the fountainhead of a new type of thinking" that "led him and his followers to the denial of . . . inerrancy."[17] Gordon Lewis, in a paper entitled "The Human Authorship of Inspired Scripture," calls Berkouwer's view of Scripture "both inadequate and unorthodox."[18] John Gerstner says Berkouwer's view of Scripture "does more than 'damage reverence for Scripture,' " it "damages reverence for God."[19] If the battle is for the Bible, then Berkouwer is a major combatant!

15. Krabbendam, Summit Papers, p. 15.3, n. 6.
16. Lindsell, *The Battle for the Bible*, p. 13.
17. Krabbendam, Summit Papers, 15.1.
18. Gordon R. Lewis, "The Human Authorship of Inspired Scripture," in Summit Papers, p. 9.11.
19. John H. Gerstner, "The Church's Doctrine of Biblical Inspiration" in *The Foundation of Biblical Authority*, ed. James Montgomery Boice (Grand Rapids: Zondervan, 1978), pp. 49-50.

Our study of Berkouwer's view of Scripture requires two qualifying comments. First, we will be very selective, simply because of the amount of material. But we will also be selective in dealing with problem areas. We will not spend time recounting all the good things Berkouwer had to say, but will purposely choose the material that suggests deviation from the more generally accepted Reformed doctrine of verbal inerrancy.

The other qualification concerns the way Berkouwer writes. When he treats the historical development of a doctrine along with the exegetical and theological questions to be considered, he usually exhibits great clarity. But when it comes to a direct statement of his own view on an area of controversy within the Reformed heritage, there is a studied lack of forthrightness. The issue of biblical inerrancy is a prime example. Though Berkouwer has been more candid in recent years, one still does not find blatant denials of inerrancy. It is there in rhetorical questions and by implication. He is not interested in the "battle for the Bible" as Lindsell and others might formulate it. Berkouwer does not wish to state boldly that there are errors in the Bible, but under that assumption he wants us to see the questions of authority and certainty from a different perspective.

Berkouwer's hesitation to be drawn into a commitment on the inerrancy issue is illustrated by an incident related by Lindsell in his recent book. With reference to Berkouwer he writes:

> He was a contributor to the Current Religious Thought Column of *Christianity Today* for some years. When readers raised the question about his belief in biblical inerrancy, I wrote to him for clarification. Despite extended correspondence, I could get no answer from him either affirming or denying inerrancy. When a man refuses to reply to a direct question about his continued acceptance of inerrancy, the only conclusion that can be drawn is obvious.[20]

We believe it is increasingly obvious, and for those who see that as a critical issue the time is past for giving his "no comment" the benefit of the doubt.

That is not to say that Berkouwer does not wish to subject him-

20. Lindsell, *The Battle for the Bible*, p. 135.

self to the Word of God. Theology for him is "relevant" only when it is "relative to the Word of God. . . . Theology is occupied in continuous attentive and obedient listening to the Word of God."[21] For Berkouwer, however, that is in opposition to inerrancy, not in its support. Berkouwer believes his view is really honoring God's Word while the inerrantist's is not. "Some," he says, "are fascinated by a miraculous 'correctness,' " but "in the end it will damage reverence for Scripture more than it will further it."[22] "In appealing to its authority we are not dealing with a formal principle but with a deep spiritual witness to Jesus Christ. . . ."[23] Thus, a person who operates with "a certain theory of inspiration [i.e., inerrancy] is almost certainly going to cry 'It stands written' and still come out with something that misses the truth and power of Scripture."[24] "To speak of *errors* . . . is to speak out of an unhistorical approach."[25] The slogan "It stands written" is not "a magic wand that can be waved to eliminate all problems. . . ."[26] Reflecting on his 1938 work on Scripture, Berkouwer affirms that he is no less committed to the significance of "It stands written,"[27] even though his present understanding of what that means has changed considerably.

Of course, anyone may claim obedience to Scripture and may do so with utmost integrity.[28] The neo-orthodox, no less than

---

21. G. C. Berkouwer, *Faith and Justification*, trans. Lewis B. Smedes (Grand Rapids: Eerdmans, 1954), p. 9.
22. G. C. Berkouwer, *Holy Scripture*, trans. Jack B. Rogers (Grand Rapids: Eerdmans, 1975), p. 183.
23. Berkouwer, *Half Century*, p. 138.
24. Ibid., p. 139.
25. Ibid., p. 140.
26. Ibid., p. 141.
27. Ibid., p. 139.
28. It is interesting to note that on the assumption that Berkouwer is not willfully deceiving us, his writing is inerrant as he defines it. According to Berkouwer, the biblical notion of error is not incorrectness but deception, as in intentional lying, cf. Berkouwer, *Holy Scripture*, p. 181. Therefore, unless he is willfully trying to deceive us, Berkouwer's writing is "inerrant." Following that lead, Rogers distinguishes "the biblical notion of error as willful deception" from "error" in the sense of technical accuracy (Rogers, *Biblical Authority*, p. 46). Thus, error concerns the writer's intent. Paul D. Feinberg, "The Meaning of Inerrancy," Summit Papers, p. 10.21, shows how such a definition says too much with this telling comment: "If we accept Rogers' understanding of error as 'willful deception,' then almost every book that has ever been written is inerrant."

neo-evangelicals, claim to be those who are truly honoring and reverently listening to God's Word.[29] Van Til, acknowledging some validity in Berkouwer's criticism that Van Til was not sufficiently exegetical, nevertheless makes this timely observation: "One can be 'exegetical' in terms of the neoorthodox schematism of thought and this is, after all, to be speculative first, and biblical afterwards."[30]

As we turn to the historical development of Berkouwer's doctrine of Scripture, we will see why there is a growing consensus on an "early" and "late" Berkouwer. Yet it is also true that the seeds of what he would consider his "mature" view were present in those early years. It is interesting that in his most recent publication he chooses not to repudiate his early work on Scripture but to see it as a different emphasis.[31]

The historical, or chronological, exposition of Berkouwer's doctrine of Scripture must begin with a book published over forty years ago and continue through his recently published work, in which he surveys the past fifty years of theology as he has experienced it. We will conclude with a look at some disciples of Berkouwer who dramatically illustrate the bearing of his doctrine of Scripture on the current debate over inerrancy.

In 1938 Berkouwer's first of two major works on Scripture appeared. Almost four hundred pages long, *Het Probleem der Schriftkritiek* is a positive statement of the Reformed doctrine of Scripture in relation to the debates raging at that time. A central theme was the contrast of the Reformed doctrine to the "subjectivism" of the increasingly popular biblical criticism. According to Berkouwer, "the modern Scripture examination stands in sharp antithesis with that of orthodoxy," and "if the Scripture is lost the

29. Cf. Rogers, *Confessions of a Conservative Evangelical*, pp. 103-4, where he claims Warfield "diverted attention" from a true listening of Scripture because of his concern for inerrancy. That criticism of defenders of inerrancy is implicit in the slogan emblazoned on the cover of *Biblical Authority*: "Turn your Bible from a battleground into a source for spiritual strength." So also Hubbard (*Biblical Authority*, p. 167): "The Hodge-Warfield brand of Reformed theology with its rationalistic defense of Scripture, comes close to jeopardizing the solid principle that Scripture is sufficient."
30. Cornelius Van Til, *Toward a Reformed Apologetics* (N.p: n.d.), p. 27.
31. Berkouwer, *Half Century*, p. 139.

context of the Christian faith is lost."[32] He apparently saw the deception of the modern critic of Scripture. "The battle against petrification of orthodoxy," says Berkouwer, "was in reality a letting go of Scripture revelation," and the "self-sufficient autonomous subject" dominates the "modern" reflection on Scripture.[33]

We should pay attention to the striking contrast that affords to his later work. It is precisely the battle against the petrification of orthodoxy that became his battle, but now he affirms that it does *not* involve a "letting go of Scripture revelation." That contrast is put in bold relief by Berkouwer's more recent doubts about the early chapters of Genesis. In the 1938 work, opposing those who questioned the historicity of those early chapters, his position is quite orthodox. Modern theology distinguishes, he says, "between form and content or between the kernel and the husk, between fact and the clothing of that fact."[34] Such a form-content distinction is part and parcel of most of Berkouwer's dogmatical studies and especially his work on Scripture, but hear what he said about it in 1938. "The natural question is what remains of the religious significance when the historical surroundings are considered doubtful."[35] The crux of the matter is how one receives certainty in the "*religious* connection" if the "religious relation's indissoluble connection to the historical givens is devalued."[36] A few pages later he writes: "According to Scripture the character of sin cannot be established apart from the historic fact of the fall and the surrounding trustworthy communications given to us."[37]

The prevailing message of that early work is clear. A modern "subjective" viewpoint is clearly set in opposition to the orthodox view of Scripture as the revelation of God. There was resistance to all forms of subjectivism that denied the indissoluble connection between the form and the content. Basically, one may say that in the early work, Berkouwer is opposed to the neo-orthodox view of Scripture, a view he increasingly came to embrace.

32. G. C. Berkouwer, *Het Probleem Der Schriftkritiek* (Kampen: J. H. Kok, 1938), p. 44.
33. Ibid.
34. Ibid., p. 129.
35. Ibid., p. 131.
36. Ibid.
37. Ibid., p. 135.

It was almost thirty years later that Berkouwer wrote an even larger work on the doctrine of Holy Scripture. Entitled *De Heilige Schrift*, it appeared in two volumes in 1966 and 1967, the next to last in his *Studies in Dogmatics*. The English translation appeared in a somewhat abridged one-volume edition in 1975. The translation was done by Jack Rogers of Fuller Seminary, and it is from that edition that we will be citing.

It would be a serious error to suppose that that work represents anything other than the combined development of Berkouwer's thinking during those thirty years, set down in a somewhat systematic fashion. Berkouwer's view of Scripture was not unknown prior to the 1966 publication. Indeed, one could without too much difficulty ascertain his position from his other writings during that time, not the least of which would be his books and articles on the Roman Catholic church and the "new theology" emerging there. For the sake of space, however, we will concentrate specifically on his work *Holy Scripture*.

The fact that Berkouwer's view of Scripture was generally known prior to that publication is significant. The author was living in the Netherlands at the time, and there was an air of expectancy as people wondered to what extent Berkouwer would repudiate his 1938 book. It was my impression that in both church and university circles no one really doubted that Berkouwer had moved considerably from his earlier work. What made that new book newsworthy was the anticipation of whether he would ignore, repudiate, or reinterpret the earlier book. Those familiar with Berkouwer's style were not surprised to find that he did a lot of ignoring, some reinterpretation, and a studied avoidance of explicit repudiation.

A common denominator in the modernist-fundamentalist debate in the early part of this century and the "battle for the Bible" today is the question of certainty with regard to our faith. Berkouwer begins his book with a chapter on Holy Scripture and the certainty of faith. For him, the certainty of one's faith is not grounded in an infallible Scripture but in a recognition that Scripture is the Word of God, a recognition that grows out of one's existing faith-certainty. It is "an incorrect conception of theology," according to Berkouwer, "which considers it possible to discuss Holy Scripture apart from a personal relationship of belief in it."[38] He acknowledges that "for a long time during church history certainty of faith was specifically linked to the trustworthiness of Holy Scripture as the Word of God,"[39] but that traditional view is "an incorrect conception of theology." The correct view is a correlation between faith and the object of faith, namely, God and His Word. "Only God himself can give us definite and indubitable certainty and place us for time and eternity on an immovable foundation."[40] Berkouwer does not tell us how God does that. He says he does not mean "a miraculous voice of God," and he strongly denies charges of mysticism, spiritualism, or subjectivism. Yet his correlation concept is strongly influenced by the existential character of modern theology, what Berkhof calls Berkouwer's third phase of "the existential direction of Scripture" with its kerygmatic-existential correlation.[41]

Berkouwer sees a strong parallel with the struggles within Roman Catholicism over the certainty question and sympathizes with the approach of neo-orthodox-type liberal Roman Catholics. The final chapter of *A Half Century of Theology* is entitled "Concern for the Faith" and discusses the certainty theme. Some people feel betrayed and threatened, he says. "For Protestants it is tied to a fear that the complete trustworthiness of Scripture is somehow being subverted. For Catholics, it is related to a loss of respect for the authority of the church as the last word for questions of faith."[42] Both books by Berkouwer on the Second Vatican Council and subsequent developments are illustrative of that. But one page from *A Half Century of Theology* will illustrate dramatically how the parallel between Rome and Protestantism functions.

Hans Küng, according to Berkouwer, "called for a hard look at the actual history of papal statements in which error was, as a matter of fact, mixed with truth. He wanted complete honesty and integrity."[43] We, of course, agree with Küng that there is a great deal of error in papal statements. But remember, Berkouwer is

38. Berkouwer, *Holy Scripture*, p. 9.
39. Ibid., p. 11.
40. Ibid., p. 15.
41. Berkhof, *Ex Auditu Verbi*, pp. 48ff.
42. Berkouwer, *Half Century*, p. 215.
43. Ibid., p. 222.

drawing a parallel with the Protestant doctrine of Scripture. "The *church* is, Küng insisted, indefectible. But that does not require, as a *conditio sine qua non*, that its *teachings* are infallible nor that the church's path is marked by irrevocable statements."[44] The church is "indefectible," but the particular teachings are fallible. If that concept is understood, you will be prepared to understand what men like Berkouwer mean when they say that Scripture is infallible but not inerrant!

Berkouwer continues to paraphrase Küng with words very similar to the neo-orthodox banner—follow the living Lord, not a dead book. "We should rather think in terms of being guided and sustained by the Spirit as he leads us through the valleys of possible error. . . . Küng talked in the same vein as Bavinck did and as the Belgic Confession does: the church is preserved by God as it walks amid enemies (Article XXVII)."[45] That is a remarkable statement. Küng's view of an infallible church with fallible teaching is likened to the Belgic Confession's teaching that the church is preserved by God as it walks amid enemies. Here Berkouwer equates enemies with errors, so that in the parallel to the Roman Catholic discussion, the infallible purpose of Scripture is preserved by God as it dwells amid error.

In chapter 1 of Berkouwer's *Holy Scripture* we find another theme that will be frequently repeated—"the transition from a more 'mechanical' to a more 'organic' view of Scripture."[46] He sees a continuity between the traditional view in which "certainty of faith was specifically linked to the trustworthiness of Holy Scripture" and what he calls a mechanical view of inspiration. By contrast the rise of historical criticism focused attention on the human aspect. That resulted in taking seriously the human "organ" of revelation, and thus came the preference for an organic view of inspiration, which is almost self-evident according to Berkouwer. With that also came problems, which Berkouwer recognizes. "Students of Scripture began to wonder . . . whether Holy Scripture as God's Word was truly beyond all criticism," and

---

44. Ibid.
45. Ibid.
46. Berkouwer, *Holy Scripture*, p. 11.

questions were raised concerning the meaning of "is" in the confession: Holy Scripture is the book of God.[47]

Again, Berkouwer's sympathy with Roman Catholic parallels is interesting. His chapter entitled "Exegesis and Doctrinal Authority" in his book on the Second Vatican Council deals with the tension within the Roman Church growing out of two encyclicals. The 1943 encyclical, *Divino Afflante Spiritu*, "carries a hint of new directions" for biblical studies. In it Pius XII introduced "the question as to the nature" of scriptural authority, granted an area of freedom, and "emphasized the necessity of interpreting the Bible according to its own intent and purpose."[48] Without denying inspiration, the door was nevertheless opened. One of the results was a challenge to the accuracy of the Genesis stories while emphasizing their religious intent. One is reminded of Barth's comment that the literal existence of the serpent is not important, but what the serpent said is! A 1950 encyclical, *Humani Generis*, was necessitated by the erosion of previously proclaimed infallible doctrines regarding the origin of human life. The expected loss of fallible form was resulting in the loss of "infallible" content as well.

This is a fascinating area of study with a wealth of material; the Roman Church will probably never be the same because of it. It is important to us in understanding Berkouwer, since he is not only sympathetic with the new and unorthodox Roman exegetes, but sees Protestantism faced with the same issue.

> We must acknowledge that we are not able to look on the tensions within the Roman Catholic Church on this point from a restful Reformed eminence, as though Reformation theology is untouched by similar problems. One could maintain such an illusion only by supposing that exegesis is an individual and not a Church concern and that exegesis is secured against error by the motto, *sola Scriptura*. Actually, the question of Scriptural authority is a most pressing one within Reformed churches. Ever since they abandoned a mechanical view of Scripture's inspiration and came to terms with an "organic" view, they have been faced, wittingly or not, with

47. Ibid., pp. 13, 17.
48. G. C. Berkouwer, *The Second Vatican Council and the New Catholicism*, trans. Lewis B. Smedes (Grand Rapids: Eerdmans, 1965), pp. 113-14.

problems parallel to Catholicism's problem of the Church's teaching authority and free exegesis of Scripture. Pius XII wrote in his encyclical, *Divino Afflante Spiritu*, of the writers of Scripture as "organs" and "living, rationally gifted instruments" of the Spirit. He emphasized the authority of Scripture, but his acknowledgement of the human writers as "organs" opened the question of how the organs functioned in the service of revelation and how their dynamic function affects the character of Scripture's authority. Evangelical theology faces the same question. The witness of Scripture itself along with the "biblical studies of our time" faces evangelical churches with problems that only a docetic view of Scripture can ignore.[49]

Berkouwer's commitment to a confessional church gives him great empathy with the liberal Roman Catholics who want their heritage and changes too, and the solution for both is sought not in orthodoxy but a "neo"-orthodoxy.

It is clear that Berkouwer is not satisfied with past formulations. There is a move, he says, from a mechanical to an organic view of Scripture. And it is important to understand something of his criticism of the alleged enemy, mechanical inspiration, as well as who the enemy is, before moving on with his own view. Unhappily, Berkouwer does not clearly identify the enemy. There are hints; there are indicators. Yet many readers will surely be asking themselves, "Who is he referring to," or, "Is he implying that I am guilty of that?" The task of identification is further complicated by what Berkouwer himself acknowledges, namely, that "no one deliberately takes the side of a mechanical idea of inspiration.[50] Thus, his criticism of persons holding a "mechanical view," if they are not to be straw men, are persons who deny that theirs is a mechanical view.

It is thus necessary to make an assumption that some may not like, but one that we believe to be valid, and one that would be confirmed by those who espouse Berkouwer's doctrine of Scripture. That assumption is this: when Berkouwer speaks of a mechanical view of inspiration, or fundamentalism, or a formal-

49. Ibid., pp. 141-42.
50. Berkouwer, *Holy Scripture*, p. 153.

ized doctrine of Scripture, he is in the broad sweep referring to those of us who hold to the classical Reformed doctrine of biblical inerrancy. That means Warfield and Old Princeton. On the contemporary scene that means John Gerstner, J. I. Packer, Cornelius Van Til, and many others who hold to an inerrant Bible. It is important to say that, since it is very easy to read Berkouwer's criticisms with approval, assuming that he is attacking the same abuses the inerrantist would, while in reality he is attacking that very position. It is to some of those charges that we now turn.

Part and parcel of the nonorganic, mechanical view of inspiration was an overemphasis on the supernatural or divine aspect. According to Berkouwer, the tendency in the church was "to minimize the human aspect of Scripture." Arguing from a false dichotomy he says, "The human element of Scripture does not receive the attention it deserves if certainty of faith can only be grounded in the divine testimony, for then it can no longer be maintained that God's Word came to us in the form of human witness."[51] In that context the word *Docetism* appears. Docetism was the heresy of stressing the divine nature of Christ to the neglect of His human nature. Berkouwer raises the question "whether a kind of Docetism possibly lay behind the so-called theory of mechanical inspiration" and assures us that it is a "totally wrong concept of Scripture" that thinks "that the trustworthiness of Scripture is protected by means of a docetic view."[52]

From a discussion of certainty that is grounded in a docetic view of Scripture, Berkouwer moves into a discussion of fundamentalism. He is critical of the "very defensive character" of fundamentalism.

> To be sure, many expressions from the fundamentalist camp frequently give the impression that the acceptance of a fundamental truth and a certainty that cannot be subjectified are at stake, especially when its members gladly accept the name "fundamentalist" to set them apart from those who have fallen victim to the influ-

51. Ibid., p. 18.
52. Ibid., pp. 18-19.

ence of subjectivism. This, however, terminates the discussion at the point where it actually should begin.[53]

Berkouwer claims the same "simple and childlike acceptance of Scripture" as the fundamentalist. The problem is that the fundamentalist fails to see the complexity of the problem.

The fact that Berkouwer sees implicit Docetism in the inerrancy of fundamentalism is illustrated in the following quote:

> I believe that I am judging no one unfairly when I say that fundamentalism, in its eagerness to maintain Holy Scripture's divinity, does not fully realize the significance of Holy Scripture as a prophetic-apostolic, and consequently human, testimony. It is true that fundamentalists do not deny the human element in Scripture, but they allow their apologetics to be determined by the fear that emphasis on the human witness may threaten and overshadow Scripture's divinity.[54]

According to Berkouwer the real point at issue is not the acceptance or rejection of the voice of God, as the fundamentalist insists. In a statement that many fundamentalists would see as grossly unfair, if not slanderous, he writes:

> They suggest that . . . an *a priori* acceptance of Scripture's infallibility precludes all dangers. Thus, they manifest great tolerance for all who maintain the fundamentalist view of Holy Scripture. They tend to relativize concrete obedience in understanding Scripture. The result is that their apologetic, which is meant to safeguard Scripture's divine aspect, threatens in many respects to block the road to a correct understanding of Scripture, which is normative, by ignoring and neglecting its human aspect.[55]

We need to pursue that theme in some detail, because those charges are serious. Here are some more of Berkouwer's extreme charges against the fundamentalist or inerrant view of Scripture. The fundamentalist sees Scripture "as though it were a string of

53. Ibid., p. 21.
54. Ibid., p. 22.
55. Ibid., pp. 22-23.

divine or supernaturally revealed statements, ignoring the fact that God's Word has passed through humanity and has incorporated its service." The fundamentalist is said to be guided by the "wholly divine or wholly human" dilemma, opting for the former. "Thus to them the human aspect of Holy Scripture lost all constitutive meaning and became blurred through the overwhelming divine reality of God's speaking." The fundamentalist "greatly obscures the contexts in which God himself gave us Scripture." There is "an unconscious wish not to have God's Word enter the creaturely realm," and "this background . . . determines fundamentalist apologetics."[56]

Berkouwer takes another line of attack against the psychological fundamentalism of defenders of inerrancy. Citing critics of post-Reformation theology with apparent approval, he describes the danger thus:

> An incorrect connection between Scripture and certainty of faith can be made by proceeding *a priori* from the premise that for our certainty of faith we need an immovable basis to the conclusion that we can find this only in an infallible Scripture. It is especially the so-called of orthodox view of Scripture that came to the fore in this analysis.[57]

Verbal inspiration is thus "an attempt to make the basis of certainty of faith immovable by an *a priori* preclusion of every element of uncertainty because of the unique, supernatural, divine quality of Holy Scripture."[58] Faith in Scripture is called a "religious postulate," and the "religio-psychological explanation" of a need for absolute certainty is seen as the source of the doctrine of inerrancy.

What should disturb us about such an attack is its apparent disregard for the question of truth. Do defenders of inerrancy take that position because of a psychological need for certainty? They are categorized with "Islam's evaluation of the Koran" and Roman Catholicism's evaluation of the pope, with the common

56. Ibid., pp. 24-25.
57. Ibid., p. 30.
58. Ibid., p. 31.

denominator being a need for certainty. Berkouwer says, "Faith is not and cannot be based on a theoretical reflection on what, according to our insights, must be the nature of the divine revelations."[59] None of my teachers on inerrancy ever claimed to arrive at his conclusion on the basis of what his "insight" told him it must be. They believed, with good reason, that inerrancy was taught by God and was not an idea of their own creation. The traditional doctrine appears to be on firm ground between the existential direction of Berkouwer and the straw man of human wisdom envisioned in his criticism.

Next we must consider the testimony of the Spirit at least to see how it functions in Berkouwer's doctrine of Scripture. His treatment of that doctrine is something quite different from what is generally understood by the testimony of the Holy Spirit.

Berkouwer sees traditional apologetics and inerrancy as exemplifying the same problem, and he raises the issue in the context of the testimony of the Spirit. He is using Bavinck to summarize his criticism. (Berkouwer continually cites Bavinck with deep appreciation. He sees himself as in line with Bavinck's thought.) Here then is what Berkouwer writes:

> The doctrine of the testimonium was somehow revived again when it was realized that rationalism was untrustworthy and apologetics unfruitful. In this connection he mentions Kant's criticism of the proofs for the existence of God. Once again there was room for the conviction that it is meaningful to speak of a testimony of the Spirit, because it was seen that the ultimate basis of faith cannot lie outside of us in proofs and arguments, the church, or tradition, "but can be found only in man himself, in the *religious* subject."[60]

The relevancy for inerrancy should be obvious. Whether in apologetics in general or Scripture in particular, certainty is denied any possibility in the phenomenal world. Certainty—religious certainty, is possible only in the Kantian noumenal realm of suprahistory and existentialism.

59. Ibid., p. 33.
60. Ibid., p. 47.

According to Berkouwer, "Only the Holy Spirit himself can give certainty and conquer all doubts."[61] The certainty of Scripture is not in the realm of reason; we cannot speak of its objective truth apart from a believing subject. Are we not in the realm of existential theology's "truth as encounter?" Berkouwer mentions that view approvingly in *The Second Vatican Council* where it is said that revelation "is not a reservoir of intellectual propositions" but rather "a personal self-disclosure by God in which He encounters the total person."[62] It is obvious, says Berkouwer, "that there are not two separate kinds of witness, one that must be called the outer and the other the inner testimony."[63] He states further: "A merely natural recognition of Scripture as a supernatural phenomenon with the consequent 'rational' proofs is not possible."[64] In that framework the question of inerrancy is irrelevant.

We also find in Berkouwer a confusion between "faith" in Scripture and "faith" in Christ, or saving faith, which affects many areas. But he confuses them intentionally via his exposition on the testimony of the Spirit. According to Berkouwer, "there can be no splitting of the *testimonium* into two separate *testimonia*, namely, one regarding our sonship, and another concerning the truth of Scripture."[65] It is certainly true that the regenerating, light-giving, eye-opening work of the Holy Spirit wins our acquiescence in both Scripture and the Savior. The issue, however, is not our "faith" *in* Scripture but the truth *of* Scripture, whether we acquiesce or not. Is it objectively true or only existentially true?

For Berkouwer the message, if not the medium, determines the medium's veracity. "On the basis of the New Testament, the confession of the Spirit is first of all related to salvation in Christ; and *then* the Word of God is discussed."[66] He can use the same full meaning of faith with regard to both Scripture and Christ, since faith in Scripture is really not in Scripture at all, but in the message of Scripture, namely Jesus Christ. This is what Berkouwer says: "True belief in Scripture is possible and real only

61. Ibid., pp. 47-48.
62. Berkouwer, *Second Vatican Council*, p. 68.
63. Berkouwer, *Holy Scripture*, p. 58.
64. Ibid., p. 63.
65. Ibid., p. 52.
66. Ibid., pp. 52-53.

in relation to the message of Scripture. . . . When the 'acceptance' of Holy Scripture as the Word of God is separated from a living faith in Christ, it is meaningless and confusing to call such an acceptance belief in Scripture or an 'element' of the Christian faith."[67] But again the issue is not whether we should call acceptance of Holy Scripture as the Word of God a "belief" or "faith," but whether it *is* the Word of God or only *becomes* the Word of God when one is related to it as a Christian. Berkouwer's position is clear. "The confession of the *Testimonium Spirtus Sancti* once and for all precludes every separation of faith in Christ from faith in Scripture. Faith in Scripture is not a separate belief that must be complemented by trust."[68]

Berkouwer has two chapters on the God-breathed character of Holy Scripture, and within those chapters the fundamental issues are raised, some of which we have already touched on. Berkouwer's concern for the intent or purpose of Scripture predominates. The word *inspiration* may be difficult to fully grasp, but the "functional character of Scripture" that concerns salvation and the future is what we must comprehend. "Scripture is the Word of God," says Berkouwer, "because the Holy Spirit witnesses in it of Christ."[69] "Seen from the perspective of *sola Scriptura*, that will not be an abstract and empty confession. The concreteness of the goal idea is of great importance."[70] John's words are cited: "These things are written that you may believe that Jesus is the Christ" (John 20:31). In *A Half Century of Theology* Berkouwer calls that a "religious pragmatic," an "awareness that the gospel records were portraits of Jesus Christ rather than ordinary historical reporting," with the result that "closer attention had to be paid to the purpose of the Gospel writers."[71] Though *defenders* of inerrancy would make a similar statement, Berkouwer places the purpose in *opposition* to inerrancy. He says that "the mystery of the God-breathed Scripture is not meant to place us before a theoretical problem of how Scripture could possibly and conceivably be

67. Ibid., p. 54.
68. Ibid., p. 55.
69. Ibid., p. 162.
70. Ibid., p. 124.
71. Berkouwer, *Half Century.*, p. 121.

both God's Word and man's word, and how they could be 'united.' It rather places us before the mystery of Christ."[72]

The *scopus*, or intention, of Scripture is Berkouwer's primary thrust over against "verbal inspiration", and its concomitant "inerrancy." "Believing Scripture does not mean staring at a holy and mysterious book but hearing the witness concerning Christ."[73] There is room for error growing out of the fact that Scripture is time-bound. The concept of "accommodation" is introduced in making a "distinction between *essential content* and *time-related form.*"[74] "The *scopus* of Scripture," according to Berkouwer, means "a concentrated attention . . . to the Word in the midst of many words, to its intent and purpose."[75] He then cites the Pharisees' misunderstanding of the Sabbath commandment as an example of missing the "intent" of the Sabbath. But that text teaches that the Pharisees had a faulty understanding of the law, not that the law was an errant statement pointing to an inerrant intention. Berkouwer implies an either/or choice between his *scopus* idea and Scripture as "many words without the goal" in which "its God-breathed character is thereby neglected."[76] Happily we are not confronted with such a dilemma.

Berkouwer, in criticizing inerrancy as set forth by Warfield, will speak of an inerrancy in the sense of "sin and deception." But inerrancy as Warfield advocates it is a "serious formalization" that is "far removed from the serious manner with which erring is dealt in Scripture."[77] Recognizing the good intention of inerrancy, Berkouwer nevertheless maintains that "the formalization of inerrancy virtually destroys this intention" by ignoring the organic nature of Scripture and its testimony.[78] Inerrancy in addition to infallibility is not needed "to guarantee the full and clear message of Scripture."[79] Inerrantists then, according to Berkouwer, are "fascinated by a miraculous 'correctness' that forever disregards

72. Berkouwer, *Holy Scripture*, pp. 162-63.
73. Ibid., p. 166.
74. Ibid., p. 175.
75. Ibid., p. 184.
76. Ibid.
77. Ibid., p. 181.
78. Ibid., p. 182.
79. Ibid.

every problem of time relatedness," and "in the end it will damage reverence for Scripture more than it will further it."[80]

It is undoubtedly a long way from Berkouwer's 1938 book on Scripture to his contemporary writings. Reflecting on that earlier book, he remarks that the appeal "It stands written" made a powerful impact on him. In 1974 he wrote: "As I reread my book of 1938, I sense that the difference between then and now is not that I was at that time impressed with 'It stands written' and that later, in my volume on the Scriptures, I was less committed to it. I still wish to stand, attentively and devoutly, by that appeal, made by Christ."[81] Who will question, however, that the phrase "It stands written" functions differently for Berkouwer now?

In 1938 he rejected the form-content distinction. The intention, the religious meaning, was inseparable from the historical surroundings. Later, such a distinction was the key to the *scopus* or intention of Scripture. In 1938 he defended the historicity of Genesis 3, as the *Gereformeerde Kerken* had done in 1926. The *Gereformeerde Kerken* officially abandoned that position forty years later, and Berkouwer saw no break with the church's past. In 1971 Berkouwer publicly asked the question, "Is there room in the Reformed Churches for persons—and I reckon myself among them—who at this stage of their reflection have great hesitations concerning the historicity of Adam?"[82]

One begins to see why Lindsell calls it a battle rather than an intramural skirmish. It is not just how we get the message, but it is a conflicting message. Berkouwer speaks of the same infallible content in the fallible form. But in time what he said in 1938 proves correct. The form and content are bound together, and we see new content emerging. His new position on the historicity of Adam and its relationship to Genesis 3 and Romans 5 is but one of several problems. The whole question of Paul's statements on womanhood and marriage is also involved. "At one time," says Berkouwer, "virtually no attention was given to time-boundness in these passages." They were read out of context, with a faulty view of inspiration, creating insoluble problems. "But Paul, in

---

80. Ibid., p. 183.
81. Berkouwer, *Half Century*, p. 139.
82. Quoted in Lindsell, *The Battle for the Bible*, p. 135.

contrast, did not in the least render timeless propositions concerning womanhood."[83]

Berkouwer is not unaware of the uneasiness surrounding these developments. In chapter one of *Holy Scripture* and in the concluding chapter of *A Half Century of Theology* he speaks of the fear, uncertainty, and alarm within the church. The last page of his *Holy Scripture* affirms that his approach "is the true and only way to obedience."[84] The last page of *A Half Century of Theology* encourages us not to lose courage and "lapse into skepticism," but to be stimulated by the promise "Seek and ye shall find."[85] Berkouwer is convinced that his way most honors the authority of Scripture. The question that must be asked, however, is this: If part of God's truth is surrendered will the time not come when the gospel itself will also be surrendered?

CONFESSIONS OF A DISCIPLE

We have elsewhere referred to Berkouwer as the "hole in the dike" through which a flood would come.[86] Of the many small streams that are making up that flood Jack Rogers of Fuller Theological Seminary has been selected for particular reference. A variety of circumstances has made him something of a spokesman for Berkouwer's thought in this country. The inclusion here of a disciple is justified in that disciples are sometimes quicker to draw conclusions and thus are frequently bolder in stating their goals than are their masters.

Rogers is certainly a zealous supporter of Berkouwer, and he has impressive credentials. His doctoral dissertation on the doctrine of Scripture in the Westminster Confession was under Berkouwer's supervision, and he is the translator of Berkouwer's *Holy Scripture*. Furthermore, he sees himself as leaving behind his "conservative" background and its "rigidity" while finding deliverance in Berkouwer. "It is possible to avoid the extremes of both

---

83. Berkouwer, *Holy Scripture* p. 187. Cf. Rogers, *Confessions of a Conservative Evangelical*, p. 116: "Jesus was a feminist."
84. Ibid., p. 366.
85. Berkouwer, *Half Century*, p. 263.
86. Carl Bogue, *A Hole in the Dike* (Cherry Hill, N.J.: Mack Publishing, 1977), pp. 25-26.

conservatism and liberalism and yet develop into an outstanding evangelical theologian. My example is G. C. Berkouwer of the Netherlands."[87]

Rogers claims to have been "a straight, uptight, conservative Christian." Though his self-description often sounds like pietistic moralism rather than healthy orthodox Christianity, his critique does not distinguish the two. He wants to be "less conservative and more evangelical." Before being enlightened by Berkouwer he "needed an idealized Bible."[88] No more:

> I can no longer be conservative and talk about what the Bible must be, or ought to be—reasoning logically from some idealized human notion of perfection. I want to be evangelical and accept the Word that God has given me, with all its magnificent surprises in both content and form.[89]

The reason there are such "surprises" for Rogers is found in the subjectivism of his philosophical presuppositions. Convinced of Hume's skepticism, he finds a way to "keep the faith" in Kant's philosophy that "turns our attention from the objective world outside to what we subjectively bring to it."[90] The "way out" becomes the "way up" to "suprahistory" where one is not bound to the logic of space and time, cause and effect. Or, to use Berkouwer's expression, he is seeing things "in faith."

The imprint of Berkouwer on Rogers was clearly seen in 1966 when his published dissertation, *Scripture in the Westminster Confession*, appeared. It evidenced tremendous research, giving us important information on the background of the Confession. In my judgment, however, it is most significant as a reinterpretation of the Confession, making it read like Berkouwer on Scripture. The difference is that the attack was fully in the open. According to Rogers, "Princeton Theology's . . . emphasis on the inerrant original autographs of the Bible signaled a change from the approach of the "Westminster Divines."[91] How was it different?

87. Rogers, *Confessions of a Conservative Evangelical*, p. 134.
88. Ibid., pp. 9, 12.
89. Ibid., p. 26.
90. Ibid., p. 125.
91. Rogers, *Scripture in the Westminster Confession*, p. 448.

"Princeton Theology undervalued the witness of the Holy Spirit" and relied on rationalism. There was "a lack of emphasis on the living dynamic Word of God in preaching," and there was "an under-emphasis on the *scopus* or purpose of Scripture." There was "an under-valuation of the human element in Scripture."[92] Furthermore, the New-Princeton theologians, in the then proposed "Confession of 1967" for the United Presbyterian Church "acted rightly in restoring the emphasis on the witness of the Holy Spirit and on Jesus Christ the Savior as being the central content of Scripture," an emphasis Rogers thought lost in "American Presbyterian orthodoxy."[93]

Not surprisingly, Jack Rogers looms large in the current battle for the Bible. Significantly, he is the editor of *Biblical Authority*, a collection of articles specifically attacking Lindsell's book by men opposed to inerrancy. Roger's own article purports to be a historical survey of biblical authority. In reality it is a vehement polemic against inerrancy that is open to challenge on almost every page. Apart from exhibiting an amazing zeal to promote a Platonic-Augustinian philosophical foundation for his doctrine of Scripture,[94] the article is characterized by repeated quotes or para-

92. Ibid., p. 449. American Presbyterian orthodoxy "under-emphasized the witness of the Spirit and the saving purpose of Scripture" (pp. 449-50). "While the Princeton theology felt obligated to defend Scripture's statements on every subject, the Westminster Divines emphasized that Scripture did not deal with matters of art and science" (p. 452).
93. Ibid., p. 453: "The proposed Book of Confessions, including the 'Confession of 1967,' offers the United Presbyterian Church in the U.S.A. a fresh opportunity to understand its heritage and confess its faith" (p. 454.).
94. Rogers, *Biblical Authority*, pp. 18-45: "Post-Reformation Protestants" used "the same Aristotelian-Thomistic arguments which Roman Catholics used. . . . Thus a significant shift in theological method occurred from the neo-Platonic Augustinianism of Luther and Calvin to the neo-Aristotelian Thomism of their immediate followers" (p. 29). "The old Princeton tradition . . . is a reactionary one . . . wedded to a prior commitment to Aristotelian philosophy" (p. 45). Norman L. Geisler, *Summit Papers*, pp. 11.2-4, gives some elementary philosophical teaching that destroys the credibility of much of what Rogers has to say. Concerning "the alleged Aristotelian background of inerrancy" Geisler lists several inconsistencies. "First, the 'aristotelian' Turretin did not originate the doctrine of inerrancy. The platonic Augustine . . . clearly held to inerrancy. . . . Secondly, Augustine . . . was not the fideist Rogers would make him to be. . . . Thirdly, Rogers speaks as if Aristotle invented the law of non-contradiction. . . . Fourthly, even Rogers and other errantists use the law of non-contradiction as a pillar of their position. . . . Finally, it was not Aquinas nor Turretin who first applied logic to God's revelation. The biblical writers themselves warned the believers to

phrases of Berkouwer's work on Scripture. The primary conclusion, aimed at Lindsell's *The Battle for the Bible*, is that "it is historically irresponsible to claim that for two thousand years Christians have believed that the authority of the Bible entails a modern concept of inerrancy in scientific and historical details."[95] However one might view Lindsell's book, it is apparent that Rogers has entered the battle in opposition to inerrancy.

To return again to Rogers's "confessions," we find him asserting that Berkouwer did indeed change his position on Scripture and that in doing so he was following the "good" Dutch Reformed tradition as opposed to the "bad" American Reformed tradition. Of Berkouwer's *Holy Scripture* he writes: "I believe that this work on Scripture really does break the liberal-conservative dilemmas we have wrestled with for a century. It offers a genuinely evangelical middle way." Then, referring to Berkouwer's early work on Scripture he says:

> It encourages me to see how his thinking has changed and developed in this mature work. . . . The extremes—formalism and subjectivism, rationalism and existentialism—have been rejected. We do not have to choose one or the other of these extremes as so much of our American theology has suggested.[96]

"Warfield left on his followers the imprint of the apologist and polemicist. Bavinck influenced the generations after him to be theological scientists and churchmen. Berkouwer reflects this influence."[97] "In the nineteenth century, while Hodge and Warfield were building defenses against Biblical criticism, Kuyper and

---

'avoid . . . contradictions' and anything 'contrary' to sound doctrine." Geisler then makes this telling critique of Rogers's preference for Platonic presuppositions: "A further irony in Rogers' position is his assumption of the relative harmlessness of platonic presuppositions as they bear on the inerrancy of Scripture. While Rogers consciously rejects Turretin's 'aristotelian rationalism,' he unconsciously adopts a kind of platonic 'spiritualism.' . . . Now Rogers is apparently not aware of the fact that this dualistic separation of the material and spiritual worlds is a philosophical presupposition at the root of the errancy position." The implications of Rogers's philosophical preference is indeed manifest throughout much of what he writes.
95. Ibid., p. 44.
96. Rogers, *Confessions of a Conservative Evangelical*, p. 136.
97. Ibid., p. 135.

Bavinck were meeting the issue openly and constructively."[98] "G. C. Berkouwer has taught that the choice between conservatism and liberalism is a false dilemma."[99] Rogers has thus found a comfortable Platonic, Kantian home in Berkouwer's "evangelical" middle way.

On the theory that reading Berkouwer into the Westminster Confession salvaged it from the "conservatives," Rogers collaborated with one of his former students to work the same "magic" on much of church history. Desiring to demonstrate to the reader that inerrancy is not the historic position of the church. The book *The Authority and Interpretation of the Bible* has been accurately described by Norman Geisler as "the most complete attempt by non-inerrantists to reinterpret church history in their favor."[100] Again, Berkouwer provided the model.

Though spoiled by the Aristotelian Scholasticism of Aquinas, Rogers and McKim see a basic consensus in the early church in Neoplatonic Augustinianism with no thought of inerrancy.[101] After a bad Scholasticism in the Middle Ages, nominalism and mysticism "helped pave the way for a return to Neoplatonic Augustinianism."[102] The Reformers focused attention, not on inerrancy, but on the Bible's saving function.[103] Reflecting the neo-orthodox view, Rogers and McKim write: "For Calvin, the Bible was God's Word. But he knew that God did not address human beings directly with divine words."[104] The Bible is God's Word but not divine words! In contemporary terms, The Word is manifest in human (i.e., errant) words.

The real villain emerges in post-Reformation "Protestant scholasticism"[105] with its Aristotelian-Thomistic approach where "Scripture came to be treated as a compendium of propositions

---

98. Ibid., p. 137.
99. Ibid., p. 141.
100. Norman L. Geisler, "A Critical Review " I.C.B.I. Update (Summer 1980), p. 1. That review, though brief, is a devastating critique of the philosophical presuppositions and inconsistencies of Rogers and McKim.
101. Rogers and McKim, *Authority and Interpretation*, pp. 3-71.
102. Ibid., p. 73.
103. Ibid., pp. 73-145.
104. Ibid., p. 116.
105. Ibid., pp. 147-98.

from which logical deductions could be drawn."[106] Remarkably, the Westminster Divines were exempted from such scholasticism, but Great Britain generally went the way of the Continent via Owen, Bacon, Newton, Locke, Thomas Reid, and John Witherspoon, who imported errant inerrancy to America.[107]

In America, Reformed Scholasticism was continued preeminently in Princeton Theological Seminary with the teaching of Turretin's theology and under the leadership of A. Alexander, the Hodges, B. B. Warfield, and J. G. Machen.[108] Rogers and McKim assert that though the leaders of that tradition thought themselves to be followers of Calvin and the Westminster Standards, "in actuality they believed and taught a theological method regarding the authority and interpretation of the Bible that was rooted in a post-Reformation scholasticism, an approach almost the exact opposite of Calvin's own."[109]

The direction that such historical revisionism takes for Rogers and McKim, as well as Berkouwer's influence, becomes evident when the more modern counterparts of Rogers's approved theologians are named. Charles Briggs, suspended from the Presbyterian ministry, is said to be "historically correct."[110] The Auburn Affirmation is implicitly approved in opposition to Machen and the conservatives.[111] T. M. Lindsay and James Orr in Scotland are praised as "evangelical reactions to Reformed Scholasticism," and so also are Kuyper and Bavinck (not Hepp) in the Netherlands and P. T. Forsyth in England.[112]

More recently Barth, Berkouwer, and the Confession of 1967 carry the banner for Rogers and McKim. Karl Barth "founded the authority of the Bible on its divine function" and in so doing "provided a way back to the Reformation focus."[113] Berkouwer's difference from Barth is that he reacted to Scholasticism while Barth had reacted to Liberalism.[114] They both arrived at a Refor-

106. Ibid., pp. 187-88.
107. Ibid., pp. 200-60.
108. Ibid., pp. 265-379.
109. Ibid., p. xvii.
110. Ibid., p. 358.
111. Ibid., pp. 364-65.
112. Ibid., pp. 380-405.
113. Ibid., p. 425.
114. Ibid., pp. 426-37.

mation focus on the Bible's saving function" in a way that excluded inerrancy. In the United Presbyterian Church "Barth provided a core of consensus," and the Confession of 1967 restored "the Reformation focus on Christ as the content of Scripture."[115] With pride Rogers and McKim declare the confession of 1967: "The final document was a worthy modern version of the Reformation vision of the Bible."[116]

CONCLUSION

A look at the disciple has produced nothing to alter our evaluation of the professor. Armed with Berkouwer's view of Scripture, one who professes to be a conservative evangelical in time embraces Briggs and Barth as the true descendants of the Reformation. Not surprisingly, neo-orthodox and liberal Roman Catholics have increasingly embraced Berkouwer, while relations are strained within his own tradition. Rogers is "encouraged" by the change in Berkouwer and finds support for his hostility to American Presbyterianism in what he calls Berkouwer's "evangelical middle way." But is it really "a way," an alternative, or is it an illusion? Will there not always be but two alternatives—the absolute, authoritative bedrock of God's inerrant Word and the many variations of a humanistic, subjectivistic judgment of errant men about what is and is not authoritative within that written Word?

Almost twenty years ago an esteemed seminary professor told us that in fifty years Karl Barth would be but a footnote in the history of doctrine. In the early sixties that was an incredible statement. Now, in less than half that time, it seems almost a reality. "Modern" theologians, like the Athenians of Paul's day, "spend their time in nothing other than telling or hearing something new." Thus does Rogers, after over four hundred pages of effort to justify the neo-orthodox, Barthian, and even Berkouwerian "consensus" out of which the Confession of 1967 was born, painfully acknowledge new theological fads leading United Presbyterians along with "every wind of doctrine." Trying to keep

115. Ibid., pp. 437 and 439.
116. Ibid., p. 442.

the illusion alive, Rogers and McKim conclude their book with a plea that Berkouwer's model is indeed a sound alternative to "conservative and liberal" rather than merely another subjective, liberal theology of similar nature to the process theology and liberation theology that replaced it.[117]

Directly and indirectly, Berkouwer is a prominent figure in the battle for the Bible in the English-speaking world. To many who are convinced that modern criticism destroyed an authoritative and inerrant Bible but who still crave an evangelical atmosphere, Berkouwer has provided what sounds like an answer. The language sounds "conservative," but there is no longer the danger from flesh and blood critics. Revelation is placed in what Kant called the "noumenal" realm where logic is not applicable, and therefore all theology must be done "in faith" (i.e., above the historical, critical battles). "For Berkouwer, the model by which we understand Scripture should be functional, not philosophical."[118] "The function of human reason is not to investigate revelation but to draw logical conclusions."[119] All revelation is thus lifted out of the rational, logical, causal investigation and placed in the "noumenal" realm. For Berkouwer the only religious knowledge worthy of the name was personal or relational knowledge.[120] That applies to theology in general and to the doctrine of Scripture in particular.

Berkouwer, then, has anchored his ship in the "storm-free harbor of supra-history" to be safe from the "critical historical flood tide." But if Berkouwer's "middle way" is utterly illusive by the very nature of its subjectivism, the storm-free nature of his harbor is no less so. For in that harbor the only standard by which we may test anything is our own experience with "every man doing whatever is right in his own eyes." In that harbor there is no safety from being "tossed here and there by waves, and carried about by every wind of doctrine, by the trickery of men by craftiness in deceitful scheming" (Eph. 4:14).

---

117. Ibid., pp. 440-43, 457-61.
118. Ibid., p.433.
119. G. C. Berkouwer, *General Revelation* (Grand Rapids: Eerdmans, 1955), p. 75.
120. Rogers and McKim, *The Authority and Interpretation of the Bible*, p. 434.

Index of Subjects

413

Index of Persons

Abelard, Peter, 75-76
  on authority of Scriptures, 76
  on inspiration, 76
Alexander, J. A., 371
Alexander, A., 409
Ambrose, 40
Anselm, 74
  on faith, 74-75
Aquinas, Thomas, x, 68, 69, 110
  and Augustinian Platonism, 92
  as Bible scholar, 80-84
  hermeneutics of, 90-96
  on human reason, 90
  on inspiration, 82, 90
  on knowledge, 86-88
  on reason, 86
  on revelation, 87
  and Scholasticism, 84
  on truth, 86, 90
  view on biblical authorship, 92-93
  view of God, 86-89
  view of Scripture, 85-90
Aristotle, 68
  effect on theology in Middle Ages, 77-80
Arnett, William, on inerrancy, 318
Athanasius of Alexandria, 5, 12, 26-27

Athenagoras, 7, 14
Augustine, x, xi, 28, 166, 183
  and allegory, 64
  defines error, 51-53
  effect on Middle Ages theology, 70-74
  on faith, 60-65, 72
  and gospel writers, 53-54, 63
  on gospel writers, 45-46, 49, 51
  on history, 55-60
  on Holy Spirit, 50-51
  on inerrancy, 35, 37-65, 48-50
  on inspiration, 42-48
  on John 19:14, 51
  life of, 39-42
  on Mark 15:25, 51
  on Matthew 27:9, 43-44, 50
  and reason, 70-74
  on science, 55-60
  on truth, 71-72
  view of Scripture, 39-42

Backus, Isaac, 346-47
Barth, Karl, x, xi, 147, 383-84, 410
  on inerrancy, 187
Basil of Caesarea, on inerrancy, 27
Bassett, Paul, 314

418

Moody Press, a ministry of the Moody Bible Institute, is designed for education, evangelization, and edification. If we may assist you in knowing more about Christ and the Christian life, please write us without obligation: Moody Press, c/o MLM, Chicago, Illinois 60610.